DROUGHT

DROUGHT
A Global Assessment

VOLUME II

EDITED BY
DONALD A. WILHITE

London and New York

First published 2000
by Routledge
11 New Fetter Lane, London EC4P 4EE

Simultaneously published in the USA and Canada
by Routledge
29 West 35th Street, New York, NY 10001

Routledge is an imprint of the Taylor & Francis Group

Typeset in Galliard by Solidus (Bristol) Limited
Printed and bound in Great Britain by
Butler and Tanner Ltd, Frome and London

British Library Cataloguing in Publication Data
A catalogue record for this book is available from the British Library

Library of Congress Cataloging in Publication Data
Drought : a global assessment / edited by Donald A. Wilhite.
p.   cm. — (Hazards and disasters : v. 2)
1. Droughts.   I. Wilhite, Donald A.   II. Series.
QC929.24.D74   2000
363.34′929dc21   99–10302

ISBN 0-415-16833-3 (2-volume set)
ISBN 0-415-16834-1 (Volume I)
ISBN 0-415-21418-1 (Volume II)

CONTENTS

VOLUME II

FIGURES

PLATES

TABLES

BOXES

PART V

ADJUSTMENT AND ADAPTATION STRATEGIES

EFFECTIVE DROUGHT MITIGATION

Linking micro and macro levels[1]

Susanna Davies

INTRODUCTION

Poor people living in drought-prone environments are consummate risk managers. They often have successful track records in managing drought, even though the effectiveness of indigenous coping strategies to protect food and livelihood security has been undermined by successive droughts and impoverishment. Research into the characteristics and needs of drought-prone people in sub-Saharan Africa (SSA) is paying off, and there are a number of clear indications of what is required to address their needs and to reinforce what they already do to mitigate drought. There have also been significant improvements in the ability to predict the consequences of drought on people's access to food, through the establishment of famine early warning systems (EWS). Much less progress has been made in using this information to improve preparedness and to trigger timely and appropriate responses, at either national government or donor level.

Institutional barriers to effective drought preparedness and mitigation (DPM) in SSA are manifold.[2] Failure to link local-level capacities to national-level planning and implementation continues to characterise most episodes of drought in SSA. Outsiders' imperfect understanding of local-level responses to drought exerts key influences on external perceptions of what happens before and during droughts, and hence on the policy prescriptions they advocate. A range of policy tools has been developed to mitigate the effects of drought, but their effective implementation has proved elusive. National organisations to manage and plan for drought relief have proliferated in SSA, often in alliance with donor agencies, and have met with varying degrees of success. Many have drafted drought contingency plans, but these tend to remain at the level of theory. The failure of national organisations to respond effectively to drought has led to international non-governmental organisations (NGOs), supported by donors, stepping into the breach to deliver emergency aid.

Stages of risk management

DPM may be defined as a planning and response process to predict drought and establish timely and appropriate responses to mitigate negative consequences of that drought on lives and livelihoods. In developing more effective DPM, it is important to differentiate between drought (an unusual and significant decline in the anticipated level and distribution of rainfall) and the consequences of this shock for people and their livelihoods. Risk management is at the heart of effective DPM. This can be divided into four stages, which operate (albeit incompletely) both at the level of donor and state policies and at community and household levels. Indigenous household and community strategies and external interventions by the state, donors, or NGOs can conflict with or complement each other. The four stages are:

1 *preparedness* (information and diagnosis, contingency planning, and post-crisis evaluation);
2 *mitigation* (insurance strategies/interventions, accumulation, and diversification undertaken before a shock);
3 *relief* (concurrent strategies/interventions undertaken whilst a crisis is under way, but if planned for

in advance, these can be part of mitigation activities); and

4 *rehabilitation* (rehabilitation or recovery strategies/ interventions undertaken once conditions begin to return to normal, but, again, planned for in advance).[3]

Neither the relationship between these stages nor progression through them is linear. When the threat of drought is endemic, the stages are best conceptualised as part of a continuous cycle in which shocks are part of the 'normal' portfolio of types of change. The lines between each phase need to be blurred to ensure that activities undertaken in different stages are integrated with previous and subsequent ones and to guard against the compartmentalisation of resources. Risk management needs to be understood within the broader development continuum, implicit in which are overlapping time frames and the simultaneous pursuit of different activities of varying duration. Preparedness is taken as the starting point because it refers to those informational and diagnostic activities that underpin subsequent stages. Relief is regarded as an *outcome* of preparedness and mitigation. Mitigation does not necessarily come after preparedness in all circumstances; indeed, it may run in parallel with it, but it nevertheless presupposes some preparedness. Relief may also run concurrently with mitigation and, to be effective, rehabilitation would link on to anterior mitigation activities and inform preparedness for subsequent droughts. The objective of these four stages is not, therefore, to create artificial barriers around sets of activities which may be almost indistinguishable on the ground, but instead to indicate that the motivation for and timing and sequencing of interventions are of critical importance in effective risk management.

This chapter focuses on three aspects of DPM in SSA, in the context of these stages of risk management:

*   rural household- and community-level strategies to confront drought;
*   progress in government and donor activities, and why these limited successes have not been translated into coherent DPM strategies;
*   ways in which local people's strategies can lead to

the elaboration of more effective national-level initiatives, including a mechanism to bridge the gap between local- and national-level strategies.

The impact and consequences of drought on the rural poor

Drought affects vulnerable people in different ways. They may be directly dependent on rainfall (cultivators, pastoralists, riverine fishers), or indirectly so (landless or displaced labourers searching for work in rural areas and all those who are dependent on the market for their food, including the urban poor and refugees). For the first category, the impact of drought is determined by a combination of the natural resources they exploit in their livelihoods; the type of household or individual in question (principally how poor, old, young, or healthy); and the assets, stores, and claims over which the individual or household has command. Widespread drought affecting all resources in agroecological areas where most people are poor has the most serious consequences, but frequently the interaction of reduced rainfall and its distribution can have differing effects on, say, pastoral and agricultural production. A single year of drought rarely leads to famine. The worst of SSA's drought-induced recent famines (in the mid-1970s and mid-1980s) were preceded by a number of years of low rainfall. But, as people become poorer and more vulnerable to drought, future famines may be caused by a single failure of the rains (von Braun 1991).

Declining access to food – sometimes degenerating into famine – is the most common short-term consequence of drought, although production failures caused by drought do not cause famine unless there are other determining socioeconomic factors. In Africa, war is increasingly associated with tipping the balance between drought-induced food insecurity and full-blown famine (Duffield 1990a). India had its worst drought in a hundred years in 1987, but there was no famine: preventing the 'inevitability' of drought leading to famine – even in conditions of chronic poverty – is the essence of successful DPM. In this context, food security is most appropriately defined as access to enough food at all times for an active, healthy life, and at household level rather than in terms of aggregate national self-sufficiency (World Bank 1986). Although the national food (im)balance will be critically affected by drought, Sen's (1981) classic study of famines in Africa and Asia demonstrated that famine can occur in conditions of apparent plenty if people cannot afford to buy. The consequences of drought for vulnerable groups can be ascertained only by considering people's *entitlement* to food as well as food availability.

Defining famine is more problematic. In recent years, opinions have shifted from an emphasis on widespread increases in mortality due to starvation toward more multidimensional definitions, incorporating loss of livelihood as well as of life and the breakdown of social and economic ties that bind households and communities, leading to the conditions under which fatal epidemics can thrive – the so-called health crisis model of famine (de Waal 1989, Dyson 1993). The relationship between drought and increased undernutrition does, however, remain central to most definitions of famine, despite controversy as to what increased prevalence of undernutrition (growth faltering in children and weight loss in adults) indicates (von Braun 1991). In both Africa and Asia, studies of local responses to drought show how people choose to go hungry in periods of drought, cutting consumption early on in the process of impoverishment to preserve assets for future production until the point of destitution, when all options have been exhausted (Corbett 1988, de Waal 1989). Increased prevalence of undernutrition may therefore be quite an early indicator of the likelihood of famine (Young and Jaspars 1994).

These findings suggest that, although drought and famine mitigation in SSA will continue to be preoccupied with reducing undernutrition to prevent starvation, there is a wider agenda that needs to be addressed. This includes creeping impoverishment, the declining productivity of the natural resources on which people depend in areas where the frequency of drought may be increasing, and the inability to recover economically and socially from drought. These effects undermine the environmental and economic sustainability of livelihoods and engender increasing vulnerability to subsequent droughts. Such vulnerability has two dimensions: greater sensitivity to the shock of drought, and reduced resilience or capacity to bounce back to a predrought state. Over time, a vicious circle is set in train: people become more vulnerable to drought and less able to recover from its consequences (Davies 1996).

Against this background, the shock of drought is mitigated by the level of insurance provided either by the individual and community (e.g., assets, stores and claims, or reciprocal self-help mechanisms) or by the state (e.g., safety nets, public works, or free food distributions). The provision of such insurance has undergone two major changes in SSA since the drought of the early 1970s. First, whereas household and community mechanisms have worked reasonably well in many cases, there is some evidence to suggest that they are now so strained as to cause great concern about their viability in the next cycle of drought. In particular, the ability of indigenous strategies to secure longer-term livelihood needs – including resilience to drought – has been severely undermined (Duffield 1990b, Davies 1996). Second, and in contrast, the array of state mechanisms increased substantially in the 1980s, although interventions still tend to be in the form of emergency food aid distributions. State insurance mechanisms have thus focused principally on the immediate consequence of low rainfall: reduced food security. There are few links between these two levels, which severely compromises the effectiveness of DPM.

THE MICRO LEVEL

Preparedness

People who live in drought-prone areas have highly developed information systems which they use to predict disruptions in rainfall and to diagnose appropriate responses. It is the *informed* decisions they make that give rise to their mitigation and relief (coping) capacities. All local strategies – whether adopted at individual, household, or community level – are part of wider contingency plans, reinforced by indigenous information and diagnosis. Although there has been little systematic documentation of local people's contingency plans, there is evidence to suggest that the use of local strategies is far from random (Longhurst 1986, Watts 1983 and 1988, Corbett 1988). Populations in marginal environments are probably much better equipped to cope with periods of food stress than those accustomed to more secure conditions (Reardon and Matlon 1989). This has led to the suggestion that monitoring indigenous coping strategies is an essential and effective element of famine EWS, and indicators have been developed accordingly (Frankenberger 1992). Although increasingly advocated, examples are rare. Monitoring coping strategies is a tricky process. The interpretation of such indicators is problematic and necessitates detailed understanding of local livelihood systems (Davies 1996). This approach is often rejected by national planners on the grounds of cost, time, and lack of representativeness and comparability. Since famine EWS are preoccupied principally with full-blown famine, not with preparedness as such, some question the relevance of local preparedness.

Mitigation

Insurance strategies are those activities undertaken to reduce the likelihood of production failure, whilst at the same time trying to maximise income. Production-based insurance strategies are livelihood system specific. Cultivators use seed mixes that include drought-resistant varieties, early-maturing seeds to break the hungry season, and others that, although more productive in good years, are prone to failure in times of drought. In many drought-prone parts of SSA, cultivators try to diversify into livestock, and pastoralists may shift from cattle to goats (which have a higher resistance to drought). Community-level insurance mechanisms consist primarily of transferring assets or lending resources between richer and poorer households through a range of reciprocal ties (e.g., employing poorer households to work on richer ones' land in return for seed or a share of the crop), or in building up communal reserves that can be used in times of stress (Swift 1989a). Reciprocal ties between different livelihood systems further reinforce insurance strategies, for example via bartering arrangements that are mutually beneficial in helping to iron out fluctuations in the seasonal terms of trade between different products (e.g., milk and cereals) (Adams 1993). There is, however, nothing intrinsically welfarist about such reciprocal ties: they tend to mirror existing social hierarchies and inequalities (Gore 1993). One consequence of prolonged drought is the intensification of exploitative community ties (e.g., calling in outstanding dues rather than making new loans) and the breakdown of more welfarist measures to support the most vulnerable members of the community. Women and children are frequently particularly adversely affected by these changes (Agarwal 1990).

Relief

Coping strategies are the bundle of producer responses to declining food availability and entitlements *in abnormal seasons or years*, and they are employed once principal sources of production have failed to meet expected levels and people have to cope until the next harvest. The ten most commonly observed responses to food crisis are: collect famine foods, borrow grain from kin, sell labour power, engage in dry-season farming, sell small livestock, borrow grain or money from merchants/money-lenders, sell domestic assets, pledge farmland, sell farmland, and migrate out permanently (Watts 1983). There has been much less systematic documentation about the downstream effects of drought. For those dependent on the market for all their food needs, coping amounts to being able to increase household cash income. Households do not pursue these strategies one after the other, but rather juggle different activities simultaneously and in response to the seasonal options available to them. In the case of sales of assets, for example, rural people are highly conversant with the seasonal terms of trade between goods, and will seek to maximise their revenue over a drought year by playing the market to the extent possible. There is also a range of community-based coping mechanisms to help people withstand periods of drought. These include gifts of food to impoverished kin, credit to buy food and other necessities, and fostering of children by wealthier households. Coping strategies are highly gendered: women and men ensure against and cope with drought in very different ways, reflecting their differing entitlements. Women, for example, invest more heavily in social networks than men, especially when their access to labour markets is constrained (Agarwal 1990). This is true at all stages of risk management, but gendered differences increase as the crisis intensifies.

Rehabilitation

Recovery or rehabilitation strategies are those undertaken once the immediate crisis has passed, to regain lost ground (e.g., restocking, reinvesting in production, reconstitution of stocks). Recovery and rehabilitation are implicit in the tradeoff between immediate and longer-term needs. Households that have managed to preserve productive assets can recover. Destitution implies not only that insurance and coping have failed, but also that there is no scope for rehabilitation within the household or community. At community level, just as for insurance and coping strategies, reciprocal mechanisms exist to redistribute assets after droughts to aid poorer households. These include the loaning of animals to reconstitute herds; the loaning of seed, tools, and food; and other informal credit mechanisms.

How successful is indigenous risk management?

There are several important reasons not to overestimate the capacity of poor people to manage the effects of drought. First, risk management is harder in vulnerable livelihood systems in which coping strategies have to be used to fill the food gap in some seasons of every year. When drought strikes, their use can only be intensified. Secure livelihood systems, in contrast, have coping strategies that are *reserved for* periods of unusual food stress (akin to 'relief'), which enables them to bounce back after drought. If these become absorbed into normal activity patterns, this resilience declines. Similarly, sensitivity to drought will be greater if coping strategies cannot be used to cushion the shock. Vulnerable livelihood systems, characterised by properties of low resilience and high sensitivity, thus find it hard to cope (Davies 1996).

Second, people cannot always manage risk. Overemphasis on local risk management capacity can mask the collapse of livelihoods that are no longer viable. In Sudan, for example, there are parts of the country where the combination of agroclimatic conditions, civil war, and impoverishment from repeated famine has rendered some groups incapable of surviving,

even when rainfall returns to normal (Duffield 1990b). These are precisely the circumstances in which famine risks becoming endemic and rural people need to alter their livelihoods radically to survive subsequent droughts. Further, the poor are harder hit by drought than the better-off. In the highlands of Ethiopia, for example, households with incomes in the top third had cereal yields in a drought year that were 60 per cent higher than those in the poorest third. Milk yields were also higher. This is explained by richer households having both more successful insurance strategies and greater access to community-based claims when times are tough (Webb and Reardon 1991).

Third, not all coping strategies are sustainable. They can become exhausted as more and more people turn to them. Both the economic and the environmental sustainability of strategies needs to be carefully assessed. It is necessary to distinguish between 'non-erosive' and 'erosive' coping to differentiate between those strategies that use extra sources of income and avoid eroding the subsistence base of the household, and those that do not and thereby compromise future livelihood security (de Waal 1989). There is as yet little evidence to show how the tradeoff between subsistence and sustainability works in striking a balance between immediate food needs and longer-term livelihood ones. Most studies of how people deal with drought cover a single cycle of drought (and less often recovery). An exception is a longitudinal study of villages in northern Nigeria over a twenty-year period, which shows huge and highly localised variations in how different households adapt to drought (Mortimore 1989). Sahelian livelihoods in Mali have undergone a transition from security to vulnerability since the drought cycle of the early 1970s, and local people's ability to manage the risk of the effects of drought is increasingly compromised (Davies 1996).

Fourth, permanent risk management may be bad for development, and not all coping strategies are worth reinforcing. Implicit in coping strategies is the idea that the entire working life of subsistence producers is taken up in acquiring some stock of food, enabling people to stand still but preventing them from moving ahead. All too often, future livelihoods are no more secure as a result of coping with drought, implying that there is no saving in the household and that livelihoods are taken up in avoiding risk – including the risk of investing in production. The overwhelming characteristic of strategies pursued is that they offer uncertain, piecemeal, and poorly remunerated means of filling the annual food gap (Davies 1996). Support for them is often advocated in preference to imposing external, often late, inappropriate and unsustainable solutions to food crises, epitomised by emergency food aid distributions (WFP 1989). But if such strategies simply allow people to stand still, or to fall back more slowly, reinforcing them may lock people into a vicious circle of subsistence and coping. If, on the other hand, insurance is provided for the very poor, it enables them to be economically active (to take risks, to save). Institutional support for coping strategies may thus at times be inefficient because it will reinforce the risk-averse survival orientation of poor people: it is insurance or mitigation and rehabilitation strategies that need to be strengthened.

THE MACRO LEVEL

Institutional responses to drought at the national level in SSA have focused on food security aspects of the impact of drought, most obviously via the establishment of famine EWS and relief and rehabilitation commissions, which proliferated in the 1980s. National-level institutions regard relief as exceptional and plan for it in isolation from wider development concerns. Their responses are crisis driven, reflecting a lack of preparedness and a failure to respond sensitively to changing livelihoods confronted with drought. Divisions between relief and development inherent in both state and donor bureaucracies persist, as does the divergence between what appears to exist on a bureaucratic level and what actually happens when drought strikes.

The emphasis here is on public institutions, but it is important to note that their private counterparts can both contribute to DPM and be adversely affected by drought. Weak private sector marketing networks can collapse and other local businesses be destroyed by falling effective demand. The destruction of private sector institutions can have especially deleterious consequences (e.g., inability to deliver essential goods and services or to provide off-farm employment) for post-drought recovery. Recently – and at times incompletely – liberalised marketing sectors are often ill-equipped to withstand the risk of drought. Private traders may be unable to continue supplying remote drought-affected areas with cereals if market demand suddenly increases or if the supply of cereals from elsewhere declines and there is insufficient access to credit to increase imports.

Preparedness

Substantial progress in establishing famine EWS in SSA in the 1980s means that – once it is clear that there is a drought – famines are now quite easy to predict (although prediction remains highly uncertain when war is also a factor). These EWS range from being highly centralised and top-down, in both their methods of data collection and their institutional structure, to being decentralised and more people-oriented. The former tend to focus on food availability decline and the need for emergency food aid; the latter use a more comprehensive range of socio-economic indicators to track the impact of drought on food entitlements and can suggest a more flexible range of responses. Whereas more comprehensive local-level systems are indicated for accurate tracking of the consequences of drought, institutional constraints favour more top-down and minimalist approaches to early warning. These constraints include a lack of resources for, and priority attached to, preventive data collection; inadequate training and personnel to analyse large volumes of data in a timely manner; and, in many cases, the coexistence of several EWS, which give conflicting signals (and some of which by-pass government structures). Centralised information systems concentrate almost exclusively on the short-term consequences of drought for people's access to food. Most are designed to target emergency food aid, not wider famine mitigation responses. Arguments against expanding the remit for famine EWS to be able to predict earlier and recommend more varied responses are made on the grounds of cost, feasibility, and institutional capacity. Relief departments in donor agencies tend to be structured to respond to relief, not mitigation, and government bureaucracies mirror this divide.

Many drought-prone countries have some form of drought contingency plan on paper, but most have not been translated into effective policy covering the range of activities required to address short- and longer-term consequences. There is a 'missing link' between improved capacities to predict famine and famine prevention. In a five-country comparative study, a number of institutional constraints to response have been identified (Buchanan-Smith and Davies 1995). Information is not linked to response, and the use of information that is available is partial and unsystematic. Response takes place in a highly politically charged context, and where donor/government relations are already strained, contingency planning counts for very little. Coordination between different actors involved in response planning is poor and at times impossible. There is disagreement as to who is ultimately responsible for DPM when governments have inadequate resources to respond alone, especially if government and donor interests are at variance. Donor and government bureaucracies are ill-equipped to respond in a timely fashion, with a lack of synchronisation between need and bureaucratic procedures and a tendency to respond only to crisis indicators rather than to earlier signs of stress.

Failures to plan adequately for response are much better documented than successes.[4] One success is in Turkana, Kenya, where a decentralised system of response planning has been developed, offering a range of responses in addition to food aid, including intervention in livestock markets and restocking (Swift 1989b). Recent experience, however, indicates that implementation is still flawed, owing to inadequate decentralisation of resources for response as well as preparedness (Buchanan-Smith and Davies 1995). Sudan is an example of a country where a lack of institutional memory and an inability to learn from past mistakes has prevented the improvement of response.

Response planning should be enacted only when planned mitigation has failed. In fact, response planning is what tends to happen by default, even if mitigation planning exists on paper. Drawing on evidence of the success of mitigation planning in South Asia, it is argued that famine in Africa is due, in large part, to the failure of public action to prevent and contain it (Drèze 1990). Such public action is the essence of mitigation planning, which needs to address both food availability decline and food entitlement decline through entitlement promotion and entitlement protection, implicit in which are the longer-term as well as the immediate consequences of drought. Entitlement promotion is a much broader enterprise than famine relief and might include, for example, interventions to promote more drought-resistant crops. Entitlement protection is epitomised by the provision of public works once food security is threatened.

The institutional constraints to such an approach to mitigation planning are intimately bound up with the national political economy, and weak, resource-poor states are unlikely to be able to sustain effective public action to combat drought. It has been argued that public action is much more likely to emanate from government bureaucracies if they are democratically accountable (Drèze and Sen 1989). But this view, developed in the context of India, has been contested in SSA, because democratic freedoms in SSA as such are less important than a specific politically negotiated right to be free from famine, which has had little or no opportunity to emerge in Africa because famine has never been politicised in SSA in the same way it has in India (de Waal 1996).

Mitigation and relief

A potentially wide array of policy instruments (summarised in Table 28.1) is available to national governments embarking on mitigation and relief interventions. They fall into three broad categories: insurance, concurrent, and recovery/rehabilitation. All require developed institutional capacities. Flexible responses, such as public works offering food or cash, presuppose substantial decentralised institutional capacity. On the other hand, weak marketing infrastructures and poorly integrated markets reduce the effectiveness of most income-based response options. Interventions need to complement strategies pursued at household and community levels. This might include: research into drought-resistant crops, improvement of marketing networks (insurance/mitigation); provision of seasonally appropriate off-farm employment, facilitation of migration by provision of transport, information about employment opportunities, and better mechanisms for sending remittances (concurrent/ mitigation); livestock price maintenance (relief); provision of seed, tools, and credit (rehabilitation). Relief interventions would be required only as fall-back mechanisms once mitigation had failed. The choice of appropriate mixes of interventions can be assessed according to criteria of scale, consistency with wider government policy, speed, administrative feasibility, cost effectiveness, sustainability, and equity. The principal lessons for effective food security planning are also relevant to DPM: integrated planning but independent implementation; the importance of a bias toward action over planning; the value of risk-taking and innovation; and the importance of addressing explicitly the need for new modes of organisation in multidisciplinary teamwork (Maxwell 1990).

Rehabilitation

The roots of poor post-drought rehabilitation are grounded in unsuccessful relief and mitigation, and rehabilitation encounters many of the same institutional constraints. When rehabilitation does happen, it tends to be seen as the tail end of relief, rather than as a link between relief and future development. Relief operations tend to be evaluated according to their own internal logic: they need to be justified retrospectively, which obscures lessons that could be learnt for subsequent droughts. Evaluations of the failure to respond early and effectively to drought are rare; post-drought evaluations of the impact on livelihoods even more so (Riely 1991). This is exacerbated by the lack of an institutional 'home' for rehabilitation, and so it remains outside established aid planning and organisation. If rehabilitation is to

Table 28.1 Tools for drought preparedness and mitigation

Level	Type of strategy/ intervention	Food	Nonfood
National	Insurance/ mitigation	National food security reserve Price stabilisation reserve	Old-age pensions Subsidised loans for asset acquisition
		Agricultural research into drought-resistant crops	
	Mitigation/ relief	Public food distribution National food-for-work scheme	National public works programme
Local government	Insurance/ mitigation	Investment in food marketing infrastructure	Primary health care provision Improved water supply
	Mitigation/ relief	Local food-for-work Supplementary feeding	Cattle camps Local works schemes
Community	Insurance/ mitigation	Village grain banks	Improved common property resource management Village seed banks Tax holidays
	Mitigation/ relief	Redistribution of food or household members within community	Health measures
Household	Insurance/ mitigation	Grain stores Make farming systems resilient to shock	Acquire assets Develop social bonds Develop mitigation activities Livestock restocking
	Recovery/ rehabilitation	Send household members to urban areas to generate savings	

Source: Adapted from Maxwell 1992

be effective, governments and donors need to incorporate it into their existing institutional arrangements for policy design and aid delivery (Brigaldino 1996).

How successful is macro risk management?

Macro-level drought risk management encounters many obstacles in SSA. In most instances, response is reactive, not proactive. If contingency plans exist, there is no guarantee that they will be used. Increasingly, there is overreliance on private cereal-trading sectors in the face of substantial production failures. If external trade remains controlled despite liberalisation, food imports are not available in sufficient quantities. When an emergency response is launched, food aid dominates and there are few examples of tried and tested flexible response options. Inadequate primary health care and inability to respond quickly to emergency health problems can undermine any increase in access to food. The burden of taxation and other forms of state extraction from the community can offset many of the benefits of safety nets and other state insurance mechanisms, especially if such demands are made when the value of assets that poor people have to sell plummets. Few African governments can afford tax holidays, even if these often happen by default when people cannot pay. There is little input by local people into decision making.

National constraints are exacerbated by the tendency for donors and NGOs to set up parallel structures in order to deliver relief as fast as possible once a crisis is under way. In Darfur, Sudan, in the mid-1980s, this approach had deleterious effects not only on the relief operation itself, but also on fragile local institutions (Buchanan-Smith 1990). When contingency plans do not exist, or are by-passed by emergency donor operations, local institutions are weaker in the aftermath of drought than at its outset. Contingency plans are of little value if the resources to respond quickly are unavailable and donors are reluctant to pre-position resources. Far from improving institutional capacity, emergency operations have the potential to undermine it. This underlines the need to strengthen national institutions well in advance of drought, rather than trying to build local capacity for DPM simultaneously with emergency relief operations.

This list of constraints paints a gloomy picture, the more so because it implies a need for wide-ranging institutional capacity building in most sectors of government (health, foreign trade, domestic marketing, etc.). Nevertheless, mitigation and relief strategies do not always fail. The drought in southern Africa in the early 1990s is widely held to have been managed much better than its predecessors in the Sahel and the Horn in the mid-1980s, although success was not unqualified and the strategic importance of southern Africa at the time encouraged a timely response by donors.[5]

Table 28.2 summarises common interventions used in successful episodes of famine mitigation in a number of drought-prone countries where drought has historically been associated with famine but no longer is (India, Botswana, Kenya, Cape Verde, and Zimbabwe). It also shows the institutional implications of successful mitigation activities, indicating where institutional capacity building needs to focus. Such an exercise would need to be carried out on a country-by-country basis, but in starting from what has worked in the past, institutional priorities can be identified. Some of the implications relate to wider political and economic factors, which cannot be addressed by institutional capacity building alone. The most important of these factors is the absence of civil war.

CONCLUSIONS: LINKING MICRO AND MACRO LEVELS

The key elements of local risk management in confronting drought are, first, that people vulnerable to drought know what is happening and have a highly developed portfolio of strategies to plan for and mitigate its adverse consequences. Mitigation or insurance strategies are bound up with wider livelihood security considerations, balancing the need to meet immediate consumption with preserving future capacity to produce. This tradeoff works, up to a point, but the most vulnerable households and communities may be reaching a threshold, beyond which their livelihoods cannot be secured against drought. Second, coping strategies habitually used only in times of drought are the local equivalent of 'relief' interventions, used only when insurance strategies

Table 28.2 Common elements in cases of successful macro-level famine mitigation

Elements of mitigation	Institutional implications
Formal EWS backed up by free press and active political debate	Greater transparency of information (political accountability)
Government plays predominant role; donors and NGOs in secondary position	Strong coordination and leadership by government, based on adequate planning capacity
Efficient system of food supply and distribution, with appropriate mixture of public and private measures	Portfolio of preplanned responses and means of implementation
Commercial imports	Appropriate licensing and/or foreign exchange allocation system
Food aid available on time when needed	Planned food aid shipments and multiannual pledging
Storage reserves work well	Small-scale storage (e.g., some pre-positioning of stocks) Cooperative management between government and donors of these reserves, if supplied by food aid
Traditional 'relief' measures important (e.g., direct feeding); but implemented *before* famine happens	Contingency planning, early response, pre-positioning of resources
Successful public works programmes	Dependent on effective local bureaucracy
No civil war	(Political stability)

Source: Based on Longhurst 1992

have failed or to complement them when crisis threatens. Capacity to cope is increasingly compromised by the need to draw on these strategies in nondrought years and by creeping impoverishment. This tendency is further exacerbated by incomplete recovery from recent droughts: rehabilitation strategies, although also highly developed, cannot function when livelihoods lose their resilience to drought.

At the macro level, institutional constraints to effective mitigation and relief are legion. They include overcentralisation of planning and resources; over-ambitious goals given weak planning capacities; an inability to translate improved preparedness into better mitigation and relief; institutional amnesia and failure to learn from past mistakes, including the costs of not being prepared; DPM policies that can conflict with other policy objectives; incomplete, over-enthusiastic, or insufficient market liberalisation; lack of synchronisation between international relief systems and internal ones; overreliance on foreign NGOs, which can weaken government structures; over-emphasis on relief (emergency food aid); failure to link relief and development; domestic and external

political constraints, frequently confused with institutional constraints; and lack of consultation with and participation of drought-prone people. Political constraints, although usually central to the success or failure of timely response to drought, are rarely systematically incorporated into DPM analyses.

The analysis of micro-level risk management suggests the following implications for macro-level policy makers in improving their own risk management of food crises. First, more needs to be known about the longer-term consequences of drought on local livelihoods to identify what prevents people from managing risk. Planners need to tap indigenous knowledge about the likelihood and effects of risk, and the potential for improving its management. The remit of EWS needs to be widened to the collection and analysis of data that reflect how people are affected by drought. As long as EWS are principally or exclusively concerned with recommending free food distributions, risk management of food crises will continue to focus on emergency relief.

Second, an inventory of institutions and capacities is needed. A major drawback of the proliferation of famine-driven institutions and plans in the 1980s was a lack of systematic documentation of what each component could and could not do when crisis strikes. Such documentation would facilitate the development of institutional memory and indicate where opportunities exist for macro-level interventions and institutions to reinforce local risk management. An estimate of the cost of poor risk management should be included. In the context of declining aid flows to Africa, systematic documentation of the costs of emergency operations, compared with those of effective risk management, would greatly strengthen the case for the latter.

Third, active and continuous contingency planning needs to be promoted. There is more to contingency planning than simply drawing up a document. If institutional capacity is to be strong enough to withstand the pressures of crisis and relief operations, it must be continually reinforced – in times of plenty as well as dearth. This implies involving local people, training of personnel, field testing flexible responses in advance of emergencies and designing interventions that can be taken 'off the shelf' when needed, updating plans and evaluating risk management enhancing activities, and pre-positioning or advance allocation of resources that will enable timely response.

Fourth, ways of supporting local strategies need to be tried and tested, by systematic piloting of different options in a variety of localities. Enlisting the participation of drought-prone people in this process is essential. Planners need to recognise the basis on which local people's choices are made: protecting future livelihoods is as important as – if not more important than – sustaining immediate consumption above the minimum level required for survival. Interventions need to build on – rather than ignore, by-pass, or overwhelm – indigenous institutions that underpin local risk management. These vary in their institutional capacity and significance, but a detailed assessment of such structures is an essential prerequisite for understanding and reinforcing local risk management strategies.

Fifth, appropriate and flexible institutional arrangements are needed. Opinions are divided as to whether purpose-built planning units are the most appropriate, or whether the emphasis should be on coordinating existing structures more effectively. Much depends on the local context. There is a need for greater respect of these institutions from donors and NGOs, in the sense of not by-passing or steam-rolling them in the name of humanitarian objectives. Reinforcing indigenous risk management capacities is a tall order given that national planning and implementation capacities are often chronically weak, resource-limited, and difficult to build up in a hurry. Institutional arrangements need to be sustained: the tendency for a flurry of activity immediately after a crisis can create overambitious structures in which interest wanes. A model is needed whereby quite light structures can be geared up quickly in the event of need.

Finally, it is unlikely that most African governments will be able to bear the costs of comprehensive risk management enhancing strategies, so donor support needs to be long term. This should not be confused, however, with responsibility for management, which must be firmly vested in national government hands. Donors can support national institutional arrangements by better coordinating their own activities, and by reducing the time lags in responding. Institutional amnesia needs to be overcome, so that lessons are learnt in each cycle of drought crisis and recovery.

How does the enhancing of indigenous risk management fit with the wider policy climate? Table 28.3 shows a matrix for the different actors in risk management, operating at different levels: the micro level (individuals/households, community institutions); the meso level (district or provincial government, NGOs); and the macro level (national government, international donors). Policy instruments operate in different parts of the matrix. Free food distributions, for example, link most of the cells, being funded by donors, facilitated by government, and executed by NGOs to reinforce individual and household food security. Community-based safety nets have only very localised effects and, when functioning properly, are largely independent of the wider policy environment, whereas macroeconomic tools (e.g., market interventions to stabilise food prices) are concentrated in the hands of government. Action is currently concentrated in the 'relief' cells. How can the other cells be filled? Effective risk

Table 28.3 Risk management matrix

STAGES	ACTORS					
	Micro		*Meso*		*Macro*	
	Individuals and households	*Community institutions*	*District or provincial government*	*NGOs*	*National government*	*International donors*

PREPAREDNESS
  Information and diagnosis
  Contingency planning
  Post-crisis evaluation						

MITIGATION
  Insurance
  strategies/interventions						

RELIEF
  Concurrent
  strategies/interventions						

REHABILITATION
  Recovery
  strategies/interventions						

Source: Adapted from Davies 1994

management is likely to comprise a mixture of policies and interventions linking different parts of the matrix. Preparedness is essential if the quite complex range of responses that this implies are to be successfully implemented.

There is great variation between countries in the relative capacity of different actors. Varying agro-ecological and politico-economic conditions require that efforts be concentrated in different parts of the matrix for particular countries. Where local response capacity is already highly evolved, it should be strengthened; elsewhere, reinforcing the role of the state may be more appropriate. Just as the capacity of actors varies, so too will the appropriateness of particular components in the matrix. Where drought and other shocks are frequent occurrences, emphasis on preparedness and mitigation is indicated. Where these occur, say, once every fifty years, relief measures may be more sensible, with much less comprehensive preparedness and mitigation, the premium for such insurance being too high. The matrix is intended, therefore, not as a hard and fast structure to be imposed across a range of widely differing situations, but as a tool for helping to identify those cells that should be accorded priority in a given context.

The institutional tendency to respond to the short-term effects of drought as if they were hermetically sealed from wider poverty reduction and development concerns needs to be redressed. Most of the above measures will facilitate this process, but it is unlikely that this divide can ever be entirely bridged without decentralisation of risk management. Given the complexity of options when local strategies are taken into account, scope for merging micro- and macro-level initiatives at the meso level needs to be explored. National risk management strategies are, by their very nature, incapable of being sufficiently finely tuned to fulfil this role, implying the need for greater decentralisation of planning and resources if local strategies are to be complemented. Decentralisation would make different elements of risk management more manageable and more location specific. Monitoring the likelihood and consequences of drought, and response capacity, closer to the action is more feasible with decentralised risk management. This, in turn, would increase the probability of locally appropriate and timely response at mitigation, relief, and rehabilitation stages and of these being linked to wider development objectives.

Decentralisation of risk management planning would reinforce current trends within many African governments toward more general decentralisation. It does not mean that all such activities are divorced from national-level planning, which will of necessity continue to play a key role in negotiations with donors and in resource allocation issues. The principle of subsidiarity, or the allocation of policy-making decisions and implementation tasks to the lowest possible administrative level, is useful in this respect. It does not imply mandatory decentralisation of all decision making and tasks, but instead suggests that these should be carried out *as close to the user or beneficiary as is feasible* (Swift 1994). Subsidiarity makes sense because international and national institutions are unlikely to be able to reform sufficiently to meet fully the multiplicity of tasks inherent in supporting local risk management. Their comparative advantage lies in creating the material and political conditions under which institutions closer to the ground can react. Further, the greatest scope for building on what already exists and functions reasonably well is at the local level, within the parameters of civil society (Davies 1994). It is in this middle ground – close to where crisis hits, but not entirely separate from national planning and resources – that local constraints and opportunities stand the greatest chance of being systematically addressed.

NOTES

1 This chapter is based on two earlier publications (Davies 1993a and 1994) and an unpublished report to UNSO (Davies 1993b).
2 The term *institutions* is used in the sense of regularised patterns of behaviour or prevailing rule systems, as distinct from actual organisations that operate within them (see North 1990).
3 Davies 1994, based on OFDA 1990.
4 See Curtis *et al.* 1988 for 1984–5; Buchanan-Smith and Davies 1995 for 1991–2.
5 See Amstader and Eriksen 1994, Berger and Koons 1994a and 1994b, Pushpanath 1994, SADC 1994, and, for a more critical view, Green 1993.

REFERENCES

Adams, A. (1993) 'Food insecurity in Mali: Exploring the role of the moral economy', *IDS Bulletin* 24, 4: 41–51.

Agarwal, B. (1990) 'Social security and the family in rural India: Coping with seasonality and calamity', *Journal of Peasant Studies* 17, 3: 341–412.

Amstader, I. and Eriksen, J. (1994) 'Evaluation of US Government response to 1991/92 Southern Africa drought – Country report: Botswana', report sponsored by Agency for International Development Bureau for Humanitarian Response, Washington, DC, and United States Agency for International Development/Namibia, Windhoek, Washington, DC: Management Systems International, Inc.

Berger, R. and Koons, A. (1994a) 'Evaluation of US Government response to 1991/92 Southern Africa drought – Country report: Malawi', report sponsored by Agency for International Development Bureau for Humanitarian Response, Washington, DC, and United States Agency for International Development/Malawi, Lilongwe, Washington, DC: Management Systems International, Inc.

—— (1994b) 'Evaluation of US Government response to 1991/92 Southern Africa drought – Country report: Zambia', report sponsored by Agency for International Development Bureau for Humanitarian Response, Washington, DC, and United States Agency for International Development/Zambia, Lusaka, Washington, DC: Management Systems International, Inc.

Brigaldino, G. (1996) 'Rehabilitation: A bridge between relief and development', *Development in Practice* 6, 4: 367–9.

Buchanan-Smith, M. (1990) 'Food security in the wake of an emergency relief operation: The case of Darfur, Western Sudan', *IDS Discussion Paper* No. 278, Brighton, UK: Institute of Development Studies.

Buchanan-Smith, M. and Davies, S. (1995) *Famine Early Warning and Response: The Missing Link?*, London: Intermediate Technology Publications.

Corbett, J. E. M. (1988) 'Famine and household coping strategies', *World Development* 16, 9: 1,009–12.

Curtis, D., Hubbard, M., and Shepherd, A. (1988) *Preventing Famine: Policies and Prospects for Africa*, London: Routledge.

Davies, S. (1993a) 'Are coping strategies a cop out?', *IDS Bulletin* 24, 4: 60–72.

—— (1993b) 'Preparing for and mitigating drought: Linking macro and micro levels', report to United Nations Sudano–Sahelian Office, New York.

—— (1994) 'Public institutions, people and famine mitigation', *IDS Bulletin* 25, 4: 46–54.

—— (1996) *Adaptable Livelihoods: Strategic Adaptation to Food Insecurity in the Malian Sahel*, Basingstoke, UK: Macmillan.

de Waal, A. (1989) *Famine that Kills: Darfur, Sudan, 1984–1985*, Oxford: Clarendon Press.

—— (1996) 'Social contract and deterring famine: First thoughts', *Disasters* 20, 3: 194–205.

Drèze, J. (1990) 'Famine prevention in Africa: Some experiences and lessons', in J. Drèze and A. Sen (eds), *The Political Economy of Hunger. Vol. 2: Famine Prevention*, Oxford: Oxford University Press.

Drèze, J. and Sen, A. (1989) *Hunger and Public Action*, Oxford: Oxford University Press.

Duffield, M. (1990a) 'War and famine in Africa', *Oxfam Research Paper* 5, Oxford: Oxfam.

—— (1990b) 'Sudan at the cross-roads: From emergency procedures to social security', *IDS Discussion Paper* 275, Brighton, UK: Institute of Development Studies.

Dyson, T. (1993) 'Demographic responses to famines in South Asia', *IDS Bulletin* 24, 4: 17–26.

Frankenberger, T.R. (1992) 'Indicators and data collection methods for assessing household food security', in S. Maxwell and T.R. Frankenberger, *Household Food Security Concepts, Indicators, Measurement*, New York: United Nations Children's Fund and Rome: International Fund for Agricultural Development.

Gore, C. (1993) 'Entitlement relations and "unruly" social practices: A comment on the work of Amartya Sen', *Journal of Development Studies* 29, 3: 429–60.

Green, R. (1993) 'The political economy of drought in Southern Africa 1991–3', *Health Policy and Planning* 8, 3: 255–66.

Longhurst, R. (1986) 'Household food strategies in response to seasonality and famine', *IDS Bulletin* 17, 3: 27–35.

—— (1992) 'Country experiences in famine mitigation', *Famine Mitigation Occasional Paper*, Washington, DC: United States Agency for International Development, US Office of Foreign Disaster Assistance, Prevention, Mitigation and Preparedness Division.

Maxwell, S. (1990) 'Food security in developing countries: Issues and options for the 1990s', *IDS Bulletin* 21, 3: 2–13.

—— (1992) 'Famine prevention', paper prepared for conference 'Food Aid and Famine', CARE (UK), London, 2 November 1992. Brighton, UK: Institute of Development Studies (mimeo).

Mortimore, M.J. (1989) *Adapting to Drought: Farmers, Famines and Desertification in West Africa*, Cambridge: Cambridge University Press.

North, D. (1990) *Institutions, Institutional Change and Economic Performance*, Cambridge: Cambridge University Press.

OFDA (1990) 'Report: Drought Disaster Mitigation Workshop', 30 April–2 May 1990, Emmitsburg, Maryland, Washington, DC: Office of US Foreign Disaster Assistance.

Pushpanath, K. (1994) 'Disaster without memory: Oxfam's drought programme in Zambia', *Development in Practice* 4, 2: 81–91.

Reardon, T. and Matlon, P. (1989) 'Seasonal food insecurity and vulnerability in drought-affected regions of Burkina Faso', in D.E. Sahn (ed.), *Seasonal Variability in Third World Agriculture: The Consequences for Food Security*, Baltimore: Johns Hopkins University Press for International Food Policy Research Institute.

Riely, F. (1991) 'Household responses to recurrent drought: A case study of the Kababish pastoralists in Northern Kordofan, Sudan', in *Famine and Food Policy Discussion Paper* 6, Washington, DC: International Food Policy Research Institute.

SADC (1994) 'Drought Management Workshops in Southern Africa: Final Report', Southern African Development Community Food Security Technical and Administrative Unit.

Sen, A. (1981) *Poverty and Famines: An Essay on Entitlement and Deprivation*, Oxford: Clarendon Press.

Swift, J. (1989a) 'Why are rural people vulnerable to famine?', *IDS Bulletin* 20, 2: 8–15.

—— (1989b) 'Planning against drought and famine in Turkana: A District Contingency Plan', in T.E. Downing, K.W. Gitu, and M.K. Crispin (eds), *Coping with Drought in Kenya*, Boulder and London: Lynne Rienner.

—— (1994) 'Dynamic ecological systems in the administration of pastoral development', in I. Scoones (ed.), *Living with Uncertainty: New Directions in Pastoral Development in Africa*, London: Intermediate Technology Publications.

von Braun, J. (1991) 'A policy agenda for famine prevention in Africa', *IFPRI Food Policy Report*, Washington, DC: International Food Policy Research Institute.

Watts, M. (1983) *Silent Violence, Food, Famine and Peasantry in Northern Nigeria*, Berkeley: University of California Press.

—— (1988) 'Coping with the market: Uncertainty and food security among Hausa peasants', in I. de Garine and G.A. Harrison (eds), *Coping with Uncertainty in Food Supply*, Oxford: Clarendon Press.

Webb, P. and Reardon, T. (1991) 'Drought impact and household response in East and West Africa', Washington, DC: International Food Policy Research Institute (mimeo).

WFP (1989) 'Review of food aid policies and programmes: Anti-hunger strategies of poor households and communities: Roles of food aid', Report No. WFP/CFA:27/P/INF/1 Add.1, Rome: World Food Programme.

World Bank (1986) *Poverty and Hunger: Issues and Options for Food Security in Developing Countries*, World Bank Policy Study, Washington, DC: World Bank.

Young, H. and Jaspars, S. (1994) *Nutrition Matters: People, Food and Famine*, London: Intermediate Technology Publications.

PRODUCTIVE WATER POINTS AS A MEANS OF COPING WITH DROUGHT

Charles Batchelor, Chris Lovell, and Isiah Mharapara

INTRODUCTION

In recent years, it has become fashionable to advocate indigenous soil and water conservation practices as a primary means of reducing environmental degradation and increasing agricultural production in the dryland areas of Africa. For example, Reij *et al.* (1996) describe twenty-seven case studies in which a range of different soil and water conservation practices have been promoted in different parts of Africa. Although adoption of these practices can result in a range of benefits during nondrought years, they produce minimal or no benefits during drought years. In areas with accessible and reliable water resources, the obvious solution to maintaining agricultural production during drought years is to irrigate crops both for human and livestock consumption. Although irrigation of small plots, particularly vegetable gardens, is an indigenous practice, promoting irrigation has become unfashionable during the last decade for a number of reasons, the main one being that large irrigation schemes in Africa, and many small-scale irrigation schemes for that matter, have proved to be expensive, relatively inefficient, and difficult to reconcile with traditional farming systems (Underhill 1990). In addition, large irrigation schemes, in many cases, have led to a range of health-related and environmental problems.

Disenchantment with irrigation as a means of increasing agricultural production and coping with drought is illogical and misguided. Experience from Zimbabwe and elsewhere in southern Africa has shown that informal garden irrigation does not suffer from many of the problems that affect large irrigation schemes. Experience from Zimbabwe has also shown that informal garden irrigation can be economically viable and appropriate for farmers, especially women farmers, for whom it is already a traditional component of the farming system. It should be noted also that the majority of farmers in southern Africa, given half a chance, are keen to incorporate irrigated cropping into their farming system. In 1988, a programme of research and development was started in southern Zimbabwe with the main objectives of studying the feasibility of using shallow crystalline basement aquifers as a source of water for small-scale irrigation and assessing the potential of using *productive water points* as an initial step toward establishing community-based sustainable management of natural resources. In this context, productive water points are considered to be community-based water points that are designed and implemented to provide water for both domestic use and income-generating activities such as small-scale vegetable production. This chapter gives a brief description of the main elements of this programme. More information can be found in Lovell *et al.* (1996 and 1998) and Murata *et al.* (1995).

Background to the project

Drought is a natural and recurring phenomenon in Zimbabwe. Traditional drought coping strategies have become much less effective as a result of population increases during the last century; consequent competition for land, water, and other natural resources; and changes in landownership and tenure. In the nineteenth century, before the arrival of

European settlers, the limited scale of subsistence agriculture imposed little stress on the environment, except on the fertile and well-watered but steep slopes of the Eastern Highlands (Moyo *et al.* 1993). Elsewhere, rotational methods of resource utilisation meant that the natural resource base was not damaged. Periodic drought had a serious impact on the quality of life of rural people, but the effects of drought were ameliorated by migration and by recourse to a variety of food sources that did not succumb rapidly to drought.

The political history of Zimbabwe has resulted in the country being divided into areas that have distinctly different land management systems. These areas include large tracts of land that are owned and farmed predominantly by white commercial farmers and large areas of communal land, in which the majority of the rural population of Zimbabwe live (Moyo *et al.* 1993). The problems of communal areas of southern Zimbabwe typify those problems now facing people and the environment in many semiarid parts of Africa. Prime constraints on sustainable development are the low and erratic rainfall and the availability of ground and surface water resources. Rain-fed crop production provides the main source of staple foodstuffs. Since 1980, the government of Zimbabwe has adopted policies aimed at improving the management of resources in rural areas. However, the successful implementation of these policies remains elusive, as does the goal of sustainable agricultural development. Although the situation in the drier communal areas of Zimbabwe appears gloomy, there are good reasons to believe that more sustainable production systems can be developed. One approach that could be used would be to make more effective use of water from crystalline basement aquifers, which are, for much of the country, underexploited.

Crystalline basement aquifers

Crystalline basement aquifers, which are present over much of Africa (see Figure 29.1), provide a limited but extensive resource that has the potential for greater use (Wright 1992). Lovell *et al.* (1996) estimated, on a regional long-term basis, that groundwater use from these aquifers in communal areas of southeast Zimbabwe is only around 4 per cent of average annual recharge. Although extremely variable in space and time, recharge is estimated to be in the range of 2–5 per cent of annual rainfall (Houston 1988).

In general, water in basement aquifers is found within the weathered residual overburden (or regolith) and the fractured bedrock. In Zimbabwe, current development is generally carried out by digging wells within the regolith or drilling boreholes to intercept fractures in the bedrock. Research during the last twelve years has demonstrated that collector wells can be used to increase groundwater abstraction from the regolith (Wright 1992). A collector well is a shallow hand-dug well of large diameter with horizontal boreholes drilled radially from the base to a distance of approximately 30 m, typically in four directions (see Figure 29.2). Because collector wells are shallow, normally 5–15 m depth to water, and have low drawdowns, hand pumping from the wells is less arduous than is the case for boreholes. In addition, the wide diameter vertical shaft also provides increased volume of storage and allows two or more hand pumps to be installed. This enables relatively high pumping rates to be achieved using hand pumps rather than motorised pumps, which also reduces the risk of water shortages from pump breakdowns.

Results of research studies in Zimbabwe, Malawi, and Sri Lanka have shown that collector wells can be

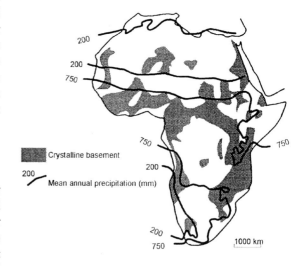

Figure 29.1 Distribution of basement aquifers in Africa
Source: Wright 1992

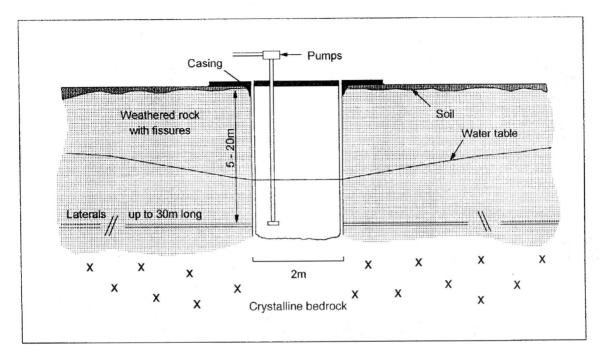

Figure 29.2 Schematic diagram of a collector well

used to maximise and optimise groundwater abstraction from basement aquifers that are not suited to slim boreholes. This work has demonstrated that, in these areas, higher average yields can be obtained from collector wells than from slim boreholes, with the added advantage of small drawdowns. Mean safe yield from eight collector wells in Zimbabwe and Malawi and twenty wells in Sri Lanka has been calculated at $2.7 \, ls^{-1}$ (ranges of 1.1–6.6 and 0.5–8.0 ls^{-1}, respectively) with drawdowns of 2–3 m. These results can be compared with typical yields of 0.1–0.7 ls^{-1} for slim boreholes at pumping drawdowns in excess of 30 m (Wright 1992).

DESIGN OF IRRIGATED GARDENS

In organisational terms, a number of different types of irrigated gardens can be found in dryland areas of Africa. These include *private gardens*, whereby one farmer or one household fence and manage their garden using water from their own well, a river, or a public water point; *community* or *allotment-type*

gardens, whereby a number of farmers or households have plots within a fenced area and water is obtained from a public water point; and *collective gardens*, whereby a garden is operated by the community and the produce is shared. The type of gardening practised depends on a number of factors, including availability of water resources, social and institutional considerations, and the advice given to communities by extension services.

Availability of water is a major constraint to gardening in crystalline basement aquifer areas, to the extent that few individual farmers are able to implement groundwater-based private gardens either because there is insufficient groundwater beneath their land or because the cost of accessing groundwater is prohibitively expensive. These factors tend to encourage the development of community or collective gardens, and in Zimbabwe, most rural communities, when given the choice, prefer some type of community garden.

Assuming that sufficient water resources are available, the main advantages of private gardens versus community or collective gardens are all related to the relative ease with which they can be set up and managed. Decision making is made by a single household, and leadership disputes, which are inevitable with community gardens, are less common. However, if water resources are scarce, as is the case in much of southern Zimbabwe, private gardens tend to promote inequality between the relatively richer garden owners and relatively poorer non-garden owners. Apart from improving equity at the village level, community or allotment gardens have the advantage over private gardens that they can reduce competition for water resources between private farmers. Community gardens also have the important advantage that they can provide communities with confidence and organisational experience that can be used to tackle other resource management problems at the village level. Many of these problems, such as reducing over-

grazing of communal grazing areas or reducing runoff from hill slopes, can only be tackled effectively by community or collective action.

DESCRIPTION OF THE COLLECTOR WELL GARDEN PROGRAMME

In 1989, a collector well and irrigated garden (1 ha in area) were installed at the Chiredzi Research Station in southeast Zimbabwe (21° S, 31° E, elevation 429 m). These were used for demonstration purposes and also as the location for a series of replicated irrigation trials that were aimed at comparing and developing improved methods of irrigation suitable for use on small irrigated gardens (Batchelor et al. 1996). In 1990, the first off-station collector well garden or productive water point was constructed in the Romwe Catchment with the participation of members

Plate 29.1 Aerial view of the Romwe collector well garden during the 1991–2 drought

Plate 29.2 A productive water point during the 1991–2 drought

of three villages. Ninety-eight households have been using this well as a primary source of drinking water and forty-six households have been growing vegetables on 100 m² allotments on the garden. The success of this garden, particularly during the 1991–2 drought, prompted the implementation of a further eight schemes during 1992–5. These schemes were implemented as part of a pilot project that studied the technical, socioeconomic, and institutional aspects of locating, implementing, and managing productive water points. Many valuable lessons were learnt with regard to well design and siting and with regard to ensuring the participation of the communities and local institutions (Lovell *et al.* 1996). These lessons were used as a basis for developing a series of decision trees that are to be used as guidelines in the execution of a project that will implement a further one hundred gardens and water points in southern Zimbabwe during the next five years.

One innovative approach adopted to minimise confusion over scheme ownership and community participation was the use of informal contracts. These contracts were drawn up and discussed by communities and project staff before the commencement of groundwater exploration. The main benefit of such contracts has been that they clearly define responsibilities for scheme implementation, operation, and maintenance. Informal contracts also play an important role in guaranteeing transparency and openness in discussions between project staff and community members, in outlining obligations, and in clarifying misconceptions. Another important factor in determining sense of ownership was the fact that project staff did not place time constraints on negotiations. It was recognised that, whenever possible, rural development should be process oriented and not target oriented.

In 1992, work started in the Romwe Catchment

on a project to study the processes and mechanisms that control groundwater recharge in dryland areas underlain by crystalline basement geologies. In 1994, additional monitoring equipment was installed to monitor the effects of land use and management on groundwater recharge and quantify the physical and socioeconomic benefits of taking an integrated approach to the management of natural resources. The Romwe Catchment Study has been set up with the participation of local communities and institutions, and most of the data collection is carried out by members of the local community. This data collection includes keeping records of agricultural output, groundwater levels, soil erosion, and surface runoff as measured by a number of weirs and flumes (Lovell *et al*. 1998). Figure 29.3 is a typical output from the participative monitoring that shows the important influence of land use and soil type on surface runoff as measured by weirs located in three subcatchments within the Romwe Catchment.

PERFORMANCE OF COLLECTOR WELL GARDENS

Data collected by scheme members and surveys taken before and after productive water points were implemented give an indication of the wide portfolio of benefits that arise from community gardens and from other income-generating activities such as brick making or beer brewing (Waughray *et al*. 1995 and 1997). Internal rates of return for gardens are 11–15 per cent, with an overall average gross margin for 1994–5 of Z$67,433 ha[-1], Z$310 per member, and Z$10.8 per labour day (in February 1995, Z$13 = £1). Of those who took up allotments on the garden, 80 per cent are women and 49 per cent, on average, are

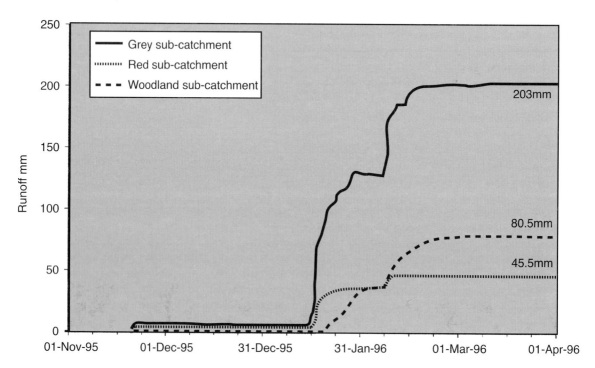

Figure 29.3 Effects of land use and soil type on runoff
Notes: In this example, over 200 mm runoff from a cultivated sub-catchment with grey sandy soils over clay occurred due to the formation of a perched water-table. Runoff from the woodland exceeded that from the sub-catchment with red clay soils as significant baseflow was captured at the gauging site.
    Monitoring the hydrology of catchments with contrasting characteristics and land use helps provide fundamental data for assessing the effects of land use change and for developing policies that lead to improved resource management
Source: Lovell *et al*. 1998

among the very poorest in the communities. Gardens supply fresh vegetables that are consumed as a relish by both garden members and nonmembers. Whilst some gardening continues during the rainy season when rain-fed cropping is taking place, garden production is highest and returns are greatest during dry seasons and during periods of drought. Figure 29.4 shows the nonavailability of vegetables before and after the implementation of gardens. This figure shows that scarcity of vegetables during normal dry seasons is much reduced for both garden members and nonmembers.

The schemes possess considerable potential for income generation and income diversification for garden members. The average income per member obtained by selling excess produce during 1994–5 was Z$225 in an area where 50 per cent of households have an income of less than $400 per year. Women are controlling the saving and investment of cash generated. At least 50 per cent of all garden members were found to be involved in savings clubs and revolving funds. Only one fund was said to have existed before the collector well gardens existed, and this has expanded. Savings from these funds are being spent on education and household necessities or on initiating other income-generating activities.

The users of productive water points can be separated into three groups: households that were involved in scheme implementation and that use the well as a source of water for domestic use and income-generating activities; households that were probably not involved in scheme implementation but use the well as a source of domestic water; and a more

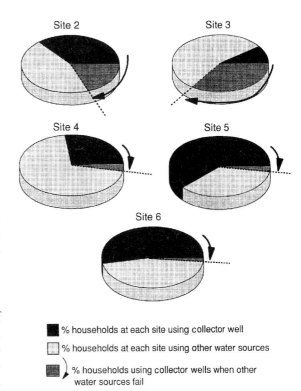

% households at each site using collector well

% households at each site using other water sources

% households using collector wells when other water sources fail

Figure 29.5 Surges in collector well use as other water sources fail

peripheral group that uses the well during periods of drought when other wells or water sources fail. It has become clear that collector wells are, in general, a more reliable water source than other well designs during periods of drought. Figure 29.5 shows the surge in collector well usage that occurs at five of the wells that have been monitored as part of the Collector Well Garden Programme. It is clear that the collector wells become extremely important for the peripheral group of users during periods of drought.

COMMUNITY-BASED INTEGRATED NATURAL RESOURCE MANAGEMENT

Many institutions and international agencies are showing considerable interest in community-based integrated natural resource management (INRM) as a practical means of mitigating the effects of drought and reducing environmental degradation.

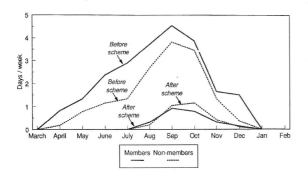

Figure 29.4 Before and after vegetable consumption

The exact nature of the economic, social, and physical feedback mechanisms that lead to environmental degradation has been under debate for many decades (Thomas and Middleton 1994). One shortcoming of many attempts to identify key feedback mechanisms has been the lack of recognition of the fact that social and economic (or human) feedback mechanisms can take place at the same temporal and spatial scales as physical feedback mechanisms and that these two feedbacks are often mutually reinforcing. Thomas and Middleton (1994) proposed feedback cycles, based on Scoging (1991), that acknowledge the intimate links between human and physical feedbacks. Figure 29.6 is based on this work.

The logic behind the negative human feedback cycle in Figure 29.6 is that vegetation reduction, which may be a result of increased human pressure, drought, or poor management, will lead to shorter fallows and cropping of marginal lands. This, in turn, will lead to a reduction in soil fertility, and productivity per unit area and per land holding will decline. The resulting income reduction and poverty will encourage further vegetation reduction as a result of increased overgrazing and clearance of remaining forestry. The physical feedback, which is discussed in more detail by Wallace (1994), is based on the fact that loss of vegetation cover may trigger feedback mechanisms that can propagate further land degradation via the land surface–atmosphere feedback. This occurs when a decrease in evaporation and an increase in the amount of radiation reflected back to the atmosphere (albedo) reduce cloud formation and rainfall, causing a negative feedback, which may further reduce vegetation. Another possible mechanism contributing to dryland degradation is hydrological. This can occur when a decrease in ground cover associated with poor land management results in increased and more rapid runoff, decreased soil moisture storage, and reduced groundwater recharge. In this situation, less of the rain that does fall on degraded land is available for plant growth, the risk of severe soil erosion is increased, and less groundwater will be available either for deep-rooting trees or as a resource that can be used by rural communities. The hydrological feedback can also exist in the absence of any climatic change, which is another mechanism that can

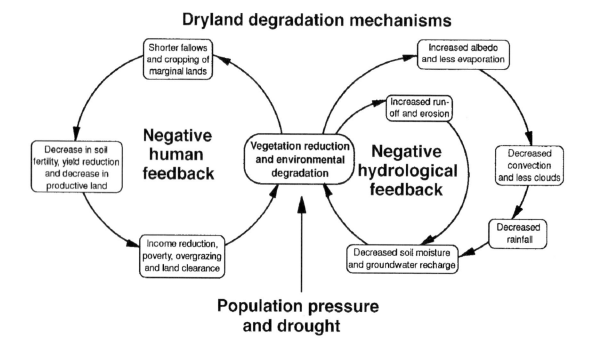

Figure 29.6 Negative feedback

contribute to degradation. Here, 'external' influences stemming from sea-surface temperature anomalies, humid tropical deforestation, and/or CO_2-induced climate change are thought to be associated with drought and degradation in arid zones such as the West African Sahel. Another example of a possible linkage between sea surface temperatures and rainfall is the correlation observed between rainfall and crop yields in southern Africa and sea temperatures in the eastern equatorial Pacific Ocean (Cane *et al.* 1994).

A failing of many community-based INRM strategies has been that, although they have been able to articulate the right aspirations for the management of resources, they have not been able to bring about improvements in resource management at the catchment scale (Blackmore 1994). One of the main hypotheses behind the Collector Well Garden Project is that the implementation of community-based productive water points is the ideal initial step toward the implementation of community-based INRM on a wide scale. Although it is too early to be totally confident that this hypothesis is correct, there is evidence that a first productive water point can provide the initial step that brings about a reversal of the feedback loops described in Figure 29.6. The evidence and arguments are as follows:

- Unlike many improved resource management practices, productive water points produce a range of benefits to garden members in a short space of time. The immediacy of these benefits is crucial because they provide the incentive for communities to overcome leadership or other social problems that are inevitable with community-based projects (Waughray *et al.* 1997).

- Having successfully implemented a scheme and started to benefit from the scheme, communities are more likely to recognise the need to protect this scheme by managing the recharge zone around the water point. In some cases, this intrinsic awareness needs to be reinforced by external agents such as extension workers.

- As well as providing an incentive for taking a long-term view of managing natural resources, productive water points provide an alternative to income-generating practices that might provide some level of short-term drought mitigation but lead to long-term resource depletion. As noted earlier, the Romwe collector well garden scheme was a vital source of domestic water, fresh vegetables, and income during the 1991–2 drought.

- Experience and social capital gained from a first community-based garden can be used to establish other improved resource management practices. It is also clear that confidence gained from implementing a first scheme inspires communities to tackle other natural resource problems, either themselves or with the help of external agencies. Ideally, communities, working with appropriate assistance, will develop their own INRM strategy and start a programme of integrated catchment management. In some cases, this INRM strategy might be developed before the establishment of a community garden as part of a consultative village inventory or participatory rural appraisal exercise.

- Gardens enable income to be generated by individuals and by the garden committee. Lack of income is a huge impediment to entrepreneurial activity. Revolving or community funds can be used to initiate a range of activities, with some related to agriculture and others related to commerce or cottage industries.

- Gardens provide a regular meeting place for informal discussion and problem solving. Women working in the garden and pumping and collecting water are able to discuss and plan either proposals emanating from within the community or from outside agencies. Gardens also provide an ideal meeting place for discussions with agricultural extension workers.

Figure 29.7 attempts to show that a first productive water point can lead to improved resource management practices that will lead to increased vegetation cover at a village and catchment scale, which, in turn, will lead to a reversal of the physical feedback (although the sequence of steps may vary). However, the reversal of this feedback will not be straightforward if climate change has occurred because of external factors. Similarly, if the human feedback is being strongly influenced by external factors (e.g.,

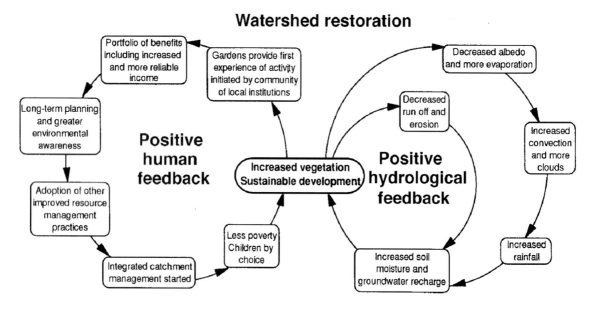

Figure 29.7 Positive feedback

economic structural adjustment programmes, changes in the law relating to land tenure), then reversal may not be possible.

Collective responsibility for water and other natural resources

The degree of collective responsibility for water and other common property resources has a significant bearing on the ability of a rural community to mitigate the worst effects of drought. A second hypothesis behind the Collector Well Garden Programme has been that appropriate implementation of a first community-based productive water point can improve or establish collective responsibility for water and other environmental resources. To date, scheme monitoring has shown that productive water points are effective in establishing collective responsibility for the maintenance of pumps. In contrast to community-based and water sanitation projects in southeast Zimbabwe, pumps on the productive water points are being maintained and repaired by the users. Managing the water resource at each water point has entailed some degree of collective responsibility and decision making, particularly during periods of drought. Collector well gardens are having an impact

on the surrounding farming system in that income from the gardens is being used to purchase livestock, seeds, and agrochemicals and to hire labour for tasks such as weeding on rain-fed fields (Waughray *et al.* 1997). However, to date, this impact has not formed part of any efforts to establish collective responsibility for, say, improving groundwater recharge in areas around the collector wells.

A number of researchers have identified the conditions under which joint management of common property can be successful (e.g., Wade 1987, Evans 1996). These conditions, which are related to both the resource and the user group, include the following:

- the resource is small and clearly defined;
- there is a close physical proximity between the resource and the users;
- the users have a high level of dependence on the resource;
- a small and defined set of users already have established arrangements for discussing common problems;
- decision-making power within the user community is in the hands of subgroups favouring communal action;

- cheating with regard to resource use is easily noticed; and
- the costs of exclusion from the resource are high.

It is clear that the majority of these conditions either prevail or can be created when implementing productive water points in dryland areas. Hence, there has to be some optimism that, with appropriate facilitation, productive water points can lead initially to the establishment of collective responsibility for water resources.

CONCLUSIONS

Provisional findings of the Collector Well Garden Programme have shown that collector wells and productive water points provide a wide range of benefits during both drought and nondrought years. Provisional findings also suggest that productive water points can provide an ideal first step to the development of community-based integrated natural resource management (INRM). The development of productive water points in sub-Saharan Africa is constrained by the availability of water resources. However, the Collector Well Garden Programme has demonstrated that innovative drilling techniques can be used to develop water resources in the weathered surface zone of crystalline basement aquifers in areas that are not suited to more conventional drilling techniques. Because crystalline basement aquifers are present over large areas of sub-Saharan Africa, further development of these aquifers may be the key step to initiating community-based INRM in much of this region.

REFERENCES

Batchelor, C.H., Lovell, C.J., and Murata, M. (1996) 'Simple microirrigation techniques for improving irrigation efficiency on vegetable gardens', *Agricultural Water Management* 32: 37–48.

Blackmore, D.J. (1994) 'Integrated catchment management – The Murray-Darling Basin experience', in C. Schonfeldt, P. Saunders, and M. Knight (eds), *Water Down Under '94*, Vol. 1, Silver Spring, MD: Accents Publications Service, Inc., pp. 1–7.

Cane, M.A., Eshel, G., and Buckland, R.W. (1994) 'Forecasting Zimbabwean maize yield using eastern equatorial Pacific sea temperature', *Nature* 370: 204–5.

Evans, B. (1996) 'Institutional incentives and urban sanitation', in WEDC, *Reaching the Unreached: Challenges for the 21st Century*, Proceedings of the 22nd WEDC Conference (New Delhi), Leicestershire, UK: Water, Engineering and Development Centre, Loughborough University, pp. 38–40.

Houston, J.F.T. (1988) 'Rainfall-runoff-recharge relationships in the basement rocks of Zimbabwe', in I. Simmers (ed.), *Estimation of Natural Groundwater Recharge*, Dordrecht and Boston, MA: D. Reidel Publishing Co., pp. 349–65.

Lovell, C.J., Batchelor, C.H., Waughray, D.K., Semple, A.J., Mazhangara, E., Mtetwa, G., Murata, M., Brown, M.W., Dube, T., Thompson, D.T., Chilton, P.J., Macdonald, D.M.J., Conyers, D., and Mugweni, O. (1996) 'Small scale irrigation using collector wells pilot project – Zimbabwe: Final Report', *IH Report* ODA 95/14, Institute of Hydrology, Wallingford, UK, p. 106.

Lovell, C.J., Butterworth, J.A, Moriarty, P.B., Bromley, J., Batchelor, C.H., Mharapara, I., and Mugabe, F.T. (1998) 'Romwe Catchment Study: Final Report', *IH Report* DFID 98/3, Institute of Hydrology, Wallingford, UK.

Moyo, S., O'Keefe, P., and Sill, M. (1993) 'Zimbabwe', in S. Moyo, P. O'Keefe, and M. Sill, *The Southern African Environment: Profiles of the SADC Countries*, London: Earthscan, pp. 303–39.

Murata, M., Batchelor, C.H., Lovell, C.J., Brown, M.W., Semple, A.J., Mazhangara, E., Haria, A., McGrath, S.P., and Williams, R.J. (1995) 'Development of small-scale irrigation using limited groundwater resources: Fourth Interim Report', *IH Report* ODA 95/5, Institute of Hydrology, Wallingford, UK.

Reij, C., Scoones, I., and Toulmin, C. (1996) *Sustaining the Soil: Indigenous Soil and Water Conservation in Africa*, London: Earthscan Ltd., p. 260.

Scoging, H. (1991) 'Desertification and its management', in R. Bennet and R. Estall (eds), *Global Change and Challenge. Geography for the 1990's*, London: Routledge, pp. 57–79.

Thomas, D.S.G. and Middleton, N.J. (1994) *Desertification: Exploding the Myth*, Chichester, UK: Wiley, pp. 194.

Underhill, H.W. (1990) *Small-scale Irrigation in Africa in the Context of Rural Development*, Bedford, UK: Cranfield Press.

Wade, R. (1987) 'The management of common property resources: Finding a cooperative solution', *Research Observer* 2: 2, IBRD.

Wallace, J.S. (1994) 'Hydrological processes and dryland degradation', *WMO Bulletin* 43, 1: 22–8.

Waughray, D.K., Mazanghara, E.M., Mtetwa, G., Mtetwa, M., Dube, T., Lovell, C.J., and Batchelor, C.H. (1995) 'Small-scale irrigation using collector wells: Return-to-households survey', *IH Report* ODA 95/13,

Institute of Hydrology, Wallingford, UK, p. 107.

Waughray, D.K., Lovell, C.J., Moriarty, P.M., Batchelor, C.H., Nangati, F., Keatinge, D., Mtetwa, G. and Dube, T. (1997) 'Community resource management and livelihood strategies phase I', *IH Report* ODA 97/1, Institute of Hydrology, Wallingford, UK, p. 82.

Wright, E.P. (1992) 'The hydrogeology of crystalline basement aquifers in Africa', in E.P. Wright and W.G. Burgess (eds), *The Hydrogeology of Crystalline Basement Aquifers in Africa*, London: Geological Society of London (Geological Society Special Publication No. 66), pp. 1–28.

RESPONSE STRATEGIES OF LOCAL FARMERS IN INDIA

A.R. Subbiah[1]

INTRODUCTION

High rainfall variability and drought are common phenomena in semiarid and arid regions of India. The Indian farmers of various agroclimatic regions evolved numerous strategies to live with droughts. Even in normal years, Indian farmers remain aware of the possibility of drought. They undertake water management, crop management, contingency crop planning, and alternate enterprises to minimise recurrent drought impacts. Although farmers treat both positive (normal) and negative (drought) rainfall variations as an integral part of climatic variation and manage the situations in a holistic manner, the public policies of many countries perceive drought as a discrete and unexpected event and deal with the negative side (drought) of rainfall variation. As such, drought relief programmes are designed to respond to drought by treating it as a transient phenomenon, and response efforts, therefore, are undertaken to provide relief during the crisis period. Recent public policy instruments, however, do recognise the significance of farmers' strategies for mitigating the impacts of droughts.

THE CLIMATIC CONSTRAINTS OF DRYLAND AREAS

The principal source of water for sustaining dryland farming systems in India, as elsewhere, is rain. About 80 per cent of the annual precipitation is received during summer monsoon periods (June–September). A drought frequency of less than three years occurs over 13.2 per cent of India's total geographical area, and drought frequencies of three, four, and five years occur over 11.6 per cent, 36.5 per cent, and 30.9 per cent, respectively, of India (Jodha *et al.* 1988).

The most significant attribute of rainfall variation is concentration of rains in a few spells in the dry tropics. Over vast tracts of semiarid and arid regions, monsoon conditions last barely sixty to seventy-five days, with ten to fifteen effective rainy days. Moisture availability crucial for crop growth is short eight to ten months a year in these seasonally dry areas. Heavy precipitation exceeding 200 mm in two to three days usually entails quick runoff that carries top soil with it, causing silting in reservoirs. Quick rainwater runoff, even though it can cause flash floods, reduces moisture availability during critical stages of crop growth and drastically reduces crop yields.

High rainfall variability and drought are common phenomena in semiarid and arid regions. The rainfall variability-induced uncertainties shaped the farming system in these drought-prone regions. Even in normal years, the possibility of drought influences both the options and strategies of the villagers (Chen 1991). The basic principle guiding dryland farmers' adaptation to climatic risks is to capture opportunities provided by good monsoon conditions to build buffers against rainfall-related uncertainties in subsequent years. Farmers treat normal and drought years as an integral part of climatic variation, and drought-related risk is built into their livelihood response system. Farmers in India evolved many resource management practices to survive recurrent droughts. Some of these strategies are described below.

WATER MANAGEMENT

In response to highly uneven concentrations of rain-storms, farmers harvest runoff through water harvesting structures and recycle the collected water for irrigating crops. Efficient and timely use of rainwater makes all the difference between adequate and poor harvests during the worst droughts. Farming communities devised practices to conserve rainwater and preserve soil moisture through location specific water-harvesting structures and agronomic practices. Both small-scale and large-scale water harvesting structures have been built over the centuries. The basic principle behind this strategy is to collect and store rainwater to raise crops. Some of the rainwater harvesting systems are:

- *Khadim* (mostly in low rainfall regions – less than 500 mm per annum): Wherever possible, cultivators raise tiny embankments around their fields to conserve rainwater. The practice of raising earthen embankments across gullies in low rainfall areas (areas having less than 500 mm annual rainfall) to recharge root zones for a successful winter crop has been used for many years.

- *Tanks* (in the medium rainfall zones – 700–1,000 mm per annum): Influenced by geographic features and climatic conditions, farmers of peninsular India evolved tank irrigation practices. These tanks are small water-harvesting structures to impound water during the peak rainy season for use in irrigation in dry periods. The special feature of these tanks is that they lie in a row, formed by earthen embankments at different elevations. The purpose of such an arrangement was to facilitate collection and storage of surplus water overflowing from one tank (on a higher level) to the next (on a lower level). In this arrangement, surplus water in the upper-level tank not only reaches the next tank at the lower level but also ensures continuous seepage to recharge groundwater in the area. In Tamil Nadu alone, more than 38,000 such tanks, which were built centuries ago, exist today.

- *Kunta* (in the high rainfall regions – more than 1,000 mm per annum): Small community ponds are the predominant devices for providing supple-mental irrigation to rain-fed paddy during long breaks in rainfall.

Farmers watch every season's early rainfall and its variability and intensity, and then attempt to predict rainfall for the remainder of the season. To measure the volume of rainfall received as the season progresses, they use the 'tank watch' method – that is, they estimate, by observation, the amount of water in small reservoirs during different phases of the season – the beginning, the middle, and the end (Tennakoon 1986). The farmers select a suitable crop to plant based on the amount of water available in the rainwater storage structures.

CROP MANAGEMENT

Crop diversification and mixed/inter cropping

Growing a number of crops anticipating yield compensation is one method of minimising weather-induced risk. In certain areas, farmers cultivate seven to ten crops on their farms. Farmers view the system of mixed/inter cropping as providing stability against weather-induced fluctuations in yields and incomes. This mixed cropping system is based mainly on groundnut, consisting of redgram, horsegram, cowpea and/or mungbean, corn, and pearl millet. This combination is believed to ensure food requirements of cereals and pulses as well as fodder requirements of cattle. Groundnut meets the financial needs of the farm family. The underlying logic behind the mixed/inter cropping system, besides meeting food, fodder, and financial needs of the farm family, is to incorporate leguminous crops into the farming system to improve soil fertility and prevent pest and disease infestation.

Although modern developments, like the introduction of high-yielding varieties (HYV) through Green Revolution practices, disturbed mixed economy practices in some areas, the farmers are reverting to traditional crop diversification practices. For instance, a study in certain areas of the Indian state of Karnataka revealed this trend (Bandyopadhyay 1987).

Before 1965–6, the cropping pattern in the semiarid region of Karnataka state was maize, cotton, groundnut, and pearl millet as the main crops, mixed and in rotation with other crops. Maize was mixed with pulse in proportions of 1 : 10 to 1 : 5. The mixed crop provided insurance against drought. Further insurance against unexpected crop failure due to low rainfall was the cultivation of a hardy food crop called 'samey'. In the early 1960s, HYV maize was introduced under irrigated conditions. The new crop attracted pests previously unknown to the region. Pesticide was used as part of the Green Revolution, but it merely transferred the pests to neighbouring fields and created a new pest for the originally pest-free indigenous strains of maize. This indigenous variety was a tall, fodder-producing variety, and the crop was normally 10–12 ft. high. Thus normal pesticide spraying equipment failed to reach the crop. The farmers, after a few failures, were forced to stop cultivating traditional varieties from 1975–6 onward, on a large scale. For example, in Kurugund village in Dharwad district of Karnataka state, the area under traditional maize varieties in 1965–6 was 839.12 acres. In 1970–1, it was 973.84 acres. By 1975–6, it was just four acres, and since 1980–1, no area has been sown with traditional maize. From 1970–1 on, the area under HYV maize gradually increased. In 1970–1, it was 99.06 acres; in 1975–6, 401.74 acres; and in 1980–1, 835 acres.

HYV maize does not allow mixed cropping, and hence the HYV monoculture is more vulnerable to drought than the indigenous mix. The HYV also has low nongrain biomass yield. It is not an attractive fodder, and as a result, recycling the organic matter into the soil, a critical mechanism for moisture conservation and drought proofing, has gone out of practice. This combination of vulnerabilities resulting from the Green Revolution has created more frequent crop failures even under conditions of normal rainfall. The farmers are thus being compelled to try to cultivate the indigenous varieties again. For example, in Kurugund village the area under HYV maize, which was 832.24 acres in 1982–3, dropped to 461.36 acres in 1984–5 and 460.14 acres in 1985–6.

Crop rotation

Crop rotation is an important feature of traditional farming systems in the semiarid tropics. Important agronomic considerations for farmers making crop rotation decisions are the maintenance of soil fertility, control of soil-borne diseases, beneficial residual effects of certain crops, and protection of soil through periodic resting (Jodha and Singh 1990). Balancing food and cash supplies and protecting subsistence needs over time are other primary considerations underlying crop rotations. Crop rotation has three distinguishing characteristics: (1) crop (or cropping system) successions (i.e., a change from one crop to another on the same plot); (2) crop successions involving specific orders and intervals; and (3) the repetition over time of a cropping sequence, based on (1) and (2).

Contingency crop planning

Under rain-fed conditions, the farmers have learnt to keep their cropping practices flexible so that corrective measures can be introduced, depending on the type of weather aberrations. Normally, the following kinds of aberrations are observed under rain-fed conditions:

- delayed onset of monsoon rains;
- long break in rainfall during the middle of the rainy season;
- lack of rainfall during the post-rainy season; and
- high soil temperature at sowing time (in case of post-rainy season crops).

In response to late onset of rainfall conditions, farmers change from long-duration high-yielding crop varieties to short-duration low-yielding varieties.

The mid-season correction for each aberration varies from place to place, depending on the rainfall pattern, soil type, choice of crop, and so forth. Corrective measures include reducing the plant population by thinning crops to reduce crop competition for available moisture and providing supplemental irrigation in case there is a long break in rainfall during the crop season.

ALTERNATE ENTERPRISES

Farmers tend to avoid high-risk enterprises and opt for low-risk enterprises by keeping options open to ensure high flexibility in their production plans and schedules. They rely on enterprises that are relatively stable against rainfall fluctuations. A ranking of enterprises, based on coefficient of variation (CVT) and probability of failure, reveals that farmers in the dry regions prefer dairy enterprise and low remunerative, low water-consuming crops over high water-consuming crops with high risk potentials (Table 30.1) (Gajana and Sharma 1990).

Farmers in drought-prone areas usually combine subsidiary enterprises like dairy, poultry, sheep rearing, and sericulture with crop cultivation. Off-farm income-generating alternatives, like labour sale (for wage earning) and businesses like petty shops, are also common in such areas.

Engaging in multiple activities is an important way of promoting flexibility and countering risk and

Table 30.1 Ranking of enterprises based on coefficient of variation (CVT) and probability of failure (PF)

CVT of enterprises yields (%)		CVT of enterprises (PF) returns (%)	
Haraka	39.53	Redgram	45.55
Redgram	35.29	Pearl millet	45.32
Navane	34.82	Haraka	39.53
Pearl millet	30.53	Navane	34.82
Horsegram	29.45	Paddy	30.48
Maize	29.20	Groundnut	29.68
Paddy	24.58	Horsegram	25.26
Korle	21.81	Ragi	21.35
Sericulture	20.11	Maize	18.74
Groundnut	19.38	Sericulture	15.59
Ragi (Fingermillet)	19.22	Dairy (Cow)	8.44
Dairy (Buffalo)	10.12		
Dairy (Cow)	6.16		

Source: Gajana and Sharma 1990

Table 30.2 Rainfall and income variations in arid zones (Rajasthan, India)

Zone	Mean annual rainfall (in mm)	% income from:		
		Crop	Livestock	Nonfarm
I	185.0	13	49	48
II	361.4	25	35	40
III	429.9	40	29	31

Source: Venkateswarlu 1990

uncertainty. Rainfall fluctuations are easily weathered by those who have at least one or more secondary activities. Analysis of income sources reveals that, although crop-based income decreases with increasing aridity, dependence on livestock and other less rainfall-dependent sources increases with increased aridity (Table 30.2) (Venkateswarlu 1990).

Table 30.3 illustrates that the degree of diversification of enterprise is in tune with rainfall regimes of various agroclimatic regions in India (Jodha *et al.* 1988).

RESOURCE MANAGEMENT CYCLE

Farmers' measures to contain the damage potential of adverse seasonal conditions and droughts include divesting earlier investments, drawing down inventories, drawing on resources from social relationships and common lands, modifying consumption, calling in loans, disposing of nonproductive assets, and migrating. Although it is not possible to establish an order or schedule of events, farmers generally sequence their strategies in response to the prolongation of the crisis, and the logic behind sequencing strategies is to safeguard productive assets. The aim is to live with droughts without losing productive assets (such as land and livestock) and return to the pre-crisis stage quickly, to take advantage of opportunities associated with the return of good monsoon conditions.

The sequencing of strategies depends on the asset base of households and the spread, duration, and intensity of droughts. Households with surplus assets handle the situation better than resource-poor households, at least in initial stages of drought conditions. When drought conditions are localised, people from the affected area migrate to adjoining areas to eke out a living. When drought conditions are widespread, employment opportunities in adjoining areas also shrink. When the duration of drought is longer, even households with a surplus are forced to take up alternate employment opportunities, and the market becomes overcrowded and the wage level drops. With prolonged drought conditions, certain options open to resource-poor households at initial stress periods are closed or limited under peak drought conditions (Chen 1991).

To cope with prolonged droughts, household

Table 30.3 Indicators of farmers' long-term strategies against weather risk in three districts with different degrees of weather risk in the dry tropical regions of India

Details of degree of risk and adaptations	Situation in the villages of		
	Akola	Sholapur	Jodhpur
(a) Characteristics of weather risk			
Annual average rainfall (mm)	820	690	382
Probability of favourable soil moisture conditions for rainy season cropping	0.66	0.33	0.21
Length of growing season (days)	200	155	60
Incidence of crop failure (average of three years)			
– plots with complete crop failure (%)	4	17	33
– plots with partial crop failure (%)	7	24	–
(b) Indicators of spatial diversification			
Scattered land fragments per farm (no.)	2.8	5.8	7.3
Split plots per farm (no.)	5.0	11.2	–
Fragments per farm by distance from village (no.)			
– up to 0.8 km	1.5	1.4	1.2
– 0.8 to 1.6 km	1.1	3.4	4.3
– Above 1.6 km	0.2	1.0	1.8
(c) Indicators of crop-based diversification			
Extent of intercropping (%)	83	35	100
Total single crops planted (no.)	20	34	12
Total combinations of mixed crops planted (no.)	43	56	30
(d) Crop/livestock-based mixed farming			
Ratio of land and livestock values	93.7	91.9	63.4
Ratio of crop and livestock incomes	80.2	71.3	69.3
(e) Occupational and institutional adjustments			
Occupations (source of income) per household (no.)	1.5	2.3	2.9
Households with more than two occupations (%)	14	18	39
Households with incidence of seasonal outmigration (%)	2	24	33
Cases of land tenancy induced by risk-sharing/management considerations (no.)	9	66	–

Source: Jodha *et al.* 1988

response mechanisms must address one central question: whether the response action can be reversed. Households start with responses that involve the smallest commitments of domestic resources and the greatest degree of reversibility (Chambers *et al.* 1981). Farming communities prefer easily reversible strategies to less reversible strategies in anticipation of the return of normal conditions. Without a productive resource base, they may not recover quickly even when climatic conditions are favourable. Table 30.4 shows the sequencing of community drought strategies in the order of quickest reversibility (Chen 1991).

Individual households also attempt to sequence recovery, although in a different order. On the return of normal conditions, households generally begin by returning home, acquiring or redeeming productive assets, repaying loans, building up reserves, stockpiling disposable assets and investing in social relationships, and acquiring nonproductive assets. The reserve building, reserve drawdown, and reserve replenishment cycles, in consonance with good, bad, and not-so-bad rainfall years, form core survival strategies against the uncertainties of climatic conditions.

Many countries perceive drought as a discrete and unexpected event; their drought relief programmes treat it as a transient phenomenon, and response efforts therefore are undertaken to provide relief during the crisis period. This situation emphasises the

Table 30.4 Consequential crisis management strategies in order of quickest reversibility

Strategy	Order of reversibility
Drawing down inventories	1
Drawing on common property resources	2
Drawing on social relationships	3
Reducing or modifying consumption	4
Borrowing	5
Mortgaging nonproductive assets	6
Disposing of nonproductive assets	7
Migrating	8
Mortgaging productive assets	9
Disposing of productive assets	10
Drastic measures	*

Source: Chen 1991
Note: *Only when all strategies are exhausted. Involves the disengagement of all normal systems of survival, particularly during acute famine conditions

need for long-term drought mitigation measures, keeping in mind the local farmers' experiences in managing resources. Some recent public policy instruments do recognise the significance of local farmers' strategies for mitigating the impacts of drought, such as a micro watershed development begun in the 1990s that explicitly incorporates the viable components of farmers' drought mitigation strategies.

NOTE

1   Views expressed by the author are his personal views and are not necessarily the views of the organisation to which he is attached.

REFERENCES

Bandyopadhyay, J. (1987) 'Political ecology of drought and water scarcity – Need for an ecological water resource policy', *Economical Political Weekly* 22, 50: 2,159–69.

Chambers, R., Longhurst, R., and Pacey, A. (eds) (1981) *Seasonal Dimensions to Rural Poverty*, London: F. Pinter and Totowa, NJ: Allanheld, Osmun.

Chen, M. (1991) *Coping with Seasonality and Drought*, New Delhi: Sage Publications India Pvt. Ltd.

Gajana, T.M. and Sharma, B.M. (1990) 'Technologies for minimising risk in rainfed agriculture', Indian Council of Agricultural Research, New Delhi, pp. 47–59.

Jodha, N.S., Virmani, S.M., Gadgil, S., Huda, A.K.S., and Sing, B.P. (1988) 'The effect of climatic variation on agriculture in dry tropical regions of India', in M.L. Parry, T.R. Carter, and N.T. Konijn (eds), *The Impact of Climatic Variations on Agriculture*, Vol. 2, pp. 499–576, Dordrecht, Netherlands: Kluwer Academic Publications.

Jodha, N.S. and Singh, B.P. (1990) 'Crop rotation in traditional farming systems in selected areas of India', *Economic Political Weekly* 25, pp. A.28–A.35.

Tennakoon, M.U.A. (1986) *Drought Hazard and Rural Development*, Central Bank of Sri Lanka, Cylone.

Venkateswarlu, J. (1990) 'Technologies for minimising risk in rainfed agriculture', Indian Council of Agricultural Research, New Delhi.

31
ADAPTATION TO DROUGHT IN MEXICO

Diana M. Liverman

The country of Mexico (Figure 31.1) has a long and varied experience with drought, whether described by early historical chronicles or contemporary climatic data and disaster declarations. With more than 85 per cent of the Mexican land area defined as arid or semiarid (Reyes Castañeda 1981), interannual rainfall

Figure 31.1 Regions of Mexico

is highly variable. The experience of drought has resulted in a wide range of adaptations to climate variability, yet today many Mexicans are still extremely vulnerable to lower-than-average rainfall.

This chapter provides an overview of the nature, causes, and consequences of drought in Mexico, focusing on how vulnerability and adaptations vary over time and space. Some preliminary results of a case study of the recent drought in northern Mexico illustrate the state of vulnerability and the limits of adaptation in contemporary Mexico.

THE CLIMATIC ORIGINS OF DROUGHT IN MEXICO

Mexican climate spans the hot, dry conditions of the northwestern Sonoran desert (annual average rainfall less than 100 mm) to the wet tropical climates that characterise the forest regions of southern Mexico, especially Chiapas and the Gulf coasts (average annual rainfall can reach 2,000 mm). These climates originate in latitudinal belts of atmospheric circulation that shift seasonally and range from the westerlies that bring precipitation to northern Mexico in winter, to the subtropical highs associated with stable, dry conditions, to the intertropical convergence zone (ITCZ) and trade winds that deliver summer rainfall to the central and southern regions of the country. Other key influences on precipitation are fall hurricanes on both Caribbean and Pacific coasts, the summer monsoons in the north, and summer high pressure that disrupts the flow of moist air and creates a period of dry conditions known as the *canicula*, or midsummer drought. The mountainous and varied topography of Mexico dominates many other climatic influences, producing cooler temperatures and higher rainfall in the highlands and central plateau, and rain shadows behind coastal mountains (Metcalfe 1987, Mosino and Garcia 1973).

Meteorological data have been available for some parts of Mexico since the nineteenth century (Servicio Meteorologico 1980), and centuries of Mexican climatic history have been reconstructed using tree rings, pollen, and lake levels. Marine and pollen records suggest much drier periods before 9000 BP and around 2000 BP (Brown 1985). Analysis of tree rings from northern Mexico (where narrower annual growth rings are associated with drier conditions) indicates some intense periods of drought during the last 500 years. For example, Figure 31.2 shows a tree ring chronology from northern Mexico that indicates severe drought in the latter part of the sixteenth century (1545–1600), 1752–68, 1801–13, 1859–68, and, most recently, the 1950s.[1]

For the period of reliable instrumental records, Douglas (1996) has calculated the Palmer Drought Severity Index (PDSI) for eighteen climatological divisions in Mexico. PDSI plots for selected regions

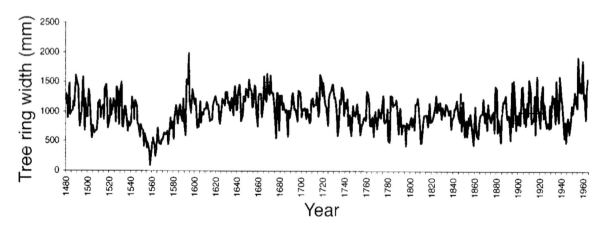

Figure 31.2 Sierra Madre–Los Angeles Sawmill dendrochronology. Data from the Laboratory for Tree Ring Research, University of Arizona. See also Cleaveland *et al.* 1992, Scott 1996

are shown in Figure 31.3. Severe drought is usually identified with PDSI values of –2 and below. In region 3, roughly contiguous with the northwestern state of Sonora, several extended periods of severe drought are apparent, particularly the intense drought of 1942, the 1950s, 1973–4, 1983, and 1987–8. The mid-1980s were relatively wet. In region 11, which includes parts of the important agricultural states of Guanajuato, Jalisco, and Michoacan in west central Mexico, severe droughts occur in the early 1950s, 1969–79, and the summers of 1976, 1979, 1982, and 1988. In region 16, which includes the state of Oaxaca in southern Mexico, there were intense droughts in 1934–5, 1940–1, 1949, 1957–8, 1977, 1982–3, and 1987. Several of these droughts coincide with the variations in Pacific sea surface temperatures associated with El Niño. El Niño conditions (warmer Pacific) correlate with the 1957–8, 1977, 1982–3, and 1987 droughts in Oaxaca. La Niña conditions (colder Pacific) seem to correspond to droughts in the 1950s, 1974, and 1988 in northern Mexico. Significant correlation between El Niño years and drought have also been observed in Oaxaca, associated with a southward displacement of the ITCZ and diminished hurricane frequency in the Gulf of Mexico during El Niño years (Dilley 1996). Cold events have been linked to lower-than-average winter rainfall in northern Mexico and higher-than-average summer rainfall in central Mexico because of northward shifts in the ITCZ and weaker trade winds (Cavazos and Hastenrath 1990).

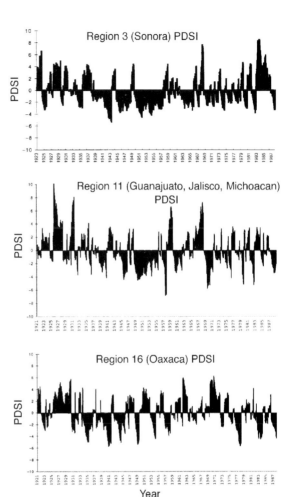

Figure 31.3 PDSI plots for various regions of Mexico. Data from Douglas 1996

THE HUMAN AND ECOLOGICAL IMPACTS OF DROUGHT IN MEXICO

Drought has played a significant role in the human history of Mexico. Archaeologists have investigated the impacts of drought on pre-Columbian populations, and have debated the possibility that drought may have played a role in the collapse of Mayan and other Meso-American civilisations (Culbert 1973, Dahlin 1983, Deevey 1944, Hodell *et al.* 1995). The evidence is inconclusive and it is likely that, although drought-induced harvest failures and water shortages may have stressed regions such as the Yucatan and central Mexico, the reasons for political and demographic decline were more complex. Nevertheless, it

is clear that drought was a concern in pre-Columbian Mexico. Several important deities – such as the Aztec god of rain Tláloc – were worshipped to ensure that rainfall would be timely and abundant, astronomical observatories were built to help predict the weather, and extensive irrigation works and reservoirs were constructed to store and transport water. The Codex Ramirez documents a terrible drought from 1450 to 1454 causing famine and outmigration from the valley of Mexico. Although the Aztec empire distributed maize from central granaries in times of hunger, the drought of 1454 was so severe that people sold themselves or their children into slavery and human sacrifices were made to the gods of rain (Musset 1991, Sancho y Cervera and Pérez-Gavilán Arias 1981).

The arrival of the Spanish in 1519 altered climatic risks in important ways. There was a tremendous expansion of irrigation, which increased the range and reliability of crop production whilst increasing competition for limited water supplies in some regions. However, the Spanish often controlled the best land and water, and their cattle and wheat replaced the more moisture-conserving agriculture of the indigenous people. Historians have blamed drought for famine and social unrest during the colonial period. Between 1521 and 1821, eighty-eight droughts were recorded, with the worst in 1695, 1749, 1771, 1785, and 1809. Production declines were accompanied by price increases in corn and meat, death of livestock, and reduction in subsequent planting because of lack of draft animals. There is also evidence of large-scale migration, epidemics, unemployment, deaths of indigenous and farming peoples, and social unrest (Sancho y Cervera and Pérez-Gavilán Arias 1981). In 1785, drought triggered the starvation of more than 300,000 people – mostly members of the indigenous Indian population (Florescano 1980). Florescano has linked variations in the price of maize in the sixteenth and seventeenth centuries to droughts and other climatic events (Florescano 1969). He claims that the majority of price rises were preceded by a severe drought, but he also notes the role of speculation and economic arrangements in triggering price rises and associated famines. He suggests that the economic and land tenure relations imposed by the Spanish crown and church created a tremendous vulnerability to drought among the poorer and indigenous *campesino* populations. The colonial political economy allowed the larger landholders and merchants to manipulate the price of staples in drought years to the disadvantage of poor consumers and small producers.

The impacts of drought in twentieth-century Mexico can be seen in declines in production and exports of crops and livestock and corresponding increases in imports; reductions in yields and area in production; declines in livestock production; and increases in forest fires and losses. For example, the impacts of drought, interacting with other factors

such as economic conditions and prices, can be seen in the variations in overall maize production and imports for Mexico since 1960 (Figure 31.4). Production was low in 1973–6, 1979, 1982, and 1986–9, partly because of droughts in those years, but exacerbated by economic crises. Imports have grown steadily in response to increasing population demand, but they increased sharply following the drought and production decline in the early 1970s, 1982, and the late 1980s. Government responses have included grain imports, extension of credit payments, dam construction, and, in 1969, the Drought Combat Plan to provide jobs in disaster zones.

The geography of drought impacts is also revealed in the reports of crop losses in Mexican agricultural censuses and statistics. In 1930 the agricultural census reported a total of 1.2 million ha lost to natural disasters, a total of 17 per cent of the area planted, with the most serious losses in northern and north central states such as Nuevo Leon (40 per cent loss) and San Luis Potosi (50 per cent). A similar area was lost in 1940, with northern states losing 20–40 per cent of their planted area. The 1950 census was the first to report losses from specific hazards, and of the 1.43 million ha lost, 1.1 million suffered from drought in regions such as the Bajio and Quintana Roo. The 1960 census reports a drought loss of 0.8 million ha,

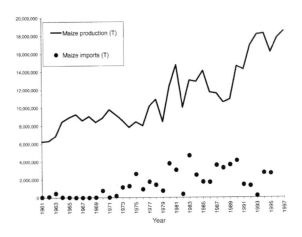

Figure 31.4 Overall maize production and imports for Mexico since 1960. Data from INEGI, Mexico, 'Estadisticas historicas de Mexico', Mexico, D.F.: Instituto Nacional de Estadistica, Geografia e Informatica: Instituto Nacional de Antropologia e Historia, Sep, 1985

lower than previous census reports, with states averaging only about 10 per cent losses. However, the 1970 census, which separates winter and summer growing seasons, includes some very high drought losses, with 22 per cent of the growing area lost to drought in summer (2 million ha). The drought impacts were most severe in Aguascalientes (70 per cent loss), Zacatecas (65 per cent), and Chihuahua (53 per cent) (Figure 31.5). General patterns emerging from this historical analysis suggest that drought impacts are frequent and often severe in Mexico, with 10–20 per cent of the total planted area lost, especially in northern Mexico. The states of Aguascalientes, Nuevo Leon, and San Luis Potosi seem particularly vulnerable.

VULNERABILITY

Vulnerability to drought in Mexico is determined by both biophysical and social conditions (Liverman 1994). Biophysical vulnerability is greatest in the northern and north central regions of the country, where rainfall is most variable, and in the highlands, where frost limits the growing season and the timing of rainfall and extent of the midsummer drought are critical. Biophysical vulnerability to drought may also be increasing as a result of deforestation and over-grazing, which result in increased temperatures and reduced soil moisture (Bahre and Bradbury 1978, Balling 1988, Bryant *et al.* 1990, Medellin-Leal and Anaya-Garduno 1978). And, of course, anthropogenic greenhouse gas emissions to the atmosphere are likely to result in global warming that would bring warmer, drier conditions to much of Mexico (Liverman and O'Brien 1991).

Social vulnerability to drought varies greatly by region and social group, and has changed over time as a result of technological, economic, and demographic changes. Mexico's rapid economic and population growth has increased demand for both food and water, especially as consumption increased in urban areas and irrigated agriculture expanded. For example, the states bordering the United States saw an expansion of their irrigated acreage from about 700,000 ha in 1930 to 2.4 million ha in 1980 (Figure 31.6). Mexico's overall population grew from 16 million to more than 80 million people during the same fifty-year period. One estimate projected a doubling of water use between 1970 and 2000.

The restructuring of agriculture has resulted in increased water use as producers shift from basic grains, such as maize, to forage and vegetable production. In the irrigation districts of northern Mexico, acreage has shifted from maize and wheat to crops such as alfalfa and tomatoes that consume more water (Liverman 1995). In the valley of Oaxaca, some farmers have purchased mechanical pumps to irrigate alfalfa for dairy cows and cheese production, and this has resulted in a drop in the groundwater levels. Poorer farmers have found it increasingly difficult to reach water using traditional manual techniques to irrigate their subsistence crops. Groundwater supplies have also declined as a result of the deforestation of hill slopes surrounding the valley and urban pumping for the expanding city of Oaxaca (Dilley 1993, Lees 1976, Liverman 1995).

Some groups and sectors are much more vulnerable to drought than others. More than 50 per cent of Mexican cropland is operated by *ejidos*, a form of cooperative land tenure established to allocate land in the aftermath of the Mexican Revolution. A comparison of drought losses on *ejidos* and private farms at national and state levels using data from the agricultural censuses for 1950, 1960, and 1970 suggests that *ejidos* tend to experience much higher crop

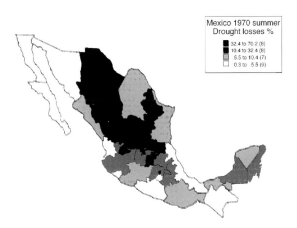

Figure 31.5 1970 summer drought losses in Mexico. Data in Table 8, INEGI, 1976, 'Resumen General: Censo Agricola, Ganadero y Ejidal 1970', Mexico, D.F.: Instituto Nacional de Estadistica, Geografia e Informatica

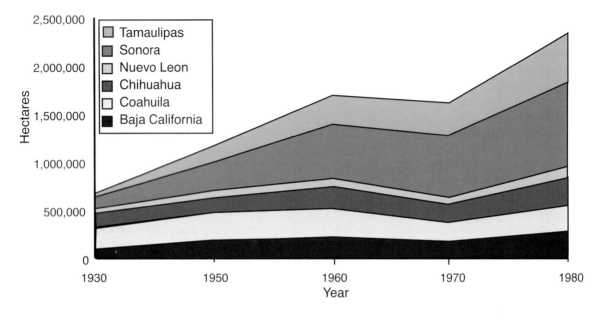

Figure 31.6 Irrigation in northern Mexico, 1930–80. Data from INEGI, Mexico, 'Estadisticas historicas de Mexico', Mexico, D.F.: Instituto Nacional de Estadistica, Geografia e Informatica: Instituto Nacional de Antropologia e Historia, Sep, 1985

losses from drought than private landowners of more than 5 ha (Figure 31.7). At the state level, the differences are even larger. In Nuevo Leon in 1950, drought losses were 11 per cent on private land and 29 per cent on *ejidos*; in 1960, the loss was 20 per cent on private land and 28 per cent on *ejidos*. In winter 1970, private land in Nuevo Leon lost 14 per cent of the crop area to drought and *ejidos* lost 39 per cent; in summer 1970 the loss on private land was 26 per cent and on *ejidos*, 50 per cent.

Several factors explain the relative vulnerability of *ejido* land. Land reforms tended to give less productive and drier land to the new cooperative sector, except in regions where those claiming land were particularly aggressive in their demands. In many regions, the *ejidos* do not have as much irrigated land and also have problems in getting access to credit, improved seeds, or other resources (Liverman 1990, Nguyen 1979).

ADAPTATION AND RESPONSE TO DROUGHT

Local communities in Mexico developed many tra-

ditional technologies for coping with drought. As in many semiarid regions, sophisticated irrigation systems have developed over centuries to store and transport water to settlements and agriculture. Archaeologists and others have described prehispanic water control systems such as the *chinampas* – the highly productive raised fields in the wetlands around Mexico City – and the *galeria* tunnels, which bring water from the hillside aquifers to the valley of Tehuacan, Puebla (Enge and Whiteford 1989, Wilken 1987).

The heterogeneity of the Mexican landscape and the high interannual climate variability also promoted a diversity of crop varieties, especially of maize, and many farmers still plant several different varieties to minimise risk from drought, frost, and diseases (Altieri and Trujillo 1987, Bellon 1991, Brush et al. 1988, Mangelsdorf 1974). Traditional farmers in Oaxaca adjust to drought by selecting a maize variety appropriate to expected rainfall conditions, altering the ratio of beans and maize planted, and adjusting the planting density of crops (Kirkby 1973).

Indigenous social institutions and traditions also served as drought adaptations and risk management strategies. Rituals following the agricultural calendar

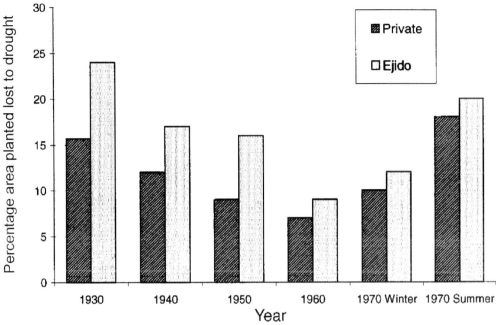

Hazard losses on private and ejido cropland 1930-1970

Figure 31.7 Hazard losses on private and *ejido* cropland, 1930–70. Data from the five 'Resumen General: Censo Agricola, Ganadero y Ejidal' (1930, 1940, 1950, 1960) 1970 Mexico. D.F.: Instituto Nacional de Estadistica, Geografia e Informatica

invoke rain and other key influences on harvests. Traditional weather prediction techniques monitor the first days of January or phases of the moon as ways to predict growing season weather (H. Eakin, personal communication, 1997; Signorini 1994). The harvest can be redistributed through social events such as the *guelaguezta* of Oaxaca, where local leaders are responsible for sharing food with other members of the community (Kirkby 1973, Murphy 1991). In drought years, some communities rely on traditional sources of famine food and liquid such as cactus, agave, and mesquite fruit (Minnis 1991).

Many of these traditional drought adaptations survived the ecological and social transformations associated with the arrival of the Spanish, although, as noted earlier, some scholars believe that drought vulnerability increased as a result of Spanish changes in land use and economy.

In the twentieth century, new forms of adaptation have accompanied the expansion and intensification of Mexican agriculture. Irrigation reduced short-term vulnerability to drought whilst increasing water use and vulnerability to multiyear droughts, such as those that occurred in the 1950s and 1990s in northern Mexico and brought reservoirs to very low levels. For example, three years of drought resulted in reservoirs at only 10 per cent of capacity across most of northern Mexico at the beginning of the 1995 growing season (Figure 31.8).

In those districts that rely on groundwater, increased demand and sustained drought have contributed to declines in the water table and to saline intrusion (Aceves-Navarro 1985, Cummings 1972, 1989). Over the longer term, improvements in irrigation efficiency have reduced drought vulnerability in some irrigation districts, and new proposals for decentralised management and water pricing may allow more flexible adjustment to water supply variations (Casasus 1994).

In the 1950s, the 'Green Revolution' brought

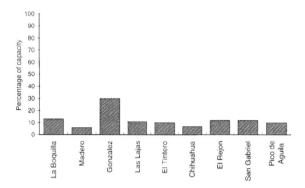

Figure 31.8 Reservoir levels in northern Mexico, 25 May 1995

improved seeds, fertiliser, and mechanisation to Mexican agriculture. Plant breeders developed new, higher-yielding varieties of maize and wheat that increased production, especially for those farmers with irrigation and access to credit and fertiliser. Although some new varieties were drought resistant, there are some indications that the Green Revolution increased the sensitivity of agricultural production to climatic variations and drought (Michaels 1979). In Puebla, where development projects focused on increasing yields of rain-fed maize, drought and economic crisis interacted to bring the yields of those using the new technologies below those of traditional farmers in some years (Diaz-Cisneros 1994). Because the new commercial technologies sometimes require farmers to go into debt to purchase them, drought-induced harvest failure can be more serious for these farmers than for farmers using traditional techniques without purchased inputs (Appendini and Liverman 1994).

Urban areas have responded to drought and increased demand by constructing storage reservoirs and rationing water. Mexico City now pumps water at great expense from an area 100 miles distant and a thousand feet lower (Aguilera Gomez 1989, Zenteno and Benigno Morelos 1988). Many northern cities compete for water with agriculture and had severe water rationing during the recent drought. Many rural communities required water to be trucked in at considerable expense. In Chihuahua, forty-two deaths were attributed to the lack of drinking water because of drought and poverty (Correspondents 1996).

Institutional response to drought in contemporary Mexican agriculture includes a complex set of agricultural subsidies and emergency relief measures. Mexican agricultural policy has varied quite dramatically in terms of guaranteed support price, and year-to-year crop area is very sensitive to relative prices for different crops. In 1981, for example, prices for growing basic grains were increased to promote national food self-sufficiency, and production increased (Appendini 1992). In the last decade, however, financial restructuring and the liberalisation of trade have resulted in a decline in the guaranteed prices for producers (Figure 31.9), and this has increased the economic uncertainty and associated environmental risks (Appendini and Liverman 1994). In the early 1980s, subsidies for agricultural inputs were reduced from 27.5 per cent of the cost of grain production in 1985 to only 6.5 per cent in 1990 (De Janvry *et al.* 1995). The fertiliser parastatal FERTIMEX was privatised in the early 1990s, and fertiliser prices are now near those of the international markets.

Less than 10 per cent of Mexican producers have crop insurance, although some coverage is increasingly required as government credit declines and producers turn to private lenders for loans. But the recent collapse of the peso and associated surge in interest rates has made access to both credit and insurance difficult for the majority of farmers.

THE 1996 DROUGHT IN NORTHERN MEXICO

Four years of below-normal rainfall produced severe drought conditions in northern Mexico by 1996. By June, reservoirs were at fifty-year lows, below 5 per cent of capacity in some cases; more than 4.6 million ha of cropland was damaged; and 6 million ha remained unplanted because of the drought. Ranching, important to the economy and culture of states like Sonora, was suffering great losses as herds died off or were sold at prices 40 per cent lower than in 1995. An estimated 300,000 cattle died and 700,000 were sold at very low prices. By the end of the year, Mexico's livestock herd had declined one-third from 1990 levels. The Federal Agricultural department estimated farm losses at more than US$1 billion and planned to import an extra 4 million metric tonnes of

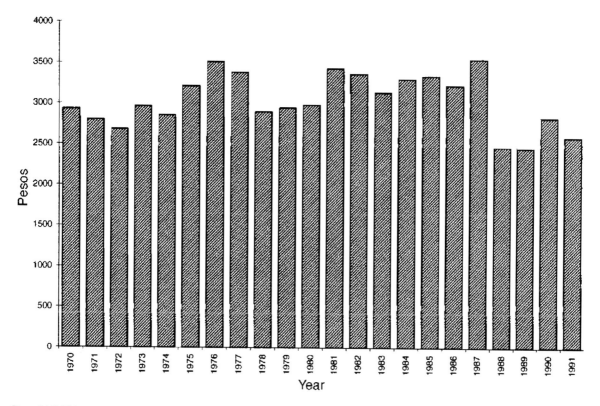

Figure 31.9 Maize support prices, 1970–91. See Appendini and Liverman 1994

basic grains for a total grain import of about 11.25 million metric tonnes in 1996, compared to 6 million metric tonnes in 1991. Farmers' groups estimated the loss to producers at nearer US$2.5 billion (SourceMex 1996, Agricultural Trade Office 1996). The drought provoked interstate political conflict, with Sonora and Sinaloa competing for the water from the Huites Dam; Nuevo Leon and Tamaulipas competing for the remaining water in the El Cuchillo dam; and even Mexico, as a nation, requesting Rio Grande water from Texas, and being refused (Patterson 1996).

The government responded to the drought with 1.147 billion pesos (US$155 million) in drought aid for feed purchases, drinking water supplies, and jobs in infrastructural improvements, as well as with ongoing price support programmes such as Procampo, which made direct cash payments to farmers for area planted. State government and local producers' organisations also provided drought relief. For example, in Sonora, the state government joined with irrigators to invest US$500,000 in cloud seeding, and also provided feed to ranchers (Notimex 1996).

Individual responses to the drought varied widely, with some farmers planting and then praying for rain or government relief, and others deciding to abandon their land and migrating to find work in other regions of Mexico or in the United States (Velasco 1996). Many ranchers and rain-fed crop producers found the combined impact of the drought and economic crisis overwhelming, with the low rainfall, high input prices, low producer prices, and high interest rates placing them at great risk. Smaller landholders were disproportionately affected, especially those who were in debt, or who farmed or ranched more biophysically marginal land (Liverman and Rosenberg 1996).

CONCLUSIONS

The 1996 drought in northern Mexico drew attention to the overall and differential vulnerability of Mexican agriculture and society to climate variability. Although agriculture contributes less than 10 per cent to Mexico's gross national product, it is important to rural stability and national political strategy. Drought exacerbated the effect of economic crises in the agricultural sector and stressed the water supplies of rapidly growing cities and communities. Partly as a result of the drought, the Mexican government is now undertaking a major review of water resources management, including decentralisation of management, improvements in infrastructure, and potential for seasonal climate forecasting. Agricultural production in many irrigation districts increased in 1997 and, overall, the Mexican economy was recovering (American Embassy 1997). But the future of the most vulnerable farmers and ranchers on rain-fed and marginal land is less clear in the face of the decline in support prices, the continuing difficulties in access to input and credits, and the unequal participation in economic recovery (Quintana S. 1996).

NOTE

1   Tree ring data from the Laboratory for Tree Ring Research, University of Arizona. See also Cleaveland *et al.* 1992; Scott 1966.

REFERENCES

Aceves-Navarro, E. (1985) 'Salinity problems in food production of the Mexican irrigation districts', in W. Jordan (ed.), *Water and Water Policy in World Food Supplies: Proceedings of the Conference, May 26–30, 1985*, College Station, TX: Texas A&M University.

Agricultural Trade Office (1996) *Economic Consequences of the Mexican Drought*, Mexico City, Mexico: American Embassy.

Aguilera Gomez, M. (1989) 'Las ciudades mexicanas en la ultima decada del siglo XX', paper delivered at the 3rd Seminario de Economia Urbana, 1988, Mexico City.

Altieri, M.A. and Trujillo, J. (1987) 'The agroecology of corn production in Mexico', *Human Ecology* 15, 2: 198–220.

American Embassy (1997) '1997 Mexican agricultural situation and outlook', 26 September.

Appendini, K. (1992) *De la Milpa los Tortibonos : La restructuracion de la politica alimentaria en Mexico*, Mexico: El Colegio de Mexico.

Appendini, K. and Liverman, D.M. (1994) 'Agricultural policy and climate change in Mexico', *Food Policy* 19, 2: 149–64.

Bahre, C.J. and Bradbury, D.E. (1978) 'Vegetation change along the Arizona-Sonora boundary', *Annals of the American Association of Geographers* 68, 2: 145–65.

Balling, R.C. (1988) 'The climatic impact of a Sonoran vegetation discontinuity', *Climatic Change* 13: 99–109.

Bellon, M.R. (1991) 'The ethnoecology of maize variety management: A case study from Mexico', *Human Ecology* 19, 3: 389–418.

Brown, R.B. (1985) 'A summary of late quaternary pollen records from Mexico west of the isthmus of Tehuantepec', in V. Bryan and R. Holloway (eds), *Pollen Records of Late Quaternary North American Sediments*, Dallas: American Association of Stratigraphic Palynologists, pp. 71–93.

Brush, S.B., Corrales, M.B., and Schmidt, E. (1988) 'Agricultural development and maize diversity in Mexico', *Human Ecology* 16, 3: 307–28.

Bryant, N.A., Johnson, N.F., and Brazel, A.J. (1990) 'Measuring the effect of overgrazing in the Sonoran Desert', *Climatic Change* 17, 2–3: 243.

Casasus, C. (1994) 'Privatizing the Mexican water industry', *Journal of the American Water Works Association* 86, 3: 69–73.

Cavazos, T. and Hastenrath, S. (1990) 'Convection and rainfall over Mexico and their modulation by the Southern Oscillation', *International Journal of Climatology* 10, 4: 377–86.

Cleaveland, M.K., Cook, E.R., and Stahle, D.W. (1992) 'Secular variability of the Southern Oscillation detected in tree-ring data from Mexico and the southern United States', in H. Diaz and V. Markgraf (eds), *El Niño: Historical and Paleoclimatic Aspects of the Southern Oscillation*, New York: Cambridge University Press, pp. 271–91.

Correspondents (1996) 'Por el calor, 42 muertos en 15 dias en Chihuahua', *La Jornada*, 26 May.

Culbert, T.P. (1973) *The Classic Maya Collapse*, Albuquerque: University of New Mexico Press.

Cummings, R. (1972) *Water Resource Management in Northern Mexico*, Baltimore and London: The Johns Hopkins University Press.

Cummings, R.G. (1989) *Waterworks: Improving Irrigation Management in Mexican Agriculture*, Washington, DC: World Resources Institute.

Dahlin, B.H. (1983) 'Climate and prehistory on the Yucatan Peninsula', *Climatic Change* 5, 3: 245–64.

De Janvry, A., Gordillo, G., and Sadoulet, E. (1995) *Reformas del sector agricola y el campesino en Mexico*, San Jose, Costa Rica: Fondo Internacional de Desarollo Agricola y Instituto Interamericano de Cooperacion para la Agricultura.

Deevey, E.S. (1944) 'Pollen analysis and Mexican archaeology: An attempt to apply the method', *American Antiquity* 10: 135–49.

Diaz-Cisneros, H. (1994) 'The impact of support prices for corn on small farmers in the Puebla Valley', in C. Hewitt de Alcantara (ed.), *Economic Restructuring and Rural Subsistence in Mexico: Corn and the Crisis of the 1980s*, Transformation of Rural Mexico, No. 2, San Diego: Center for US–Mexico Studies.

Dilley, M. (1993) 'Climate and agriculture in the Valley of Oaxaca, Mexico', PhD dissertation, Pennsylvania State University, State College, Pennsylvania.

—— (1996) 'Synoptic controls on precipitation in the valley of Oaxaca, Mexico', *International Journal of Climatology* 16: 1,019–31.

Douglas, A. (1996) *Mexican Temperature, Precipitation and Drought Database*, Asheville, NC: National Climate Data Center, 1996.

Enge, K.I. and Whiteford, S. (1989) *The Keepers of Water and Earth: Mexican Rural Social Organization and Irrigation*, Austin: University of Texas Press.

Florescano, E. (1969) *Precios del Maiz y Crisis Agricola en México: 1708–1810*, Mexico City: Ediciones Era.

—— (1980) 'Una historia olvidada: La sequía en México', *Nexos* 32: 9–18.

Hodell, D.A., Curtis, J.H., and Brenner, M. (1995) 'Possible role of climate in the collapse of Classic Maya Civilization', *Nature* 375: 391–4.

Kirkby, A.V.T. (1973) 'The use of land and water resources in the past and present valley of Oaxaca, Mexico', *Memoirs of the Museum of Anthropology, University of Michigan* 5, 1.

Lees, S. (1976) 'Oaxaca's spiralling race for water', *The Ecologist* 6: 20–2.

Liverman, D.M. (1990) 'Vulnerability to drought in Mexico: The cases of Sonora and Puebla in 1970', *Annals of the Association of American Geographers* 80, 1: 49–72.

—— (1994) 'Vulnerability to Global Environmental Change (Ch. 26)', in S. Cutter (ed.), *Environmental Risks and Hazards*, Englewood Cliffs, NJ: Prentice Hall, pp. 326–42.

—— (1995) 'Economic and environmental change in Mexico', paper delivered at the First Open Conference on the Human Dimensions of Global Environmental Change, Duke University, Durham, NC.

Liverman, D.M. and O'Brien, K.L. (1991) 'Global warming and climate change in Mexico', *Global Environmental Change* 1, 4: 351–64.

Liverman, D. and Rosenberg, J. (1996) *Preliminary Assessment of the 1996 Drought in Sonora*, Tucson, AZ: Latin American Area Center.

Mangelsdorf, P.C. (1974) *Corn*, Cambridge, MA: Harvard University Press.

Medellin-Leal, F. and Anaya-Garduno, M. (1978) *La desertificacion en Mexico*, San Luis Potosi: Instituto de Investigacion de Zonas Deserticas, Universidad Autonoma de San Luis Potosi.

Metcalfe, S.E. (1987) 'Historical data and climate change in

Mexico: A review', *The Geographical Journal* 153, 2: 211–22.

Michaels, P.J. (1979) 'The response of the Green Revolution to climatic variability', *Climatic Change* 5: 255–79.

Minnis, P.E. (1991) 'Famine foods of the Northern American Desert Borderlands in Historical Context', *Journal of Ethnobiology* 11, 2 : 231–57.

Mosino, P. and Garcia, E. (1973) 'The climate of Mexico', in H. Flohn (ed.), *World Survey of Climatology*, Vol. 2, London: Elsevier.

Murphy, A.D. (1991) *Social Inequality in Oaxaca: A History of Resistance and Change*, Philadelphia: Temple University Press.

Musset, A. (1991) *De L'eau Vive à L'eau Morte: Enjeux Techniques et Culturels dans la Vallée de Mexico (XVIe – XIXe siècles)*, Paris: Éditions Recherche sur les Civilisations.

Nguyen, D.T. (1979) 'The effects of land reform on agricultural production, employment and income distribution: A statistical study of Mexican states 1959–1969', *Economic Journal* 89: 624–35.

Notimex (1996) 'Preven inducir lluvias', *El Imparcial*, 15 May.

Patterson, J. (1996) *Drought Alert Report: Nuevo Leon*, Mexico City: American Embassy.

Quintana S., V.M. (1996) 'La séquia de todos tan temida', *Infosel*, 26 May.

Reyes Castañeda, P. (1981) 'Historia de la Agricultura: Informacion y Sintesis', Mexico City: AGT Editor, S.A.

Sancho y Cervera, J., and Pérez-Gavilán Arias, D. (1981) 'A perspective study on droughts in Mexico', *Journal of Hydrology* 51: 41–55.

Scott, S.D. (1996) *Dendrochronology in Mexico*, Tucson: University of Arizona Press.

Servicio Meteorologico (1980) *Normales Climatologicas 1940–71*, Mexico City: Servicio Meteorologico.

Signorini, I. (1994) 'Rito y mito como instrumentos de prevision y manipulacion del clima entre los huaves de San Mateo del Mar, Oaxaca, Mexico', *La Palabra y el Hombre* 90.

SourceMex (1996) 'Agriculture Secretariat estimates direct losses from drought at 8 billion pesos this year', *SourceMex*, 12 June.

Velasco, E. (1996) 'Se tendran que importar 8 Millones de Ton. de Granos', *Excelsior*, 26 May, p. 4.

Wilken, G.C. (1987) *The Good Farmers: Traditional Agricultural Resource Management in Mexico and Central America*, Berkeley: University of California Press.

Zenteno, R.B. and Benigno Morelos, J. (1988) *Grandes Problemas de la Ciudad de Mexico*, Mexico: Plaza y Valdes.

AGRICULTURAL DROUGHT MANAGEMENT FOR SUSTAINED AGRICULTURAL DEVELOPMENT

A.S.R.A.S. Sastri

INTRODUCTION

Despite considerable advances in technology, agriculture is still subject to the vagaries of weather in all parts of the world. Among weather factors, rainfall is the most critical because about 70 per cent of the net sown area is still unirrigated. Erratic rainfall during the crop-growing season results in water stress conditions. The impact of water stress or drought is different for different crops and at different growth stages. Abnormalities like delayed onset of monsoon, aberrant behaviour of monsoon, and prolonged dry spells are some of the causes for decreased food production, especially in developing countries. The cost of development of irrigation in India is about US$1,700 per ha. Under such conditions, increasing irrigation potential is also a difficult task, not only in India but also in other developing countries. According to Datta (1992), food production in India has significantly dropped during years of aberrant weather that have been preceded by a good production year (Table 32.1).

However, in recent years, the national capacity to deal with the deleterious consequences of drought has increased. According to Sastri (1993), the productivity of rice in the Chhattisgarh region in central India increased over the years in given moisture stress conditions, and this can be attributed to technological changes.

Although crops and cropping patterns are adjusted to given climate and physiographic conditions, intermittent drought spells or recurring drought conditions in a given area can be managed with the help of different strategies (Figure 32.1).

For example, recurring drought conditions can be managed primarily by crop variety adjustments, either by planting early-maturing varieties that can escape drought or by planting drought-resistant varieties. If drought occurs during the crop growing season, it can be alleviated with either soil water conservation techniques or supplemental irrigation. This can be done by harvesting rainwater during a wet spell and recycling the same water during the subsequent dry spell.

In some cases, groundwater can be used for supplemental irrigation. However, each strategy to be adopted should be time, space, and socioeconomic condition specific. Some of these strategies are discussed in case studies in this chapter.

CROP ADJUSTMENT FOR ALLEVIATION OF DROUGHT

Moisture stress leads to drought, which, in turn, affects crop production adversely. Efforts were made to stabilise dryland agriculture by evolving contingent crop production strategies in rain-fed areas. One of the best methods that was evolved is the adjustment of a suitable crop to the rainfall quantum and distri-

Table 32.1 Food production in India in years of aberrant weather

Year	Food grain production	Year	Food grain production
1964–5	89.00	1978–9	131.00
1965–6	72.00	1979–80	109.00
1971–2	105.20	1983–4	150.00
1972–3	97.00	1986–7	143.00

Source: Datta 1992

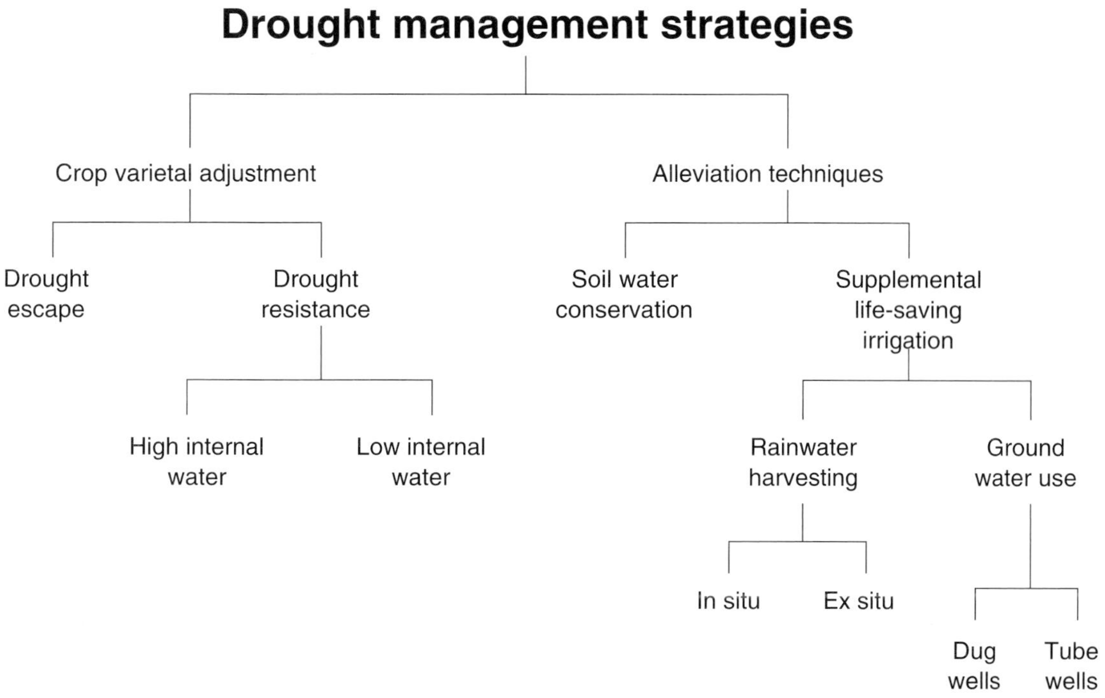

Drought management strategies
Crop varietal adjustment
Alleviation techniques
Drought escape
Drought resistance
Soil water conservation
Supplemental life-saving irrigation
High internal water
Low internal water
Rainwater harvesting
Ground water use
In situ
Ex situ
Dug wells
Tube wells

Figure 32.1 Drought management strategies
Source: Sastri 1993

bution in a given area. For example, in the Madhya Pradesh state of India, which is centrally located, the annual rainfall varies from more than 1,600 mm in the southeastern parts to less than 900 mm in the westernmost parts (Figure 32.2). The whole state is divided into five crop zones: (i) rice, (ii) rice–wheat, (iii) wheat, (iv) sorghum–wheat, and (v) sorghum–cotton zones (Figure 32.3). These five crop zones are further divided into twelve agroclimatic zones (AcZs).

Using years of experience, crops have been chosen to suit the zones, based on rainfall and physiographic features. However, certain crops often are grown more for convenience, by convention, or for family needs. With more and more commercialisation of agriculture, the attitude of the farmers is changing. As a consequence, the sorghum area in the state is slowly being replaced by soybeans. In the last five to six years, soybean area has increased from a mere thousand ha to more than 1 million ha. This is one of the best

800 mm
GWL
1,000
STN
800
BHP
1,200
1,400
IND
AMB
1,600
1,600
800
BTL
800
1,600
BSP
1,600
800
1,200
1,200
800
1,000
RPR
1,600
1,400
1,200
1,400
JGP
1,600
1,600 mm

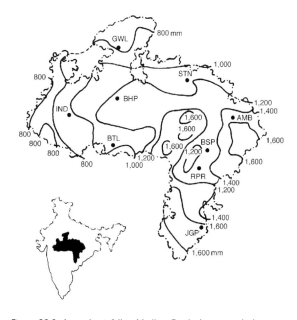

Figure 32.2 Annual rainfall in Madhya Pradesh state in India
Source: Sastri 1998

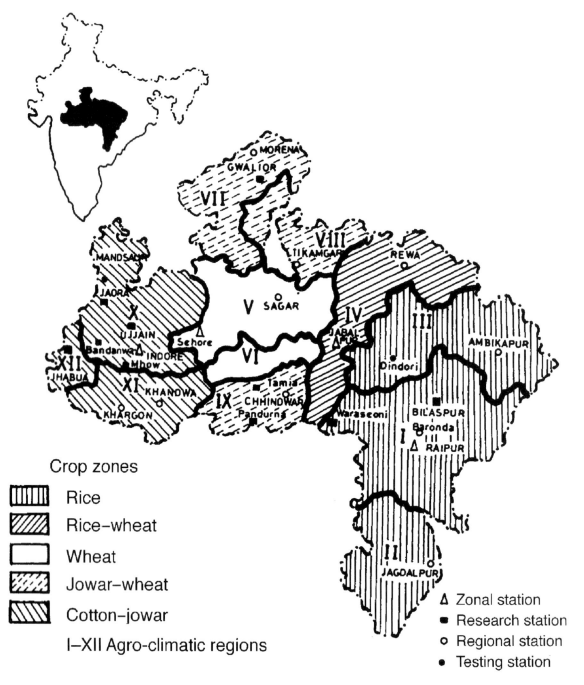

Figure 32.3 Crop zones (CZ) and agroclimatic zones (AcZ) of Madhya Pradesh state in India. 'Status Report', Zonal Agricultural Research Station, Jawaharlal Nehru Agricultural University, Raipur

examples of crop choice to suit the rainfall pattern. Such changes in other dryland areas of India have been studied by Singh and Ramana Rao (1988), and the details are shown in Table 32.2.

Thus, selection of a crop suitable for the rainfall quantum and distribution can contribute to sustainable agriculture.

SELECTION OF CROP VARIETIES

Sometimes rainfall spatial variability necessitates the selection of suitable crop varieties for different locations of a given crop zone. This depends on the rainfall quantum and variability, which determine the stability of rainfall.

Stable rainfall periods

The selection of suitable rice varieties can be based on stable rainfall periods that can be defined as 'periods when the weekly average rainfall is greater than 50 mm and corresponding coefficient of variation is less than 100 percent' (Sastri 1992). In the rice zone of Madhya Pradesh, the daily evapotranspiration (ET) and percolation losses in rice fields account for 6-8 mm and therefore a minimum rainfall of 50 mm per week is considered the stable rainfall quantum. If the coefficient of variation (CV) is greater than 100 per cent, it is considered unstable, and hence the CV of the corresponding week with more than 50 mm of rainfall should also be less than 100 per cent. Those weeks with total weekly rainfall greater than 50 mm

and corresponding CV less than 100 per cent are considered stable rainfall weeks for rice. With this criterion, the stable rainfall periods for different districts of the rice zone of Madhya Pradesh are shown in Figure 32.4.

Figure 32.4 shows that the stable rainfall period for Raipur is from 22 June to 13 September (eighty-four days) while for Bilaspur it is from 22 June to 15 September (eighty-six days). However, for Durg the stable rainfall period occurs in two parts – 15 June– 6 July (sixteen days) and 31 July–11 September (forty-three days), with instability (higher CV values) in between, from 7 July to 30 July (twenty-four days).

In other words, in Durg district there is a chance of water stress due to instability of rainfall during the seedling stage of the rice crop. Thus, a variety that is drought tolerant during the seedling stage is suggested for Durg. Similarly, the stable rainfall period at Rajnandgaon is from 22 June to 24 August (sixty-four days), which is about twenty days shorter than the same period at Raipur. This suggests that an early-maturing rice variety, which can escape drought at the reproductive stage, is needed for Rajnandgaon.

Drought resistance

Drought-resistant plants are those varieties that are able to grow and yield satisfactorily in areas liable to periodic drought (Hounam *et al.* 1975). May and Milthorpe (1962) identified three types of drought resistance. They are:

Table 32.2 Relative yields of traditional and efficient crops in dryland areas of India

Region	Traditional crop	Yield (t/ha)	Efficient crop	Yield (t/ha)
Bellary (Deccan Rabi region)	Cotton	0.20	Sorghum	2.60
Varanasi (East UP)	Wheat	0.86	Chickpea	2.85
Ranchi (Upland of Bihar)	Upland rice	2.88	Corn	3.36
Indore (Malwa Plateau)	(i) Greengram	1.18	Soybean	3.36
	(ii) Wheat	1.12	Safflower	2.42
Agra (West UP)	Wheat	1.03	Mustard	2.04
Hissar (NW India)	Wheat	0.32	Taramira (*Eruca Sativa*)	1.61
Udaipur (SE Rajasthan)	Maize	1.80	Hybrid Sorghum	2.80
Rewa (North MP)	Soybean (Black)	0.40	Soybean (Yellow)	1.20

Source: Singh and Ramana Rao 1988

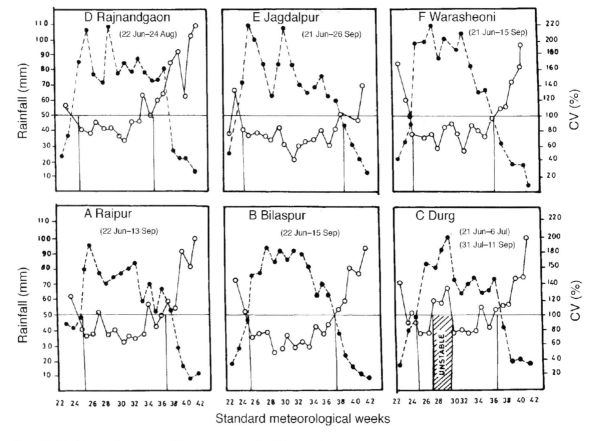

Figure 32.4 Stable rainfall periods at different stations in the Chhattisgarh region
Source: Shrivastava *et al.* 1986

1 drought 'escapability' – the ability of a plant to complete its life cycle before being subjected to serious water stress;
2 drought endurance with high internal water content, enabling a plant to survive drought by virtue of a deep root system or reduced transpiration; and
3 drought endurance with low internal water content during the period of drought but the ability to recover and grow when soil water is replenished.

Thus for Durg district the third type of drought tolerance is needed in the rice variety at the seedling stage because the root has not penetrated to deeper layers, while for Rajnandgaon district, the first type (drought-escaping) is needed in the rice variety, which completes its reproductive stage by 25 August.

In areas where prolonged dry spells occur, varieties of the second type of drought tolerance are needed. For example, sorghum is more drought resistant than corn because of differences in root concentration. Greater drought resistance is shown by these plants with deeper and more extensively branched root systems. Root extension virtually ceases in most species during flowering and podding stages and hence the plants with faster maturity can survive during a drought spell.

Experiments conducted (Jaggi *et al.* 1986) at the research farm of Indira Gandhi Agricultural University, Raipur, on different genotypes of rice grown under rain-fed conditions revealed that a local predominant variety, *Safri-17*, has the highest root density in the top 10 cm (Figure 32.5). Hence, this

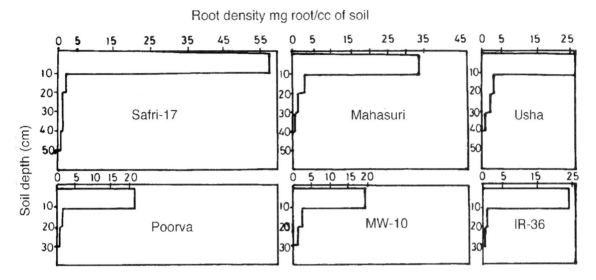

Figure 32.5 Rooting pattern of six cultivars of rice
Source: Jaggi *et al.* 1986

variety recovers fast even with only a small drizzle after a prolonged dry spell. That is one of the reasons for the predominance of this variety in the rice zone of Madhya Pradesh.

In another experiment (Sharma *et al.* 1986) at the same place, the drought tolerance of the cultivar MW-10 was higher than other hybrids that were tested. Drought tolerance was examined according to the evaluation system developed by the International Rice Research Institute in the Philippines.

Soil variability

The availability of water for plants also depends on soil type. In sand, most of the water is readily available and plants grow rapidly until transpiration depletes the supply. They then suffer from a sudden and severe deficit, and death may follow if the water in the root zone is not replenished. On the contrary, in clay soils, water is held with progressively increasing tension as the water content is reduced below field capacity. Plants then experience transient water deficits that reduce the rate of growth, but water continues to be released as the tension progresses, to the wilting point (Hounam *et al.* 1975). Thus, after rains cease, water is available for longer periods in clay than in sandy soils.

In rice fields that are diked, deep percolation losses are lower in clayey soils than they are in light soils. In view of this, in the rice zone of Madhya Pradesh, recommendations for rice varieties have been made according to the soil types, as shown in Table 32.3 (Alam and Sastri 1997).

CROP MANAGEMENT TO ALLEVIATE DROUGHT CONDITIONS

In the case of drought incidence during the growing season, the ill effects of drought, to a considerable extent, can be alleviated by adopting proper crop management strategies. These strategies may vary from moisture conservation to manipulation of plant population, fertilisation, and even some midseason corrections. Some of the strategies that can be adopted are discussed below. However, one point to be noted is that no one strategy can be applied to every situation. In fact, every strategy is location, crop, time, and socioeconomic condition specific.

Plant population management

If water stress conditions occur at the time of or immediately after germination, it would be best to

Table 32.3 Rice variety recommendations according to the soil types in the rice zones of Madhya Pradesh

Serial no.	Soil type	Suitable duration (days)	Varieties	Maturity (days)
1	Lateritic	80–90	i) Vanprabha	90
			ii) Kalinga-3	85
			iii) Aditya	90
2	Sandy loam	90–110	i) Tulsi	105
			ii) Poornima	105
			iii) Annada	105
			iv) IR-64	105
3	Clay loam	110–30	i) IR-36	115
			ii) Krant	128
			iii) Mahamaya	130
			iv) Abhaya	125
4	Clay	130–40	i) Kranti	128
			ii) Mahamaya	130
5	Semideep water	140–50	i) Safri-17	140–5
			ii) Mahsuri	140–5
			iii) Swana	145–50

Source: Alam and Sastri 1997

resow the crop, preferably with some early-maturing variety. On the other hand, if water stress occurs around forty to fifty days after crop emergence, ratooning and thinning need to be considered. According to Venkateswarulu (1992), ratooning of a drought-affected sorghum crop with a subsequent rain resulted in a grain yield of 0.8 t/ha, compared to 0.2 t/ha for the same crop without ratooning. Similarly, pearl millet had a yield of 2.51 t/ha with ratooning, whereas the non-ratooned crop yielded 1.6 t/ha. Thinning the plant population by removing every third row at the time of drought increased the productivity of sorghum from 1.55 t/ha to 2.11 t/ha at Bellary in south India. When the plants started to recover after the return of rainfall, a 2–3 per cent urea spray was also found to be beneficial.

Rainfall distribution modelling and contingency planning

The corrective measures that can be taken in the event of moisture stress depend on the period during which drought occurs. If the rains fail immediately after sowing, resulting in a heavy mortality of seedlings, resowing has to be done. On the other hand,

if water stress occurs during the midseason, other measures, like ratooning crops such as sorghum or pearl millets or thinning plant populations, must be adopted. Such contingency plans can be prepared only if rainfall distribution models are prepared for different situations and are made available. For example, at Raipur, the probability of early, normal, and late onset of southwest monsoon is 22, 58, and 20 per cent, respectively. The conditional probability of drought in July (JD), August (AD), and September (SD) and corresponding rainfall distributions in different weeks under each situation are studied by Sastri and Chaudhary (1990) and are shown in Figure 32.6. Such information for each location/area is highly useful in developing contingency plans for midseason corrections.

Weed management

During a dry spell or stress conditions, weed competition is a problem for crops because weeds also use the little moisture that is available. In an experiment on drought management on a traditionally grown rice crop in the Chhattisgarh region of eastern Madhya Pradesh, it was found that when a prolonged dry spell

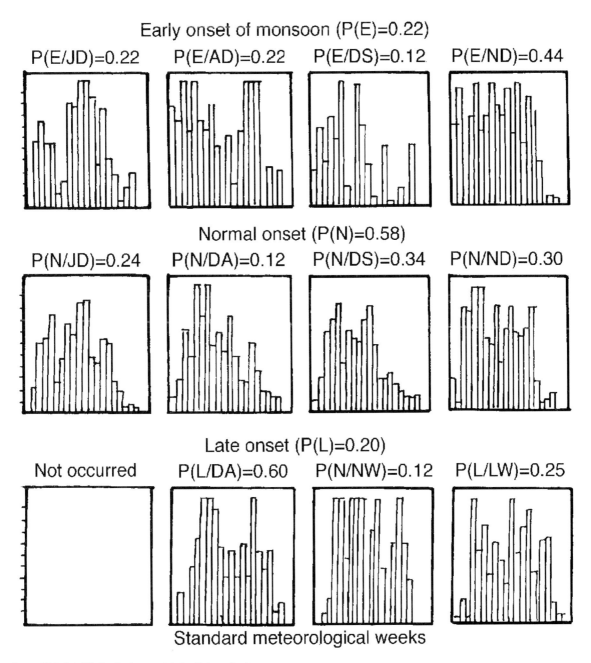

Figure 32.6 Rainfall distribution models for Raipur district
Source: Sastri and Chaudhary 1990

occurs immediately after the germination of the crop under rain-fed conditions, weeds infest the entire field. *Bushening*, one of the traditional practices of weed control and a means of creating semipuddled conditions (a condition of partially pulverised soils), cannot be done under dry conditions.

Under such conditions, at thirty to thirty-five days after sowing, harvesting the entire field (weeds and rice together) can economically reduce the weed problem (Sastri *et al*. 1990). Even with a small amount of rainfall, the rice crop, which at this point would have just entered the vegetative growth stage, would suppress the weeds, which would have completed the vegetative stage and entered the flowering stage at that time. Even in dryland crops sown in line, weed control through interculture operation was found to be beneficial under water stress conditions.

LIFESAVING IRRIGATION

In drought-prone areas, although there are no irrigation facilities, technological developments have been made to harvest, conserve, and recycle excess rainwater for use during water stress. Such techniques are in vogue in almost every dryland area of the world. However, in recommending a particular practice of harvesting rainwater for providing lifesaving irrigation, care should be taken to match the practice to the available natural resources. Land, soil types, physiography, rainfall quantum, rainfall distribution and intensity, and cropping patterns must all be considered in this process. Some of the techniques that have been developed in Chhattisgarh and other parts of India are discussed below.

Rainfall cistern system

A rainfall cistern system is nothing but a series of alternating raised and sunken beds laid across a slope. The raised beds act like donor catchments for the sunken beds, where high-duty crops like rice, sugar-cane, and maize are grown, while in raised bed areas, lower or moderate water requirement cross-like legumes are grown (Padmahabhan 1992). The sunken beds, in the case of rice, are made zero grade, and for other crops a gentle gradient is provided.

To properly utilise the assured rainfall of 1,000–1,200 mm in the Chhattisgarh region of Madhya Pradesh in India, which is inadequate for rice and excessive for other dryland crops, a rainwater cistern system was developed for assured rice production (Sastri and Urkurkar 1988, Urkurkar 1990). Soybeans were grown in the raised bed and rice was grown in the sunken bed. The excess rainwater from the soybeans drained off and was automatically collected in the sunken beds with rice crop. The study revealed that 45–48 per cent of the rainwater is runoff and is collected in the sunken bed. The results of the experiment showed that in 1986, under severe water stress conditions during flowering and reproductive stages, soybean productivity was 63 per cent higher because of better drainage while rice productivity increased by 76 per cent because of excess water collected through runoff. The results of the two-year study are shown in Table 32.4.

Farm ponds

Farm ponds are bodies of water made by constructing an embankment across a water course or by excavating a pit, or by a combination thereof. Farm pond design takes into account the quantum of lifesaving irrigation needed for the crop in that area. At Indira Gandhi Agricultural University in Raipur, farm pond technology has been developed to alleviate the drought conditions in the rice crop during the grow-

Table 32.4 Water balance and grain yields of soybeans and rice under the rainwater cistern system

| Year | Rainfall during growing season (mm) | Runoff (mm) | Total water available for: | | Yields (t/ha) | | | |
| | | | Soybean (mm) | Rice (mm) | Cistern systems | | Traditional systems | |
					Soybean	Rice	Soybean	Rice
1985	1,395.5	313.0	1,082.5	1,708.5	2.06	4.27	1.57	3.50
1986	648.5	173.3	475.2	821.8	1.85	2.43	1.13	1.38

Source: Urkurkar 1990

ing season (Anonymous 1996). The technology has been developed for harvesting rainwater from a field of 1 ha in a farm pond of 0.09 ha, dug in the field in such a way that two-thirds of the area falls above the pond as catchment area and one-third of the area falls below the pond. In the catchment area, crops like soybeans and pigeon pea are grown, while rice is grown in the lower area. About 28–37 per cent of the total rainfall is collected as runoff and is harvested in the farm pond. The productivity of upland crops increased significantly because of better drainage, and rice yields improved because of lifesaving irrigation during stress periods. After meeting the lifesaving requirements of rice, the collected water was also used for providing irrigation to establish a second crop, like chickpea. This increased the double-cropped area and thereby the cropping intensity. The results of the experiments (Table 32.5) indicated that even in a severe drought year like 1992–3, rice productivity could be increased by 81 per cent, and chickpea productivity was about 1.1 t/ha.

During the rainy season of 1996, there was severe drought in some pockets of the Chhattisgarh region in general and the Raipur district in particular. In on-farm experiments on rain-fed rice in Tarpongi village of the Raipur district, there was a severe drought during the growing season. Some farmers participating in the experiments used the rainwater that collected in the roadside ditches as lifesaving irrigation, and this small amount of irrigation could improve the productivity of two rice varieties in heavy soils. In light soils, the plants died at a very early stage because of heavy infestation of weeds (Koshta *et al.*

1997). The results are shown in Figure 32.7. Thus, lifesaving irrigation through so-called farm ponds can, to a great extent, improve the productivity of crops.

Village tanks

In the Chhattisgarh region, especially in the Chhattisgarh plains, irrigation tanks were developed in every village to provide one or two irrigations to rice to alleviate the effects of drought (Sastri 1992). The number of tanks and corresponding irrigated area in different districts of the Chhattisgarh region are shown in Table 32.6.

The efficiency of tank water use varies significantly with space and time. During drought years, only the area around the tank is irrigated, but during a good rainfall year the tank water is also used for a second crop in the winter season. However, during the rainy season, with rice as the main crop, tank water use efficiency is quite low because there is little good water management practice. Farmers near the tank fill their fields up to a depth of at least 30 cm and then let out the water. During drought years when there is even less water stored in the tank, efficiency decreases further.

Water harvesting potentials

To assess the runoff potential for water harvesting during excess, normal, and deficit rainfall years in the catchment areas of different tanks at different stations of the Raipur district, an index known as storage index (SI) has been developed (Sastri 1996).

Table 32.5 Yields of different crops during rainy and post-rainy seasons under farm pond technology

Season	Crop	Grain yield (t/ha)					Mean
		1990–1	1991–2	1992–3	1993–4	1994–5	
Rainy	(a) Rice:						
	(i) With lifesaving irrigation	4.30	4.60	2.68	3.86	4.78	4.04
	(ii) Without irrigation	2.90	2.72	1.72	2.13	3.35	2.56
	(b) Soybean	2.40	2.70	3.07	2.73	2.28	2.64
Post-rainy	(a) Chickpea after soybean	0.92	1.89	1.12	0.82	2.05	1.36
	(b) Chickpea after rice	0.86	1.41	1.04	1.19	1.91	1.28
	(c) Mustard after soybean	0.51	1.05	0.86	0.53	1.36	0.86
	(d) Mustard after rice	0.34	0.61	0.73	0.24	0.74	0.53

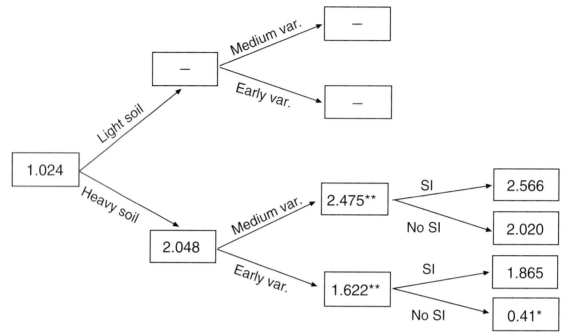

* Poor yield due to poor germination; resown on 27 July, 1996
** Weighted average

SI: Supplemental life-saving irrigation

Figure 32.7 System analysis for productivity (t/ha) of early- and medium-duration rice varieties under severe drought conditions in two types of soil
Source: Koshta et al. 1997

Table 32.6 Number of tanks and corresponding irrigated area in different districts of the Chhattisgarh region

Serial no.	District	No. of tanks	Total tank irrigated area (in thousands of ha)	Irrigated area per tank (ha/tank)
1	Raipur	12,737	29.1	2.3
2	Durg	2,156	8.7	4.0
3	Rajnandgaon	187	6.1	32.6
4	Bilaspur	15,681	16.3	1.4
5	Bastar	138	1.3	10.0
6	Surguja	2,368	4.1	1.7
7	Raigarh	2,995	2.5	0.9
8	Balaghat	6,138	35.3	5.7

Source: Directorate of Agriculture, Government of Madhya Pradesh, Bhopal (India) 1995

$$\text{Storage Index (SI)} = \frac{\text{Annual surplus water}}{\text{Annual average rainfall}} \times 100$$

Based on SI, the water harvesting potentials at different stations in the Raipur district during excess, normal, and deficit rainfall years have been worked out and are shown in Table 32.7. During drought years, the chances of collecting runoff water and providing supplemental irrigation are much lower.

CONCLUSIONS

The productivity of a crop is drastically reduced by water stress conditions. In unirrigated areas, especially in developing countries, failure of rains causes prolonged dry spells, which, in turn, result in drought conditions that reduce crop productivity. Sustainable strategies must be developed to alleviate the impact of drought on crop productivity.

In areas of recurring drought, one of the best strategies for alleviating drought is varietal manipulation, through which drought can be avoided or its effects can be minimised by adopting varieties that are drought-resistant at different growth stages.

If drought occurs during the middle of a growing season, corrective measures can be adopted; these vary from reducing plant population to fertilisation or weed management. In high rainfall areas where there are a series of wet and dry spells, rainfall can be harvested in either farm ponds or in village tanks and can be recycled as lifesaving irrigation during a prolonged dry spell. The remaining water can also be used to provide irrigation for a second crop with a lower water requirement, like chickpea.

However, no one strategy can be adopted universally. In fact, all such strategies are location, time, crop, crop stage, and (to some extent) socioeconomic condition specific. Developing such strategies for each specific condition can help make agriculture sustainable.

Table 32.7 Storage indices in different stations of Raipur district during excess, normal, and deficit rainfall years (data base 1901–90)

Serial no.	Station	Storage Index (%)			Annual average rainfall (mm)
		Excess	Normal	Deficit	
1	Raipur	87.6	39.9	3.0	1,149.4
2	Dhamtari	86.4	35.4	2.3	1,388.4
3	Simga	63.5	27.6	2.5	1,185.7
4	Balodabazar	74.9	33.8	3.5	1,269.2
5	Gariyaband	83.0	40.2	6.6	1,521.3
6	Arang	78.3	34.4	8.2	1,342.8
7	Rajim	72.8	35.0	10.5	1,351.8
8	Mahasamund	89.3	38.4	5.5	1,367.6
9	Deobhog	67.4	25.5	2.7	1,345.2
10	Kurud	75.3	27.9	0.0	1,276.0
11	Brindanavagarh	76.8	24.2	0.0	1,353.1
12	Kusrangi	80.4	32.7	0.0	1,327.4
13	Khairadatan	66.3	30.2	0.5	1,276.5
14	Pithora	73.7	37.1	8.2	1,532.6
15	Lakholi	78.8	27.4	0.0	1,404.0
16	Rudri	68.5	32.8	0.0	1,462.3
17	Muramsilli	77.1	35.0	2.6	1,550.1
18	Bhatagaon	75.0	34.4	11.4	1,453.2
19	Kondapur	72.5	30.2	0.0	1,422.1
20	Kanki	62.9	32.1	2.4	1,394.1
21	Saraipali	75.5	35.7	0.0	1,389.0

Source: Sastri et al. 1997

REFERENCES

Alam, A. and Sastri, A.S.R.A.S. (1997) 'Water management strategies for enhancing agricultural production in Eastern Madhya Pradesh', Seminar on Harnessing and Management of Water Resources for Enhancing Agricultural Production in Eastern Region, 15–17 February, Orissa University of Agriculture and Technology, Bhubeneswar, Orissa.

Anonymous (1996) 'Impact of National Agricultural Research Project on the agricultural development of Eastern Madhya Pradesh', *Indira Gandhi Agricultural University*, Raipur, p. 107.

Datta, R.K. (1992) 'Role of weather forecasting in agriculture', lecture notes in the *First SERC School on Agrometeorology*, Indira Gandhi Agricultural University, Raipur (India), 14 September–30 October.

Directorate of Agriculture, Government of Madhya Pradesh, Bhopal (India), 1995 'Agricultural Statistics of Madhya Pradesh'.

Hounam, C.E., Burgos, J.J., Kalok, M.S., Palmer, W.C., and Rodda, J. (1975) 'Drought and agriculture', *WMO Technical Note* 138, World Meteorological Organization, Geneva, p. 127.

Jaggi, I.K., Das, R.O., and Bisen, D.C. (1986) 'Evaluation of six genotypes of rice growing under rainfed conditions', *Journal of the Indian Society of Soil Science* 34: 445–50.

Koshta, V.K., Sastri, A.S.R.A.S., Urkurkar, J.S., Sahu, V.N., and Baghel, S.S. (1997) 'On farm research on rice and rice-based cropping systems', *Annual Report. IGAU-IRRI Collaborative Project IFAD Project IGAU*, Raipur, India, p. 28.

May, L.H. and Milthorpe, F.L. (1962) 'Drought resistance of crop plants', Commonwealth Bureau of Pastures and Field Crops, *UK Field Crops Abstracts*, pp. 171–9.

Padmanabhan, M.V. (1992) 'Soil and water conservation measures in watersheds', lecture notes in the *First SERC School on Agrometeorology*, Indira Gandhi Agricultural University, Raipur (India), 14 September–3 October.

Sastri, A.S.R.A.S. (1992) 'Traditional drought management techniques in Central India', *Drought Network News* 4, 2: 3–4.

—— (1993) 'Agricultural drought management strategies to alleviate impacts: Examples from the arid and subhumid regions of the Indian subcontinent', in D.A. Whilhite (ed.), *Drought Assessment, Management, and Planning: Theory and Case Studies*, Boston, MA: Kluwer Academic Publishers, pp. 65–86.

—— (1993) 'Climate fluctuations and changes in Central India and their impact on agriculture', in Proceedings of the International Symposium on 'Climate Change, Natural Disasters and Agricultural Strategies', Beijing, People's Republic of China, pp. 54–7.

—— (1998) 'Water balance studies of bunded rice fields in Chhattisgarh region of Central India and some strategies to improve the lowland rainfed rice productivity', *Proceedings of the International Symposium on Hydrology in Humid Tropics*, Jamaica, 17–24 November 1996, IAHS Publication 253: 93–100.

—— (1998) 'Agroclimatic Features', in Reference to Madhya Pradesh, Deshbhandhu Publications, Raipur, India, pp. 79–83.

Sastri, A.S.R.A.S. and Chaudhary, J.L. (1990) 'Models on climate for increased productivity in rainfed rice', *Proceedings of the International Symposium on Rice Research: New Frontiers*, pp. 392–3.

Sastri, A.S.R.A.S., Chaudhary, J.L., Shrivastava, A.K., and Naidu, D. (1997) 'Water harvesting potential in Chhattisgarh Plains: A hydroclimatic analysis', *Bhagirath* 44, 1: 15–21.

Sastri, A.S.R.A.S., Siddique, M.R.H., and Urkurkar, J.S. (1990) 'New approaches for drought management of rainfed rice in Central India', *Drought Network News* 2, 1: 12–13.

Sastri, A.S.R.A.S. and Urkurkar, J.S. (1988) 'Rainwater management for rainfed rice in Chhattisgarh region of Madhya Pradesh', *Oryza* 26: 342–3.

Sharma, D.K., Shrivastava, M.N., Shrivastava, P.S., and Sastri, A.S.R.A.S. (1986) 'Drought tolerance under varied moisture levels during seedling stage of rice crop', *Oryza* 23: 135–6.

Shrivastava, P.S., Sastri, A.S.R.A.S., and Shrivastava, M.N. (1986) 'Selection of suitable rice varieties to different soils and agroclimatic regions using rainfall characteristics and climatic water balance – A case study for Chhattisgarh region', presented to Second Indian Agrometeorological Congress, 10–12 March 1986, Anand, India.

Singh, R.P. and Ramana Rao, B.V. (1988) 'Adjustments to weather variation through efficient cropping systems', *Fertilizer News* 33, 4: 21–7.

Urkurkar, J.S. (1990) 'Studies on growth, development and productivity of rice soybean and blackgram in relation to water management in poorly drained soils', unpublished Ph.D. thesis, Pt. Ravishankar Shukla University, Raipur.

Venkateswarulu, J. (1992) 'Steps to mitigate moisture stress in crop production', lecture notes of *First SERC School on Agrometeorology*, Indira Gandhi Agricultural University, Raipur (India), 14 September–3 October.

33

'SHE'LL BE RIGHT, MATE'. COPING WITH DROUGHT

Strategies old and new in Australia

R.L. Heathcote

INTRODUCTION

The extensive droughts in eastern Australia that began in 1994 and ended effectively with extensive flooding in February 1997 and the associated national drought relief packages are reminders of the continuing relevance of drought to resource management in Australia. While the phenomenon of drought can be recognised as a continuous theme in Australian history, the relief packages were supposed to reflect revised disaster relief policies resulting from the proposals in the Final Report of the Federal Drought Policy Review Task Force (DPRTF 1990). In fact, as this chapter hopes to show, the revisions appear to have been at best cosmetic, and for the drought 'victims', the old confidence in official drought relief handouts seems still to be secure. 'She'll be right, mate'.

DROUGHT AND THE AUSTRALIAN ECOSYSTEM

Drought has been a long-time companion to resource management in Australia. Aboriginal legends include reference to it, and since 1788 its impacts, both positive and negative, have concerned Australian society. In 1813 it helped push settlers over the Blue Mountains into the continental interior; in 1865 Surveyor General Goyder delimited that year's drought in South Australia and initiated a regional resource management policy that is still relevant today (Heathcote 1981); in 1888 – the centennial year of European settlement – it was devastating southeastern Australia; in the 1930s it added to the miseries of the Depression years; in February 1983 it helped to bring the Victorian Mallee soils to Melbourne in a dust storm, as it had similarly in 1902; in the Bicentennial Commonwealth Year Book it merited a six-page article (ABS 1988); and, more recently, it has been shown to cause economic and environmental degradation in Queensland and New South Wales.

Defining drought, however, has been difficult, and without reviewing all the arguments noted earlier (Heathcote 1969), it is necessary to remind ourselves that most definitions are relative – that is, the shortage of moisture (whether rainfall, soil moisture, or groundwater) is assessed in relation to the demand for that moisture, and drought is defined when that imbalance causes human hardship – usually, in the Australian context, an economic hardship. Given that context, the problems of definition arise when we realise that human management of the resources can either reduce or enhance the risk of drought occurring by reducing or increasing the demand for water – be it on a sheep/cattle property, on a wheat farm, or in an urban water supply system. Different thresholds of water need and different management systems create different potentials for drought occurrence.

Conventionally, however, research into the general effects of drought on the Australian community and ecosystems has compared reports of drought occurrences with the most readily accessible climate statistics – rainfall data – and suggested that meteorological droughts (annual rainfalls in the lowest 10 per cent of values on record), when occurring over at least 10 per cent of the continent, have in the past coincided with damaging agricultural droughts (shortfalls of moisture causing significant economic losses of crops and livestock) (Gibbs and Maher 1967, ABS 1988). Following this convention, therefore, I will focus on such meteorological droughts, their associated societal and environmental impacts, and management strategies.

PATTERNS OF DROUGHT IN SPACE AND TIME

Using the Commonwealth Bureau of Meteorology's annual maps of rainfalls by deciles to supplement the earlier study by Gibbs and Maher (1967), it is possible to survey the temporal and spatial patterns of the occurrence of meteorological drought in Australia (Heathcote 1991).

At the continental scale, drought has occurred somewhere on the continent in 80 per cent of the 108 years of record from 1885 to 1993. For 32 per cent of that time, more than 10 per cent of the continent has been affected, with some significant societal impact likely. The maximum sequence of years (four) with more than 10 per cent of the continent drought-affected was 1926–9, a period of considerable stress for new farming settlements in southeastern and Western Australia. Conversely, at the continental scale, the maximum sequence of years relatively free of drought (eleven years) has occurred recently – from 1983 to 1993, inclusive. Such a long period relatively free of drought is unprecedented in our history; it was broken in 1994, as noted above.

At the regional scale of the states, the picture is different. Although no more than 46 per cent of the continent has experienced drought in any one year, the whole of Victoria was affected in 1982; 90 per cent of Tasmania and the Northern Territory was affected in 1961; 81 per cent of New South Wales was affected in 1940; 70 per cent of Queensland and South Australia was affected in 1902 and 1961, respectively; and 66 per cent of Western Australia was affected in 1936. This varying spatial impact reflects the latitudinal contrasts between the tropical and temperate weather systems, since it has been rare for the summer rains of northern tropical Australia to fail in sequence with the winter rains of southern temperate Australia. This probably accounts for the low maximum area affected by drought in Western

Australia, since it is the only state to span both temperate and tropical zones.

The spatial variation in drought occurrence is not merely latitudinal, however, for there is evidence of longitudinal contrasts between droughts in eastern and western Australia. Of the one hundred years from 1888 to 1987, New South Wales had droughts in seventeen years when Western Australia was drought free, and Western Australia had droughts in twenty-six years when New South Wales was drought free. The most recent example of this longitudinal 'oscillation' of droughts occurred in 1982, when 58 per cent of New South Wales was in drought but Western Australia was completely drought free.

What conclusions can we draw from this brief review of the historical record of drought in Australia? First is the obvious comment that meteorological drought is a frequent event, occurring somewhere in the continent every three out of four years and having the size to cause serious economic hardship on average every one in three years. Second, it is extremely unlikely that the whole of the continent will be affected in any one year, and thus regional drought impacts in one part of this continental nation may be offset by normal seasons in other areas – as witness the good harvests in Western Australia in 1982 when the harvests in eastern Australia generally failed. For individual states, however, drought may affect most of their area and result in major economic and environmental impacts, requiring major drought relief strategies.

CHANGING DROUGHT IMPACTS

The historical background of meteorological droughts is paralleled by significant historical evidence of both positive and negative drought impacts on society and the environment. Summarising earlier papers (Heathcote 1969 and 1988), the sizeable historical losses attributed to drought included shortfalls in agricultural and pastoral production leading to adverse national balance of payments and reduced gross domestic product (GDP). Service costs were increased for water provision (both urban and rural), and farm and road maintenance costs were increased because of drought-accelerated soil erosion. There was also some evidence of retreat of rural settlement from the riskier sites inland. Droughts did bring some benefits: drought-reduced domestic, feral, and wild livestock numbers gave the hard-pressed grazing lands a breathing space to make at least a partial recovery; the private transport industries generally benefited from accelerated livestock and fodder movements in droughts; and official drought relief measures often channelled funds into areas that otherwise would not have benefited. In many cases the money spent, for example, on public road construction and maintenance was of considerable long-term benefit to the rural communities.

Taking into consideration the complexities of the accounting noted in the original review – particularly, for example, the inclusion of losses from wheat not sown and livestock not conceived – there is continuing evidence of high economic losses (Dury 1983). The economic costs of one of the last major droughts (1982) were claimed to have multiplied up to A$7,500 million (Allan and Heathcote 1987, Martin 1983, Oliver 1986: 304), and this despite a declining share of GDP by the agricultural and pastoral sectors – from 18 per cent in the 1950s to about 4 per cent currently (Chisholm 1992). More recent estimates of the costs of the 1992–5 drought have suggested about A$4,000 million, with a decline of 8 per cent in the gross value of farm output (McLennan 1996: 116).

The social and demographic effects of the 1982 drought have also been shown to resemble those of the droughts of the 1930s – particularly in rural communities already suffering from declining incomes and rising prices (Burnley 1986, Gregory 1984). The onset of drought appeared to have speeded up the processes of rural change already present in those communities.

Added to the undisputed socioeconomic impacts is increasing concern for the environmental effects of droughts. National concern for resource conservation issues in Australia in the 1970s and 1980s has reflected the wider concerns of western societies. Thus the appearance in 1965 and subsequent work of the Australian Conservation Foundation (ACF), the first national survey of soil conservation needs (DEHCD 1978), the adoption of a National Conservation Strategy in 1986, and the joint ACF–National Farmers Federation proposal for the National Land Care Pro-

gram in 1989 (subsequently adopted by the Commonwealth Government) were evidence of increasing awareness of land degradation or desertification, loss of natural and cultural heritage items, and quality of life issues (Chisholm 1992).

Earlier, at the turn of the century and in the 1930s and 1940s, there had been fears that severe droughts were responsible for 'desert outbreaks' – desertification as it would now be called – on eroding arid range lands in eastern Australia (Heathcote 1987). The national soil survey of 1978 showed that 29 per cent of the land in agricultural or pastoral use needed soil conservation works or a change in land use (three-quarters of this being arid grazing land), and the United Nations World Map of Desertification of 1977, although criticised in detail, again raised the spectre of the spread of the desert lands.

The linkage between drought and wildfires (bush fires) has been clearly demonstrated (Luke and McArthur 1978, Pyne 1991). It was reinforced by the series of massive bush fires covering 500,000 ha of the tinder-dry drought-stricken countryside in South Australia and Victoria in 1983, which killed seventy-two people, more than 300,000 domestic animals, and an unknown number of wild and feral animals, and caused property damage of approximately A$400 million. The coincidence with drought was clear enough. Less clear was the link between drought and soil erosion (up to 48 tonnes lost per hectare) from some of the burned areas in the drought-breaking rains of March 1983 (Allan and Heathcote 1987).

A complicating factor is that reports of drought occurrence may be rising because of increased pressure on the land as a result perhaps of economic necessity, ignorance, or greed on the part of the resource managers. Historically, in the pastoral industry in Australia, overstocking the range initially paid off but made subsequent operations more vulnerable to drought, since the drought reserves of edible scrub were destroyed. The advance of the wheat farmers inland into areas where rainfall was not only lower but less reliable effectively increased their vulnerability to drought, despite the efforts of the plant breeders to produce more drought-resistant crop varieties. In Western Australia, the official reports of drought occurrence certainly seem to favour the drier edge of the wheat country (Heathcote 1988). In

New South Wales, the disparity between drought occurrences, as defined by soil moisture criteria and as declared at the request of local rural producers, has been noted by Smith and Callahan (1988). As graphed in Figure 3 of Heathcote 1991, as the annual rainfall along a transect inland decreased, over the period 1976–82 the plotted disparity between the observed frequency of soil moisture (Palmer Index) droughts and the higher frequency of officially declared droughts along that transect increased. It may be that drought, not rain, has 'followed the plough' in Australia (de Kantzow and Sutton 1981), a theme recently documented in a wider global context (Glantz 1994).

DROUGHT COPING STRATEGIES

Australian responses to the stress of drought may be classified into two groups: private (the strategies of the settlers themselves) and official (the policies of governments).

Private strategies

Whether Australians have ever fully accepted drought as endemic to the continent is debatable (Heathcote 1969), but there is no doubt that as settlement spread down the rainfall gradient into the continental interior, pragmatic, often technologically based strategies to cope with the increasing incidence of 'agricultural drought' were evolved by the settlers independent of any official inputs.

For the pastoralists with a good sense of geography and the finances to back it, a favoured strategy was an interregional spread of their properties from summer to winter rainfall areas, helping to create millionaires such as Sir Sidney Kidman (1857–1935) and James Tyson (1819–98). Technological responses were also favoured, such as fencing to control access to the range, excavation of tanks to store the fleeting surface runoff, deep drilling to tap the Great Artesian Basin, and (more recently) drought-resistant livestock breeds. Storage of surplus feed, however, has only proved economic for valued breeding stock (Dillon and Lloyd 1962, Powell 1963). Evacuation of starving stock to purchased grazing lands (agistment) beyond the drought area or

exploitation of the public 'long paddock' – the official travelling stock routes (wide grassed road reserves) – were also possibilities.

A recent review of various pastoral regions suggested that traditional strategies to cope with drought would provide economic benefits, provided they included some of the following:

- reduced stocking rates;
- destocking of all but essential breeding stock in drought;
- rapid build-up of stock numbers after drought;
- diversification, but only after the optimisation of existing management; and
- recognition that drought was a seasonal risk.

(Buxton and Stafford Smith 1996: 306)

The economic benefits of such strategies were demonstrated, but the environmental consequences, particularly after rapid restocking after drought, were less clear.

For farmers, the march out onto the droughty plains has been hard-fought, with human ingenuity stretched to its limits to cope with the variable seasons. The optimal time for seeding was learned by trial and error; fallowing of land to save moisture from one season to the next began privately in South Australia in the 1880s before the technique received official blessing following official contacts with the Campbell Dry Farming System of the US Great Plains in 1906. Machinery to harvest drought-stunted crops – Ridley's 'Stripper' of 1843 – was developed in South Australia before diffusing rapidly through Victoria and New South Wales. South Australian farmers also were experimenting with drought-resistant wheat varieties (Williams 1974) before William J. Farrer began to cross drought-resistant Indian wheats with good-quality Canadian baking wheats and the well-established, high-yielding but vulnerable Purple Straw wheats. The results, especially 'Federation' (produced during the last years of the 1895–1902 drought), were to push the wheat fields further down the rainfall gradient into the semiarid lands over the next twenty-five years.

The apparent success of highly mechanised broad acre grain farming using controlled fertilisers and associated pastures in the semiarid portions of South Australia led to the formation of a specialised government agency in the 1970s (South Australian Agricultural Research Investment Company – SAGRIC), which was invited to develop dry farming systems in north Africa and southwest Asia (SAGRIC n.d.). The emphasis was on adapting successful technologies developed in South Australia to areas of similar climate around the world, but the success has been limited (Chatterton and Chatterton 1996).

An earlier private strategy for water management on farm, by which an attempt was made to conserve all the rainfall falling on the property and spread it evenly over the land surface, had been developed in New South Wales in the late 1940s. Despite strong support from the professor of geography at Sydney University (Macdonald Holmes 1960), it appears to have been forgotten.

For the urban investor in rural Australia, however, drought in the past may have served a useful purpose in that drought losses on rural properties could usually be offset by profits on urban enterprises, for taxation purposes. In the vernacular, 'Collins Street farmers' (Victoria) or 'Rundle Street farmers' (South Australia) traditionally have written off losses against their non-farm city business interests, so that drought impacts may be less economically significant in *their* overall strategies.

On Australian farms, however, when the crop starts to wilt there is little to be done if irrigation is impossible. When the crop has died and the soil begins to blow, there is only emergency tillage (deep ploughing to bring moist subsoil to the surface as protection) to stave off disaster, and that only as long as the subsoil is moist enough to hold the clods together. When that fails, the next step has often been to appeal for official drought relief.

Official policies toward drought

Official policies toward drought have traditionally seen it as a natural disaster, to be met by a variety of strategies. These have included direct assistance in subsidies for in-drought emergency measures (water provision for humans and domestic stock; feed or evacuation provision for starving livestock; low-interest loans and even cash grants). Post-drought measures have included replacement seed, public works employment for victims, support for pre-

drought research into drought-resistant crops and animal species, rain-making experiments, support for irrigation schemes (particularly in the Murray Darling Basin), and subsidies for surface water storage for both urban and rural needs (Heathcote 1986).

For drought, as with all other 'natural disasters', the states had to bear the initial costs, with the Commonwealth providing further support for costs above a threshold tied to the states' gross revenue (Australia 1996). In effect, drought relief has been for many years the largest component of official disaster relief – from 1962–3 to 1987–8 it absorbed 57.6 per cent of Commonwealth disaster payments (Smith and Callahan 1988), and for South Australia from 1977 to 1983 drought relief absorbed 82 per cent of the state's disaster payments.

Since the occurrences of drought, as we have seen, tended to be regional and the *claims* of the occurrences tended to be more frequent in the climatically marginal semiarid country (Smith and Callaghan 1988), over the years the provision of public funds via the states and Commonwealth probably has been a fairly regular subsidy for resource users in those areas. Further, this subsidy has in the main been provided irrespective of whether their management systems adequately reflected the constraints of their environment (Smith 1989, Smith *et al.* 1992). The irrational character of this traditional policy was exacerbated by significant variation in the procedures for drought declaration between the states – the responsibilities for declaration ranging from local government authorities to rural producer groups – and the potential to 'cry wolf' seems to have been exploited on occasion.

The appointment of the Commonwealth Drought Policy Review Task Force in 1989 marked an acceleration of an already established trend toward a revision of longstanding official policies on drought. The 1970s and early 1980s had witnessed a series of natural disasters with severe impacts on Australian society: the destruction of Darwin by Cyclone Tracy and massive flooding in eastern Australia in 1974, serious bush fires in 1981 and 1983 and the drought of 1982–3. Various conferences and symposia brought together academics, civil defence personnel, and disaster victims to share experiences and try to mitigate any future impacts (Heathcote and Thom 1979,

Minor and Pickup 1980, Oliver 1980, Pickup 1978, Reid 1979, Smith *et al.* 1979). Among these meetings was some evidence of rethinking, particularly on drought.

The first evidence was in the national review of water resources to the year 2000. This recognised the inevitability of drought in Australia and the political relevance of the associated problems:

> Water supply restrictions in periods of severe rainfall deficiencies must be expected in Australia with its high rainfall variability, and the resultant inconvenience and losses must be expected by all classes of users . . . The acceptable degree of restrictions is essentially a matter for political decision, as is the extent of public investment in storage to reduce the impact of drought.
>
> (DRE 1983: 61)

Significantly, the review also suggested that irrigation not only did *not* protect agriculture against drought, but might exacerbate the effects by encouraging maximum use of available water resources without adequate reserves. This, coming after the final abandonment of cloud-seeding rain-making trials by the CSIRO in 1981, seemed to mark the end of a purely technological approach to the problem of drought (Heathcote 1986).

In 1984 two separate activities to promote a national policy on drought were initiated, one of which was to fade away (Heathcote 1991), the other to result in a policy statement. The policy statement came from the National Drought Consultative Committee (NDCC), which had been formed in 1984. This committee, comprising officials from each state and territory and the Commonwealth Departments of Primary Industry and Finance, along with three private representatives of primary producers, was formed to advise the Commonwealth Minister of Agriculture on drought matters, and its first report appeared in 1985 (NDCC 1985). The objectives of drought policy were 'to encourage the efficient allocation of national, regional farm resources; and to minimise the economic hardship to individuals resulting from drought'. These general objectives were to be embodied in the specific national objectives of the policy:

1   maintenance of land resources;
2   maintenance of breeding herds, at a level which would enable post-drought recovery of livestock industries within a reasonable period;
3   enable post-drought sowing of crops and pastures;
4   maintenance of minimal living standards for farmers assessed as viable in the long term;
5   short-term income support for farmers assessed as nonviable in the longer term; and
6   minimisation of stock distress.

(NDCC 1985: 2)

To achieve this policy, a series of measures was proposed for the various levels of government. Joint action by the Commonwealth and states was to take the form of the traditional concessional loans and freight rebates for transport of livestock, feed, and water, along with soil conservation programmes and other possible measures to be determined. The Commonwealth alone, through its basic control of the national income tax, was to apply taxation measures, the Income Equalisation Deposits Scheme (by which the highly variable annual incomes are smoothed for income tax purposes and which replaced an earlier unsuccessful Drought Bonds scheme), and 'household support and rehabilitation' under the Rural Assistance Scheme. The states, in addition, were to develop and provide information on the policies to the rural managers. Finally, a proposal for crop and rainfall insurance was referred to the Commonwealth Industries Assistance Commission for investigation, and a working party of the NDCC was set up to review the principles relating to the declaration and revocation of drought, which, as we have seen, varied considerably between the states.

Much of this was a continuation of traditional policies, but there were some innovations. Concern about the links between drought and land degradation was evident in the effort to maintain the land resource and associated soil conservation measures. For the first time also, drought relief measures were linked with broader policies on rural restructuring – with the implication that farmers nonviable economically in the longer term would only get short-term income support – that is, they would be expected to leave the industry eventually. Earlier drought relief policies had attempted to maintain the rural population through the crisis; now the poorer managers were to be encouraged to leave.

Concern about the distress to livestock was re-emphasised, and it was proposed that crop and/or rainfall insurance should be considered. A national natural disaster insurance scheme had been considered (and rejected as too costly) as part of the response to the heavy insurance losses from the cyclone and flood disasters of 1974. Drought in fact was not included in the hazards (DNDE 1980). The specific new proposal for insurance was considered, but initial reactions have been negative, arguing that this would be difficult to implement and would be economical only if it were to replace the existing drought relief policies (BAE 1986, RMSAB 1986).

Just to confirm the impression that officialdom was beginning to look more carefully at the principles of drought relief, a subsequent statement by the NDCC in May 1986 noted what had been evident throughout Australia's history, namely that drought vulnerability is a function of resource management:

> Production systems fail at different rainfall depending on the nature of the components and the intensity at which it (sic) is operating. This feature makes the distinction between normal production risk and 'drought, worthy of public assistance' difficult to define. Declaration processes should not encourage individuals to adopt production strategies which result in inappropriate use of particular land systems and declarations made at a greater frequency than one might otherwise expect.
>
> (NDCC 1986: 2)

The gamblers on the environmental margins were not to be encouraged.

In this context, therefore, it was not really surprising that evidence of rorts (confidence tricks or schemes) in the application of drought relief measures in Queensland in April 1989 was used as the excuse by the Commonwealth minister for finance to remove drought assistance from the national Natural Disaster Relief Arrangements, and led to the setting up of the Drought Policy Review Task Force a month later.

The final report of the Drought Policy Review Task Force set quite clear guidelines for the national policy:

> The objectives of a national drought policy are to:
>
> – encourage primary producers and other segments of rural Australia to adopt self-reliant approaches in managing for climatic variability;
> – facilitate the maintenance and protection of Australia's

agricultural and environmental resource base during periods of increasing climate stress;
– facilitate the early recovery of agricultural and rural industries, consistent with long-term sustainable levels.

(DPRTF 1990 [1]: 13–14)

The report specifically stressed that drought was a 'natural, recurring and endemic feature of the Australian environment' and 'the prospect of variable seasonal conditions is a normal commercial risk that must be incorporated into the management of Australian rural enterprises' (DPRTF 1990 [1]: 14). Obviously, governments were being encouraged to look more critically at any future calls for public disaster relief funds from drought-affected farmers. Sustainable farm management in the future was expected to be able to withstand drought impacts without official relief efforts.

However, despite its banishment from the ranks of the officially recognised natural disasters, drought has crept back in. The 1996 review of the Natural Disaster Relief Arrangements program noted that although drought had been removed from the list of eligible disasters on 1 July 1989 and in future 'should be treated as a normal risk factor rather than a natural disaster as such', it went on to state:

> These [new] arrangements also recognise the occurrence of extraordinary drought events for which specific assistance is made available under the Exceptional Circumstances provisions of the Rural Adjustment Scheme . . . the Commonwealth has formulated specific exceptional circumstances assistance packages to address severe and sustained drought.
>
> (Australia 1996: 19)

Entry now appeared to be by the back door rather than the front.

The identification and monitoring of these 'exceptional circumstances' has proved to be very difficult and is the subject of current officially funded research projects (White 1997). However, preliminary reports indicate that on-farm management – a vital factor in environmental conditions that is itself a major component in drought declarations – is not adequately factored into the assessment process, which still seems to focus on the rainfall, soil moisture, and plant linkages in the search for 'objective' natural science rather than social science criteria (White 1996, White and Bordas 1997).

Future management for drought, however, may be easier for both officials and private resource managers if the current hopes for the prediction of meteorological drought are realised. What are the implications?

DROUGHT FORECASTS AND DROUGHT MANAGEMENT

Drought forecasts have appeared as part of the current high-profile scientific concern for climate change, receiving a significant stimulus from the El Niño–Southern Oscillation (ENSO) of 1982–3 (Glantz *et al.* 1987). Nicholls has claimed that the 1982 drought could have been predicted from the Darwin mean sea level air pressure positive anomalies from a few months previously (Nicholls 1983). He subsequently went on to suggest that major Australian droughts (particularly the failure of the winter–spring rains, June to November, which are essential for the cereal grain crops), might be predicted by cooler sea surface temperatures and higher air pressure anomalies off northern Australia near the start of the calendar year (Nicholls 1985a and 1986), and later studies have confirmed this (Whetton 1989).

Despite some reservations about the stability of these teleconnections (Pittock 1984), support has come from global modelling exercises (Voice and Hunt 1984), and Nicholls has suggested that Australian crop production in general is related to the ENSO phenomenon:

> Observing the SST [sea surface temperature off northern Australia] anomaly change from September–November to March–May seems to provide a means for predicting yields of some Australian crops [wheat, barley, oats and sugar cane] and also the gross value of Australian crops.
>
> (Nicholls 1985b: 559)

The key is the dependence on rainfall for most of Australia's crop production.

More recently, a 'national drought alert strategic information system' has been proposed, arising from the apparent dysfunctional relationship between meteorological observations and community claims of drought occurrence, both underestimates and overestimates being reported (Brook and Carter 1996).

The intention is to produce 'land condition alerts' for local government areas based on the 'best combination of rainfall analysis, seasonal climate forecasts, satellite and terrestrial monitoring, and simulation models of meaningful biological processes' (Brook and Carter 1996: 13).

Despite the recognition of high stocking rates in the process leading to an alert, the focus is still on the physical condition of the land as the trigger for drought recognition; land management again seems to have been overlooked. How such studies will prove 'exceptional circumstances' and justify the recognition of a 'natural disaster' is not clear.

But what are the real possibilities for, and implications of, drought forecasting? In 1985 a gathering of drought researchers concluded that three avenues for drought forecasting existed. These were probabilistic forecasts, thought useful for small-scale and short periods of drought; statistical forecasts, useful for regional and severe droughts; and deterministic forecasts, based on climate modelling for periods up to two to three months ahead (Hunt 1985: 3).

It would seem that the chances for *regional* drought forecasts sufficiently in advance of crucial management decision making – e.g., crop planting times (or possibly animal mating times?) – are good, and the Commonwealth National Climate Centre has already begun to issue seasonal weather forecasts. Scientific probability forecasts for those able to interpret them have existed for some time (Verhagen and Hirst 1961), and I suspect individual farmers and pastoralists make use of their own 'probability forecasts' based on their personal assessment of the rainfall records, which they all keep anyhow.

If improved forecasts, of whatever type, are becoming available, what effect will they have on the community? Will the forecast of a drought mitigate its potential impact? The answer is not as simple as it might appear, and depends first on the accuracy of the forecast, second on the form it takes, and finally on the response of the decision makers, given the commercial context of their activities.

Resource managers may or may not accept the forecasts – and in either case they could be in error (Pittock 1986)! The resource managers, however, face not only the problems of the accuracy of the forecast and whether or not he/she believes it, but also what might happen if it *were* accurate, if he/she *did* believe and act on it and find that the future market was glutted by produce from other resource managers who had also believed and also acted on the forecast. The forecasters attempt to predict only the weather, which might affect production but not the value of that production in the free market!

CONCLUSION: SHE'LL BE RIGHT, MATE!

Historically, drought has played a significant role in the development of Australian resources. Traditionally it has been viewed as a national disaster, the victims deserving of public disaster relief, the response being crisis management. Technology has been harnessed to try to buffer society against drought, but the recognition that the real threat to the society is the continental aridity and its associated rainfall variability has been learned only at substantial cost – both economic and social. Public funds have allowed the continued use of resources on lands both economically and climatically marginal, and at the cost of land degradation. Unscrupulous operators have exploited official drought relief policies, while the better managers have coped with the drought stresses, neither asking for relief nor receiving any official recognition for their skills.

What of the future? The meteorological droughts will continue. When these droughts return, what will happen? We can be certain that agricultural production will decline and consequent economic processes will force some primary producers into bankruptcy, others into gambling unsuccessfully on the seasons or pushing cropping or grazing into unsuitable locations. We can also be certain that some urban areas will experience water shortages as water demand continues to escalate, existing storages prove inadequate, and popular 'Green' opposition to further big dam construction grows. Further, if the global climate change effect occurs as projected, the temperate cereal-growing areas will be more vulnerable to the failure of the winter rains.

The impacts, however, may be reduced by the continued reduction of the GDP share provided by agriculture, by more off-farm income sources for primary producers, by diversification and better management strategies on the rural properties (helped by the removal of the failed managers), by soil conservation measures undertaken as part of the National Land Care Program, by advance warnings through drought forecasting, and perhaps most of all by the removal of traditional official drought relief policies.

However, the prospects of the latter are not good, for the National Drought Relief Package (A$164 million) announced by the Commonwealth Government on 21 September 1994 (Australian 1994) and the drought-related assistance packages of A$260 million (1995–6) and A$135 million (1996–7) (Australian 1996), although officially focused on regions experiencing 'exceptional circumstances', contained many of the traditional subsidies. These subsidies will continue to reward the poor managers, who are basically bankrupt, and fail to reward the better managers whose paddocks are not bare and whose bank accounts are still in credit and who as a result will not qualify for drought assistance!

Perhaps the problem is not so much physical or economic as social or psychological. Recently, the possible role of 'drought discourses in Australian culture ... as a moral drama' has been suggested (West and Smith 1996: 97). In this argument, drought is seen as a symbolic 'national enemy' against which national energies can be galvanised as part of the '(national and personal) character-building qualities of drought' (West and Smith 1996: 99). One reason offered, which appears to hold merit, is 'because it [drought] is recognised as a *natural fact* rather than correctly perceived as a *socially constructed fact*' (West and Smith 1996: 99).

Thus, from a combination of national concern for an environmental threat, plus popular sympathy for the resultant victims and the general concern for the increasing general pressure on water supplies in both rural and urban contexts, it seems likely that changing traditional Australian attitudes to drought and its management will be more difficult than initially thought. She'll be right, mate!

ACKNOWLEDGEMENTS

Research for this chapter was funded by Flinders University Research Committees and the Australian University Research Committees.

REFERENCES

ABS (1988) *Year Book Australia 1988*, Canberra: Australian Bureau of Statistics.

Allan, R. and Heathcote, R.L. (1987) '1982–83 Drought in Australia', in M. Glantz, R. Katz, and M. Krenz (eds), *The Societal Impacts Associated with the 1982–93 Worldwide Climate Anomalies*, Boulder, CO: National Center for Atmospheric Research, pp. 19–23.

Australia (1996) *Commonwealth Disaster Relief: Review of National Disaster Relief Arrangements Program*, Canberra: Department of Finance, Primary Industries and Environment.

Australian (1994) 'Farmers welcome $164m drought fund', *The Australian*, 22 September, p. 1.

—— (1996) 'Welfare to replace farm drought aid', *The Weekend Australian*, 28–9 September, p. 11.

BAE (1986) *Crop and Rainfall Insurance: A BAE Submission to the IAC*, Commonwealth Bureau of Agricultural Economics, Canberra: Australian Government Publishing Service.

Brook, K.D. and Carter, J.O. (1996) 'A prototype national drought alert strategic information criteria information system for Australia', *Drought Network News* 8, 2: 13–16.

Burnley, I. (1986) 'What we can learn from drought and depression', *Inside Australia* 2, 3: 7–10.

Buxton, R. and Stafford Smith, M. (1996) 'Managing drought in Australia's rangelands: Four weddings and a funeral', *Rangeland Journal* 18, 2: 292–308.

Chatterton, L. and Chatterton, B. (1996) *Sustainable Dryland Farming. Combining Farmer Innovation and Medic Pasture in a Mediterranean Climate*, Cambridge: Cambridge University Press.

Chisholm, A.H. (1992) 'Australian agriculture: A sustainability story', *Australian Journal Agricultural Economics* 36, 1: 1–29.

de Kantzow, D.R. and Sutton, B.G. (eds) (1981) *Cropping at the Margins: Potential for Overuse of Semi-arid Lands*, Sydney: Australian Institute of Agricultural Science and Water Research Foundation of Australia.

DEHCD (1978) *A Basis for Soil Conservation Policy in Australia*, Report No. 1, Department of Environment, Housing and Community Development, Canberra: Australian Government Publishing Service.

Dillon, J.L. and Lloyd, A.G. (1962) 'Inventory analysis of drought reserves for Queensland graziers: Some empirical evidence', *Journal of Agricultural Economics* 6: 50–67.

DNDE (1980) Policies and practices for adjustment to natural hazard risk, Report of the (Natural Hazards) Mitigation Committee, Canberra: Commonwealth Department of National Development and Energy, unpublished draft.

DPRTF (1990) *National Drought Policy. Final Report*, Canberra: Australian Government Publishing Service, 3 volumes.

DRE (1983) *Water 2000. A Perspective in Australia's Water Resources to the Year 2000*, Commonwealth Department of Resources and Energy, Canberra: Australian Government Publishing Service.

Dury, G.H. (1983) 'Step-functional incidence and impact of drought in pastoral Australia', *Australian Geographical Studies* 21, 1: 69–96.

Gibbs, W.J. and Maher, J.V. (1967) 'Rainfall deciles as drought indicators', *Commonwealth of Australia Bureau of Meteorology Bulletin*, No. 48, Melbourne.

Glantz, M.H. (ed.) (1994) *Drought follows the Plow: Cultivating Marginal Areas*, Cambridge: Cambridge University Press.

Glantz, M., Katz, R., and Krenz, M. (1987) *The Societal Impacts Associated with the 1982–83 Worldwide Climate Anomalies*, Boulder, CO: National Center for Atmospheric Research.

Gregory, G. (1984) *Country Towns and the Drought*, Armidale: Australian Rural Adjustment Unit, University of New England.

Heathcote, R.L. (1969) 'Drought in Australia: A problem of perception', *Geographical Review* 59: 175–94.

—— (1981) 'Goyder's Line – A line for all seasons?', in D.J. and S.G.M. Carr (eds), *People and Plants in Australia*, Sydney: Academic Press, pp. 295–321.

—— (1986) 'Drought mitigation in Australia: Reducing the losses but not removing the hazard', *Great Plains Quarterly* 6: 225–37.

—— (1987) 'Images of a desert? Perceptions of arid Australia', *Australian Geographical Studies* 25: 3–25.

—— (1988) 'Drought in Australia: Still a problem of perception?', *GeoJournal* 16, 4: 387–97.

—— (1991) 'Managing the droughts? Perception of resource management in the face of the drought hazard in Australia', *Vegetatio* 91: 219–30.

Heathcote, R.L. and Thom, B.G. (eds) (1979) *Natural Hazards in Australia*, Canberra: Australian Academy of Science.

Hunt, B.G. (ed.) (1985) *Report on Drought Research in Australia*, meeting held in Melbourne, 1985, Aspendale: CSIRO, Division of Atmospheric Research.

Luke, R.H. and McArthur, A.G. (1978) *Bushfires in Australia*, Canberra: Australian Government Publishing Service.

Macdonald Holmes, J. (1960) *The Geographical Basis of Keyline*, Sydney: Angus and Robertson.

McLennan, W. (1996) *Australians and the Environment*, Canberra: Australian Bureau of Statistics, Cat. No. 4601.10.

Martin, B.R. (1983) 'The 1982 drought in Australia', *Desertification Control Bulletin*, No. 9, Nairobi: United Nations Environment Program.

Minor, J. and Pickup, G. (1980) 'Assessment of research and practice in Australian natural hazards management', *North Australian Research Unit Bulletin*, No. 6, Darwin, North Australian Research Unit.

NDCC (1985) *Report by the National Drought Consultative*

Committee on Drought Policy, Canberra: Commonwealth Department of Primary Industry.

——— (1986) 'Note on the nature of drought and issues in drought declaration and revocation procedures: Drought relief and policy committee', Canberra: National Drought Consultative Committee, mimeo.

Nicholls, N. (1983) 'Predictability of the 1982 Australian Drought', *Search* 14: 154–5.

——— (1985a) 'Towards the prediction of major Australian droughts', *Australian Meteorological Magazine* 33: 161–6.

——— (1985b) 'Impact of the Southern Oscillation on Australian crops', *Journal of Climatology* 5: 553–60.

——— (1986) 'Use of the Southern Oscillation to predict Australian sorghum yield', *Agriculture and Forest Meteorology* 38: 9–15.

Oliver, J. (ed.) (1980) *Response to Disaster*, Townsville: James Cook University.

——— (1986) 'Natural hazards', in D.N. Jeans (ed.), *The Natural Environment, Australia – A Geography*, Vol. 1, Sydney: Sydney University Press, pp. 283–314.

Pickup, G. (ed.) (1978) *Natural Hazards Management in North Australia*, Darwin, North Australian Research Unit.

Pittock, A.B. (1984) 'On the reality, stability, and usefulness of southern hemisphere teleconnections', *Australian Meteorological Magazine* 32: 75–82.

——— (1986) 'Climate predictions and social responsibility – Guest editorial', *Climatic Change* 8: 203–7.

Powell, A.A. (1963) 'A national fodder reserve for the wool industry: An economic and statistical analysis', University of Sydney, *Department of Agricultural Economics, Paper No. 3*, Sydney: University of Sydney.

Pyne, S.J. (1991) *Burning Bush: A Fire History of Australia*, New York: H. Holt.

Reid, J.A. (ed.) (1979) *Planning for People in Natural Disaster*, Townsville: James Cook University.

RMSAB (1986) *Report and Recommendations of the Drought Workshop, May 1986*, Melbourne: Royal Meteorological Society (Australian Branch).

SAGRIC (n.d.) *Changing Horizons*, Adelaide: SAGRIC International.

Smith, D.I. (1989) 'Should there be drought subsidies? Droughts and drought policy in Australia', *Search* 20, 6: 188–9.

Smith, D.I. and Callahan, S.D. (1988) 'Climatic and agricultural drought, payments and policy, a study of New South Wales', *CRES Working Paper*, 1988/16, Centre for Resource and Environmental Studies, Canberra: The Australian National University.

Smith, D.I., Den Enter, P., Doling, M.A., Jellife, P.A., Munro, R.G., and Martin, W.C. (1979) *Flood Damage in the Richmond River Valley New South Wales: An Assessment of Tangible and Intangible Damages*, Northern Rivers College of Advanced Education, Lismore and Centre for Research and Environmental Studies, Canberra: Australian National University.

Smith, D.I., Hutchinson, M.F., and McArthur, R.J. (1992) 'Climatic and agricultural drought: Payments and policy', *Centre for Resource and Environmental Studies RES 7*, Canberra: Australian National University.

Verhagen, A.M.W. and Hirst, F. (1961) 'Waiting times for drought relief in Queensland', CSIRO Division of Mathematical Statistics, *Technical Paper* No. 9.

Voice, M.E. and Hunt, B.G. (1984) 'A study of the dynamics of drought initiation using a global general circulation model', *Journal of Geophysical Research* 89, D6: 9,504–20.

West, B. and Smith, P. (1996) 'Drought, discourse, and Durkheim: A research note', *Australian and New Zealand Journal of Sociology* 32, 1: 93–102.

Whetton, P. (1989) 'SST Anomalies', *Drought Network News* 1, 2: 4–5.

White, D.H. (1996) 'Objective scientific and economic criteria for estimating the extent and severity of drought', *Proceedings 2nd Australian Conference on Agricultural Meteorology*, 1–4 October 1996, University of Queensland, pp. 78–92.

——— (1997) 'Objective criteria for exceptional circumstances declarations – Improving scientific and economic inputs to decision making', available: WWW.brs.gov.au/brs/apurb/drought/droughtnet.html.

White, D.H. and Bordas, V.M. (eds) (1997) *Indicators of Drought Exceptional Circumstances: Proceedings of a Workshop Held in Canberrra on 1 October 1996*, Bureau of Resource Sciences, Canberra.

Williams, M. (1974) *The Making of the South Australian Landscape*, London: Academic Press.

34

MANAGING SUPPLY VARIABILITY

The use of water banks in the western United States

Kathleen A. Miller

INTRODUCTION

Across the western United States, rapid population growth and increasing environmental concerns are changing the character of water demands while placing new constraints on traditional engineering approaches to managing variable streamflows. Because ranchers and farmers long ago appropriated most of the reliable streamflows in this region, newer urban uses and environmental values are disproportionately at risk to shortfalls in supply during droughts. Efforts to remedy this situation have included permanent sales of water rights from senior agricultural users to growing cities, but there also have been attempts to develop more flexible water banking arrangements. These can provide drought protection for highly valued water uses while allowing the traditional agricultural uses to continue in times of adequate supplies.

Water banks serve to mitigate the economic impacts of a drought either by increasing the reliability of water supply or by facilitating short-term reallocation of water among users. Broadly speaking, there are two types of arrangements to which the term 'water bank' has been applied. We can label one of these types 'groundwater storage banks'. These include active conjunctive use programmes whereby surface water is used to recharge an aquifer, which is then used as a source of water supply during periods when surface water is less abundant. Arizona, for example, has enacted legal provisions governing such underground water storage and subsequent delivery (Ariz. Rev. Stat. Ann §45–801 et seq.). Other groundwater storage banks allow water users to earn credits for increased pumping in the future by reducing current groundwater extractions and using certain substitute supplies, such as treated effluent. Arizona state law also allows for that type of banking under 'indirect groundwater storage and recovery' provisions (Ariz. Rev. Stat. Ann §45–853 et seq.). Groundwater banking arrangements do not necessarily entail a transfer of the use of a water right from one party to another. However, some actual and proposed water exchange agreements revolve around the storage of water by one party to the agreement, to be later extracted and delivered to the other party in times of shortage.

Another use of the term 'water bank' refers to a formal mechanism created explicitly for the purpose of facilitating voluntary changes of the use of water under existing rights. We can distinguish these as 'water transfer banks'. The defining feature of this type of water bank is that it provides an established process or procedure for accomplishing such transfers. The major examples of this type of water bank are the Emergency Drought Water Banks set up by the state of California in 1991, 1992, and 1994 and four water banks in Idaho (a statewide bank run by the Idaho Water Resource Board through the Idaho Department of Water Resources and three local rental pools, each managed by a district water master in conjunction with a local committee appointed by the Water Resource Board). These operate on the Snake, Boise, and Payette rivers.

In addition to these major water transfer banks, there are several local rental or exchange pools throughout the western states operating at the level of an irrigation district, conservancy district, project, or county. Some of these are ongoing arrangements, such as the Sacramento River Water Contractors Association Pool in California and the Roza Irrigation District Pool in Washington State. The 1991 Solano County Emergency Water Pool is an example of a local water bank established for a single year to facilitate water transfers during a drought. Privately arranged water rentals and dry-year options provide alternatives to an organised water bank (Howe *et al.* 1982, Saliba and Bush 1987, National Research Council 1992). The advantages or disadvantages of an organised water bank must be evaluated against those alternatives.

INSTITUTIONAL BACKGROUND AND THE ROLE OF WATER BANKS

The prior appropriation system of water law, which predominates in the western states, was designed to protect the oldest out-of-stream water users against streamflow depletions caused by newcomers. Under prior appropriation, water rights are ranked according to the date on which they were established. Whenever there is insufficient water to fully satisfy all rights, the most junior (newest) water users are required to curtail their uses until all senior rights have been fully satisfied. The most junior water users are therefore most vulnerable to streamflow reductions, whether due to drought or to regular seasonal fluctuations. In dual-system states like California, where the prior appropriation and riparian systems of water law co-exist, the riparian water rights of owners of streamside properties generally take priority over all appropriative rights (National Research Council 1992, Bowden *et al.* 1982). Historically, the rule of prior appropriation created an incentive for junior users to invest in 'drought insurance', primarily in the form of water storage in surface reservoirs. As that option has become increasingly infeasible, expanding urban areas and other new users have sought other forms of drought protection.

Where cities have permanently purchased senior agricultural water rights, they have often encountered stiff local opposition to those actions. In addition, such transactions typically involve substantial transaction costs. These include not only the usual costs of locating willing sellers and negotiating and enforcing agreements, but also legal fees, payments for hydrologic analyses, and other costs associated with ensuring that the transfer will not damage any other vested water right (MacDonnell 1990a).

The no-injury rule has long been a central element of western water law. It recognises the inevitable interdependence among the users of a shared water source. Shortly after the California courts approved changes of water use without loss of the priority of the right (Maeris v. Bicknell, 7 Cal. 261, 263 [1857]), they added the requirement that such a change may not damage the property of others (Kidd v. Laird, 14 Cal. 161 [1860]). The basic principle is that a 'junior appropriator has a right to the continuation of stream conditions as they existed at the time the junior appropriated the water' (Tarlock 1989: 571).

Interdependence arises because most water uses do not consume all of the water diverted from the source. Rather, some portion of the water percolates back to the stream or aquifer as return flows, then becoming part of the flow available for other users. Because water transfers may disturb the pattern of return flows, all western states regulate changes of water rights to different places or types of use to prevent damage to other users (Higginson and Barnett 1984). Such regulation may restrict the quantity transferred to the seller's historic consumptive use (e.g., that portion lost to evapotranspiration and thus not contributing to return flows), or may require that the seller provide water to sufficiently augment streamflow to offset the effects of the transfer (MacDonnell 1990b). Thus, the process of obtaining approval for a permanent transfer of a water right is often expensive, time-consuming, and difficult.

The ponderous nature of the transfer process frequently encourages buyers to seek relatively large blocks of water in advance of actual need, and to acquire additional water rights for drought insurance that may or may not be rented back to agricultural users until needed (Saliba and Bush 1987, MacDonnell 1990a, MacDonnell *et al.* 1994). These practices may dry up agricultural land unnecessarily. The potential inefficiency of such a situation, along with frequent community opposition to permanent sales of agricultural water rights, has led to increased interest in short-term water transfers to accommodate fluctuations in demand and availability.

Although the approval process for temporary transfers is often less cumbersome than for permanent sales of water rights, information requirements and potential delays can nevertheless be daunting for persons wishing to engage in the short-term rental or exchange of small quantities of water. The amount of time required for approval of a temporary transfer may be particularly critical since the value of additional water for such uses as irrigation, protection of fish or wildlife habitat, recreation, or power production may be quite sensitive to timing.

Both types of water banks (groundwater storage banks and water transfer banks) allow water users to sidestep some of the difficulties that would be involved in using the ordinary water transfer process to mitigate the impacts of a drought. Groundwater banks provide an additional source of supply, specifically reserved for use when the usual sources are insufficient. Water transfer banks can allow more efficient drought management by reducing the transaction costs of moving water from lower to higher valued uses.

The water transfer type of water bank constitutes a central clearinghouse through which the cost of locating trading partners and negotiating the terms of trade are reduced relative to the costs that might be incurred in an atomistic market. In addition, the approval process for transfers through state-sanctioned water banks appears to be more streamlined than for individually arranged transfers. The transaction cost advantage of a formal water bank is likely to be particularly great where transfers are generally uncommon and their potential volume varies greatly from one year to the next as the number of parties seeking supplemental supplies or having surplus water to sell fluctuates with precipitation amounts, streamflows, and reservoir storage levels. In such a situation, information about trading opportunities may be sparse and costly to obtain. Although the pricing practices of formal water banks may deviate considerably from a theoretical optimum, the fact that a single price or easily understood pricing rule has been established saves water bank participants the effort of acquiring market information and carrying out negotiations.

WATER BANKING EXPERIENCE IN THE WESTERN STATES

The two major examples of water transfer banks, the California Emergency Drought Water Banks and the set of four water banks in Idaho, were established for quite different purposes. As a result, they perform very differently under drought conditions. This contrasting performance provides us with an opportunity to identify those factors that can make such a bank a relatively good or poor tool for mitigating the effects of a drought.

California Emergency Drought Water Banks

In 1987, at the beginning of California's recent multi-year drought, the state had relatively little experience with privately arranged water transfers outside of the confines of individual irrigation districts and major project service areas. A comparative study of the water transfer process in six western states found very few applications for changes in water rights in California during the 1980s relative to the level of water trading activity in most of the other states examined (MacDonnell 1990b). The few transfers processed by the California State Water Resources Control Board (SWRCB) during that period were all short-term transfers of water rather than permanent sales of water rights.

The small number of documented transfers may have been partly due to the fact that the state's change of permit process does not cover all water transfer activity. The SWRCB only has jurisdiction over transfers of water rights established after 1914 under the state's permit system. Earlier rights may be transferred without formal state review, although inadequate records and possible challenges in civil courts may inhibit such transfers (National Research Council 1992). In addition, transfers of water within local irrigation districts and large projects such as the federal Central Valley Project (CVP) are also outside of the jurisdiction of the SWRCB (Gray 1993). It appears that there was a considerable amount of short-term water trading among CVP contractors during the 1980s.

The lack of market development also has been attributed to the difficulty of obtaining approval of transfers from the SWRCB (MacDonnell 1990b). Although the review process for temporary transfers was streamlined in 1988, it is still lengthy relative to the time frame of a single-year transfer. Thus, potential delays, uncertainties about transferable quantities, and lack of market information useful to private parties attempting to negotiate the price and other terms of a transfer agreement constituted significant barriers to the use of privately arranged transfers to mitigate the impacts of the drought (Macaulay 1993).

As the drought persisted, it became clear that neither within-project water transfers nor those requiring approval of the SWRCB were likely to occur in sufficient volume to alleviate the very uneven impacts of the drought on major urban centres and irrigated agriculture. In January 1991, at the beginning of the fifth year of the drought, projected streamflows were well below normal and statewide reservoir levels were near their historic lows at 32 per cent of capacity and 54 per cent of the historic average (Howitt *et al.* 1992, DWR 1991). Many urban centres as well as agricultural users served by the CVP and the State Water Project (SWP) were facing severe cutbacks in supplies. At the same time, other agricultural water users with riparian rights, senior appropriative rights, or access to storage outside of the SWP or CVP had full or nearly full supplies at their disposal.

By the end of January, many state policy makers, water managers, and water users viewed the situation as a crisis. The response of the SWRCB was to hold hearings on a variety of proposals to mandate reallocation of water through temporary regulatory modifications of existing water rights. However, on 15 February, Governor Wilson's Drought Action Task Force rejected the regulatory approach, and instead called for the creation of an emergency drought water bank to acquire water from willing sellers to meet the 'critical water needs' of the purchasers as defined by the rules of the bank.

California's Department of Water Resources (DWR) acted as the manager of the Water Bank because most of the anticipated transfers would require conveyance of the water through SWP facilities (primarily the state's pumping plant in the Sacramento/San Joaquin Delta and the California aqueduct). DWR personnel negotiated the purchase contracts,

monitored compliance with those contracts, obtained SWRCB approval where needed, and coordinated deliveries of water to the purchasers. As manager of the SWP, the DWR also committed SWP funds to cover purchases of water not sold to other entities, with that water to be held as carry-over storage in SWP facilities to provide insurance against continuation of the drought. By acting as buyer of last resort, the SWP absorbed the risk of a mismatch between purchases and sales.

Any entity that had responsibility to supply water for municipal, industrial, agricultural, or other beneficial uses could choose to become a member of the Water Bank, thereby becoming qualified to purchase water to fulfil 'critical needs'. To qualify as having critical needs, municipal and industrial suppliers had to demonstrate full utilisation of normal sources of supply (allowing for prudent carry-over storage of surface water), maximum practical use of groundwater, reclaimed water and local water exchange opportunities, and total water supplies less than 75 per cent of normal water demand (equivalent to water use in 1986, adjusted for population growth). Estimated critical needs for agricultural use were to be based on water required for the survival of trees, vines, and other high-valued crops after full utilisation of all other available supplies. Provisions were also made for water purchases by public entities for fish and wildlife protection. Given many Californians' distrust of sales of agricultural water to urban areas, the 'critical needs' criteria and active management of the Water Bank by a state agency may have been necessary to ensure political acceptability of the banking arrangement.

A 'Water Purchase Committee', representing the members of the bank, confronted the task of setting a price to be offered to prospective sellers. However, the committee had virtually no information regarding what quantities of water might be offered for sale at various prices. They chose a price of US$125 per acre-foot of consumptive use on the basis of estimates that farmers of a variety of field crops could earn slightly more by fallowing their land and selling water at that price than they would earn on net by farming the land. During the first few weeks of the bank's operation, there was speculation that the purchase price would likely rise as the season progressed. This made growers reluctant to commit themselves to sale of their water. Rather than immediately raising the offer price, Water Bank officials added a price escalation clause to the purchase contracts. This modification largely transferred the risk of price uncertainty from potential water sellers to purchasers and ultimately to the SWP. The price escalation clause guaranteed sellers that they would not receive a lower price than the price negotiated in their contracts and that if the average price paid to similarly situated sellers in contracts executed by a particular date was higher by more than 10 per cent, the seller would receive the higher price. Once that clause was introduced, sales to the Water Bank proceeded rapidly. Within approximately six weeks, DWR personnel had negotiated more than 300 purchase contracts for more than 800,000 acre-feet of water. Many observers were surprised at DWR's success in quickly acquiring such a large quantity of water. The purchases proceeded in advance of firm commitments from buyers, with the quantity purchased based on early estimates of critical needs (DWR 1992). Those estimates were obtained from eighteen suppliers who had expressed an interest in participating in the bank before it was known how much bank water would cost (Howitt *et al.* 1992).

The price to buy water from the 1991 Water Bank was set at US$175 per acre-foot at the Harvey O. Banks Delta Pumping Plant plus delivery charges from that point based on pumping costs, estimated conveyance losses, and a use-of-facilities fee for non-SWP contractors. The US$175 figure was calculated to include payment to the sellers plus cost of administration and payment for carriage water required for conveyance through the Delta.

The demand for bank water turned out to be much smaller than anticipated. Heavy rains in March improved local supplies, and various demand reduction efforts succeeded in lowering consumption. As a result, when the prospective buyers closely considered the relatively high cost of Water Bank deliveries, they revised their estimates of critical needs substantially downward. Some entities that had initially expressed interest declined to become members of the Water Bank because that would have required a substantial financial commitment. Within seven days after joining the bank, members were required to deposit 50 per

cent of the estimated cost of the quantity of water necessary to meet their critical needs. Deposit of 75 per cent of the estimated cost was to be made within fifteen days of joining, with the balance to be paid before delivery.

Ultimately, approximately 396,000 acre-feet were delivered to twelve purchasers. After subtracting the carriage water required to maintain water quality standards in the Delta and various 'technical adjustments', the Water Bank was left with an unsold inventory of 264,000 acre-feet of water (Jercich 1997). That water was held as carry-over storage at a cost to the SWP of about US$45 million (Lund *et al.* 1992).

Water for the 1991 bank came from three sources: fallowing, groundwater, and surface storage. The goal of the Water Bank was to introduce 'new water' into the surface water system, defined as 'water that would be developed by this programme that otherwise would not be in the surface water system' (DWR 1991). DWR required that parties selling water to the Water Bank have a 'provable firm water supply', and DWR staff made case-by-case determinations of the validity and ownership of the rights and entitlements involved in the transactions, as well as the quantity of 'new water' that would be produced. The SWRCB generally waived further review of these transactions (Gray 1993).

Fallowing contracts, which required growers to fallow their land or withhold the application of any irrigation water to certain normally irrigated crops, accounted for approximately half of the water acquired by the 1991 Water Bank. Payments for fallowing were based on the estimated consumptive water use of the crop planned for production in 1991. Since different crops entail different rates of consumptive use, the quantity of bankable water and thus payments per acre differed depending on the crop planned for production in 1991. For example, rice, pasture, and alfalfa were each assumed to consume 3.5 acre-feet per acre, field corn was assumed to consume 2.5 acre-feet per acre, and a crop of dry beans was assumed to consume 2.1 acre-feet per acre. Therefore, the payment was US$450 per acre for rice, pasture, or alfalfa but only US$325 for field corn and US$263 for dry beans. DWR based the fallowing payments on evidence for 1991 production plans taken primarily from acreage reports filed with the federal Agricultural

Stabilization and Conservation Service (ASCS).

DWR negotiated the majority of the fallowing contracts with owners of riparian rights. As a matter of law, these rights are unquantified and unmetered, but the ASCS cropping plans allowed reasonably accurate estimates of reductions in consumptive use. Under most circumstances, riparian water rights are not transferable, but they can be left unused for a limited period without loss of the right. For those contracts, DWR used the innovative argument that the Water Bank was not actually purchasing water from the riparian owners, but rather was keeping the water instream to meet the Delta outflow and salinity control requirements applying to operation of the SWP. This, in turn, freed other SWP water to be transferred to the Water Bank (Gray 1993).

Groundwater substitution contracts, which accounted for one-third of the water purchased, allowed farmers to sell the surface water that normally would have been applied to their crops to the Water Bank and to continue irrigating with groundwater. To qualify, the well to be used could not be drawing from groundwater immediately connected to a river. To assure that new surface water was made available through the programme, pumping was metered and the individual's water district was required to release an equivalent amount of surface water to the bank. Payments were based on actual quantities pumped up to a maximum specified in the individual contract. Water stored in reservoirs accounted for the remaining 17 per cent of the purchases of the 1991 Water Bank.

Improved water supply conditions in the southern part of the state and the substantial costs that had been incurred by the SWP for the purchase and storage of water not sold to other entities during operation of the 1991 Water Bank led to a more cautious approach to acquisitions in 1992. An important 1992 policy change required a signed contract with a buyer before the DWR would commit to purchase any water. In 1991, all members purchased water from a single 'pool'. In 1992, on the other hand, the Water Bank operated six separate pools, each of which was to sell water at a single melded price to the members of the pool. Prices for the 1992 Water Bank could have varied from one pool to the next, but in practice, there was no change in the purchase or selling price as the season progressed.

The purchase price was set at US$50/acre-foot and the selling price, net of delivery charges from the Delta at US$72. If all critical needs from one pool had not been met, the members would automatically have become members of the next pool, but sufficient water was offered to the bank so that demands for each pool were met.

As part of this policy change, purchases for the 1992 bank began somewhat later, when the water supply conditions for the year were better known than had been the case in 1991. In 1991, the DWR began buying water as soon as the formation of the Water Bank was announced in mid-February. In 1992, no agreements to buy water were concluded until the first pool was formed in mid-March. Approximately 160,000 acre-feet were sold through the 1992 Water Bank, with 24,000 acre-feet purchased for fish and wildlife purposes and 60 per cent of the sales going to agricultural uses (as opposed to 20 per cent in the previous year).

Other changes in 1992 included elimination of fallowing contracts as a source of water, so that 152,000 acre-feet of the purchased water came from groundwater contracts and the remainder from storage releases (DWR 1993). (See Table 34.1 for the sources and disposition of water for California's Emergency Drought Water Banks.) The fallowing contracts had been criticised by business and community interests in the counties from which water was sold to the 1991 Water Bank. They argued that the idling of agricultural land under the programme had contributed to increased unemployment and to reduced sales by agriculturally related businesses. However, efforts to quantify these third-party impacts suggest that they were small relative to other fluctuations in agricultural sector income and employment and to the statewide net benefits derived from the Emergency Water Banks (see, for example, Coppock and Kreith 1993, Dixon et al. 1993, DWR 1993, Holcomb 1992, Howitt et al. 1992, The Bay Area Economic Forum 1993).

After a single wet year in 1993, critically dry conditions again returned in 1994. As of 1 May, flows for most of the state's major rivers were expected to be less than 50 per cent of the long-term average (USDA 1994). As a result, the state established another water bank, closely mimicking the 1992 Water Bank. The 1994 Water Bank paid US$50 per acre-foot to

Table 34.1 Water balance of 1991, 1992, and 1994 Drought Water Banks (numbers rounded)

	1991 Water Bank amount (acre-feet)	1992 Water Bank amount (acre-feet)	1994 Water Bank amount (acre-feet)
Water source			
Fallowing	410,000	0	0
Groundwater	246,000	152,000	187,000
Surface water	164,000	38,000	33,000
Total	820,000	190,000	220,000
Delta requirements[1]	−160,000	−30,000	−50,000
Net available	660,000	160,000	170,000
Allocations			
Urban uses	297,000	40,000	25,000
Agricultural uses	99,000	96,000	145,000
Wildlife uses	0[2]	24,000	0
Carry-over storage	264,000	0	0
Total allocated	660,000	160,000	170,000

Notes:
1 Water required to remain in Sacramento-San Joaquin Delta for water quality protection and miscellaneous technical corrections
2 More than 40,000 acre-feet of water was provided in bank-related transactions (DWR 1993)
Source: Jercich 1997

acquire 220,000 acre-feet through groundwater substitution contracts and purchases of stored water in northern California. Of that quantity, 170,000 acre-feet were delivered to purchasers south of the Sacramento/San Joaquin Delta. The remainder was used for Delta carriage water. The melded price to buyers at the Delta pumps was US$68 per acre-foot (Jercich 1997).

Most of the buyers from the 1994 Water Bank were agricultural water suppliers such as the Westlands District and the Kern County Water Agency. In fact, agricultural uses accounted for 85 per cent of the water delivered through the bank. Central Valley Project contractors were major purchasers because most CVP allotments had been cut to 35 per cent of normal as a result of the drought. Urban suppliers, such as the Metropolitan Water District of Southern California (MWD), purchased only small quantities from the 1994 Water Bank.

At the beginning of 1995, DWR made preparations for another water bank by negotiating option contracts with a number of willing sellers.

DWR paid US$3.50 per acre-foot to buy options for 29,000 acre-feet of water, with prospective sellers offering water for as little as US$36.50 per acre-foot (Jercich 1997). DWR halted the option purchases and decided against activating the bank when wet spring conditions eliminated the demand for that water.

Most observers view California's Emergency Drought Water Banks as a successful response to the imbalances between availability and demand created by the drought. One study (Howitt *et al.* 1992) conservatively estimated the net benefits of the 1991 Water Bank at US$91 million, including net benefits of more than US$32 million to the agricultural sector. However, the 1991 bank did result in some losses to individuals and to agriculturally related businesses, particularly in the counties where there were numerous fallowing contracts. In no county did such losses exceed 1 per cent of county personal income, and in all but one county, the negative impacts were more than offset by Water Bank revenues (Dixon *et al.* 1993). In addition to those third-party impacts, there was some concern about the possible environmental impacts of the water transfers.

It is difficult to separate the environmental effects of the Water Bank transactions from the effects of the drought itself. Discussion focused on three types of possible environmental impacts: (1) damage to wild bird habitat and forage caused by the removal of grain crops from lands around the Sacramento Delta, (2) reductions in groundwater levels and quality and possible acceleration of subsidence, and (3) possible adverse impacts on endangered and threatened fishery resources in the Delta caused by increased operation of Delta pumping plants. The first of these impacts may be manageable by increasing the geographical scope of water acquisition efforts for any future water banks and by limiting the percentage of land in sensitive areas that can participate in fallowing contracts.

The DWR made efforts to ensure that there were no significant adverse impacts of increased groundwater withdrawals under groundwater substitution contracts by requiring that participating wells be metered and logged. Groundwater levels did decline in many areas that contributed water to the banks, but only a portion of the decline is attributable to sales to the Water Banks (McBean 1993). Recharge from both natural sources and irrigation seepage declined during the drought and other groundwater pumping increased significantly. The SRWCB has no jurisdiction over groundwater, and its use in much of California remains unrestricted. There are, however, adjudicated basins in southern California where pumping rights have been quantified on the basis of the principle of mutual prescription (Tarlock 1989). Recent changes in state law will allow increased local control over the possible long-term effects of groundwater substitution contracts. Section 1745.10 of the California Water Code, effective 1 January 1993, specifies that:

> A water user that transfers surface water pursuant to this article may not replace that water with ground water unless the ground water use is either of the following:
> (a) Consistent with a ground water management plan adopted pursuant to State law for the affected area.
> (b) Approved by the water supplier from whose service area the water is to be transferred and that water supplier, if a ground water management plan has not been adopted, determines that the transfer will not

create, or contribute to, conditions of long-term overdraft in the affected ground water basin.

Although sales to the Water Banks contributed to aquifer drawdown, there has been no evidence of increased subsidence as a result of bank-related groundwater extractions.

The possible impacts of increased Delta pumping operations on endangered and threatened species have turned out to be the most problematic of the environmental impacts of the Water Banks. The Sacramento/San Joaquin Delta is the Achilles' heel of the California water distribution system. Both the SWP and the CVP are designed largely to transport water from the relatively water-rich Sacramento Basin of northern California to the more arid southern portion of the state. These projects rely on pumping plants located in the Delta, the operation of which has proved harmful to fish populations resident in the Delta as well as to anadromous runs that must pass through the Delta to spawn. Despite the fact that a considerable portion of the purchased water was left in the river as carriage water, operation of these pumps to make Water Bank deliveries to buyers south of the Delta raised concerns about reverse flows in the vicinity of the pumps and thus increased entrainment of threatened and endangered fish. Sharp reductions in populations of winter-run Chinook salmon and Delta smelt during the drought led to stricter controls on Delta pumping operations. In addition, the Central Valley Improvement Act of 1992 (Title XXXIV of Public Law 102–575) now mandates that the CVP allocate 800,000 acre-feet of water annually for the purpose of restoring fish and wildlife habitat. Together, these changes may limit north-to-south Water Bank transfers during future droughts. This has prompted southern California water users to explore other water-banking options as an alternative to attempting to use the state's water bank to move large quantities of water across the Delta in drought years. These alternatives will be described below in the section *Groundwater recharge and storage options*.

Water banking in Idaho

The Idaho water banks function very differently from the California Emergency Drought Water Banks because drought management is not their primary purpose. Rather, the goal of the Idaho water banks is to help irrigation districts earn a modest return from the disposal of surplus stored water in wet years and to keep as much water as possible in irrigated agriculture in dry years. Like California, Idaho recently has experienced several years of drought, with 1992 being a record or near-record low water year in many basins. Unlike California, the level of water transfers through Idaho's established water banks declined as drought conditions worsened. Although the marginal value of water for nonagricultural uses (primarily hydropower production and fishery enhancement) increased during the drought, the pricing and operating rules of the banks impeded transfers to those uses. Thus, from the perspective of the broader society, the banks did not promote most efficient use of the available supplies.

The Water District #1 Rental Pool is the Upper Snake River bank. It is the oldest of the three, with informal operations beginning in the 1930s under the supervision of the District 1 Watermaster. As the use of the bank increased over the years, the process became more formal. The state legislature eventually authorised this ongoing arrangement under the Water Supply Bank Act of 1979 (Idaho Code § 42–1761).

Other rental pools are now in operation on the Boise and Payette rivers. The Boise River water bank (Water District #63 Rental Pool) began operation in 1988 and the Payette River bank (Water District #65 Rental Pool) was organised in 1990. The Idaho Water Resources Board (hereafter referred to as the Board) is empowered to appoint local rental pool committees to manage the local banks. These are comprised primarily of representatives of irrigation districts owning storage rights in the basin.

The Shoshone–Bannock Tribal Water Supply Bank was authorised by the 1990 Fort Hall Indian Water Right Settlement Agreement (1991 Idaho Sess. Laws, ch. 228, at 547). The Board adopted final rules for the tribal water bank in 1994. The Board also administers a statewide water supply bank, through the Idaho Department of Water Resources (IDWR). The three local exchange pools on the Upper Snake, Boise, and Payette rivers account for most of the water banking activity in Idaho. There have been very few transfers through the statewide bank.

Regarding operation of the rental pools, state law apportions some responsibilities to the IDWR and leaves other responsibilities to the local committees (MacDonnell 1995). The director of the IDWR is charged with (1) setting priorities among competing applicants for bank water, (2) preventing injury to other water rights and to the local public interest, (3) ensuring the conservation of water resources within the state of Idaho, and (4) ruling on applications for changes of use of rentals (Idaho Code §§ 42–173, 42–401, 42–222). Subject to the approval of the Board, each local committee manages the rental pool funds, sets annual prices and administrative fees, and establishes rules applying to transfers through the local exchange pool.

The three rental pools limit water rentals to water available under storage rights in reservoirs located in the district. Under District #1 rules, either stored water or reservoir space may be leased, but only the actual yield of water to that space can be rented. Therefore, the lessor receives no rental fee if the space does not fill or if it is not rented (MacDonnell *et al.* 1994). In each pool, those parties who commit their space to the water bank early in the year share in the rental proceeds in proportion to their commitments. Those who offer their water for rental after 1 July receive payment, on a first-come first-served basis, only if all of the water offered by the early group of lessors is rented.

The operating rules of each of these local water banks state that the primary purpose of the bank is to benefit irrigated agriculture within the District covered by the bank. Consequently, each of these banks accords preference to rentals for irrigation use. In addition, prices for rental of water through each of these banks have been kept very low and have shown little variation from one year to the next despite large interannual variations in the quantities of water offered to and requested from these banks. For example, the price for water rented for local agricultural use through the Upper Snake River Water Bank inched upward only slightly from US$2.50 per acre-foot in the early 1980s to US$2.95 for 1991–7.

There is evidence that the water may be worth considerably more for downstream power production at dams operated by the Idaho Power Company (IPC) and by the federal government, particularly in dry years (Whittlesey *et al.* 1986, Miller 1989). Throughout the history of the Upper Snake River Water Bank, IPC has been the major renter of water. The value to the company of renting this water comes from the company's ability to then shift release of the water forward in time, allowing increased generation of low-cost hydropower at downstream dams in the peak-demand summer season. The marginal value of water bank water to IPC diminishes in very wet years as flows at the dam sites in the absence of the rentals increase. In 1986, for example, the company chose to rent only 150,000 acre-feet of the more than 800,000 acre-feet that were available after irrigation rentals. In other years, administration of the agricultural preference rule has prevented IPC from renting all of the water that it sought.

IPC had been the only nonagricultural water renter until a 1992 temporary change in the Idaho code allowed water bank purchases to be used to assist salmon migration (Idaho Code § 42–1763A, as added by 1992, ch. 101, § 2, p. 319). In recent years, rentals to assist anadromous fish passage have become increasingly important (see Table 34.2).

The Upper Snake (District # 1) and Payette (District # 65) rental pools have adopted a two-tiered pricing policy, with a higher price charged for rentals outside of the district. In 1996–7, for example, the District # 1 pool charged US$10.50 per acre-foot for water rented for use below Milner Dam. (Rentals below Milner Dam are for downstream hydropower or fishery uses.) It appears that the price differential is meant to serve as insurance against the risk of a drought in the

Table 34.2 Upper Snake River rental pool (Water District 1) rental activity

Year	Water volume (acre-feet)	
1990	401,197	space assigned
	295,508	water yielded
	118,872	rented for irrigation
	63,000	rented for hydro and other uses
1991	229,172	space assigned
	201,300	water yielded
	86,140	rented for irrigation
	99,000	rented for hydro and other uses
1992	74,295	space assigned
	9,954	water yielded
	9,954	rented for irrigation
1993	209,303	space assigned
	205,970	water yielded
	38,974	rented for irrigation
	65,000	rented for hydro and other uses
	206,647	reclamation yield for salmon
1994	508,384	of space offered
	432,171	of water offered
	75,888	rented for irrigation
	356,282	rented for hydro and other uses
1995	584,293	of space offered
	582,405	of water offered
	37,197	rented for irrigation
	71,093	rented for recharge
	255,000	rented for anadromous fish passage
1996	643,335	of space offered
	636,587	of water offered
	19,024	rented for irrigation
	250,000	rented for anadromous fish passage

Note: Reservoir storage approx 4.1 million acre-feet

year following the rental, because most of the price differential is to be returned to the renter if the reservoirs fill in the following year. The lessor of such water does not receive a higher price and may, in fact, be penalised by a rule that storage space used for rentals below Milner Dam moves to last priority for refill in the ensuing year. However, if the reservoir does not refill, the lessor is compensated out of the price differential in proportion to the storage lost by this rule.

The pricing policies of these rental pools result in little year-to-year variation in the price but large inter-annual changes in the quantity of water rented. In all three cases, the amount of water trading declined sharply in 1992, a record dry year (see Tables 34.2, 34.3, and 34.4). This was particularly marked in the case of the Upper Snake River bank, where the amount of water offered for rental through the bank declined from a wet-year high of 895,642 acre-feet in 1986 to only 9,954 acre-feet in 1992. At the same time, the flow of the Snake River farther downstream at Weiser, just above the Hells Canyon hydroelectric complex, was at its record low. This suggests that prospective lessors could have earned a higher return from the water rentals if the District #1 committee had attempted to establish a market clearing price.

However, the Idaho water banks seem to be ignoring opportunities to increase returns to the storage owners by allowing the rental price to rise in water-short years. This situation may be due to the fact that the rental pool committees represent both potential water sellers and water buyers within the irrigation community. The influence of these potential buyers may generate a reluctance to allow profit from the water rentals. The policies restricting the movement of water out of local agriculture also avoid the types of third-party impacts that raised concerns in California, when land was fallowed for the 1991 Water Bank. In addition, there is concern that allowing substantial profits from sales through these water banks could reduce the security of property rights to the water involved. Some fear that such profits could invite legal challenges to a district's continued need for the water, particularly in light of growing environmental concerns over agricultural water use in the state. As in other western states, continued beneficial use is required to maintain a water right in Idaho. Under a strict interpretation of this rule, the very large storage rights of many of the irrigation districts involved in these water banks may appear tenuous. As a result of federally subsidised projects constructed by the Bureau of Reclamation, many of Idaho's

Table 34.3 Boise River rental pool (Water District 63) rental activity

Year	Water volume (acre-feet)	
1990	11,182	offered
	11,182	rented for irrigation
1991	2,927	offered
	2,758	rented for irrigation
1992	1,832	offered
	1,832	rented for irrigation
1993	23,900	offered
	23,000	rented for salmon recovery
1994	40,703	offered
	4,753	rented for irrigation
	35,950	rented for anadromous fish passage
1995	67,000	offered
	27,000	rented for anadromous fish passage
1996	38,588	offered
	575	rented for irrigation
	13	miscellaneous
	38,000	rented for anadromous fish passage

Note: Reservoir storage approx. 1.0 million acre-feet

Table 34.4 Payette River rental pool (Water District 65) rental activity

Year	Water volume (acre-feet)	
1990	65,881	offered
	63,700	rented for hydropower
1991	102,574	offered
	2,000	rented for irrigation
	100,000	rented for salmon recovery
1992	48,615	offered
	48,615	rented for irrigation
1993	35,000	offered
	35,000	rented for hydropower
1994	5,000	offered
	3,432	rented for irrigation
	62,000	released by USBR for anadromous fish passage from uncontracted USBR space
1995*	155,915	offered
	4,061	rented for irrigation
	7,958	rented for hydropower
	145,000	released for fish passage (95,000 of the 145,000 acre-feet is from uncontracted space of the USBR)
1996*	161,485	offered
	3,790	rented for irrigation
	5,951	rented for hydropower
	151,300	released for fish passage (95,000 of the 151,300 acre-feet is from uncontracted space of the USBR)

Notes:
*Approximate volumes, not including prior year adjustments
Reservoir storage approx. 815,000 acre-feet

irrigation districts control storage space that, in all but the driest years, yields far in excess of the districts' normal annual diversions. Given the recent listing of some Snake River salmon stocks as endangered or threatened species, and California's experience with congressionally mandated reallocation of CVP water for environmental purposes, fear of loss of control over that storage space may not be unreasonable.

It would be ironic if such fears are indeed a driving force behind the pricing policies of these water banks, because these policies have the effect of reducing the availability of water to assist salmon migration past the power dams in low water years. In April 1993, the Bureau of Reclamation attempted to convince the Committee of Nine, which controls the Upper Snake River Bank, to allow the Bureau to buy water early in the season to be used to assist salmon migration. The Committee refused to set aside the agricultural preference rule and rejected the Bureau's request because,

as of the end of April, irrigators had already requested to rent 65,000 acre-feet at US$2.95 per acre-foot while only 50,000 acre-feet had been offered for sale through the bank (Associated Press 1993). Later in the season, additional water was placed in the bank, partly as a result of unusually high summer precipitation. This ultimately allowed IPC to purchase 65,000 acre-feet from the Upper Snake Bank. Under the 1992 temporary change in the Idaho code, IPC was allowed to transfer that water to the Bonneville Power Administration for fish flows, after first using it to produce hydropower in Idaho (MacDonnell *et al.* 1994). In addition, the Bureau's control over water for maintaining power heads in the Upper Snake reservoirs allowed it to release 206,647 acre-feet for fish flows (MacDonnell 1995).

Texas water bank

The Texas water bank is another example of a state-managed water transfer bank. The Texas legislature authorised a water banking programme in 1993, designating the Texas Water Development Board (TWDB) as administrator of the programme. TWDB has developed rules governing transfers of water deposited into the bank. The transfers may be either temporary or permanent, and they must follow the regular process for obtaining approval of the change from the Texas Natural Resource Conservation Commission. The bank rules, however, impose an additional restriction by allowing only 50 per cent of a water right to be transferred through the bank (Water Bank Rules at § 359.6[a]). To date, the bank has seen little activity, perhaps because it offers few advantages over privately arranged transfers. These, in fact, may be promoted by a 'bulletin board' service maintained by TWDB as part of the water banking programme. Prospective buyers and sellers use the bulletin board to post offers, but TWDB does not track the actual transactions that are facilitated by that service (personal communication, Dan Beckett, Water Bank Manager, 28 May 1997).

Other water transfer banks

In addition to the water banks administered or supervised by a state agency, there are also local water banking initiatives, some of which facilitate transfers of water among users served by a single supply entity and others that involve transfers of water from one service area to another.

Dolores project bank

The Dolores Water Conservancy District Water Bank is an example of the first of these types. The purpose of the bank is to make most efficient use of the available water by allowing it to move around (or rotate) among irrigators within the district. The bank operates through a price incentive system. Irrigators who use more than their baseline allocations pay a higher price, and those revenues are pooled and paid to irrigators who use less than their baseline allocations. The bank has been in operation since 1991. The refund per acre-foot of underuse appears to rise in dry years and fall in wet years, thus providing an appropriate conservation incentive (MacDonnell *et al.* 1994).

Palo Verde – MWD

The Metropolitan Water District of Southern California (MWD) provides an example of the second type of local bank with its Palo Verde programme. The Palo Verde irrigation district has the most senior California water right on the Colorado River. In 1992 and 1993, MWD paid farmers in the Palo Verde district not to grow crops. That reduced consumptive use by an estimated 4.6 acre-feet per acre on 22,000 acres (most of the land in the district), allowing MWD to bank 186,000 acre-feet in Lake Mead. The terms of the arrangement specified that MWD would own that water until the year 2000 unless Lake Mead spilled, in which case the banked water would be the first water to be spilled. Lake Mead did spill in the spring of 1997, so MWD lost that water. According to MWD, an expenditure of US$30 million went down the river, but they view it as analogous to health insurance. If you stay healthy, there is no reason to regret paying the insurance premium. The important thing was that the insurance was there in case it had been needed (personal communication, Tim Quinn, Deputy General Manager – MWD, 9 June 1997).

In retrospect, however, the arrangement resulted in unnecessary loss of crop output. The parties are now trying to negotiate a three-way arrangement between Palo Verde, MWD, and the Bureau of Reclamation that will both avoid unnecessary fallowing and eliminate the risk of losing the purchased water to a spill. Under the proposed agreement, MWD would borrow water from Lake Mead when needed in a dry year, to be repaid within two to three years by fallowing land in the Palo Verde district. This is a better arrangement for farmers because it does not require them to fallow their land on short notice. The proposed arrangement will give them enough notice to plan their finances and fallow in the most efficient manner. Under the arrangement, MWD would make up-front payments to the farmers to secure their commitments to the programme. MWD and the Palo Verde district have not yet finalised the exact terms of the agreement.

Groundwater recharge and storage options

The other operating water banks in the West involve storage of water in an aquifer, to be retrieved and used during droughts or future periods of increased demand. Several such arrangements have been developed or are under negotiation by MWD. These include within-state agreements and one contract involving the storage of Colorado River water in groundwater basins within the Central Arizona Water Conservancy District. In addition, in 1996, the state of Arizona passed legislation establishing a state groundwater banking programme.

MWD groundwater banking programmes

MWD's efforts to provide secure water supplies during droughts (and other emergencies) include a conjunctive use programme involving storage of water in groundwater basins within Metropolitan's service area. When imported water from the Central Valley or Colorado River is plentiful, that water is either used to directly replenish local groundwater supplies or is delivered to users in place of the groundwater that would otherwise be pumped. The latter practice provides 'in-lieu' replenishment. Metropolitan will use the replenished groundwater to meet seasonal, dry year, and emergency demands. MWD reports that 'since 1980, direct replenishment and in-lieu replenishment of imported supplies have ranged between 125,000 and 450,000 acre-feet per year, with in-lieu replenishment playing an increasingly important role' (MWD 1996a: 2, 4–10). In planning for long-term supplies, MWD estimates that ultimately 1.45 million acre-feet of storage capacity could be available within its service area for the conjunctive use programme, with a maximum yield of 962,000 acre-feet over a twelve-month period (MWD 1996a).

One element of this programme is an agreement between MWD and one of its member agencies, the Calleguas Municipal Water District, to store water in the District's North Las Posas Groundwater Basin. Under the agreement, MWD will provide US$16 million to Calleguas for the construction of up to thirty aquifer storage and recovery (ASR) wells and facilities to connect the wells to the District's distribution system. MWD then will use these facilities to store water in the aquifer, allowing additional dry-year production of 45,000 – 70,000 acre-feet (MWD 1994 and 1995).

MWD is also a party to agreements to store groundwater outside of its own service area. The Semitropic Water Storage District is currently taking delivery of a portion of MWD's State Water Project Entitlement supplies and is placing that water in storage for later delivery to MWD. Approximately 150,000 acre-feet have been put into storage under the programme. There is substantial potential to increase this quantity, given the estimated one million acre-feet of storage capacity available in Semitropic's groundwater basin. At present, MWD is actively looking for additional water to store in the basin. Metropolitan would purchase the water from entities in northern California and transport it south through the California Aqueduct at times when the environmental costs of Delta pumping operations are low (personal communication, Tim Quinn, Deputy General Manager – MWD, 9 June 1997).

Recently, MWD concluded an agreement with the Arvin-Edison Water Storage District, after several years of negotiations and false starts. The current agreement is pending approval by the SWRCB. Under the agreement, Arvin-Edison will finance the $10 million cost of constructing new spreading basins and extraction wells, while MWD will advance $12 million to the District for construction of a pipeline and intertie with the California Aqueduct. Arvin-Edison has agreed to then acquire a minimum of 250,000 acre-feet of nonfirm CVP water on behalf of MWD and to place that water in storage in the District's aquifer. The maximum quantity that would be stored at any one time is capped at 350,000 acre-feet, and MWD's annual withdrawals are to range from a minimum of 40,000 acre-feet up to a maximum of 75,000 acre-feet. The payment formula for the first 250,000 acre-feet is calculated to reimburse MWD for the cost of the pipeline while providing Arvin-Edison with a net payment for the water of US$80 per acre-foot. Afterward, the net payment will be US$100 per acre-foot, half of which will be paid when the water is acquired and put into storage and half when it is returned to MWD (MWD 1996b).

MWD and the Southern Nevada Water Authority (SNWA) are each 50 per cent participants in an active interstate groundwater storage agreement with the Central Arizona Water District (CAWCD). Under the terms of that agreement, CAWCD uses the conveyance facilities of the Central Arizona Project (CAP) to move Colorado River Water from Lake Mead to central Arizona for underground storage (see CAWCD and MWD 1992). CAWCD either uses this water to recharge its aquifer or substitutes it for groundwater that would otherwise be pumped within the District. Depending on how CAWCD chooses to use the water, it is counted either as an Underground Storage and Recovery Project (US&R) credit or as an Indirect Storage and Recovery Project (IS&R) credit under Arizona state law. Payments are made by MWD and SNWA to CAWCD when the water is put into storage, with a slightly higher price paid for US&R water to reflect the cost of injecting the water into the aquifer and subsequently retrieving it.

These groundwater credits are then assigned to an interstate underground storage (IUS) account. The ownership of the right to withdraw the credits depends on the availability of water in the Colorado River. If the flow of the Colorado is large enough that the Secretary of the Interior declares a surplus or releases water from Lake Mead for flood control purposes, then all or a portion of the IUS credits are assigned to MWD and SNWA. They may then take delivery by exchange through diversion of Colorado River water at any time at which sufficient water is available to satisfy Arizona's 2.8 million acre-foot entitlement, subject to a limit on the monthly rate of such diversion. If critically dry conditions prevail, however, the Secretary of the Interior may declare a shortage on the Colorado River. When a declared shortage results in the availability of at least 300,000 acre-feet less than the Lower Basin's 7.5 million acre-foot entitlement, then any IUS credits that have not already been permanently assigned to MWD and SNWA can be taken by CAWCD to cover its apportioned share of the shortage.

Recent Arizona groundwater banking legislation

In 1996, Arizona enacted legislation creating a state water banking programme (State of Arizona Forty-second Legislature, House Bill 2494 – Chapter 308). The legislation creates the Arizona Water Banking

Authority, to be managed by a five-member commission, including the director of the Arizona Department of Water Resources and the president of CAWCD. The Authority will annually acquire a portion of Arizona's unused Colorado River allotment and pay the costs of transporting that water through CAP facilities and storing it in underground aquifers in central Arizona. Funding is to be provided by existing groundwater pumping fees, a storage tax levied by CAWCD, State General Fund appropriations, and revenues from interstate sale of the banked water (Ariz. Rev. Stat. Ann § 45–2425; § 48–3715 et seq.). The initial General Fund appropriation was US$2 million. The water is to be used to recharge depleted aquifers, provide drought protection, and facilitate implementation of Indian water right settlements. In addition, the programme is to provide opportunities for California and Nevada to store water in Arizona for their future needs. The 'declaration of policy and purpose' in the legislation reveals that the programme is meant to secure Arizona's rights to the currently unused portion of its Colorado River entitlement against a possible 'water-grab' by California and Nevada (Ariz. Rev. Stat. Ann § 45–2401 et seq.). According to MWD, the legislation does not interfere with the existing interstate water banking agreement (personal communication, Tim Quinn, Deputy General Manager – MWD, 9 June 1997).

CONCLUSIONS

In all cases, water banks must comply with existing water law. Water to be banked in underground storage or transferred to another user through a water transfer bank must be legally available to the party storing or selling the water. For prior appropriation rights, the right must either be 'in priority' (i.e., there is sufficient streamflow to satisfy that particular right, given its position in the priority hierarchy) or the water must have been previously stored in accordance with the terms of the right. The conditions under which riparian rights can be used for water banking are considerably more restricted. In addition, the operation of the water bank may not harm any other vested water right. To operate efficiently, water banks must find relatively low-cost methods to ensure that these legal requirements are satisfied. In addition, efficiency requires that pricing policies and other bank rules do not unduly interfere with the movement of the resource to its most highly valued use.

In some cases, active management of a water bank by a state agency, as in the case of California's Emergency Drought Water Banks, appears to be the most effective alternative. In other cases, local management under clear state guidelines may be most appropriate. The Idaho examples suggest, however, that to truly serve the interests of the entire public, care must be taken in designing the guidelines and determining who is to exercise local control over operation of the bank. Finally, there are some water banks for which little state involvement may be required, other than a supportive state administrative environment. This appears to be the case for some groundwater banking arrangements and for small water transfer banks operating within a limited geographical area.

Water banks, in all their varied forms, represent important emerging tools for drought management. If the population of the West continues its rapid growth, we can expect water banking to play an increasingly prominent role in the water resource planning and drought mitigation strategies of western water users.

REFERENCES

Associated Press (1993) 'Endangered species: Bureau wants to buy water from farmers', *The Idaho Statesman*, Boise, April 30.

Bay Area Economic Forum and Metropolitan Water District of Southern California (1993) *Water Marketing in California: Resolving Third-Party Impact Issues*, San Francisco: Bay Area Economic Forum, and Los Angeles: MWD.

Bowden, G.D., Edmunds, S.W., and Hundley, N.C. (1982) 'Institutions: Customs, laws and organizations', in E.A. Englebert and A.F. Scheuring (eds), *Competition for California Water*, Berkeley, CA: University of California Press.

CAWCD and MWD (1992) *Agreement between the Central Arizona Water Conservation District and the Metropolitan Water District of Southern California for a Demonstration Project on Underground Storage of Colorado River Water*, October 15, Phoenix, AZ: CAWCD, and Los Angeles: MWD.

Coppock, R.H. and Kreith, M. (eds) (1993) *California Water Transfers: Gainers and Losers in Two Northern Counties*, Proceedings of a conference sponsored by Agricultural Issues Center, Water Resources Center, Davis, CA: University of California.

Dixon, L.S., Moore, N.Y., and Schechter, S.W. (1993) *California's 1991 Drought Water Bank: Economic Impacts in the Selling Regions*, Santa Monica, CA: Rand.

DWR (1991) *General Negotiating Principles and Provisions*, Sacramento: State of California, Department of Water Resources, March 4.

DWR (1992) *The 1991 Drought Water Bank*, Sacramento: State of California, Department of Water Resources.

DWR (1993) *Draft Program Environmental Impact Report: State Drought Water Bank*, Sacramento: State of California, Department of Water Resources.

Gray, B.E. (1993) 'Water rights, laws and institutions', in R.H. Coppock and M. Kreith (eds), *California Water Transfers: Gainers and Losers in Two Northern Counties*, Proceedings of a conference sponsored by Agricultural Issues Center, Water Resources Center, Davis, CA: University of California.

Higginson, R.K. and Barnett, J.A. (1984) *Water Rights and Their Transfer in the Western United States*, report to the Conservation Foundation, Bountiful, UT: Higginson-Barnett Consultants.

Holcomb, V. (1992) *Buying and Selling Water in California: Issues, Experience and Policy Options*, Conference Summary Analysis, UCLA Extension Public Policy Program, Sacramento: Water Education Foundation.

Howe, C.W., Alexander, P.K., and Moses, R.J. (1982) 'The performance of appropriative water rights systems in the western United States during drought', *Natural Resources Journal* 22, 2: 379–89.

Howitt, R., Moore, N., and Smith, R.T. (1992) *A Retrospective on California's 1991 Emergency Drought Water Bank*, report prepared for the California Department of Water Resources, Sacramento.

Jercich, S.A. (1997) 'California's 1995 Water Bank Program: Purchasing water supply options', *Journal of Water Resources Planning and Management* 123, 1: 59–65.

Lund, J.R., Israel, M., and Kanazawa, R. (1992) *Recent California Water Transfers: Emerging Options in Water Management*, Report No. 92-1, Davis, CA: Department of Civil and Environmental Engineering, University of California.

Macaulay, S. (1993) 'Successes and problems with water transfer and marketing programs', speech presented 7 June at meeting of Southern California Water Committee's Task Force on Water Transfers and Marketing.

MacDonnell, L.J. (1990a) 'Transferring the uses of water in the West', *Oklahoma Law Review* 43: 119–30.

MacDonnell, L.J. (Principal Investigator) (1990b) *The Water Transfer Process as a Management Option for Meeting Changing Water Demands*, Vol. II, USGS Grant Award No. 14-08-0001-G1538, Boulder, CO: Natural

Resources Law Center, University of Colorado.

MacDonnell, L.J. (1995) 'Water banks: Untangling the Gordian knot of western water', *Rocky Mountain Mineral Law Institute* 41: 22.1–22.63.

MacDonnell, L.J., Howe, C.W., Miller, K.A., Rice, T.A., and Bates, S. (1994) *Water Banks in the West*, Boulder, CO: Natural Resources Law Center, University of Colorado School of Law.

McBean, E. (1993) 'Environmental effects', in R.H. Coppock and M. Kreith (eds), *California Water Transfers: Gainers and Losers in Two Northern Counties*, Proceedings of a conference sponsored by Agricultural Issues Center, Water Resources Center, Davis, CA: University of California.

Miller, K.A. (1989) 'Hydropower, water institutions and climate change: A Snake River case study', *Water Resources Development* 5, 2: 71–83.

MWD (1994) *Conjunctive Use in the North Las Posas Groundwater Basin, Report to Board of Directors* (August 5), Los Angeles: Metropolitan Water District of Southern California.

—— (1995) *Agreement with Calleguas Municipal Water District for Groundwater Storage Program and System Reliability Development and Appropriation No. 712 for $6 Million to Finance the First Phase of the Program*, memorandum from MWD General Manager to Board of Directors (May 30), Los Angeles: Metropolitan Water District of Southern California.

—— (1996a) *Southern California's Integrated Water Resources Plan – Vol 1: The Long-Term Resources Plan; Vol 2: Metropolitan's System Overview*, Report # 1107 (March), Los Angeles: Metropolitan Water District of Southern California.

—— (1996b) *Authorization to Implement Initial Friant-Kern Water Transfer Program*, memorandum from MWD General Manager to Board of Directors (June 13), Los Angeles: Metropolitan Water District of Southern California.

National Research Council (1992) *Water Transfers in the West: Efficiency, Equity and the Environment*, Washington, DC: National Academy Press.

Saliba, B.C. and Bush, D.B. (1987) *Water Markets in Theory and Practice: Market Transfers, Water Values and Public Policy*, Boulder, CO: Westview Press.

Tarlock, A.D. (1989) *Law of Water Rights and Resources*, New York: Clark Boardman.

USDA (1994) *Water Supply Outlook for the Western United States*, Portland, OR: Soil Conservation Service.

Whittlesey, N., Hamilton, J., and Halverson, P. (1986) *An Economic Study of the Potential for Water Markets in Idaho*, Moscow, Idaho: University of Idaho, Idaho Water Resources Research Institute.

PART VI

DROUGHT MANAGEMENT: MITIGATION, PREPAREDNESS, AND POLICY

35

PREPARING FOR DROUGHT

A methodology

Donald A. Wilhite

INTRODUCTION

Preparedness was defined in Chapter 1 as predisaster activities designed to increase the level of readiness or improve operational and institutional capabilities for responding to an emergency. Drought preparedness has encountered increasing support from governments in recent years at various levels because of escalating impacts and the ineffectiveness and costs of emergency assistance programmes that have little noticeable return. For example, between 1970 and 1984, state and federal government in Australia expended more than A$925 million on drought relief under the Natural Disaster Relief Arrangements (Wilhite 1986). The Republic of South Africa spent R2.5 billion for drought relief from the mid-1970s to the mid-1980s (Wilhite 1987). Both of these nations have now adopted national drought policies that promote self-reliance and more of a risk management approach to drought management.

Coping strategies for responding to and preparing for drought are numerous and range from individual or household level to national level. The series of chapters included in this section of the book provide case studies of these approaches at various levels of government. Government policy responses to drought can be broadly classified into three types (Parry and Carter 1987): pre-impact programmes for impact reduction; post-impact government interventions; and contingency arrangements or preparedness plans. Pre-impact government programmes are defined as those that attempt to mitigate the future effects of drought. Specific drought-related examples include the development of an early warning system, augmentation of water supplies, demand reduction (such as water conservation programmes), and crop insurance.

Post-impact government interventions refer to those reactive programmes or tactics implemented by government in response to drought or some other extreme climatic event. This includes a wide range of reactive emergency measures such as low-interest loans, transportation subsidies for livestock and livestock feed, provision of food, water transport, and drilling wells for irrigation and public water supplies. This reactive crisis management approach has been criticised by scientists, government officials, and many relief recipients as inefficient, ineffective, and untimely (Wilhite 1993). More recently, the provision of emergency relief in times of drought has also been criticised as being a disincentive to the sustainable use of natural resources because it does not promote self-reliance (Bruwer 1993, White *et al.* 1993). In fact, this approach may increase vulnerability to drought, as well as to other natural hazards.

Contingency arrangements refer to policies and plans that can be useful in preparing for drought. These are usually developed at national and provincial levels, with linkages to the local level. The ultimate goal of these preparedness plans is to reduce vulnerability to future episodes of drought. Until recently, nations had devoted little effort to drought preparedness, preferring instead the traditional reactive or crisis management approach.

Deficiencies of previous drought assessment and response efforts are well documented (Wilhite 1992). They include (1) lack of appropriate climatic indices and early warning systems, as well as lack of triggers for initiating specific actions; (2) insufficient data bases for assessing water shortages and potential impacts; (3) inadequate tools and methodologies for early estimates of impacts in various sectors; (4) insufficient information flow within and between levels of government on drought severity, impacts, and appropriate policy responses; (5) inappropriate or untimely emergency assistance programmes; (6) poorly targeted emergency assistance programmes that do not reach vulnerable population groups and economic sectors; (7) meagre financial and human resources that are poorly allocated; (8) lack of emphasis on proactive mitigation programmes aimed at reducing vulnerability to drought; (9) institutional deficiencies that inhibit effective emergency response; and (10) lack of coordination of policies and programmes within (horizontal) and between (vertical) levels of government.

Increasingly, nations are pursuing a more proactive approach that emphasises the principles of risk management and sustainable development. Because of the multitude of impacts associated with drought and the numerous governmental agencies that have responsibility for some aspect of monitoring, assessment, response, mitigation, and planning, developing a policy and plan must be an integrated process, involving all levels of government. This chapter provides an overview of a planning process that can be adopted by governments to develop a more comprehensive and proactive approach to drought management and planning. This process has been used widely at various levels of governments throughout the world as a model for preparation of a drought contingency plan. As the number of drought plans increases, governments can also refer to these plans as functional models, drawing from the experiences (i.e., lessons learned) of others. Given the increased emphasis on natural hazards management as a result of the declaration of the 1990s as the International Decade for Natural Disaster Reduction, models such as the one presented here are useful for those who want to initiate the drought planning process. Drought contingency or preparedness planning also interfaces with the current global emphasis on sustainable development (i.e., UN Conference on Environment and Development and the UN Commission on Sustainable Development) and its obvious linkages to natural hazards management, as well as to the goals of the international convention on combatting desertification. This convention has as one of its cornerstones the task of fostering development of preparedness plans for drought-prone nations. A discussion of this programme is included in the chapter by Jallow in this volume (see Chapter 44).

DEVELOPING A DROUGHT PREPAREDNESS PLAN

The factors that may stimulate governments to develop drought plans are numerous and vary from one country to another. In 1986, a call by the Secretary General of the World Meteorological Organization (WMO) for the development of drought plans (Obasi 1986) likely resulted in greater attention to drought preparedness by some governments. However, internal factors, such as the occurrence of severe drought and concomitant economic, social, and environmental impacts, are more apt to stimulate the planning process at the national or provincial level. Although both external and internal factors are important, internal support ultimately must be present for the process to move forward.

Wilhite and Rhodes (1994) recently concluded that the increase in the number of states with drought plans in the United States could not be explained on the basis of the climatology of drought. This is understandable since the impacts associated with drought are a product of both the occurrence of meteorological drought and the demand placed on water and other natural resources by human activities. Wilhite and Rhodes found that social, political, and institutional influences may be more important than recent drought experiences, speculating that the increase in state drought planning activities may also have been the result of improved capabilities of state governments in conjunction with the Reagan administration's 'New Federalism' initiative and concurrent federal regulatory mandates to state and local governments, states' concerns about federal intrusion into state-level water resource planning and water rights, and some states' early experiences in working with the newly formed Federal Emergency Management Agency (FEMA). Drought climatology and these other factors likely combine to explain the large increase in state drought plans between the early 1980s and late 1990s. In 1997, twenty-seven of the fifty states had prepared drought plans, and another six are in the early stages of plan development (see Figure 39.2). Only three states had developed drought plans in 1982. The planning process in New Mexico, Texas, and Oklahoma is a direct result of the severe drought that affected the southwestern and southern Great Plains states during 1996.

The decision to prepare a drought plan almost always rests with a high-ranking political official. If this official does not initiate the plan development process, the person must be convinced of the need for a plan and the benefits that will accrue if the process is to go forward. This may be a formidable and time-consuming task. Proponents of a plan must begin by determining support for the planning process within key government agencies and assessing what expertise exists to assist with the process. Consensus building is an important part of the process that (if done properly) will enhance the chances of successfully initiating and completing the plan. In some cases, a national or regional water resources management or development plan may already exist and a drought plan, once completed, could be incorporated into this broader strategy.

Although the principles of drought planning have been known for some time, progress toward preparedness in most countries has been conspicuously absent. This lack of progress would indicate that impediments or constraints to drought planning exist and must be addressed if the planning process is to be successful.

Constraints to drought planning

Institutional, political, budgetary, and human resource constraints often make drought planning difficult (Wilhite and Easterling 1987a). One major constraint that exists worldwide is a lack of understanding of drought by politicians, policy makers, technical staff, and the general public. Lack of communication and cooperation among scientists and inadequate communication between scientists and policy makers on the significance of drought planning also complicate efforts to initiate steps toward preparedness. Because drought occurs infrequently in some regions, governments may ignore the problem or give it low priority. Inadequate financial resources to provide assistance

and competing institutional jurisdictions between and within levels of government may also serve to discourage governments from undertaking planning. Other constraints include technological limits (such as difficulties in predicting and detecting drought), insufficient data bases, and inappropriate mitigation technologies.

Policy makers and bureaucrats need to understand that droughts, like floods, are a normal feature of climate. Their recurrence is inevitable. Although we cannot influence the occurrence of the natural event (i.e., meteorological drought), we can lessen vulnerability through more reliable forecasts, improved early warning systems, and appropriate and timely mitigation and preparedness measures. Drought manifests itself in ways that span the jurisdiction of numerous bureaucratic organisations (e.g., agricultural, water resources, health, and so forth) and levels of government (e.g., national, state, and local). Competing interests, institutional rivalry, and the desire to protect their agency missions (i.e., 'turf protection') impede the development of concise drought assessment and response initiatives. To solve these problems, policy makers and bureaucrats, as well as the general public, must be educated about the consequences of drought and the advantages of preparedness. Drought is an interdisciplinary problem that requires input by many disciplines and policy makers.

The development of a drought preparedness plan is a significant step in adopting a preventive, anticipatory approach to resource management. Planning, if undertaken properly and implemented during non-drought periods, can improve governmental ability to respond in a timely and effective manner during periods of crisis. Thus, planning can mitigate and, in some cases, prevent impacts while reducing physical and emotional hardship. Planning is a dynamic process that must incorporate both traditional and emerging technologies and take into consideration socio-economic, agricultural, technological, and political trends.

It is sometimes difficult to determine the benefits of drought preparedness versus the costs of being unprepared. There is little doubt that preparedness requires financial and human resources that are, at times, scarce. This cost has been and will continue to be an impediment. Preparedness costs are fixed and occur now while drought costs are uncertain and will occur later. Further complicating this issue is the fact that the costs of drought are not solely economic. They must also be stated in terms of human suffering, damage to biological resources, and the degradation of the physical environment, items whose values are inherently difficult to estimate.

Post-drought evaluations have shown assessment and response efforts of governments with a low level of preparedness to be largely ineffective, poorly co-ordinated, untimely, and inefficient in terms of the allocation of resources. Although government expenditures for drought relief are significant and unanticipated, they are usually poorly documented. However, a few examples do exist. During the droughts of the mid-1970s in the United States, specifically 1974, 1976, and 1977, the federal government spent more than US$7 billion on drought relief programmes (Wilhite *et al.* 1986). As a result of the drought of 1988, the federal government spent US$3.9 billion on drought relief programmes and US$2.5 billion on farm credit programmes (Riebsame *et al.* 1991). A disaster relief package was also passed by the US Congress in August 1989 in response to a continuation of drought conditions. Other examples of government expenditures for drought relief were cited previously in this chapter. When compared to these expenditures, a small investment in mitigation programmes in advance of drought is a sound economic decision. The rationale for implementing preventive or pre-impact measures must be weighed not only against a retrospective analysis of relief costs but also against future relief costs and savings accrued through reduced economic, social, and environmental impacts. Though difficult to quantify, these savings will be significant.

It is equally important to remind decision makers and policy officials that, in most instances, drought planning efforts will use *existing* political and institutional structures at appropriate levels of government, thus minimising start-up and maintenance costs. It is also quite likely that some savings may be realised as a result of improved coordination and the elimination of some duplication of effort between agencies or levels of government. Also, plans should be incorporated into general natural disaster and/or water management and development plans wherever possible. This reduces the cost of preparedness sub-stantially. Politicians and many other decision makers simply must be better informed about drought, its impacts, and alternative management approaches and how existing information and technology can be used more effectively to reduce impacts at a relatively modest cost.

DEVELOPING A DROUGHT POLICY AND PREPAREDNESS PLAN: A METHODOLOGY

A planning process was developed recently in the United States to facilitate the preparation of drought plans by state government decision makers (Wilhite 1991). This process was based on methodology originally proposed in 1987 to synthesise the discussions and recommendations of participants at an international symposium and workshop on drought (Wilhite and Easterling 1987b). For the application of this methodology to states in the United States, three existing state drought plans were studied to determine the best attributes of those plans for incorporation in the process (Wilhite 1991 and 1992). This process has also been modified for application to developing countries through direct interaction with foreign governments resulting from a series of regional training seminars on drought management and preparedness, organised and conducted by the International Drought Information Center at the University of Nebraska–Lincoln (Figure 35.1). The first of these seminars was held in 1989 in Botswana for eastern and southern Africa. This seminar was followed by seminars in Asia (1991) and Latin America (1993). The ten-step drought planning methodology discussed in this chapter was used as a primary instructional resource for these meetings. These seminars were sponsored by the United Nations Environment Programme (UNEP), US National Oceanic and Atmospheric Administration (NOAA), and WMO. In Latin America, the training seminar was also sponsored by the Organization of American States. An outgrowth of these training seminars was a guidebook for developing countries, *Preparing for Drought* (Wilhite 1992), sponsored by UNEP. Workshops on drought and desertification were also held in The Gambia in 1995 for the West African region and in Israel in 1997. Both meetings were sponsored by WMO.

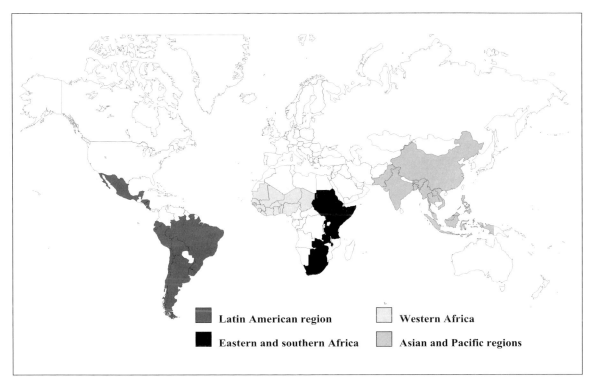

Figure 35.1 Countries participating in the four regional training seminars on drought management and preparedness, conducted between 1989 and 1995

The planning process has been used or proposed for use in other political settings and geographical scales (i.e., local, state, regional, and national – see, for example, Great Lakes Commission 1990, SARCCUS 1990, Oladipo 1993, Moran 1995). The framework described below outlines the ten steps considered essential to the planning process (Figure 35.2). The first four steps actually involve appraising the resources available to support plan development and designing tactics to gain public support for the process. The process addresses the principal issues associated with drought planning and is intended to be flexible (i.e., governments can add, delete, or modify steps as necessary).

Step 1   Appointment of national drought commission

The planning process is initiated through the appointment of a national drought commission (NDC) or authority. The appropriate name for this group (e.g., *commission, committee,* or *task force*) will vary from region to region. The NDC has two purposes. First, during plan development, the NDC will supervise and coordinate the development of the preparedness plan. Second, after the plan is implemented and during times of drought when the plan is activated, the NDC will assume the role of policy coordinator, reviewing alternative policy response options and making recommendations to political officials. The NDC is central to this planning process and will be referred to throughout the discussion of the proposed methodology.

The NDC should include representatives of the most relevant mission agencies, recognising the multidisciplinary nature of drought, its diverse impacts, and the importance of both the assessment and mitigation/response components in any comprehensive plan, and how this plan must be integrated with long-term sustainable development objectives.

Figure 35.2 The ten-step planning process

Agencies to consider for inclusion on the commission are meteorological services, agriculture, water resources, planning, public water supply, natural resources, environmental protection, health, finance, economic and rural development, emergency management, and tourism. A representative from the head of state's office should also be included. Consideration should be given to including key representatives from universities, media (or a public information specialist), and environmental and/or special public interest groups. The purpose of including a public information specialist is to guarantee that the NDC gives attention to how it will communicate information about drought severity and mitigative actions to the public during drought periods. The actual make-up of the NDC would be quite different from one country to another, reflecting different political infrastructures and the unique combination of economic, social, and environmental impacts associated with drought.

The NDC will need to consider at a later time whether it would be prudent to formalise the plan through the legislative (or some other) process. The danger in not formalising the plan is that a change in political or administrative leadership may lead to the decay of the plan's infrastructure. It must be emphasised that political interest in drought quickly wanes when the crisis is over; concern and panic during a drought are swiftly replaced by apathy once the rains have returned and drought conditions have abated. (This sequence of events is commonly referred to as the hydro-illogical cycle – see Figure 35.3.) Likewise, institutional memory is short. A drought plan (and associated infrastructure) that is ad hoc by nature may cease to exist in a relatively short time. Formalising the plan after its completion will guarantee that the infrastructure is in place to assist future generations in managing water resources during periods of scarcity.

Step 2 Statement of drought policy and plan objectives

As their first official action, the NDC must formulate a national drought policy and the objectives of the drought plan. The objectives of a drought *policy* differ from those of a drought *plan*. These differences must be made clear at the outset of the planning process. A drought *policy* is broadly stated and expresses the

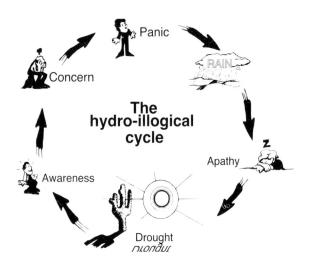

Figure 35.3 The hydro-illogical cycle
Source: Wilhite 1992

purpose of government involvement in drought assessment, mitigation, and response programmes. Ultimately, the goal of a national policy should be to reduce vulnerability to drought by encouraging sustainable development. Drought *plan* objectives are more specific and action-oriented. Typically, the objectives of drought policy have not been stated explicitly by government. What generally exists in many countries is a *de facto* policy, one defined by the most pressing needs of the moment. Ironically, under these circumstances, it is the specific instruments of that policy (such as relief measures) that define the objectives of the policy. Without clearly stated drought policy objectives, the effectiveness of assessment and response activities is difficult to evaluate.

The objectives of drought policy will differ considerably between countries. Based on a comparative analysis of drought assessment and response efforts in the United States and Australia, three objectives of a national policy have been proposed (Wilhite 1986). First, assistance should encourage or provide incentives for agricultural producers, municipalities, and other water-dependent sectors or groups to adopt appropriate and efficient management practices that help to mitigate the effects of drought. Mitigation is defined here as short- and long-term actions, programmes, or policies implemented during and in advance of drought that reduce the degree of risk to human life, property, and productive capacity. Mitigation activities must be interpreted more broadly for drought than for other natural hazards because of the nonstructural nature of most drought impacts. Emergency assistance or relief measures in Australia (White *et al.* 1993), the United States (Wilhite 1991), South Africa (Bruwer 1993), and other countries have discouraged self-reliance by encouraging the adoption of management practices that are often inappropriate or unsustainable in a particular setting. This objective emphasises accepting drought as a normal part of climate and preparing for or managing drought risks as a routine course of business.

Second, assistance, if provided, should be given in an equitable, consistent, and predictable manner to all without regard to economic circumstances, industry, or geographic region. The ultimate goal of a drought preparedness plan is to reduce vulnerability and the need for governmental intervention. However, when assistance must be provided, it will likely be provided in many forms, including technical aid. Whatever the form, those at risk must know what to expect from government during drought so that they can better prepare to manage that risk. The role of non-governmental organisations (NGOs) in assistance efforts must also be precisely defined so that they complement governmental assistance efforts.

Third, the importance of protecting the natural and agricultural resource base must be recognised. This objective emphasises the importance of promoting development that is sustainable in the long term. Clearly, many government programmes and development projects have been shortsighted, increasing vulnerability to future episodes of drought. For example, agricultural policies that encourage the expansion of agriculture into marginal land areas are not sound when evaluated in the context of sustainability. The development of a national drought policy should lead to an evaluation of all pertinent government programmes to ensure that they are consistent with the goals of that policy.

At the initiation of the planning process, members of the NDC should consider many questions pertaining to the development of a national drought policy, including the following:

- What is the purpose and role of government in preparing for drought, assessing impacts, and responding to drought?
- What should be the scope of the plan (i.e., agricultural, municipal water use, or multi-impact in design)?
- What consideration should be given to food supply and distribution or maintaining the nutritional status of various population groups?
- What are the linkages between drought and land degradation processes (i.e., desertification), natural hazards management, and sustainable development?
- What are the most drought-prone areas of the country?
- What are the most vulnerable sectors of the nation's economy?
- What are the principal social and environmental concerns associated with drought?
- Who are the most vulnerable population groups?

- Will the drought plan be a vehicle to resolve conflict between water users during periods of shortage?
- What resources (human and financial) is the government (and donor organisations) willing to commit to the planning process and in support of the plan once it is completed?
- What are the legal and social implications of the plan?

Following the development of a national drought policy, the next action of the NDC is to identify the specific objectives of the plan. Drought planning is defined as actions taken by individual citizens, industry, government, NGOs, and others in advance of drought for the purpose of mitigating some of the impacts and conflicts associated with its occurrence (Wilhite 1991). To be successful, drought planning must be integrated between levels of government, involving the private sector, where appropriate, early in the planning process. Some governments (e.g., Australia, India, South Africa, the United States) are now taking a more proactive approach to drought management. For the majority of nations, however, much remains to be done.

A general statement of purpose for a drought plan is to provide government with an effective and systematic means of assessing and responding to and mitigating the effects of drought. Drought plan objectives will, of course, vary between countries (and between political jurisdictions within countries), and they should reflect the unique physical, environmental, socioeconomic, and political characteristics of those countries (or provinces). Objectives that should be considered include the following:

- To provide timely and systematic data collection, analysis, and dissemination of drought-related information for the purpose of early warning of impending drought. The purpose of this information is to assist decision makers at all levels in making critical decisions, particularly in climate-sensitive sectors or businesses or industries.
- To establish proper criteria to identify and designate drought-affected areas and to trigger the initiation and termination of various assessment, mitigation, and response activities by governmental agencies, NGOs, and others during drought emergencies.

- To provide an organisational structure that assures information flow between and within levels of government, defines the duties and responsibilities of all agencies with respect to drought, and facilitates the decision-making process.
- To develop a set of appropriate emergency and longer-term programmes to be used in assessing, responding to, and mitigating the effects of extended periods of water shortage.
- To provide a mechanism to ensure the timely and accurate assessment of drought impact on agriculture, industry, municipalities, wildlife, health, and other areas as appropriate.
- To provide accurate and timely information to the media to keep the public informed of current conditions and appropriate mitigation and response actions.
- To establish and pursue a strategy to remove obstacles to the equitable allocation of water during shortages and to provide incentives to encourage water conservation.
- To establish a set of procedures to evaluate and revise the plan on a continuous basis to keep the plan responsive to national needs.

It is suggested that countries consider these objectives in the context of their vulnerability to drought and add to, delete, or modify them as appropriate.

Step 3   Avoiding and resolving conflict between environmental and economic sectors

Political, social, and economic interests often clash during drought conditions as competition for scarce water resources intensifies, and it may be difficult to achieve compromises under these circumstances. To reduce the risk of conflict between water users during periods of shortage, it is essential for the public to receive a balanced interpretation of changing conditions through the media and from other sources. The NDC should ensure that frequent, thorough, and accurate news releases are issued to explain changing conditions and complex problem areas that exist and situations in which solutions will require compromises on both sides. To lessen the potential for conflict, the views of citizens and environmental and other special interest groups must be considered in the drought planning process at an early stage. Although the level of involvement of these groups will no doubt vary from one setting to another, the power of these interest groups in policy making is worth noting. Public interest organisations in some countries have initiated and participated in the development of natural resource policies and plans for some time and have extensive experience with this process. The involvement of these groups in determining appropriate policy goals strengthens the overall policy and plan. Moreover, this involvement ensures that the diverse values of society are represented adequately in the policy and plan. Creating an advisory group made up of representatives of these groups is recommended as a means of addressing their concerns.

Step 4   Inventory of natural, biological, and human resources and financial and legal constraints

An inventory of natural, biological, and human resources, including the identification of financial and legal constraints, may need to be initiated by the NDC. In many cases, much information already exists concerning available resources, particularly in the natural and biological resource areas. Generally speaking, less information is available in developing countries. It is also important to determine the vulnerability of these resources to periods of water shortage that result from drought. *Resources* include, for example, physical and biological resources, human expertise, infrastructure, and capital available to government. The most obvious natural resource of importance is water: Where is it located, how accessible is it, of what quality is it? *Biological resources* refer to the quantity and quality of grasslands/rangelands, forests, wildlife, and so forth. *Human resources* include the labour needed to develop water resources, lay pipeline, haul water and livestock feed, process citizen complaints, provide technical assistance, and direct citizens to available services. In addition, representatives of government determine what local, state, or national agencies may be called into action.

Financial constraints would include costs of hauling water or livestock feed, new programme or data collection costs, and so forth. These costs must be weighed against the losses that may result in the absence of the drought plan. It should also be recognised that the financial resources available to government vary annually and from one administration to another. This may provide additional incentives for governments to formalise drought plans through the legislative or another process (see Step 1), thus assuring that funds to carry out existing programmes are available. *Legal constraints* include user water rights, existing public trust laws, methods available to control usage, requirements for public water suppliers, and emergency and other powers of political and government officials during water shortages.

An inventory of these resources would reveal assets and liabilities that might enhance or inhibit fulfilment of the objectives of the planning process. This systematic survey should include resources available at various levels of government and the often unique resources available at universities. A comprehensive assessment of available resources would provide the information necessary for further action by the NDC. The NDC may also want to undertake an examination of drought plans available in adjacent and/or climatically similar countries.

Step 5   Development of the drought plan

The NDC will be the coordinating body for the development of a drought plan. Once completed, the plan is envisioned to follow a stepwise or phased approach as water conditions deteriorate and more stringent actions are needed. Thresholds must be established such that, when exceeded, certain actions are triggered within government agencies, as defined by the structure of the plan.

A drought plan should have three primary organisational components: monitoring or early warning, impact assessment, and mitigation (including emergency response). Although these are distinct activities, formal linkages will need to be incorporated in the plan for it to function properly and be responsive to provincial and local needs and evolving conditions. These three organisational components are discussed in detail below. The names given to these components are intended to be generic, principally referring to the function of the committees. An organisational chart illustrating the linkages between these components of the drought plan is shown in Figure 35.4.

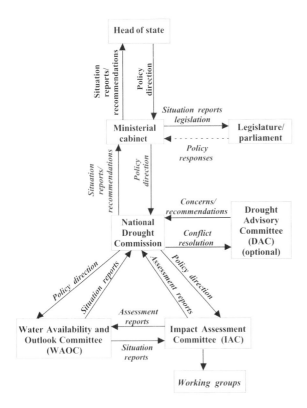

Figure 35.4 Organisational structure of a drought mitigation plan

The organisational components shown in Figure 35.4 represent the recommended structure of a national plan. It is essential that any national plan be integrated with provincial and local levels of government and also connected with food security plans, sustainable development plans, water resource plans, and so forth. These linkages are not depicted in the organisational chart. Each of the committees may have a counterpart at the provincial and local level with well-established linkages to the national committees. These provincial and local committees will facilitate not only data collection and feedback on programmes and policies, but also the dissemination of informational products and advisories and the implementation of policies.

Monitoring component: Water Availability and Outlook Committee (WAOC) A water availability and outlook committee (WAOC) must be established to monitor current and estimate likely future water availability and moisture conditions. The chairperson of this committee should be a permanent member of the NDC. The WAOC would have five primary duties during the plan development process.

1 Inventory data availability and current observational networks for all meteorological and climate-related variables (e.g., snowpack, streamflow, reservoir levels).
2 Determine primary user needs and develop and/or modify current data and information delivery systems.
3 Define drought and develop triggers for initiating action by various committees or for various programmes.
4 Develop an early warning system that incorporates all components of the hydrologic system.
5 Identify drought management areas based on the unique vulnerabilities of specific regions or population groups.

Membership of the committee should include representatives from agencies with responsibilities for forecasting and monitoring the relevant indicators of the water balance (i.e., meteorological variables such as precipitation and temperature, soil moisture, snowpack, surface water storage, groundwater, and streamflow). In some instances, many agencies at national and other levels of government may have responsibility for monitoring these indicators. It is not necessary for all of these agencies to have representation on this committee. Rather, it is recommended that data and information on each of the applicable indicators be considered in the committee's evaluation of the water situation and outlook for the country.

It is important for the WAOC to be a permanent committee, meeting regularly to determine the status of and outlook for water conditions. The committee should meet on a monthly basis throughout the year or regularly just preceding and during the period of most concern. One advantage of regular meetings is that the committee will function as a team because of continuous interaction. Another advantage is that a permanent committee can be useful in the early warning of emerging and potentially serious water problems, whether they are due to shortage or surplus situations. It is common for shortage and surplus situations to exist simultaneously within a country.

WAOC meetings will be more frequent if climatic conditions warrant.

Impact component: Impact Assessment Committee (IAC) During periods of drought, impacts will be far-reaching and cut across economic sectors and the responsibilities of various levels of government. The impact assessment committee (IAC) will represent those economic sectors most likely to be affected by drought (e.g., agriculture, transportation). The IAC should be composed of an interagency team of agency heads or their representatives, and its chairperson should be a permanent member of the NDC. It may also be advisable to include university scientists and representatives of international organisations that have expertise in early estimations of impact. The IAC should consider both direct and indirect losses resulting from drought. Often drought assistance is provided only to those experiencing direct losses while agricultural and other businesses experiencing secondary impacts are largely ignored. Because of the obvious dependency of the IAC on the WAOC, frequent communication between the two is essential.

The IAC must give significant attention to the full range of impacts associated with drought and mechanisms to lessen those impacts, and also determine how to target assistance to those economic sectors or vulnerable population groups as the need arises. One of the principal deficiencies of past response efforts has been the inability of government to direct the necessary form of assistance to the economic sector or population group in a timely manner. Assistance that is misdirected or untimely is of little or no value and is quite costly to taxpayers. The IAC must work closely with both the WAOC and the NDC to ensure that this does not occur.

Mitigation and response component: National Drought Commission The third and final element of a drought plan is the mitigation and response component. The responsibility of this component is to pursue the creation of long-term programmes to lessen vulnerability to drought while acting on the information and recommendations of the IAC. The IAC should evaluate the range of assistance available from government and other sources to assist agricultural producers, municipalities, and others during times of emergency. As people become more self-reliant, the need for government intervention will diminish.

Because this is a policy-making body, it should be composed of senior-level policy officials, precisely the same make-up as the NDC. Therefore, in addition to overseeing the development of the preparedness plan, the NDC should assume the mitigation and response role following plan development.

During the plan development process, the NDC should inventory all forms of assistance available from government and nongovernment sources during severe drought. The NDC should evaluate short-term programmes for their ability to address emergency situations and long-term mitigation programmes for their ability to reduce vulnerability to drought. The NDC may want to consider transferring this task to the IAC. The NDC (or IAC) should also recommend other forms of assistance programmes that could be developed to respond to drought. During periods of drought, the NDC will make recommendations to the head of state or appropriate representative concerning specific actions that need to be taken.

Drought assistance should be defined in a very broad way to include all forms of technical and relief programmes available from government and nongovernment sources. Rational response options must be determined for each of the principal impact sectors identified by the IAC. These options should examine appropriate drought mitigation measures on three time scales: (1) short-term (reactive or emergency) measures implemented during drought; (2) medium-term (recovery) measures implemented to reduce the length of the post-drought recovery period; and (3) long-term (proactive) measures or programmes implemented in an attempt to reduce societal vulnerability to future drought. In many instances, local input should be sought to determine the forms of assistance needed by the various impact sectors.

Societal vulnerability to drought may be influenced substantially by non-drought-related actions taken or policies implemented during nondrought periods. The national drought policy objectives formulated in Step 2 will be especially beneficial at this time. Government must consider the effects of emergency programmes on long-term development objectives and guard against implementing emergency programmes that draw resources from development programmes or interfere with their fulfilment, as has happened in Brazil (Magalháes 1993).

Emergency programmes should foster the achievement of development objectives.

Step 6 Identification of research needs and institutional gaps

Step 6 is to be carried out concurrently with Step 5. The purpose of this step is to identify research needed in support of the objectives of the drought plan and to recommend research projects to remove deficiencies that may exist. It is unlikely that research needs and institutional gaps will be known until the various committees formed in association with the drought planning process have been through the planning process. Compiling information on research needs and institutional gaps is a function of the NDC. For example, the WAOC may recommend establishing or enhancing an existing groundwater monitoring network. The NDC may find it desirable to create a multidisciplinary scientific advisory panel that could evaluate research proposals, establish funding priorities, and seek financial support from appropriate international or regional organisations, NGOs, or donor governments.

It is likely that institutional deficiencies will be identified as part of Step 6. Agency responsibilities or missions may need to be modified to support activities of the drought plan, and these modifications may require legislative action.

Step 7 Synthesis of scientific and policy issues

Previous steps in the planning process have considered scientific and policy issues separately, concentrating largely on assessing the status of the science or on the existing or necessary institutional arrangements to support the plan. An essential aspect of the planning process is the synthesis of the science and policy of drought and drought management. This is the purpose of Step 7.

The policy maker's understanding of the scientific issues and technical constraints involved in addressing problems associated with drought is often negligible. Likewise, scientists generally have a poor understanding of existing policy constraints that affect drought response. A panel of researchers and policy experts have concluded that communication and under-

standing between the science and policy communities is poorly developed and must be enhanced if the drought planning process is to be successful (Wilhite and Easterling 1987a). Direct and extensive contact is required between the two groups to distinguish what is feasible from what is desirable for a broad range of science and policy issues. Integration of science and policy during the planning process will also be useful in setting research priorities and synthesising current understanding. The NDC should consider various alternatives to bring these groups together.

Crucial to this integration process is the provision within the planning process of a means to facilitate scientific information exchange between scientists and policy makers. Since this is not their primary mission, it is unlikely that scientists will freely devote extensive attention to tailoring and otherwise making available research results on a frequent or continuous basis. One way to achieve this interaction is to appoint a specific liaison person or group to facilitate the exchange of information.

Step 8 Implementation of the drought plan

The drought plan should be implemented by the NDC to give maximum visibility to the programme and credit to the agencies and organisations that have a leadership or supporting role in its operation. As with emergency response plans for other natural hazards, all or a portion of the system should be tested under simulated drought conditions before it is implemented. A 'virtual reality' drought simulation exercise has been developed recently in the United States to assist decision makers in the decision process (Werick 1994). It is also suggested that announcement and implementation occur just before the most drought-sensitive season to take advantage of inherent public interest. In an agricultural setting, this would be in advance of planting or at some other critical time during the growing season. The cooperation of the media is essential to publicising the plan, and they must be informed fully of the rationale for the plan as well as its purpose, objectives, assessment and response procedures, and organisational framework. If a representative of the media or a public information specialist is a member of the NDC, as recommended, this person should be an invaluable resource in carrying out this step of the planning process.

Training of personnel who will be actively involved in the operation of the plan is also critical if the plan is to achieve its specified goals. This training should include not only persons in the principal national agencies involved in the activated plan, but also persons at the provincial and local levels of government who will provide valuable input in the decision-making process. The key players in the drought plan must thoroughly understand their responsibilities during drought and how these responsibilities relate to those of other organisations and levels of government. If they do not understand the plan and how it functions, it will fail.

In the absence of drought over several consecutive years, the NDC should conduct simulation exercises to keep leadership informed of their responsibilities during drought. This is a common practice in natural disaster mitigation (e.g., earthquakes, hurricanes); it should be no different for drought. Changes in political leadership, institutional change, retirements, promotions, and transfers to other positions can disrupt the integrity of the plan.

Step 9   Development of multilevel educational and training programmes

Educational and training programmes should concentrate on several points. First, a greater level of understanding must be established to heighten public awareness of drought and water conservation and the ways in which individual citizens and the public and private sectors can help to mitigate impacts in the short and long term. The educational process might begin with the development of a media awareness programme. This programme would include provisions to improve the media's understanding of the drought problem and the complexity of the management issues involved, as well as a mechanism to ensure the timely and reliable flow of information to all members of the media (e.g., via news conferences). Second, the NDC should initiate an information programme aimed at educating the general population about drought and water management and what they can do as individuals to conserve water in the short run. Educational programmes must be

long-term in design, concentrating on achieving a better understanding of water conservation issues among all age groups and economic sectors. If such programmes are not developed, governmental and public interest in and support for drought planning and water conservation will wane during periods of nondrought conditions.

Step 10   Development of drought plan evaluation procedures

The final step in the establishment of a drought plan is the creation of a detailed set of procedures to ensure adequate evaluation. To maximise the effectiveness of the plan, two modes of evaluation must be in place:

1 An ongoing or operational evaluation programme that considers how societal changes such as new technology, the availability of new research results, legislative action, and changes in political leadership may affect the operation of the plan.
2 A post-drought evaluation or audit programme that documents and critically analyses the assessment and response actions of government, NGOs, and others as appropriate and implements recommendations for improving the system.

The first mode of evaluation is intended to express drought planning as a dynamic process, rather than a discrete event. The operational evaluation programme is proposed to keep the drought assessment and response system current and responsive to national needs. Following the initial establishment of the plan, it should be monitored routinely to ensure that societal changes that may affect water supply and/or demand or regulatory practices are considered for incorporation. Accordingly, drought plans should be revised periodically.

The second mode of evaluation is the post-drought audit, which should be conducted or commissioned by governments in response to each major drought episode. Institutional memory fades quickly following drought as a result of changes in political administration, natural attrition of persons in primary leadership positions, and the destruction of critical documentation of events and actions taken. Post-drought evaluations should include an analysis of the physical aspects of the drought: its impacts on soil, groundwater, plants, and animals; its economic and social consequences; and the extent to which pre-drought planning was useful in mitigating impacts, in facilitating relief or assistance to stricken areas, and in post-drought recovery. Attention must also be directed to situations in which drought coping mechanisms worked and where societies exhibited resilience; evaluations should not focus only on those situations in which coping mechanisms failed. Provisions must be made to implement the recommendations emanating from this evaluation process. Evaluations of previous responses to severe drought are recommended as a planning aid to determine those actions (both technical and relief) that have been most effective.

The post-drought evaluation process will identify numerous topics that may require research in order for them to be more adequately addressed during future drought episodes. For example, little is known about the effects of government drought assistance programmes. Do they facilitate or hinder the recovery process? Extensive research may be required on the environmental and socioeconomic effects of prolonged rainfall deficiency on various hydrological features such as soil water and groundwater. Investigation of the effects of drought on land use, vegetation, and soil is essential to the impact assessment process.

To ensure an unbiased appraisal, governments should place the responsibility for evaluating drought and societal response to it in the hands of non-governmental organisations such as universities and/or specialised agencies or corporations. An excellent example of this practice in operation is the evaluation of India's Food for Work Programme (Sinha *et al.* 1987). Although the programme is implemented by state government, it is evaluated by an independent body, the Planning Commission (Wilhite and Easterling 1989).

DROUGHT PREPAREDNESS METHODOLOGIES: OTHER MODELS

Government entities and others interested in developing a drought plan are encouraged to consider a variety of models or methodologies. One such methodology is the product of an effort by Werick and Whipple (1994) as part of the National Study of Water Management During Drought of the US Army Corps of Engineers. This methodology recommends the following seven steps in the development of a drought preparedness plan:

1 Build a team and identify problems.
2 Develop objectives and metrics for evaluation.
3 Describe the status quo (i.e., what will happen in future droughts if the community does nothing more to prepare itself).
4 Formulate alternatives to the status quo.
5 Evaluate alternatives and develop study team recommendations.
6 Institutionalise the plan.
7 Exercise and update the plan and use it during droughts.

This process is based on federal planning principles in the United States but adds two additional steps (2 and 7) to reflect the importance of the nonfederal role in drought planning and the need for non-structural solutions in resolving water management problems associated with drought.

The American Water Works Association (1992) has created a process for developing a drought management plan that focuses on the needs of urban water managers. This process reflects a sequence of six steps:

1 Obtaining public input and involvement.
2 Defining goals and objectives.
3 Assessing water supply and demand conditions.
4 Defining drought indicators.
5 Identifying and assessing drought mitigation measures.
6 Developing a drought index and management strategy.

This report considers the primary benefit of a drought management plan, versus an *ad hoc* crisis management response, to be a reduction in the possibility of a community either over- or under-reacting to a water supply emergency. The report also notes that a drought plan can identify measured responses to a prolonged water shortage and reduce the chances the public will perceive the actions of the water utility to be arbitrary or ill-conceived. The by-product of a well-conceived plan will be to instil public confidence in the water utility and the actions taken in response to the emergency.

The similarity of this model to the ten-step process described earlier in this chapter is obvious. Each strives to obtain the same goal (i.e., improved preparedness and a reduction in impacts) through the implementation of a logical process leading to plan development. The critical issue is not which process is followed but rather whether the outcome of the process is workable and consistent with national (local or provincial) goals, and whether the process has involved stakeholders at each step. Consulting several generic models and actual operational plans being used by other groups will only serve to enhance the chances of the planning process being successful. Ultimately, each plan will be unique because of the distinct socioeconomic, political, and environmental characteristics of the region.

SUMMARY AND CONCLUSIONS

Post-drought evaluations of government response to drought have demonstrated that the reactive or crisis management approach has led to ineffective, poorly coordinated, and untimely responses. The magnitude of economic, social, and environmental losses in the past several decades in developing and developed countries has pointed out the current and apparent escalating vulnerability of all nations to extended episodes of severe drought. Increased awareness and understanding of drought has led a growing number of governments to take a more proactive approach to drought management by attempting to reduce impacts in the short term and vulnerability in the long term. This approach must integrate drought policy with issues of sustainable development.

The development of drought policies that promote risk management and the preparation of contingency plans exemplify a philosophical change by governments in their approach to drought management. Drought preparedness plans promote greater coordination within and between levels of government; improved procedures for monitoring, assessing, responding to, and mitigating the effects of severe water shortages; and more efficient use of natural, financial, and human resources.

It is recommended that the governments of all drought-prone nations formulate drought preparedness plans. The essential elements to consider in the formulation of these plans were presented in this chapter in a ten-step process to facilitate plan development. Other generic models were also discussed. A preparedness plan will lead to a more effective, efficient, and timely approach to drought management, with greater emphasis on long-term vulnerability reduction, as opposed to short-term emergency response. Governments are advised to consider the proposed planning process carefully, modifying or adapting it to their particular circumstances by adding or deleting steps as necessary.

REFERENCES

American Water Works Association (1992) *Drought Management Planning*, prepared by the Water Storage Subcommittee, Denver, Colorado.

Bruwer, J.J. (1993) 'Drought Policy in the Republic of South Africa', in D. A. Wilhite (ed.), *Drought Assessment, Management, and Planning: Theory and Case Studies*, Boston, MA: Kluwer Academic Press.

Great Lakes Commission (1990) *A Guidebook to Drought Planning, Management and Water Level Changes in the Great Lakes*, Ann Arbor, MI.: Great Lakes Commission.

Magalhães, A.R. (1993) 'Drought and policy responses in the Brazilian Northeast', in D.A. Wilhite (ed.), *Drought Assessment, Management, and Planning: Theory and Case Studies*, Boston, MA: Kluwer Academic Press.

Moran, R. (1995) 'Drought planning and management for urban water supplies in Victoria, Australia', in R. Herrmann, W. Black, R.C. Sidle, and A.I. Johnson (eds), *Water Resources and Environmental Hazards: Emphasis on Hydrologic and Cultural Insight in the Pacific Rim: An International Symposium (Proceedings)*, American Water Resources Association.

Obasi, G.P. (1986) 'Drought response plans', memo from the Secretary-General of WMO to Permanent Representatives of Members of WMO, May 14, Geneva, Switzerland.

Oladipo, E.O. (1993) 'A comprehensive approach to drought and desertification in Northern Nigeria', *Natural Hazards* 8: 235–61.

Parry, M.L. and Carter, T.R. (1987) 'Climate impact assessment: A review of some approaches', in D.A. Wilhite and W.E. Easterling (eds), *Planning for Drought: Toward a Reduction of Societal Vulnerability*, Boulder, CO: Westview Press, Chapter 13.

Riebsame, W.E., Changnon, S.A. Jr., and Karl, T.R. (1991) *Drought and Natural Resources Management in the United States: Impacts and Implications of the 1987–89*

Drought, Boulder, CO: Westview Press.

SARCCUS (1990) *Proceedings of the SARCCUS Drought Workshop*, Southern African Regional Commission for the Conservation and Utilization of the Soil, Pretoria, South Africa.

Sinha, S.K., Kailasanathan, K., and Vasistha, A.K. (1987) 'Drought management in India: Steps toward eliminating famines', in D.A. Wilhite and W.E. Easterling (eds), *Planning for Drought: Toward a Reduction of Societal Vulnerability*, Boulder, CO: Westview Press, Chapter 27.

Werick, W. (1994) 'Virtual droughts and shared visions: Some innovations from the National Drought Study', in D.A. Wilhite and D.A. Wood (eds), *Drought Management in a Changing West: New Directions for Water Policy* (Conference Proceedings), IDIC Technical Report Series 94–1, University of Nebraska, Lincoln, Nebraska, pp. 165–77.

Werick, W.J. and Whipple, W. Jr. (1994) 'Managing water for drought', *National Study of Water Management During Drought*, IWR Report 94–NDS–8, US Army Corps of Engineers.

White, D., Collins, D., and Howden, M. (1993) 'Drought in Australia: Prediction, monitoring, management, and policy', in D.A. Wilhite (ed.), *Drought Assessment, Management, and Planning: Theory and Case Studies*, Boston, MA: Kluwer Academic Press, Chapter 12.

Wilhite, D. A. (1986) 'Drought policy in the U.S. and Australia: A comparative analysis', *Water Resources Bulletin* 22: 425–38.

—— (1987) 'The role of government in planning for drought: Where do we go from here?', in D.A. Wilhite and W.E. Easterling (eds), *Planning for Drought: Toward a Reduction of Societal Vulnerability*, Boulder, CO: Westview Press, Chapter 25.

—— (1991) 'Drought planning: A process for state government', *Water Resources Bulletin* 27, 1: 29–38.

—— (1992) *Preparing for Drought: A Guidebook for Developing Countries*, Climate Unit, United Nations Environment Program, Nairobi, Kenya.

—— (ed.) (1993) D*rought Assessment, Management, and Planning: Theory and Case Studies*, Boston, MA: Kluwer Academic Press.

Wilhite, D.A. and Easterling, W.E. (1987a) 'Introduction (workshop summary)', in D.A. Wilhite and W.E. Easterling (eds), *Planning for Drought: Toward a Reduction of Societal Vulnerability*, Boulder, CO: Westview Press, Chapter 34.

—— (1987b) 'Drought policy: Toward a plan of action', in D.A. Wilhite and W.E. Easterling (eds), *Planning for Drought: Toward a Reduction of Societal Vulnerability*, Boulder, CO: Westview Press, Chapter 37.

—— (1989) 'Coping with drought: Toward a plan of action', *Eos* 70, 7: 97, 106–8.

Wilhite, D.A. and Rhodes, S.R. (1994) 'State-level drought planning in the United States: Factors influencing plan development', *Water International* 19: 15–24.

Wilhite, D.A., Rosenberg, N.J., and Glantz, M.H. (1986) 'Improving federal response to drought', *Journal of Climatology and Applied Meteorology* 25: 332–42.

36

FROM STATE DEPENDENCY TO SELF-RELIANCE

Agricultural drought policies and practices in New Zealand

Heather J.K. Haylock and Neil J. Ericksen

New Zealand is a country similar in size to Britain (270,500 km^2). Its small population (3.6 million in 1996) is primarily urban based (about 84 per cent), but its economy is heavily dependent on agriculture, especially pastoral farming. In the mid-1960s, agriculture contributed around 14 per cent to the gross domestic product (GDP) and made up nearly 90 per cent of New Zealand's overseas income. Increasing diversification of production saw a decreasing dependence on agriculture by the mid-1990s, contributing around 6 per cent of GDP and 55 per cent of overseas income.

Although meteorological drought can seriously affect urban water supplies – as when prolonged rationing was needed in metropolitan Auckland (population around 1 million) in the winter of 1994 – its main economic impact is on the rural sector. A severe agricultural drought affects not only pastoral farming, but also industries built on it. A downturn in farming and farm industries affects incomes in rural communities and provincial towns and cities. Overall, a severe agricultural drought seriously affects the regional and national economies in ways that an urban drought does not. This chapter therefore focuses on agricultural drought. It begins by summarising the physical conditions of New Zealand, with particular reference to climate, then outlines the political economy within which agriculture has had to operate. This provides a context for explaining how drought policies have evolved over time from those that engendered dependency on the state toward those seeking self-reliance in the farming industry. Prospects for the future are reflected on in the final section of the chapter.

PHYSICAL AND SOCIAL CONTEXT

Reducing vulnerability to agricultural drought cannot be satisfactorily considered in the absence of some understanding of the context within which agricultural practices have evolved. This includes the need for comment on both physical and social conditions, especially the political economy, that have stimulated farming activities, including responses to drought.

Physical setting

New Zealand is isolated in the South Pacific Ocean, nearly 2,200 km east of the Australian continent. Its two main islands run 1,600 km in a southwest/ northeast direction from 47° S latitude to 32° S (Figure 36.1). The northern part of this elongated country protrudes into the subtropical belt of anticyclones, which move west to east and bring drier weather. Southern New Zealand lies in the westerly wind belt where low pressure systems cause storminess (Figure 36.1).

The winds that blow over New Zealand come mainly from the west and southwest, and are moisture-laden as a consequence of crossing large expanses of ocean. They encounter a spine of steep mountains that decrease in altitude from south to north. These orographic conditions result in highest annual rainfalls in the south and southwest part of the South Island (up to 5,000 mm), and lowest rainfalls in sheltered basins and lowland plains to the east (down to 500 mm). This pattern is less marked in the North Island, where mountain ranges are lower (Figure 36.1). On a daily basis, wet and dry conditions differ across the country

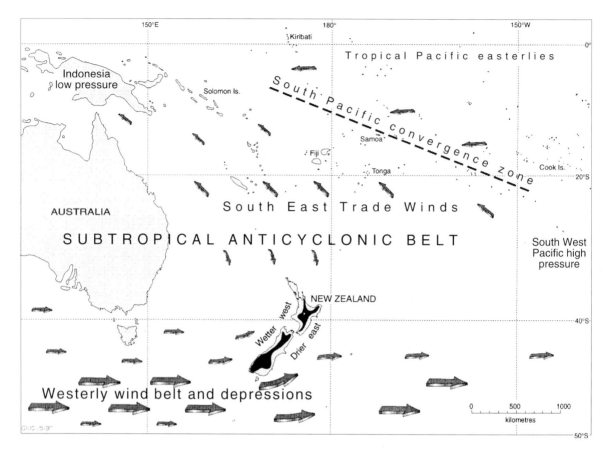

Figure 36.1 Macro climate: New Zealand protrudes north into the subtropical anticyclonic belt and south into the westerly wind belt and depressions. The mix of warm and cool air causes changeable weather. Prevailing moist westerlies are lifted by New Zealand's high axial mountains (darker shading on map), resulting in heavy rain to the west and relatively dry conditions to the east. The powerful Indonesian low pressure system and the southwest Pacific high pressure system oscillate, yielding alternate El Niño (cooler and drier) and La Niña (warmer and wetter) conditions in New Zealand, due mainly to changes in the strength of the westerly airflow. (Adapted with permission from Salinger 1988)

according to wind direction: the land area will be wetter windward than to leeward. Mean temperatures are around 16°C in northern New Zealand and around 10°C in the south (Salinger 1988).

Trends in climate and agriculture

In general, agricultural drought is more likely to occur in the drier areas of New Zealand which lie east of the axial ranges in both islands, where temperatures and evapotranspiration are also greater. Long-term records show that around 1950, temperatures for New Zealand increased as did precipitation in

northern and eastern areas. At the same time, precipitation decreased in southern and western areas (Salinger *et al.* 1992a and 1992b).

This change in long-term trends happened to coincide with a period lasting until 1975, when the El Niño/Southern Oscillation (ENSO) was more frequently in the anti-El Niño (i.e., La Niña) mode. In this phase, the subtropical high pressure belt moves southward, the westerly circulation weakens, and blocking anticyclones occur east of New Zealand. In contrast, for the decade to 1990, the El Niño mode was more frequent as the subtropical high pressure belt moved northward and the westerly and south-westerly air flow strengthened. This caused New Zealand to be wetter west and drier east of the mountain ranges, and overall a little cooler (Salinger *et al.* 1995: 286).

It is likely that the long period of La Niña dominance from 1950 to 1975 brought improved conditions for agriculture, especially to the mixed pastoral and cropping practices in the drier eastern areas of both islands. The beginning of this period coincided with rapid agricultural development in New Zealand following The Second World War and spurred on by high world prices for animal products – meat, wool, and butter – during the Korean war (1950–3). It also coincided with the expansion of agriculture onto more difficult terrain, facilitated by the advent of aerial top-dressing in 1949. Elsewhere, farming intensified in order to increase production. These were New Zealand's golden years, when it had one of the highest standards of living in the world, giving rise to the expression 'living off the sheep's back'.

Farming subsidies

The golden era closed when New Zealand's terms of trade plummeted following the 1973 oil shock and the loss of assured markets for agricultural products when Britain joined the European Common Community (EEC) the same year. Thus, as the La Niña dominance faded in the mid-1970s, so too did New Zealand's economy and standard of living relative to other developed countries.

In general, the government's response to crisis was to intervene through regulations and subsidies. Indeed, since the 1930s, when New Zealand adopted a social welfare state system, central government had introduced various mechanisms for manipulating productive activities for the wider public good (Tyler and Lattimore 1990). Faced with adverse trade conditions in the early 1970s, government intervention intensified in the hope of increasing agricultural diversification and production while at the same time propping up returns to producer boards and farmers. Farmer response to assistance was dramatic. For example, between 1968 and 1972, sheep numbers increased from 60 million to 70 million.

By the 1980s, most facets of the farming (and other) industry were heavily subsidised through tax concessions, low-interest loans, and grants. These supported, for example, forest clearance, erosion and flood control, purchase and application of fertiliser and fencing, boosting stock numbers, and income support, including drought relief. This government assistance obscured both the declining terms of trade for agriculture and the rising real rate of interest rates around the globe. At its zenith, support for agriculture increased from 15 per cent of output in 1980 to 33 per cent in 1983 (Rayner 1990).

A consequence of this assistance was that it not only continued to encourage farming in marginal hill-lands, it also helped to intensify farming in some areas that were susceptible to adverse climatic events in the form of droughts, floods, and consequential erosion. The response to losses from adverse climatic events was consistent with responses elsewhere: for government to intervene with various forms of assistance.

From state dependency to self-reliance

By the late 1970s, there were strong signs that changes were needed, but they were overwhelmed by the highly interventionist strategies of the conservative National Government led by Prime Minister Muldoon, who was also Minister of Finance (1975–84). His response to the growing crisis of rising inflation, unemployment, and adverse terms of trade was to introduce 'Think Big' energy projects (1979–81). This aimed at making New Zealand less susceptible to overseas oil shocks by expanding the local gas and oil industry and using surplus electricity to smelt imported metal ores. A wage-price freeze was also implemented (1982–3).

In 1984, the need for radical change was thrust on New Zealand when it became apparent that the fiscal deficit and overseas debt could not be sustained. The response came from a left-leaning Labour Government, which devalued the dollar, then floated it, phased out government assistance to farming and other industries, and thoroughly restructured central, regional, and local government along corporate lines. Its main aim was to reduce the deficit and control inflation, which was then around 15 per cent per year.

More specifically, new policies were aimed at

liberalising the market, removing export assistance, lowering import protection, increasing indirect taxation and widening the tax base, privatising government trading activities, and increasing government efficiency (Wallace 1990). Although many economic indicators suggest successful outcomes through to 1990, the cost was registered in escalating unemployment, declining growth, and an increased gap between rich and poor. These negative effects have slowly improved during the 1990s, although the number of poor remains a serious concern.

For farmers, incomes generally declined and expenses increased into the 1990s. Overall, the capital base of farming declined (Reynolds and SriRamaratnam 1990). Some were forced to leave their farms, especially when income was further eroded by adverse climatic events, like cyclones and droughts. Others, with more capital, sought to expand their size of operation, and agribusiness grew.

It was not therefore surprising to hear a retired hill-country sheep farmer in the mid-1980s reflect: 'Pity the poor man who took over from me. I realise now that I'd been farming subsidies.' He, like others, had been buffered from adverse trading and environmental conditions, including drought, by a complex system of government assistance.

REFORMING DROUGHT POLICY

Before 1970, relief for drought was ad hoc, and included loans, bank overdraft guarantees, tax relief on the forced sale of livestock, subsidies for regrassing, and transport subsidies for stock and fodder. In 1979, a discussion paper released by the Ministry of Agriculture and Fisheries (MAF) recommended that the balance of government assistance be shifted away from subsidies and toward loans. This took effect in February 1980, with post-drought subsidies being discontinued. Despite these changes, damage from successive drought events continued to receive greater and greater levels of government assistance throughout the early 1980s. Even though successive reforms of policy since then have aimed to increase individual and community responsibility for responding to drought, it is by no means certain that they have had the desired effect at all levels.

1986 – Review

By 1986, government assistance measures for adverse events were still seen to be strongly built into farmers' expectations, influencing their perceptions of risk (Sandrey 1990). In particular, it was considered that assistance encouraged farmers to produce according to optimum (economic and environmental) years, because it protected them from the costs associated with suboptimal years. Government assistance measures discouraged farmers from carrying out practices that would reduce their vulnerability to extreme climatic events, because the government was there to 'bail' farmers out (Dickinson and Sandrey 1986).

In October 1986, changes were announced that tightened the eligibility criteria for adverse events assistance and altered the forms of assistance that were available. The changes reflected the overall movement of central government economic policy toward a more market-led economic environment.

Meteorological criteria were developed to determine when adverse events occurred. For drought, an event had to be of such severity that it had a one in twenty chance of occurring (5 per cent annual probability of exceedence) before assistance measures would be considered. Drought was measured by the number of soil moisture deficit days occurring in the summer, or a lack of rainfall in the winter, compared with the average situation over a three-month period (Rural Policy Unit 1990). Less severe events, with higher probabilities of occurrence, were regarded as the risk management responsibility of individual farmers.

Before farmers could be eligible for climatic relief loans, the area in which their farms were situated had to be declared as an 'adverse events relief area' using the meteorological criteria outlined above. Second, to be eligible for a loan, the farms in question had to have been viable and meet certain lending criteria before the drought occurred, the event had to have rendered the farms as nonviable, and advancing the loan had to be able to return them to a viable state. Up until this time, the volume of lending through the climatic events loans had grown relatively steadily since the 1970s. Morriss (1991: 5) notes that the number of farmers eligible for the loans decreased significantly as a result of tightening the criteria, so that very few new loans were subsequently approved.

1988 – Disaster recovery plan

During 1988, a disaster recovery plan was developed to standardise the New Zealand government's response to natural disasters (Cabinet 1991). *The Recovery Plan: Natural Disasters and Emergencies within New Zealand* (henceforth Recovery Plan) was intended to coordinate the responses of a range of organisations involved immediately following a natural disaster. Policy for adverse climatic events still remained under the control of MAF, but responses to such events (as for responses to natural disasters falling under the control of other government departments) fell beneath the coordinating 'umbrella' of the Recovery Plan (Morriss 1991: 7).

The Recovery Plan is based on principles such as risk management by individuals and local communities, local response in the first instance after a disaster occurs, and central government assistance where recovery could not occur purely from local initiatives.

1988–9 – East coast droughts

In the summer of 1988–9, severe droughts developed on the east coasts of both the North Island and the South Island. At that time, the financial position of farmers in the affected areas was extremely poor, with rising costs, particularly interest rates, and low product prices. Farmers were in the midst of adjusting to significant changes in the economic environment (e.g., the removal of subsidies), and poor profits and falling land prices had reduced many farmers' equity to a very low level. Confidence levels amongst the farming community were very low, and stress being suffered within farming families was high (Morriss 1992).

In response to such factors, many farmers tried to maximise their short-term profits by increasing stock numbers to levels that were only sustainable in ideal climatic conditions. As a result, feed reserves were minimal and stock condition was poor going into the drought (Brown Copeland and Company Ltd. 1991). Thus, farmers were vulnerable to the effects of drought, in part because their capacity to absorb and recover from the effects of the extreme event was diminished.

Because the regional economies of affected areas were seen to be at risk, a drought assistance package was introduced by central government. This rationale, based on the risk to regional economies, had been used previously, to justify an agricultural assistance scheme to aid farmers on the east coast of the North Island, following significant damage caused by Cyclone Bola in March 1988. The effects of both Cyclone Bola and the 1988–9 drought were seen to be too severe for local communities to handle without central government assistance.

The drought assistance package included five main components. Adverse Events Family Income Support was available so that farm income was not run down by family living expenses (such as feeding and clothing family members). Drought Rehabilitation Loans were obtainable, dependent on the future viability of the farms in question. The loans were interest free for the first two years, with the government providing a guarantee of 80 per cent of their value for four years. Farm Appraisals were offered to assist farmers in making decisions about the future viability of their farm businesses, assess their rehabilitation needs, and plan sustainable rehabilitation and ongoing farming programmes. New Start Grants were available (up to a maximum of NZ$45,000), enabling farmers who were in an untenable financial position to vacate their properties and make a new start in another industry. The Technology Transfer Programme was designed to develop and encourage the implementation of improved dryland farming techniques, through research, educational on-farm field days, and the production of information booklets.

The assistance package may be seen as a transition between the old type of assistance policies and the new. Thus, there was a loan component, and direct monetary assistance to families, but there were also components designed to improve dryland farming techniques in the long term. Reaction to the assistance package with its transitional components was mixed, with some farmers viewing it as an attempt by the government to restructure agriculture, rather than as a package designed to help farmers cope with the drought *per se*.

A review of the effects of the drought assistance package was carried out for the South Island (Brown Copeland and Company Ltd. 1991). The effectiveness of the components of the drought assistance package varied. The Adverse Events Family Income Support was found to be effective in giving rapid assistance to those in need, and was reasonably effective in its stimulation of the local rural economy. Much of the assistance provided by the Drought Rehabilitation Loans (up to three-quarters of the money borrowed) was used to reduce debt. This meant that flow-on regional economic impacts on industries related to agriculture were much less than originally anticipated. This was similar to the effect of the agricultural assistance scheme offered following Cyclone Bola early in 1988, where many businesses were forced to close as a result of reduced spending in the affected area.

Farm Appraisals were effective in the provision of advice to farmers, making a positive contribution to the improvement of long-term viability for the farms concerned. New Start Grants were seen to provide humanitarian assistance to those in an untenable financial position. However, they were not particularly effective in changing marginal farming operations. Most of the recipients believed that they would have sold regardless of the grants, many of those farmers who sold their properties remained on them as farm managers, and only an estimated 30 per cent of the farms underwent subsequent changes in land use or scale of operations. The Technology Transfer Programme was considered to be successful in increasing awareness of the range of strategies for managing drought. The effectiveness of such programmes, though, would be increased greatly if they were continued over a longer period of time, so that long-term dryland farming strategies could be encouraged during nondrought years.

1989 Review

Even though policies had been tightened in previous years, government expenditure on adverse climatic events assistance increased significantly throughout the late 1980s (Table 36.1) and led, in December 1989, to a further review of policy.

The Recovery Plan (developed in 1988) was reviewed in 1989, and principles for assistance to the agricultural sector following adverse climatic events were closely aligned with the revised Recovery Plan. The key principles to be followed were:

Table 36.1 Annual expenditure on adverse climatic events assistance, 1968–9 to 1991–2

Year	$ (000)	Year	$ (000)
1968–9	316	1980–1	689
1969–70	477	1981–2	67
1970–1	3,541	1982–3	87
1971–2	315	1983–4	31
1972–3	192	1984–5	5
1973–4	951	1985–6	1,220
1974–5	145	1986–7	6,579
1975–6	263	1987–8	1,346
1976–7	374	1988–9	72,211
1977–8	203	1989–90	27,199
1978–9	6,054	1990–1	24,524
1979–80	314	1991–2	16,989

Source: Morriss 1992: 176

- individuals, businesses, and local authorities have a responsibility to ensure against and minimise or mitigate risk in advance of any event;
- initial and primary responsibility for recovery rests with the local community, particularly in the case of smaller-scale or localised events;
- central government has a role in the recovery process after a major natural disaster or emergency;
- any central government response programme should be designed to restore the community capacity for self-help in the future; and
- central government policies should encourage practices such as:
  - insurance of assets;
  - establishment of disaster reserve funds by businesses and local authorities; and
  - adjustment of infrastructure to limit the potential for damage.

The reviewed policies came into force 1 July 1990.

1991 – Resource Management Act

In 1988–9, a major review of the legislation relating to the management of New Zealand's natural environment occurred. At least fifteen pieces of legislation were reviewed, and one new statute was developed in their place – the *Resource Management Act 1991* (henceforth Act). The purpose of the Act is to promote the sustainable management of natural and physical resources. It gave local government agencies (regional and district councils) joint responsibility for the management of natural hazards, including drought. The legislation was drafted in a somewhat flexible manner, allowing each local government agency to decide which natural hazards are significant enough to be managed in each local area.

Successive reviews of adverse climatic events assistance, and the Recovery Plan, had alluded to the new responsibilities of local government agencies in responding to adverse climatic events. The Act formalised local government responsibilities in statute.

1993 – Contingency plans for emergencies

In December 1993, the Ministry of Agriculture and Fisheries published its *Contingency Plans for Emergencies* (henceforth Contingency Plans) (Ministry of Agriculture and Fisheries 1993: 13). The purpose of the Contingency Plans is to summarise the plans that MAF has for a number of risks and emergencies, including civil defence emergencies (where human life is in danger), agricultural disasters of national significance, and biosecurity emergencies. It is consistent with the principles of the Recovery Plan (developed in 1988 and reviewed in 1989). However, while the Recovery Plan considers agricultural emergencies only in general terms, the Contingency Plans deal with them specifically. Under the Contingency Plans, a drought may be classified and responded to as an 'agricultural disaster of national significance'. The Contingency Plans refer to and reflect the central government policies for adverse climatic events assistance outlined earlier in this chapter.

The Contingency Plans make a distinction between local events and national events. Local events are those which have impacts on the rural sector, but which are not considered severe enough to warrant central government involvement. For events such as these, producer organisations (such as Federated Farmers) representative of the affected groups are responsible for managing the local response, with the assistance of local government agencies. The Minister of Agriculture (central government) is advised by Ministry staff of the development of the adverse event and local responses to it. MAF has no direct oper-ational role, though it liaises with local organisations, and may be contracted to help such organisations develop disaster response plans.

Central government may have a role in responding to national events – those which are beyond the coping capacity of the local community. A series of actions and responsibilities operates in such cases. Local farmer organisations, in association with the local government agencies in the affected area(s), make a request for assistance to central government (through MAF). If MAF staff concur with the assessment that the impacts of the event are beyond the capacity of the local community to cope, it has to be established whether or not the event is of 'national significance'. The general criteria for an event to be of national significance include: an exceedence of meteorological norms; an extension across territorial authority boundaries; proof that responding to the event is beyond the capacity of local communities and agencies; more than one government agency is involved in the recovery operation; and considerable stock and/or property is at risk.

If it is established that the event is of national significance, an agricultural rescue coordinator may be appointed. The Contingency Plans stress that, although there is the capacity for outside assistance from the agricultural rescue coordinator, command and delivery responsibilities in the recovery operation remain with the contributing organisations. The agricultural rescue coordinator is only there to support local actions.

The responsibilities given to community organisations and local government agencies by the Contingency Plans reflect those given by adverse climatic events assistance policies and the Act. This reflects the devolution of responsibility for initial response to extreme climatic events from central government to local communities and agencies.

1996 – Further policy changes

Recent changes in policy include increasing the meteorological criteria for an event of national significance from a one in twenty year event (5 per cent annual probability of exceedence) to a one in fifty year event (2 per cent annual probability of exceedence). A new category of event has been created. Added to local and national events are regionally significant events, which may attract limited government assistance, such as social welfare grants and labour assistance.

POLICY, PRACTICE, AND PROSPECT

Since the last major reviews of drought policy and changes in responsibilities for first-line drought response, there has not been a serious drought in New Zealand to test the efficacy of the new system. Some other extreme natural events have occurred which give some indication of the way in which local and national response systems may operate. A number of issues have been identified that have yet to be fully resolved.

Determining the occurrence of severe droughts

It is still unclear what the 'trigger points' should be that would indicate a need for government assistance (Morriss 1991). Certain meteorological criteria must be met, and these have been made more stringent in recent years. But that is not the key factor. Rather, for significant central government assistance to be made available, a region's economy must be at risk. In practice, it is difficult to determine the degree and type of regional economic impacts that should be used as a threshold (Morriss 1991). The impacts of a given lack of rainfall in an area depend on a wide range of factors, including soil characteristics, type of land use, and time during the growing season. Preceding economic and social factors also affect the degree to which a lack of rainfall causes impacts at the regional level.

The degree to which central government assistance is provided can depend, to an extent, on the effectiveness of local farming lobby groups or local government bodies in persuading central government of the need for assistance. It is difficult to ascertain the extent to which central government's resolve to restrict drought relief to extremely severe events will hold in the future. In the past, in New Zealand and overseas, central government policy goals for a reduction in drought relief have sometimes been undermined as a result of various economic factors and political processes.

Long-term adjustment programmes

Consideration of New Zealand drought policies suggests that government assistance in the past has tended to promote short-term recovery, rather than long-term adjustment, to drought. Although successive governments have stated the intention to make individual citizens responsible for the management of risk associated with drought, insufficient effort has gone into the encouragement of prudent risk management practices in the long term. Indeed, Morriss (1991) suggests that there has actually been no reduction in the government's exposure to future claims for relief.

Central government does not currently have an ongoing role in the facilitation of practices that are likely to make farms less susceptible to the effects of droughts in the future. Although the Technology Transfer Programme (part of the 1988–9 drought package) did provide farmers with information on risk management techniques, programmed government funding into such programmes has now ceased. Researchers must now bid competitively for funding, but there are no guarantees that results of research are effectively disseminated to farmers.

Implementation of policies at the local level

Successive reviews of policies for adverse climatic event assistance have devolved responsibility for the management of natural hazards to local government, communities, and individual citizens. Limited research has been carried out to explore the degree to which these policies are effectively implemented by agencies at the local level. Research to date suggests that the implementation is variable (Ericksen *et al.* 1999, May *et al.* 1996).

Drought has not been included in the local government plans required by the Act to any significant degree, even in areas where recurring droughts have been experienced (Keen 1995). This may relate to the fact that before the reform of environmental legislation, local government agencies had only been charged with managing the hazards associated with flooding, erosion, and land instability. Staff and politicians in local government agencies are not accustomed to managing drought.

No severe droughts have occurred since the introduction of the Act. Many local government agency staff interviewed in Hawke's Bay, a drought-prone area of the North Island east coast in 1994, were unaware that central government had withdrawn its provisions for assistance except in the most severe cases (Keen 1995). The importance of local planning for drought may not be recognised until a serious drought occurs, where central government does not respond with financial assistance. In comparison, changes in central government policy for drought do seem to have had a significant influence on the way in which drought is managed by a sample of farmers interviewed in Hawke's Bay. Many farmers said that they supported the changes, with many noting that farming ought not be treated differently from other businesses under the government's free-market, deregulated economy (Keen 1995).

Some other extreme natural events that have occurred in recent years have seen local communities developing fund-raising mechanisms to cope with the losses experienced. Losses resulting from hail storms in Hawke's Bay in 1994 and 1996 were not significantly compensated for by central government. Limited aid was made available in the form of subsidised labour and technical assistance. Local government agencies coordinated fund-raising projects to assist affected horticulturalists. Even though assistance was limited for these events, that which was provided works against policies not to provide assistance for insurable events. Farmers may insure against hail, so government assistance after hail events has tended to work against self-help incentives.

Prospects for future drought management in New Zealand

In less than fifteen years, New Zealand has undergone a dramatic transformation from a social welfare state that controlled a mixed economy system to a commercialised state sector touting a free-market economy. Many would argue that this has meant moving people away from state dependency and toward self-reliance. Removing government assistance to entrepreneurial activities so that they respond more readily to prevailing market forces and environmental conditions was a key strategy in accomplishing this. New Zealand would thereby become an efficient producer and effective competitor in global trade.

The changing policies on drought hazard reflect these broader changes. By the 1970s, extraordinary and unforeseen natural events were the targets of large-scale public assistance programmes. For drought, this is reflected in the range of grants, tax concessions, and low-interest loans that farmers could obtain to help the recovery process.

It took a long time for government to realise that its various assistance programmes were counter-productive. In the short term they helped economic recovery, but in the long term they encouraged forms of farming in areas that were otherwise marginal. This led to a refinement in the meaning of agricultural drought, the scale at which it would trigger government response, and the criteria on which targeted assistance would be given. By and large, this meant farmers were to become much more self-reliant. Central government would only become involved if events were large-scale in nature and threatened the national economy.

Although successive policy reviews have devolved the first-line responsibility for drought response away from central government and to individuals and local agencies in the 1990s, it is by no means clear that this will result in satisfactory long-term adjustment to drought. A major drought has not happened since the policy shift was made. It is not until another major drought occurs that the ability of individuals and local agencies to cope will be tested. It is not until such a drought occurs, either, that the strength of central government's resolve not to provide assistance except in the most extreme circumstances will be tested.

ACKNOWLEDGEMENTS

The research for the thesis from which this paper is drawn was supported by student grants from the New Zealand Ministry of Agriculture and Fisheries Policy Division, the New Zealand Local Government Association, and the Centre for Environmental and Resource Studies (now The International Global Change Institute [IGCI]), University of Waikato, Hamilton. This assistance is gratefully acknowledged, as is information drawn from the work of Dr J. Salinger and his team at the New Zealand Meteorological Service (now of the National Institute of Water and Atmospheric Research [NIWA]). The views expressed in this chapter are those of the authors and not necessarily those of their institutions.

REFERENCES

Brown Copeland and Company Ltd. (1991) *The 1988/89 South Island Drought and the Assistance Package Provided by Government*, a report prepared for the Ministry of Agriculture and Fisheries, Christchurch: Brown Copeland and Company Ltd.

Cabinet (1991) *Recovery Plan: Natural Disasters and Emergencies within New Zealand*, report issued by Cabinet in July 1991 pursuant to Cabinet Minute CAB (91)M25/29 (also published as Part Two of the *National Civil Defence Plan*).

Dickinson, T.E. and Sandrey, R.A. (1986) *Government's Role in Adverse Events Assistance*, Christchurch: Agricultural Economics Research Unit, Lincoln College.

Ericksen, N.J., May, P.J., Dixon, J.E., and Michaels, S. (1999) 'Managing natural hazards in New Zealand: Is the Resource Management Act making a difference?', Hamilton, NZ: International Global Change Institute, University of Waikato, Working Paper.

Keen, H.J. (1995) *Without a Shadow of a Drought: A Hawke's Bay Case Study of Drought Policy and Implementation,* unpublished M.Soc.Sc. Thesis, University of Waikato, Hamilton.

May, P.J., Burby, R.J., Ericksen, N.J., Handmer, J.W., Dixon, J.E., Michaels, S., and Smith, D.I. (1996) *Environmental Management and Governance: Intergovernmental Approaches to Hazards and Sustainability*, London and New York: Routledge.

Ministry of Agriculture and Fisheries (1993) *Contingency Plans for Emergencies*, Wellington: Ministry of Agriculture and Fisheries.

Morriss, S.D. (1991) *Government Adverse Events Relief Assistance 1986–1991: Impact on Adjustment*, Wellington: Ministry of Agriculture and Fisheries.

—— (1992) 'Government adverse events relief assistance 1986–1991: Impact on adjustment toward sustainable land management outcomes', in P. Henriques (ed.), *Sustainable Land Management*, proceedings of the International Conference on Sustainable Land Management, Napier, New Zealand, 17–23 November 1991, Napier: Hawke's Bay Regional Council, pp. 174–80.

Rayner, T. (1990) 'The seeds of change', in R. Sandrey and R. Reynolds (eds), *Farming without Subsidies: New Zealand's Recent Experience*, Wellington: MAF, GP Books, pp. 13–24.

Reynolds, R. and SriRamaratnam, S. (1990) 'How farmers responded', in R. Sandrey and R. Reynolds (eds), *Farming without Subsidies: New Zealand's Recent Experience*, Wellington: MAF, GP Books, pp. 157–82.

Rural Policy Unit (1990) *Risk Management and Emergency Response to Adverse Climatic Events and Natural Disasters: Principles, Roles and Responsibilities*, Wellington: MAF Technology.

Salinger, M.J. (1988) 'New Zealand climate: Past and present', in Ministry for the Environment, *Climate Change: The New Zealand Response*, proceedings of a workshop held in Wellington, 29–30 March 1988, Wellington: Ministry for the Environment, pp. 17–24.

Salinger, M.J., Basher, R.E., Fitzharris, B.B., Hay, J.E., Jones, P.D., MacVeigh, J.P., and Schmidely-Leleu, I. (1995) 'Climate trends in the south-west Pacific', *International Journal of Climatology* 15, 285–302.

Salinger, J., McGann, R., Coutts, L., Collen, B., and Fouhy, E. (1992a) 'Temperature Trends in New Zealand and Outlying Islands, 1920–1990', Wellington: New Zealand Meteorological Service.

—— (1992b) 'Rainfall Trends in New Zealand and Outlying Islands, 1920–1990', Wellington: New Zealand Meteorological Service.

Sandrey, R., (1990) 'The regulatory environment', in R. Sandrey and R. Reynolds (eds), *Farming without Subsidies: New Zealand's Recent Experience*, Wellington: MAF, GP Books, pp. 98–114.

Sandrey, R. and Reynolds, R. (eds) (1990) *Farming without Subsidies: New Zealand's Recent Experience*, Wellington: MAF, GP Books.

Tyler, L. and Lattimore, R. (1990) 'Assistance to agriculture', in R. Sandrey and R. Reynolds (eds), *Farming without Subsidies: New Zealand's Recent Experience*, Wellington: MAF, GP Books, pp. 60–79.

Wallace, R. (1990) 'The macroeconomic environment', in R. Sandrey and R. Reynolds (eds), *Farming without Subsidies: New Zealand's Recent Experience*, Wellington: MAF, GP Books, pp. 43–59.

37

APPROACHES TO INTEGRATED DROUGHT RISK MANAGEMENT

Australia's national drought policy

B. O'Meagher, M. Stafford Smith, and D.H. White

Drought is a significant source of agricultural risk in many countries, affecting individual farm enterprises and those who depend on them, the locality and region within which affected enterprises are located, and whole nations. The extent and severity of impact will depend on the scale, intensity, and duration of the drought event. In extreme circumstances, particularly where food security is severely affected or where several countries are affected simultaneously, drought can have international implications. Whilst industrialised nations such as Australia do not experience widespread famine or deaths as a direct result of drought, this can be the principle impact in countries where a large portion of the population depends on agriculture for subsistence. The effective management of drought risk is therefore a matter of concern not only to those countries subject to significant climate uncertainty, but to the international community as a whole.

Drought risk encompasses human, financial, economic, social, environmental, and political aspects. These various aspects often interact in complex ways. Drought policy is therefore likely to be most effective where an integrated approach is adopted, taking into account each risk aspect and the way different aspects interact with one another. This chapter identifies the key elements of drought risk and its management, and examines the risk management approach underlying Australia's new National Drought Policy. It then describes some of the experiences of implementing this drought policy, and discusses lessons that may arise from this experience for Australia and other countries.

DROUGHT RISKS AND THEIR MANAGEMENT

Drought-related risks have been extensively documented and are therefore only summarised here (Table 37.1). The associated policy responses and techniques required to manage such risks are less extensively researched. The basic objective of drought risk management is to minimise possible adverse outcomes within the constraints of the costs involved. Given the certainty that drought *will* occur but the uncertainty about *when*, the management task encompasses anticipation of and preparation for the drought, and management of the various phases of the drought event, including drought onset, occurrence, and recovery.

Drought risks and associated impacts differ from situation to situation. For a relatively wealthy country like Australia with agricultural exports and extensive public and private social welfare mechanisms, drought is not a direct matter of life and death as it is in countries based on subsistence farming. However, the principles underlying the task of managing drought risk are similar regardless of the specific situations different countries face. In particular, the Australian experience suggests that an effective drought risk management strategy requires:

- effective information on which to base decisions;
- appropriate policy, institutional, and other arrangements for the assessment, communication, and application of that information;
- availability of an appropriate range of risk management tools for public and private decision makers; and

Table 37.1 Drought risks and impacts

Drought risks	Impacts
Financial/economic	
• personal/farm business	• personal/family disposable income
	• capital values
• local/regional economy	• farm and nonfarm incomes
	• local and regional adjustment
• national economy	• national income
	• current account
	• structural adjustment
• international	• aid expenditures
Environmental	
• biological	• native and domesticated animals
	• pests
	• vegetation
• natural resource base	• soils
	• water
Social/political	
• personal/family	• physical and mental health
	• education and personal development
• social dislocation	• suicide
	• crime
	• antisocial behaviour (alcoholism, etc.)
• political	• political pressures and uncertainties
	• policy uncertainty

• effective and consistent actions on the part of both public and private decision makers.

Given the range, complexity, and interaction of drought-related risks, and the potential range of decision makers involved, an integrated, interdisciplinary approach is required to provide a rounded appreciation of the problem (and of the appropriate management responses). Thus, the presence of a range of production and broader ecological relationships at different phases of the drought event requires close cooperation between different specialities within relevant sciences, and between scientists and economists. Again, the implications of an extended drought for fundamental adjustments to the size of an industry may demand close cooperation between economists and social analysts if efficiency and equity considerations are to be addressed adequately.

Even though the need for integrated approaches is increasingly recognised in international fora, few countries have travelled far down the track of integrating the various facets of public policy, and the integration of public and private decision making is even less well developed. An examination of the Australian experience provides some useful insights for the development of such an approach.

AUSTRALIA: A FICKLE CLIMATE

Australia, 'the lucky country', is widely regarded as a land of virtually unbounded opportunity, with its large area, low population, and predominantly sunny skies. However, the reality is that this island continent, with its ancient, fragile, largely infertile soils and predominantly arid (Figure 37.1), erratic climate, has a relatively low carrying capacity for humans and their stock. For much of the past 200 years, both farmers and policy makers have found it difficult to appreciate just how adverse the Australian environment can be and how this situation affects longer-term opportunities.

Australia has the highest rainfall variability of any

continent in the world, with variability generally increasing inland as the mean decreases (Nicholls and Wong 1990) (Figure 37.2). The continent is par–ticularly vulnerable to the influences of the El Niño–Southern Oscillation (ENSO) (McBride and Nicholls 1983), giving rise to extended periods of low rainfall ('El Niño') often followed by above-average years ('La Niña') in the northern and eastern regions of inland Australia in particular.

As a result of climatic variability and poor soils, agriculture in Australia is predominantly extensive (Figure 37.3). In small areas in southern and eastern Australia with annual rainfall above 800 mm, agri-culture is characterised by dairy and beef cattle, horti-culture, and prime lamb production. Most wheat production, in association with sheep, is located in the southeast and southwest, with annual rainfall of 300–600 mm. The balance of Australia's wool and beef production takes place in the pastoral zone, most

of which receives considerably less than 600 mm annual rainfall. Nearly half the area of inland Australia is desert or arid range lands with very low stocking rates, as well as monsoonal northern regions with leached soils and a pronounced dry season.

Eighty per cent of Australians live in cities within 200 km of the coast. However, the inland retains a significant place in the folklore and hearts of the country. Consequently, even though most of Australia's rural wealth is generated in the high rainfall and wheat–sheep areas, the more extensive inland areas often generate much more publicity when times are tough. These factors have had a profound impact on the development and implementation of drought policy in Australia.

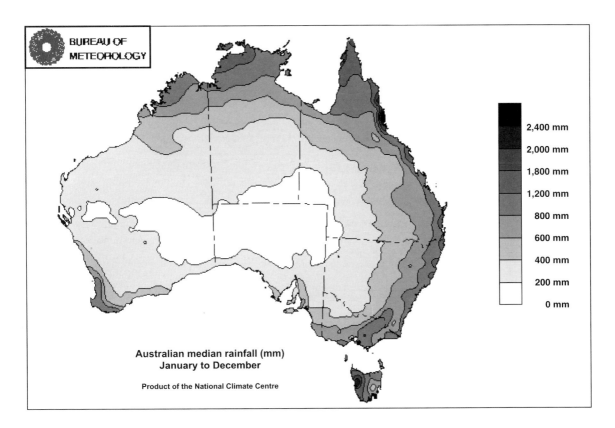

Figure 37.1 Median annual rainfall (mm) across Australia (Australian Bureau of Meteorology)

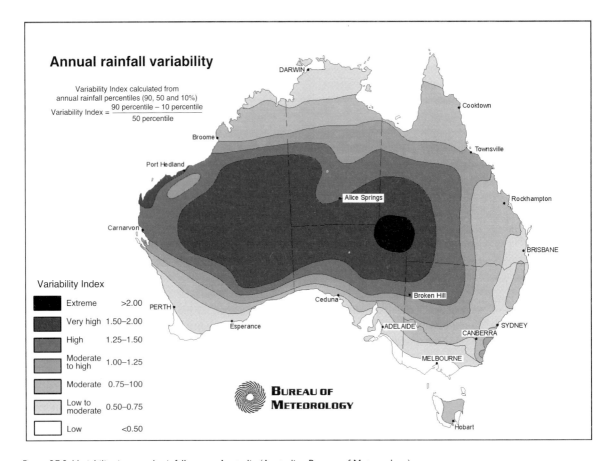

Figure 37.2 Variability in annual rainfall across Australia (Australian Bureau of Meteorology)

ATTITUDES TO DROUGHT IN AUSTRALIA: A HISTORY OF MISGUIDED OPTIMISM

The history of white land settlement in Australia is pervaded by misguided optimism, as the early settlers encountered vast native grasslands after crossing the Great Dividing Range from 1813. The interaction of false impressions, actual climatic and ecological conditions, and a frontier society's determination to unlock the land and master the environment led to extensive land clearing, overstocking, inevitable losses in productivity, and serious (and often irreversible) natural resource and environmental degradation for which we are still paying today. Early settlers and later generations failed to appreciate that what they thought of as drought was the norm, and that the application of assumptions and methods fashioned by European agricultural experience was inappropriate in this new environment.

Misapprehensions about the nature of climatic variability in Australia have been remarkably long lived, even amongst those most directly affected. During the most recent drought, for example, many farmers were unbelieving when confronted with the objective, factual data used to determine whether they qualified for drought assistance. Even for those who had kept long-term records of precipitation on their own properties, this was often the first time they had put the data into historical context. These misapprehensions, understandable in the initial decades of settlement as experience of the environmental realities of a new land accumulated, were supported long into the twentieth century by government policy

Australian broadcre zones and regions

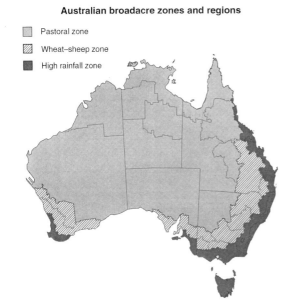

- [ ] Pastoral zone
- [ ] Wheat–sheep zone
- [ ] High rainfall zone

Figure 37.3 Australian broadcre zones (Australian Bureau of Agriculture and Resource Economics)

makers. Despite increasing warnings from scientists (e.g., Ratcliffe 1937) and other commentators (see Box 37.1), governments continued to support closer settlement, extensive clearing, and expansion of production.

At times, drought seemed to threaten these settlement objectives. For most of the nineteenth century,

dealing with the consequences of drought was largely a private matter for the individual farmer. Days of prayer during extended drought periods were not uncommon. This began to change at the end of the century when the several colonial (and sometimes local) governments began to compensate drought-affected farmers through more regular subsidy-based arrangements, although the timing and nature of such assistance was generally political.

The national (federal) government's direct involvement in providing drought assistance dates from 1934, when it helped drought-affected wheat growers. In the period to the 1960s, federal involvement was generally confined to the provision of funding to support state-based assistance schemes to stabilise the financial position of farm businesses affected by drought, through the provision of interest rate subsidies on debt, debt reconstruction, and transport, fodder, and water subsidies. Requests for involvement were still largely ad hoc.

The federal government's decision to establish the Natural Disaster Relief Arrangements (NDRA) in 1971 represented an attempt to rationalise federal involvement in drought and other disaster relief. Under the NDRA, federal funding was provided to the states after a threshold of expenditures had been exceeded; this funding was supplemented by specific measures from time to time, such as the fodder purchase and interest rate subsidy schemes in 1982–3.

BOX 37.1 WARNINGS IGNORED

- Droughts are nature's way of giving the land a rest, they should be looked on as beneficial, not a curse. [The fact that droughts are not planned for] . . . the fault is man's, not nature's
    (C. Potts, Principal, Queensland Agricultural College, 1921, quoted in Daly 1994)
- Man cannot call down rain from the heavens. . . . In the semi-desert country the intensity of grazing is the only factor that man can control; and as it happens to be the chief destructive factor operating, no programme for dealing with the deterioration of this region is worth serious consideration unless it has a scientific stocking policy as its first plank. . . . One of the most extraordinary and at the same time most discouraging aspects of the whole matter is the reluctance, amounting to almost stubborn refusal, on the part of the Australian people to recognise the inevitability of drought. The tacit assumption that drought is an exceptional visitation to the inland country has shaped and infected public thought and official policy alike.
    (Ratcliffe 1947)
- There was something radically wrong when 57% of Queensland was drought-declared every second or third year or drought-declared less frequently but for longer times.
    (Daly 1994; see Fig.6.5 in Young et al. 1984)

The NDRA gave some level of stability and predictability to the states, but it was they rather than the federal government who determined the overall thrust of drought policy. This situation changed significantly in 1989, however, when the federal government announced the withdrawal of drought from the NDRA and its intention to develop a national approach to drought policy.

A NATIONAL DROUGHT POLICY

The decision to withdraw drought from the NDRA reflected increasing concern about the cost and effectiveness of drought support (e.g., Young *et al.* 1984, Heathcote 1991, Foran *et al.* 1990). It represented a belated recognition that drought was a normal feature of Australia's agricultural and climatic situation, and that mismanagement of drought was degrading the natural resource base on which agriculture depends.

The Drought Policy Review Task Force submitted its report on a national approach to drought policy in May 1990, and its findings were largely endorsed by a bipartisan Commonwealth Senate Standing Committee inquiry in July 1992. In August 1992, the federal and state governments adopted the National Drought Policy (NDP), which marked a very substantial shift in drought policy rhetoric in Australia (Box 37.2). Reflecting the main conclusion of the Task Force, the NDP stated that 'drought is one of several sources of uncertainty affecting farm businesses and is part of the farmer's normal operating environment . . . Its effects can be reduced through risk management practices which take all situations into account, including drought and commodity price downturns.'

The goals of the NDP were to be achieved primarily by promoting self-reliance among farmers. However, it was also considered that there might be some circumstances that were beyond the capacity of normal risk management for industry. This had been a relatively small point in the Task Force's Review, but it was seized upon in the final policy-making process to justify the need for continued assistance in 'exceptional circumstances', at a time when there were signs that much of eastern Australia was heading

---

BOX 37.2   THE NATIONAL DROUGHT POLICY (NDP)

The *objectives* of the NDP are to:

- encourage primary producers and other sections of rural Australia to adopt self-reliant approaches to managing for climatic variability;
- maintain and protect Australia's agricultural and environmental resource base during periods of extreme climate stress; and
- ensure early recovery of agricultural and rural industries, consistent with long-term sustainable levels.

Specified *roles* for individual farmers and for government were defined:

Under the National Drought Policy, farmers will have to assume greater responsibility for managing the risks arising from climate variability. This will require the integration of financial and business management with production and resource management to ensure that the financial and physical resources of farm businesses are used efficiently.

Government will help create the overall environment which is conducive to this property management planning and risk management approach. We will encourage producers to adopt improved property management practices through a system of incentives, information transfer, education and training, landcare group projects and research and development.

Key *policy measures* underpinning these objectives included the following:

- Increased funding for drought research and development, and the inclusion of training about drought risk management within Property Management Planning campaigns.
- Financial support, savings incentives, and accelerated taxation depreciation, to help develop their capacity to better manage risk, including drought risk.
- Interest subsidies up to 100 per cent on debt *for farmers who could demonstrate long-term viability*, and income support (subject to income and asset test) during declared Drought Exceptional Circumstances (DEC).

into serious drought conditions. Specific arrangements for the declaration and revocation of Drought Exceptional Circumstances (DEC) were not determined until October 1994. These arrangements are detailed by White and O'Meagher (1995) and White (1997), and have been the subject of ongoing critical research (White and Bordas 1997).

For an area to be declared in DEC, its state government is required to demonstrate to the federal government that the area is experiencing a one in twenty to twenty-five year drought event that is of at least twelve months duration. Six core scientific criteria were agreed to as the basis for assessing DEC (White 1996). The meteorological state was defined as a 'threshold condition' (i.e., must apply regardless of the severity of the other criteria and must itself qualify as at least a one in twenty to twenty-five year event). The other criteria were agronomic and livestock conditions, water supplies, environmental impacts, farm income levels, and scale of the event. The process of using these criteria rapidly became more sophisticated since much of Australia around the same time had entered a genuinely severe drought period. Rainfall, agronomic, and environmental conditions were analysed to determine the number and frequency of similar events, increasingly taking into account rainfall effectiveness and defined growing seasons for different areas and farming systems. Additional information was provided by affected farmers, state and federal government agencies, and occasionally independent scientific consultants. These analyses were supplemented by visits by Commonwealth representatives to affected areas, financial farm surveys, industry data, and remotely sensed information. The final decision on whether the DEC conditions had been met was then made by the federal government following a report by the Rural Adjustment Scheme Advisory Council (RASAC) (an independent, expert advisory body). Revocation of support is made when it is assessed that conditions are such that there are reasonable prospects for a return to normal risk management by affected businesses.

The key intentions of the Australian approach may thus be summarised as follows:

- drought has been recognised and generally accepted as a normal factor of the Australian climate which must be factored into normal agricultural risk management decisions rather than as a crisis of natural disaster;
- effective drought risk management has been recognised as requiring ongoing research to provide information for improved decision making within a whole-farm planning context;
- for this change of direction to be successful, national and state governments have recognised that it will be necessary to change ingrained farmer attitudes and behaviours through measures to support a more self-reliant approach;
- a distinction has been drawn between those circumstances in which it is regarded as reasonable to expect farmers to manage risk and those exceptional cases where it is not; and
- generous income support has been provided where it can be demonstrated against specified, objective criteria that exceptional circumstances are actually being experienced.

THE POLICY APPLIED

The new policy was adopted at the start of a major El Niño event, so that the concrete policy implications of the new approach, in particular its six scientific criteria for DEC, had not been worked through by governments as the drought began to take hold. As an interim measure, all of the state of Queensland and some areas in northern New South Wales were declared to be experiencing DEC in September 1992, on essentially politically driven criteria. As pressure built up, assistance was extended to those areas of the state that had been drought-declared for at least twenty-four of the previous thirty-six months under the state declaration arrangements; although this was not a scientific criterion, it at least took drought support decision making away from purely political considerations.

The science-based objective criteria were announced in October 1994, along with new income, child education, and health support measures, as well as additional funding for drought counselling and drought research. These resulted in applications for support for all of New South Wales; much of Victoria; parts of South Australia, Tasmania, and the Northern Territory; and the Gascoyne-Murchison region of Western Australia.

Extensive areas were judged eligible (Figure 37.4), but several regions, including the Murchison-Gascoyne, Northern Territory, and significant areas of Victoria and New South Wales, were rejected on the grounds of failing to satisfy the meteorological threshold criteria.

Significant rain was received in many areas between May 1995 and March 1996. Reassessment of drought conditions by RASAC resulted in large areas being revoked for DEC purposes, with support ceasing six months after revocation. This 'recovery period' was subsequently extended to twelve months by the new national government elected in early 1996.

Table 37.2 summarises the incidence of Commonwealth support for drought-affected farm businesses and farm families in the period from September 1992 to December 1996. The total cost of all Commonwealth drought-related expenditure (including drought research) over the period is estimated at more than A$530 million (approximately US$690 million). The states are estimated to have spent more than A$200 million on drought-related activities (mainly transaction subsidies) during the same period. This compares with A$300 million expended by the Commonwealth and states during the 1982–3 drought and the A$70 million spent by the Commonwealth on drought support under the NDRA and RAS in the five years before the cessation of the NDRA in 1989 (during which time there were no significant areas of the continent which were likely to have been assessed as being eligible for support under the current science-based assessment arrangements).

LESSONS LEARNED

Although it is too early to draw definitive conclusions about the new National Drought Policy, useful observations can be made about the Australian experience within the framework of the broad

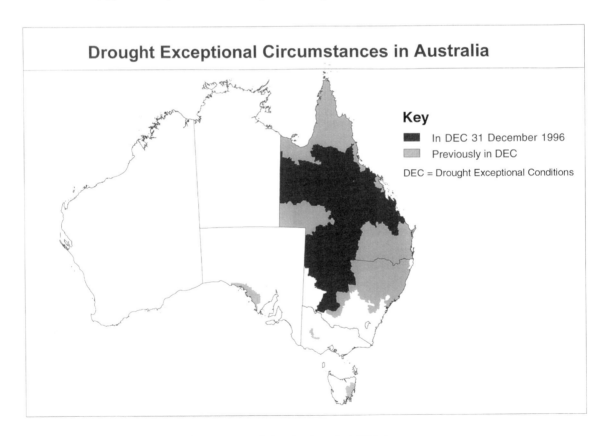

Figure 37.4 Areas of drought exceptional circumstances declared and revoked, 1995–6

Table 37.2 Cost of Commonwealth drought support measures, 1992 to December 1996 (A $million)

Type of support	1992	1993	1994	1995	1996
DEC interest rate subsidies	*	21.0	42.0	65.0	70.0
Drought relief payments			(a)	82.0	130.0
Exit assistance				0.4	1.5
Total	*	21.0	42.0	147.0	211.0

Source: Munro and Lembit, 1997
Note: *some expenditures in these years accounted for in following year

requirements for effective drought risk management strategies suggested by this paper. These are summarised in Table 37.3 and some key issues are discussed here and in the conclusions.

An integrated approach

The fact is that the implications of climatic variability, including drought, are inherently complex. An important general lesson from the Australian experience has been the lack of appreciation of the need for an integrated approach. This is particularly important for the different sciences involved (oceanographers, climatologists, and agricultural and environmental scientists, for example) and for the relationship between scientists and policy advisers. The dynamics of this latter relationship have been addressed by O'Meagher (1997).

The relationship between scientists and policy makers is weak at the federal government level and in some cases nonexistent at the state government level. At times, this meant that national scientific and policy advisers were forced to make science-based assessments for DEC triggering criteria at levels where state advisers normally would have been expected to have the relevant expertise. This meant that factors that may have enabled some areas to qualify for support may have been overlooked. Good integration between levels of government is thus also needed.

Effective and consistent policy

The need for effectiveness and consistency in policy

signals is self-evident. Too often in the past, political rhetoric favouring the development of efficient and sustainable farming practices has been undermined by the rush to provide assistance to farmers perceived to be in trouble. Wilhite (1993) has drawn particular attention to the aptly named 'hydro-illogical cycle' in the drought context.

With some important exceptions, the new direction in drought policy in Australia has been accompanied by a remarkable degree of consistency at the broad policy level, with bipartisan support within and between levels of government. However, evaluations of the impacts of some policy measures suggest that there are still internal inconsistencies (e.g., Tapp *et al.* 1995). For example, interest rate subsidies under the exceptional circumstances provisions of the Rural Adjustment Scheme are likely to distort financial markets and on-farm decision making; they could usefully be abolished. States' transaction-based subsidies also tend to distort markets and provide more effective support to service providers than to affected farmers. State and Territory governments were to have phased out these subsidies by 1998. Most have done so, but one jurisdiction has not yet done so, and another state is currently (at the time of writing) reviewing its transaction-based subsidies. More generally, the credibility of the policy depends on demonstrating to farmers that its measures genuinely accord with improved sustainability in management; this has not been carried out in a comprehensive way but could be with recent modelling developments (Milham *et al.* 1995).

Table 37.3 Major issues and lessons learned from the Australian experience

Problem/issue	Solution/opportunity
Failure to recognise that the problems are genuinely complex and require tradeoffs, and a tendency to seek simple/singular solutions	Need for interdisciplinary approaches and development of multiple tools (social, economic, and cultural) to be applied in an integrated way at multiple levels (policy, science, management); also, do not pretend that the decision-making process is trivial
Policy makers fail to use scientific information and scientists fail to provide information in an appropriate form	Need much better science/policy interface, achieved through mutual respect as a consequence of working together to address national and regional issues
Conflict between governments and government levels and lack of focus	Need firm coordination between departments and between states (perhaps an apolitical national drought committee), recognising the value of a whole-of-government approach
Bad luck arising from a drought occurring just as new policy was being implemented; inadequate time for education	Allow plenty of lead time for change in industry and among policy makers
Lack of objective confirmation of how well policy is really working, and proof of this to farmers	Establish monitoring of effects of policy in policy environment and of whether policy is really supporting sustainability on the ground
Inequity between industries and individuals	Need for transparency, equity, and consistency as policy principles (recognising limitations)
Failure to use existing planning tools, often because of cultural outlook	Need for appropriate education and communications instruments, and training and ownership in relation to the solutions; also need graduated 'drought alert' warning system to prepare people
Defining exceptional circumstances: – what is a 1:20 year event? – objective vs. subjective, rainfall vs. agricultural definitions of 'drought' – revocation	Simulation and analysis of agricultural systems to understand what these really mean in different areas of Australia; use integrated suite of triggers; open debate about the use of any trigger
Significance of regional differences and tendency to 'smear' solutions	Need to recognise differences and assess whether interventions will apply equally or appropriately to all (whether via management tactics, strategies, or government intervention)
'Lines on maps' – problems with boundaries	Spatial/temporal model of vegetative response, linked to remote sensing
Impact of 'distorted' urban views, via politics and media	Powerful opportunity for appropriate communications if done well; needs consistent communication effort with long lead times to achieve support
Banks poorly prepared, leading to poor support for structural adjustment	Important to engage them in process early and throughout
Limited links to other international and national policies	Develop collaborative opportunities, possibly brokered by a national centre for climate variability

Providing appropriate tools, warnings, and training

A significant part of the drought policy was research to ensure that risk management tools and processes were available for farmers to improve their self-reliance. Many advances have been made in this regard (reviewed in White *et al.* 1993, Bowman *et al.* 1995, Marshall *et al.* 1996, Meinke *et al.* 1996, and

Stafford Smith *et al.* 1996), encompassing both long-term matters such as stocking rates (e.g., Johnston *et al.* 1996) and the shorter-term tactics of drought management (e.g., Buxton and Stafford Smith 1996). Furthermore, the use of these tools depends on understanding the variability of the climate system itself, and generally the scientific community has been reasonably well placed for this in the monsoonal northern part of the continent (McKeon and White 1992, Stone *et al.* 1996). However, our knowledge of the dynamics of such variability in southern Australia, where weather systems are dominated by Indian Ocean effects, is somewhat more limited; considerable research is now underway on this topic, and the Australian Bureau of Meteorology has begun providing seasonal outlooks incorporating Indian Ocean sea surface temperatures.

However, many farmers are unaware of or unwilling to use either the forecast information or the financial and other risk management tools already available to them. The unfortunate timing of the recent drought in Australia meant that the intended risk management education programme was inevitably attenuated; longer lead times are required for cultural change to occur. As a result, farmers were often overwhelmed by the amount of available information during this drought. Australian farmers generally are having difficulties managing information flows effectively, and there is a critical need to develop better business management skills within an integrated, whole-farm planning framework, with an effort that is sustained over time. This must be coupled with improved information management.

An essential aspect of improved risk management is to ensure that the decisions that have to be made during drought times are not peculiar and emotionally draining – they need to become a normal part of management, simply with different outcomes in dry times (Stafford Smith *et al.* 1996). Regular decision making then needs to be associated with a graduated approach to drought warnings, comparable to cyclone warnings. A low-level drought warning causes people to start to consider their situation, but without precipitate action; as the warning level increases, greater responses should be expected until serious drought conditions are apparent. Such a comprehensive risk management approach requires some capacity to monitor conditions for drought alert purposes (Brook 1996, Hall *et al.* 1997). This is an area requiring further development, which could benefit from a greater degree of international cooperation (e.g., with South Africa [White and O'Meagher 1997, O'Meagher *et al.* 1998]).

A curious aspect of the recent discussion of drought risk management in Australia has been the absence of any substantive consideration of the role of private or public insurance as an alternative to transfer payments. As one commentator has noted, this is particularly curious given the extent to which global reinsurance technologies have developed over recent years (Mayers 1995). Certainly this would appear to be an area for further investigation.

Allowing time for communication and change

The attitudinal and behavioural changes necessary to ensure the ultimate success of Australia's new drought policy are unlikely to occur unless farmers and other stakeholders embrace the need for change. Many Australian farmers accept the need for a more self-reliant approach to drought but are as yet unconvinced that the current policy will necessarily achieve that objective in a fair, reasonable, and realistic way.

Why has this happened? The timing of the new policy could hardly have been less auspicious, given that many areas in eastern Australia were about to enter their worst drought on record. Many farmers were unaware that the drought policy had in fact changed, and others argued that they had had insufficient time to put drought preparation measures into place. By the time the new criteria for DEC were settled, public discussion proceeded in an emotionally charged atmosphere that was heavily influenced by media reportage (White and Karssies 1997).

Several lessons have emerged. Greater emphasis must be placed on a process of active engagement of farmers to build trust in government decision making and confidence in their own. This engagement should link disciplinary specialists and policy advisers with the broader agricultural community (particularly farmers and their financiers) through the establishment of regionally based consultative partnerships. These arrangements could help farmers and rural communities to understand and come to terms with the inherent complexities of the new approach and, at the same time, provide a useful feedback mechanism to governments as they seek to refine the risk management policies. The risks of politicisation of drought policy during the course of a drought would also be minimised. This process cannot be achieved overnight – it will take a decade of sustained effort to bring about a convergence of views and expectations among all the players, including farmers, their organisations, agencies, researchers, and politicians themselves.

Finally, the power of the media in implementing substantial policy change should not be underestimated. Even in an overwhelmingly urban country like Australia, city folk were fascinated by the plight of drought-stricken farmers, at least for a time, and some inconsistencies were highlighted embarrassingly. However, media coverage of the drought proved to be a net positive in policy terms' overall. As the details of policy were finalised and the science-based objectivity of the process became more apparent, media criticism ebbed and helped to legitimise that process. The media also played a crucial role in raising more than A$10 million in private donations (matched dollar-for-dollar by the national government) for farm family relief.

Extreme events and acceptable criteria

Given that the community at large comes to accept the general thrust of the drought policy, and risk management tools and training gradually become available, the continent will still be subject to extreme dry periods from time to time. Should there be such a concept as DEC with its accompanying industry support? The introduction of objective, relatively transparent, science-based triggers into the drought support decision-making process was a welcome development, which began the move away from the essentially normative approach previously used by the various states (and still used by some for state-based support measures).

Some Australian commentators have suggested the removal of the support trigger altogether, arguing that such a move should be accompanied by the removal of any special income support arrangements and that the income effects of drought, regardless of severity,

be incorporated into normal social security arrangements. On the other hand, such a social security network could be very negative for farmers, shielding them from the responsibility for effective risk management and undermining adjustment processes that respond to market signals. Furthermore, the political reality is that ad hoc support in times of severe hardship might still be hard to avoid. South African experience suggests that such concerns and the political pressures to which they give rise can never be fully overcome (White and O'Meagher 1997).

It is possible that the removal of the DEC arrangement should be a long-term goal, once the whole community is used to the objective assessment of rare extreme events. In the near term, however, there is a strong argument for retaining the current approach, but adopting a more comprehensive, frequency-of-event-based trigger, involving both rainfall and actual agronomic conditions and refined so that it is more regionally sensitive. Alternatives have been explored in White and Bordas (1997). If at the same time local farmers were to be more actively involved in the preparation of submissions against criteria on which they had been fully consulted, further objections would be met.

Some issues of equity and consistency remain, however. In general terms, cropping enterprises experience the effects of drought sooner than predominantly stock-based enterprises but, on the other hand, recover somewhat earlier, especially in cases of extended dry periods. A better approach to dealing equitably with both declaration and revocation for these different (but overlapping) sectors is needed. Additionally, one of the most vexatious issues during the Australian debate was the so-called 'lines on maps' controversy: areas defined spatially as experiencing a one in twenty to twenty-five year drought event could adjoin others that did not qualify for support yet appeared to experience virtually identical conditions. The media played a strong role in highlighting this apparent anomaly. Similar problems have been noted in South Africa (White and O'Meagher 1997).

THE WAY AHEAD

The way ahead in Australia will include better integration between the players in drought policy and management, a better ability to evaluate the success of policy measures, and a determination to improve international collaboration on this issue, which is driven by global forces.

A recurring theme in this review has been the need for greater cooperation and collaboration between the various agents and stakeholders involved – in short, the need for a more genuinely integrated approach at all levels. This must follow from a recognition that there are no simple answers to a complex question of interacting biophysical, socioeconomic, cultural, and political realities. Effective and sustained strategies for engaging relevant stakeholders and building their commitment and confidence are fundamental to finding these answers.

In these circumstances, a heuristic, continuous learning and refining approach is inevitable. Policy initiatives must continue to contribute to the prime objective of efficient and effective drought risk management, but detailed implementation will change over time. However, it is impossible to draw definitive conclusions about the success of any drought policy in the absence of a well-defined base from which to measure attitudinal and behavioural changes. This does not exist in Australia, yet the introduction of any comprehensive drought risk management regime needs to be accompanied by an objective evaluation strategy that lends itself to quantitative measurement of progress toward meeting policy objectives. Such an evaluation strategy lays the foundation needed for the continuous improvement of policy in a complex, dynamic situation. There also needs to be ongoing education of producers to ensure that they understand that climate variability is an integral component of the agricultural systems that they manage. They should be aware that government expects them to be more self-reliant than in the past in coping with climate variability, and that effective property management planning has a component of risk management that includes preparing and managing for drought and protecting the natural resource base. Many producers are probably quite aware of these issues in principle, but for various reasons may not follow this through in their current practices.

There is also a clear need for continuing drought research in Australia, which would benefit greatly from increased collaboration internationally. The climate system is a global phenomenon, and its study is a global enterprise. In particular, the Southern Hemisphere and the Asia-Pacific region share climatic characteristics with Australia, and it is likely that an international network of research on climate variability through this part of the globe will pay great dividends to all concerned. A national focus for drought research would be a useful development within Australia, perhaps with a coordinating national centre for climate variability. Such a centre could assist within Australia by integrating research and risk management across all levels of stakeholders, whilst also acting as a linchpin for international collaboration.

REFERENCES

Bowman, P.J., McKeon, G.M., and White, D.H. (1995) 'The impact of long range climate forecasting on the performance of sheep flocks in Victoria', *Australian Journal of Agricultural Research* 46: 687–702.

Brook, K. (1996) *Development of a National Drought Alert Strategic Information System*, Final report on QPI 20 to Land and Water Resources Research and Development Corporation (6 volumes).

Buxton, R. and Stafford Smith, M. (1996) 'Managing drought in Australia's rangelands: Four weddings and a funeral', *Rangelands Journal* 18: 292–308.

Daly, D. (1994) *Wet as a Shag, Dry as a Bone: Drought in a Variable Climate*, Queensland Department of Primary Industry, Information Series QI93028.

Foran, B.D., Friedel, M.H., MacLeod, N.D., Stafford Smith, D.M., and Wilson, A.D. (1990) *A Policy for the Future of Australia's Rangelands*, CSIRO Division of Wildlife and Ecology, Canberra, Australia.

Hall, W., Day, K., Carter, J., Paull, C., and Bruget, D. (1997) 'Assessment of Australia's grasslands and rangelands by spatial simulation', in A. D. McDonald and M. McAleer (eds), Proceedings of the MODSIM 97 International Congress on Modelling and Simulation, Hobart, Tasmania, 8–11 December, pp. 1,736–41.

Heathcote, R.L. (1991) 'Managing the droughts? Perception of resource management in the face of the drought hazard in Australia', *Vegetatio* 91: 219–30.

Johnston, P.W., McKeon, G.M., and Day, K. A. (1996) 'Objective "safe" grazing capacities for south-west Queensland Australia: Development of a model for individual properties', *Rangelands Journal* 18: 259–69.

McBride, J.L. and Nicholls, N. (1983) 'Seasonal relationships between Australian rainfall and the Southern Oscillation', *Monthly Weather Review* 111: 1,998–2,004.

McKeon, G.M. and White, D.H. (1992) 'El Niño and better land management', *Search* 23, 6: 197–200.

Marshall, G., Parton, K., and Hammer, G.L. (1996) 'Value of a forecast in wheat growing', *Australian Journal of Agricultural Economics* 40: 211–33.

Mayers, B. (1995) *Insurance Based Risk Management for Drought*, Occasional Paper No. CV02/95, Canberra: Land and Water Resources Research and Development Corporation.

Meinke, H., Stone, R.C., and Hammer, G.L. (1996) 'SOI phases and climatic risk to peanut production: A case study for northern Australia', *International Journal of Climatology* 16: 783–9.

Milham, N., Stafford Smith, M., Douglas, R., Tapp, N., Breen, J., Buxton, R., and McKeon, G. (1995) 'Farming and the environment: An exercise in eco-economic modelling at the farm level in the NSW rangelands', *Proceedings of the International Congress on Modelling and Simulation* (University of Newcastle, 27–30 November) 4: 221–8.

Munro, R.K. and Lembit, M. (1997) 'Managing uncertainty in the national interest: Needs and objectives', in *Climate Prediction for Agricultural and Resource Management*, Australian Academy of Science.

Nicholls, N. and Wong, K.K. (1990) 'Dependence of rainfall variability on mean rainfall, latitude and the Southern Oscillation', *Journal of Climate* 3: 163–70.

O'Meagher, B. (1997) 'Government policy and information needs on drought exceptional circumstances', in D.H. White and V. Bordas (eds), *Indicators of Drought Exceptional Circumstances*, Proceedings of a Workshop, 1 October 1996, Canberra: Bureau of Resource Sciences, pp. 11–15.

O'Meagher, B., du Pisani, L.G., and White, D.H. (1998) 'Evolution of drought policy and related science in Australia and South Africa', *Agricultural Systems*.

Ratcliffe, F.N. (1937) 'Further observations on soil erosion and sand drift, with special reference to South-Western Queensland', *CSIR Pamphlet No. 70*, Melbourne.

—— (1947) *Flying Fox and Drifting Sand*, Sydney: Angus and Robertson.

Stafford Smith, D.M., Clewett, J.F., Moore, A.D., McKeon, G.M., and Clark, R. (1996) *DroughtPlan: Full Project Report*, DroughtPlan Working Paper No. 10, CSIRO Alice Springs/LWRRDC Occasional Paper Series, Canberra.

Stone, R.C., Hammer, G.L., and Marcussen, T.M. (1996) 'Prediction of global rainfall probabilities using phases of the Southern Oscillation Index', *Nature* 384, 21: 252–5.

Tapp, N., Milham, N., Douglas, R., and Hoadley, J. (1995) 'A stochastic analysis of selected drought preparedness strategies in NSW', *39th Annual Conference of the Australian Agricultural Economics Society*, University of Western Australia, Nedlands, 13–16 February.

White, D.H. (1996) 'Objective scientific and economic criteria for estimating the extent and severity of drought', *Proceedings of the 2nd Australian Conference on Agricultural Meteorology*, University of Queensland, 1–4 October, pp. 78–82.

—— (1997) 'Risk assessment and management: Case study – Drought and risk', *Proceedings of the National Outlook Conference: 2. Commodity markets and resource management*, 4–6 February, Australian Bureau of Agriculture and Resource Economics, Canberra, pp. 98–103.

White, D.H. and Bordas, V. (eds) (1997) *Indicators of Drought Exceptional Circumstances*, Proceedings of a Workshop, Canberra: Bureau of Resource Sciences.

White, D.H. and O'Meagher, B. (1995) 'Coping with exceptional droughts in Australia', *Drought Network News* 7, 2: 13–17.

—— (1997) *Drought Policy and Drought Intensity Research in South Africa*, Canberra: Bureau of Resource Sciences.

White, D.H. and Karssies, L. (1997) 'Australia's National Drought Policy: Aims, analyses and implementation', *Proceedings of the IXth World Water Congress*, 1–6 September, Montreal, Canada.

White, D.H., Collins, D., and Howden, S.M. (1993) 'Drought in Australia: Prediction, monitoring, management, and policy', in D.A. Wilhite (ed.), *Drought Assessment, Management, and Planning: Theory and Case Studies*, Boston, MA: Kluwer Academic Publishers, pp. 213–36.

Wilhite, D.A. (1993) 'Planning for drought', in D.A. Wilhite (ed.), *Drought Assessment, Management, and Planning: Theory and Case Studies*, Boston, MA: Kluwer Academic Publishers, pp. 87–108.

Young, M.D., Gibbs, M., Holmes, W.E., and Mills, D.M.D. (1984) 'Socio-economic influences on pastoral management', in G.N. Harrington, A. D. Wilson, and M.D. Young (eds), *Management of Australia's Rangelands*, Melbourne: CSIRO, pp. 79–93.

38

WATER SUPPLY VARIABILITY AND DROUGHT IMPACT AND MITIGATION IN SUB-SAHARAN AFRICA

Ariel Dinar and Andrew Keck

INTRODUCTION

Sub-Saharan Africa (SSA) spans latitudes that include desert and tropical climate conditions. Precipitation over that part of the continent varies from near zero over the Horn of Africa and the Namib desert to more than 2,000 mm/year in the western equatorial region. The variable rainfall pattern in many SSA countries affects the entire hydrological cycle – e.g., water level in lakes, aquifers, and rivers. Agricultural productivity and livestock health in the semiarid zones are particularly sensitive to these rainfall fluctuations in already low precipitation areas. Agricultural supply in the region is thus very heavily dependent on water supply. The variability of rainfall and the problems it creates for farmers and pastoralists implies complicated management problems such as optimal water storage capacity, allocation of water among competing uses, and long-term water planning and conservation.

In addition to the naturally highly variable water supply, many countries also face periods of severe drought conditions. Droughts might be the result of long periods with low or no precipitation, or human-induced droughts that can result from, among other things, increased demand for water or poor management of water and land resources. Large parts of SSA are prone to severe drought, especially the Sahel and southern and eastern Africa.

Although variable water supplies and droughts are both hard to predict and to prevent, the adaptation of water resource management to these extreme conditions might ease their impact. It is obvious that in addition to general drought contingency plans, a comprehensive approach to water resource management may help mitigate the negative effects of water supply variability and drought. A coordinated plan should involve all stakeholders, including all affected sectors, and encompass all different water supply sources.

MEASURES OF WATER RESOURCES IN SUB-SAHARAN AFRICA

Precipitation

Four broad sources of water are often distinguished: precipitation, rivers, lakes, and groundwater. It is mainly precipitation that drives the amount of available water resources in rivers, lakes, and, to an extent, groundwater (see Keck and Dinar 1996 for data on sources other than rainfall). Table 38.1 includes estimated average annual precipitation in each country of SSA. Values of annual rainfall range from 135 mm in Djibouti (WDA 1988) to more than 3,000 mm in Liberia (FAO 1984), with nearly half the countries in Africa experiencing less than 1,000 mm of rain. Roughly speaking, the north, west, and southern semiarid areas have a single rain season, while bimodal regimes extend from southeast Ethiopia to Tanzania. Arid and semiarid zones (defined by FAO as areas with less than 75 days and 75–179 days of annual growing periods, respectively) constitute approximately 53 per cent of the continent. The semiarid areas roughly correspond to precipitation levels between 400 and 1,000 mm per year, whereas arid lands receive less than 400 mm annually.

Table 38.1 Water resources in sub-Saharan Africa

Country	Annual internal renewable water resources (million m³)	Number of stations	Precipitation: Average and range				Surface water Average and minimum river flows (cubic metres per second)			Groundwater Annual recharge (km³)
			Average annual rainfall (mm)		Range of station means (mm)					
			(a)	(b)	Low	High	MAD1[a]	MAD2	MMD[b]	
Angola	157,999	19	782	1,060	50	1,618	3,800	3,800–5,391	600	63.00
Benin	25,999	7	1,242	1,210	1,053	1,359	348		3.5	4.20
Botswana	18,001	3	501	416	470	562	406	na	5	4.70
Burkina Faso	28,004	7	891	898	534	1,182	215		55	6.70
Burundi	3,597	4	na	1,188	855	1,333	na		na	1.15
Cameroon	207,997	27	1,930	1,457	975	3,029	4,287	5,866	1,477	40.30
Cape Verde	200	26	na	214	59	432	na	na	na	na
Cent. Afr. Rep.	141,000	14	1,445	1,426	827	1,733	5,638	na	1,685	40.50
Chad	37,999	15	601	250	19	1,173	1,209	1,118	179	25.00
Comoros	1,020	3	na	1,877	1,095	2,635	na		na	na
Congo	802,001	14	1,583	1,696	1,266	2,069	42,885	42,145	38,119	101.00
Cote d'Ivoire	74,000	14	1,394	1,425	135	2,356	671	1,237	33.1	14.50
Djibouti	10	16	135	112	11	480	na	na	na	na
Equatorial Guinea	30,000	2	na	1,987	1,865	2,110	na		na	na
Ethiopia	109,977	12	750	742	239	1,778	3,257		311	30.50
Gabon	164,000	15	2,049	1,998	1,468	2,728	5,635		2,319	36.00
Gambia, The	22,000	1	1,227	938	624	2,054	153		4	0.80
Ghana	53,006	5	1,090	1,312	758	1,473	1,446	2,796	374	5.70
Guinea	225,999	8	2,224	1,937	1,334	4,305	2,582		263	28.30
Guinea-Bissau	31,000	2	2,156	2,007	1,956	2,271	259		84	6.70
Kenya	15,000	11	727	518	183	1,147	167		80	11.50
Lesotho	4,001	6	na	781	600	1,000	207	167	37	0.60
Liberia	232,000	2	3,403	2,592	3,373	3,442	505		196	31.50
Madagascar	40,005	12	1,559	1,449	409	2,731	7,794		2,094	35.00
Malawi	8,997	3	1,087	1,301	848	1,365	589	588	469	2.00
Mali	456,006	19	704	365	90	1,303	1,561		123	12.30
Mauritania	8,879	11	158	119	32	351	na		1,045	1.30
Mauritius	2,201	4	na	1,940	1,294	2,353	na		na	na
Mozambique	58,007	12	1,002	965	605	1,491	4,901	na	1,524	24.50
Namibia	9,000	3	356	280	149	563	na		na	na
Niger	43,997	7	320	187	19	701	998	1,157	53	6.30
Nigeria	308,042	13	1,562	1,265	646	3,014	1,712	5,900	204	58.70
Rwanda	6,303	2	na	1,003	824	1,182	na		na	2.20
Senegal	35,001	12	655	777	298	1,434	909		17	7.90
Seychelles		1	na	2,343	na	na	na			
Sierra Leone	160,000	13	3,310	2,878	2,161	3,700	774		97	16.25
Somalia	8,503	5	287	276	14	419	175	263	16	4.50
South Africa	49,992	43	na	522	39	1,292	na		na	na
Sudan	120,773	25	380	450	3	1,126	1,210	na	86	30.00
Swaziland	6,960	7	na	762	na	na	109	89	39	0.10
Tanzania	76,004	7	1,045	914	552	1,474	1,556	2,347	323	27.00
Togo	11,998	5	1,171	1,274	828	1,413	49		0.1	1.50
Uganda	66,008	3	1,490	1,267	1,173	1,552	1,274	na	1,207	17.50
Zaire	1,019,017	27	1,484	1,666	788	2,181	na		na	314.00
Zambia	96,004	7	973	1,029	743	1,277	na		na	160.00
Zimbabwe	22,997	4	831	618	601	1,129	2,816	4,000	1,143	4.50
							698 (excl. Vic. Falls)		140	

Source: Appendix 1 in Keck and Dinar 1996
Notes:
[a]MAD = mean annual discharge
[b]MMD = minimum monthly discharge

Rainfall and its variability as an analytical topology

Table 38.1 shows a considerable range of rainfall conditions across SSA. Based on this variation, it is unlikely that one set of water resources policies and management strategies can be effectively applied to all countries in the region. However, an analysis of conditions and water management for each and every country in SSA is not possible. For this reason, a typology has been created to group countries with similar precipitation characteristics. The typology is based on values for average annual rainfall and interannual variability. Where possible, these categories will be compared to information about drought susceptibility and mitigation presented in later sections. The chapter will also attempt to identify specific water management strategies to the different country groups.

Rainfall variability, measured as a percentage departure from long-term mean annual precipitation, has been previously calculated for all countries and presented in map form (Trewartha 1968). The map (not shown here) identifies three categories of rainfall variability (measured in interannual difference from average) in SSA: 10–20 per cent, 20–30 per cent, and greater than 30 per cent. In most cases, one category accurately describes conditions in the majority of a country. Each country was assigned a value of 1 (10–20 per cent), 2 (20–30 per cent), or 3 (more than 30 per cent), depending on which category of rainfall variability occurs in more than half of the country. Thus, although Sudan, for example, has areas that experience all three categories of rainfall variability, more than half of Sudan has rain variability greater than 30 per cent, so the country was therefore assigned a value of 3.

Two countries resist easy classification using this approach – Nigeria and Kenya. Both countries have nearly the same land area under two levels of rain variability. For Nigeria, the southern half has a low variability of 10–20 per cent, while the semiarid north experiences 20–30 per cent variability of rain. East Kenya has distinctly more variable rainfall than the west. In Nigeria's case, the relatively high average annual rainfall (1,561 mm) masks this fact. Other characteristics of each country were taken into account to select a rain variability value. Nigeria has the largest population in SSA, agriculture is its largest source of employment, and large areas within the country are susceptible to drought. Kenya, too, is relatively populous for Africa, and the semiarid characteristics that dominate the country make it susceptible to recurring drought. For these reasons, both countries were assigned a variability value of 2.[1]

For purposes of comparison, a second measure of rainfall variability within each country, the coefficient of variation (CV), was calculated from available time series precipitation data. The variables average rainfall and the two measures of rain variability were then used in a cluster analysis to identify groups of countries with similar characteristics. The cluster analysis produced four country groups. The two versions of rain variability generated the same clusters. These groups are shown in Table 38.2. Countries are listed in each group from lowest to highest average rainfall.

Generally, as one moves from left to right in the table, the average rainfall increases and interannual variability decreases (the two variables produced a correlation coefficient of –0.6365). Regression analysis was performed on all countries combined, as well as by cluster. The regressions test the statistical relationship between average annual rainfall and long-term variability of rain. The analysis produced an R^2 of 0.4052, which, combined with the correlation results, supports the hypothesis that there is a meaningful, negative relationship between average rainfall and interannual variability (not presented). Further detail can be seen in Figure 38.1, which depicts each country cluster separately. It appears that there are several countries that do not conform to the overall trend; these countries are Sudan, Botswana, Madagascar, and Nigeria. Sudan's comparatively high rainfall variability (CV = 92 per cent) skews the slope of cluster 1 to a slightly positive value. Botswana appears to experience lower rainfall variability than other countries with similar average annual precipitation. Cluster 3 also behaves somewhat unexpectedly, producing a distinctly positive slope. This is largely explained by the two outlier countries in the group, Nigeria and Madagascar, which have high rainfall as well as high variability. Both countries have climates ranging from semiarid to humid. When Nigeria and Madagascar are removed from the data set, the slope of cluster 3 becomes negative (–11.43).

Table 38.2 Results of cluster analysis of annual precipitation against interannual variability

Cluster 1 (135–380 mm/yr)	Cluster 2 (501–891 mm/yr)	Cluster 3 (973–1,583 mm/yr)		Cluster 4 (1,407–2,836 mm/yr)
		Low (973–1,242)	High (1,394–1,583)	
Djibouti (67)	Botswana (29)	Zambia (25)	Cote d'Ivoire (45)	*Comoros*
Mauritania (80)	*South Africa*	Mozambique (38)	Central Afr. Rep. (21)	Cameroon (47)
Cape Verde	Chad (67)	*Rwanda*	Zaire (25)	*Mauritius*
Somalia (71)	Senegal (57)	Tanzania (33)	Uganda (17)	*Eq. Guinea*
Niger (71)	Mali (59)	Malawi (32)	Madagascar (51)	Gabon (29)
Namibia (62)	Kenya (60)	Ghana (30)	Nigeria (53)	Guinea Bissau (17)
Sudan (91)	Ethiopia (76)	Togo (29)	Congo (23)	Guinea (41)
	Swaziland	Gambia (24)		*Seychelles*
	Lesotho	Benin (29)		*Sierra Leone* (25)
	Angola (68)			*Liberia* (21)
	Zimbabwe (33)			
	Burkina Faso (30)			

Note: Data for italicised countries are from a different source (FAO 1984), except Liberia and Sierra Leone, whose extraordinarily high annual rainfall separates them from other SSA countries in a cluster analysis. For simplicity, both countries have been included in cluster 4. The coefficient of variation is shown in parentheses after the name of each country. No data for Burundi

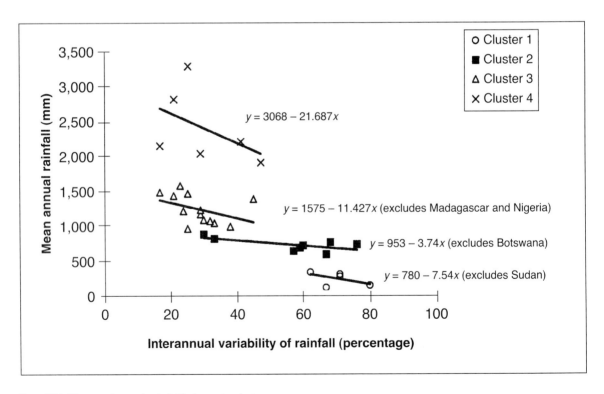

Figure 38.1 Linear estimates for individual country clusters
Source: Keck and Dinar 1996

REGIONAL WATER SCARCITY

The figures on total water resources per country presented in Table 38.1 are also those used to calculate water resources availability per capita in every country of the world. Three categories of water availability are commonly designated: water abundance (more than 1,700 m³ per capita), water stress (1,000–1,700 m³) and water scarcity (less than 1,000 m³ per capita). In 1955, only one sub-Saharan country, Djibouti, was already troubled by water scarcity (Engelman and LeRoy 1993). In 1990, seven countries (Djibouti, Cape Verde, Kenya, Burundi, Rwanda, Malawi, and Somali) were classified as water scarce, and South Africa was listed as water stressed. Based on the medium population growth projections of the UN, the number of water-scarce and water-stressed countries in SSA will grow from eight in 1990 to twenty-one in 2025 (see Table 38.3).

The water scarcity data serve as a warning to numerous African countries to give particular consideration to meeting increasing urban water demands in the next twenty-five years. Some countries, despite their arid conditions and small surface water resources (e.g., Mauritania), have relatively small populations and thus are less likely to encounter water supply problems. However, the inclusion of still-unavailable groundwater in total water resources calculations masks the fact that many arid and semiarid countries

Table 38.3 Water-scarce and water-stressed countries of sub-Saharan Africa in 2025

Water-scarce countries (less than 1,000 m³/capita)	Water-stressed countries (1,000–1,700 m³/capita)
Burundi (269)	Burkina Faso (1,237)
Cape Verde (258)	Ghana (1,395)
Comoros (620)	Lesotho (1,057)
Djibouti (9)	Madagascar (1,185)
Ethiopia (842)	Mauritius (1,575)
Kenya (235)	Mozambique (1,598)
Malawi (361)	Nigeria (1,078)
Rwanda (306)	Tanzania (1,025)
Somalia (363)	Togo (1,280)
South Africa (683)	Uganda (1,437)
	Zimbabwe (1,005)

Source: Engelman and LeRoy (1993)
Note: The values per capita are shown in parentheses

in Africa are now highly vulnerable to water shortages even though per capita resources are quite ample. Another aspect of regional water scarcity is the existence of many 'hot spots', characterised by large populations and little available water. In such cases, even though the average figures of national water availability per capita do not present any degree of water scarcity, localised situations can create big hardships. It is clear that climate and the structure of water demand also strongly influence the economic and human impact of drought when it occurs.

DROUGHT IN SSA

Drought history

Although drought is a recurring and permanent aspect of African life, that fact was not widely recognised until the drought of 1968–73, which spanned the Sahelian countries of Africa, including Ethiopia and Somalia. It is believed that drought was associated with the death of approximately 250,000 people across six Sahelian countries and led to mass migration of drought-affected refugees into unprepared African cities (Oyebande 1990). Agricultural production in Sahelian countries fell 20–70 per cent during the drought period (UNCRD 1990) and 30–40 per cent of cattle herds were lost (Oyebande 1990).

The Sahel region has experienced a near-continual decline in rainfall for about twenty-five years. Twenty-eight countries in the region experienced more than two consecutive years of drought during 1974–85, and seven countries experienced two drought events each lasting two or more years (UN 1986). The 1968–73 drought was subsequently eclipsed in severity and extent by the drought in the early 1980s, which affected countries across the continent. Finally, the 1992 drought in southern Africa has been labelled the region's worst in this century, with lost agricultural production amounting to 75 per cent for maize and almost 100 per cent for millet and sorghum (World Bank 1993).

Table 38.4 presents a partial list of drought events in SSA since 1900. The table provides a good perspective on the relative frequency of drought around the region. As mean annual rainfall decreases, the frequency of drought in a country should logically increase. A correlation analysis of mean annual rainfall and number of drought years (column 2 in Table 38.4) in each country was performed to test the validity of this hypothesis. The simple analysis produced a correlation coefficient of −0.6 when all countries are considered together. A similar negative correlation was found earlier in the analysis of mean annual rainfall and interannual variability. These findings suggest that the typology of countries developed in the cluster analysis also reflects the relative susceptibility of countries to drought. Again, the data in the table are not necessarily inclusive of all drought events, but there is sufficient information to identify countries more prone to drought.

More specifically, the table shows that Botswana, Burkina Faso, Cape Verde, Chad, Ethiopia, Kenya, Mali, Mauritania, Niger, and Senegal are the countries most likely to experience drought. These countries are followed by Namibia, Zimbabwe, Gambia, Sudan, Somalia, South Africa, Djibouti, Malawi, and Ghana. The search for data on drought history exemplifies the problems of long-term aggregate record keeping. More complete meteorological records would greatly improve the ability to predict and monitor meteorological drought.

The next two sections consider some of the impacts of drought, including the effect of drought on river flow (hydrological drought) and lake levels. Since drought is directly related to decreases in rainfall, the discussion of rainfall variability is minimal.

Water variability and drought

A basic question concerning water variability and drought is whether it is possible to predict drought based on analysis of rain station data and river flow station data. Analysis to answer this question is well beyond the scope of this chapter, as it requires detailed scrutiny and modelling of numerous climate-related variables.

The essential difficulty of predicting drought arises from the fact that drought is a gradual process whose effects accumulate slowly and whose onset and end are difficult to determine (Wilhite 1993). Nicholson (1982: 28) concluded, 'Sahelian rainfall cannot as yet be predicted on an annual or seasonal basis; long-

range forecasts of drought or even drying trends cannot be substantiated'. Writing more than a decade ago, Nicholson added that there is some optimism that 'in the not too distant future' seasonal or annual forecasts could be accurately made. Since then, the techniques and technology for climate monitoring and forecasting have become more sophisticated. Meteorological data and models, along with remotely sensed data (e.g., satellite data), are increasingly applied to the study and analysis of drought (Johnson *et al.* 1993).

Drought prediction relies on the use of long-term data to generate probabilistic climate models. Accuracy requires inclusion of numerous indices besides rainfall. These include the Southern Oscillation Index (SOI), sea-surface temperature data, remote sensing of vegetation conditions and soil moisture levels, and others.

One well-known index is the Palmer Drought Severity Index (PDSI), which generates a single number representing precipitation, potential evapotranspiration, soil moisture, and runoff (Palmer 1965). The Canadian International Development Agency has designed a similar drought monitoring system for Africa which incorporates rainfall data into simulations of crop and soil water balances (Dyer 1989). Unfortunately, many models and indices cannot accurately predict very short-term changes (daily or weekly). A more prevalent problem for any climate or drought prediction in SSA is the lack of reliable meteorological data in many areas (Dyer 1989, Bruwer 1993). A detailed assessment of hydrological data systems in West Africa concluded that in most countries, the density of rain gauges fall below the UNESCO/WMO recommended minima (World Bank and UNDP 1992).

The findings above imply that since the levels of surface water and groundwater are a function of rainfall, it is unlikely that they can be monitored for purposes of drought prediction. This does not, however, negate the importance of monitoring rivers, lakes, and other water sources. Changes in surface water levels can affect irrigation systems, livestock watering needs, urban and rural domestic uses, and industrial and energy productivity. Given the importance of surface and groundwater, what can be said about changes in the two when drought occurs?

Table 38.4 Partial list of drought years in sub-Saharan Africa since 1900

Country	Number of years	1900 to 1960	1960s	1970s	1980s	1990s	Longest consecutive drought (years)
Angola	4			75	81–2, 85	91–2	2
Benin	3			72,77	83		1
Botswana	18	1933–5	60–5,68,69	79–80	80–6	91–2	7
Burkina Faso	11		66,69	70–3, 77–8	83–4,88		4
Burundi	1	43					1
Cameroon	1			71			1
Cape Verde	13	1900,20,40,46		74,77–8	80–5		5
Cent. Afr. Rep.	1				84		1
Chad	14		66,69	70–3,76–8	80–4		4
Comoros							
Congo							
Cote d'Ivoire	3			77	83–4		2
Djibouti	6			74–5	80,83,84,88		2
Eq. Guinea							
Ethiopia	11		65,69	73–5,77–9	83,87,89		3
Gabon							
Gambia	9		68	71,76–9	80,82–4		4
Ghana	5			71,77	82–4		4
Guinea	2				83–4		2
Guinea-Bissau	9			76–9	80,82–5		4
Kenya	22	13–18,33–4,42–4	60–1,65,68	71, 74–6	83–5	91–3	3
Lesotho	6		68		81–5	91–2	4
Liberia	2				83–4		2
Madagascar	2				81,88		1
Malawi	6			79–80	82–4,86–7	91–2	2
Mali	12		66,69	70–3,78–9	80–4		5
Mauritania	15		65,69	70–9	82–4		8
Mozambique	7				80–5	91–2	6
Namibia	9			76–9	80–3	92–3	3
Niger	21	03,07,11,13	66–8,69	70–4	81–5,88		5
Nigeria	15	42,44,49,56,59	61	70,71,73,77	82–7		5
Rwanda	3	43		76–7			2
Senegal	13		66,69	70–3,77–9	80–4		5
Seychelles							
Sierra Leone							
South Africa	6		64		81–5	91–2	4
Somalia	7		64,69	74–6	87,88		3
Sudan	8			75–9	82–4		5
Swaziland	5				81–5	91–2	3
Tanzania	4		67	77	83–4	91–2	1
Togo	4			71	83–4,89		2
Uganda	5		67		83–4, 87,88		2
Zaire	2			78	84		1
Zambia	3				82–4	92	3
Zimbabwe	8				80–2, 82–4, 86	90–2	3

Note: See Appendix 1 in Keck and Dinar 1996 for list of sources

Hydrological drought, which refers to the deficit in the runoff of rivers, can be broken down into six types based on variations in the duration, season of year, or severity (see Beran and Rodier 1985 for greater detail). Different types of hydrological drought lead to sometimes very different effects. For example, if the minimum river discharge is lower or more prolonged than normal, this may have no impact on agriculture if the exceedingly low flow does not correspond with the growing season. In contrast, when there are significant deficits in the total annual runoff, both hydropower production and irrigation relying on reservoirs are likely to be negatively affected (Beran and Rodier 1985).

The results of various studies presented in Table 38.5 demonstrate the percentage deficiency of average annual river discharges during recorded drought periods. The table clearly shows that annual river flows respond to both single-year and multiyear droughts. The table does not show how great a single-year drop might be during the course of multi-year droughts. At Bakel station on the Senegal River, for example, the average deficit in annual river flow was 37 per cent over an eight-year period and flow was consistently at least 15 per cent below the long-term average, but in 1972, flow fell to 66 per cent below the mean annual discharge (Beran and Rodier 1985).

Of seventeen countries listed in Table 38.5, nine are part of typology clusters 1 or 2. These countries

Table 38.5 Percentage change from average river flows during drought periods[a]

Country	River	Station	Selected drought periods	Percentage decrease below average flow[b]
Benin	Save Bridge	Oueme	68–73, 75–7	42, 57
Burkina Faso	Black Volta	na	68–73	54
Cameroon	Benoue	Garoua	70–4, 76–7	32, 29.5
Cameroon	Sanaga	Edea	70–4, 77	18, 22
Cent. Afr. Rep.	Ubangui	Bangui	71–7	20.50
Chad	Chari	Ndjamena	65–77	22
Chad	Ba Tha	Ati	71–3, 75–7	53, 76
Congo	Congo	Brazzaville	84	21
Congo	Sanga	Ouesso	71–3, 75–7	18, 19.5
Cote d'Ivoire	Sassandra	Guessabo	69-73, 75-7	24.6, 20
Ethiopia	Shebelle	Malca	68–72	0
Gabon	Ogooue	Lambarene	70–3	11
Ghana	Volta	Senchi	71, 77, 83	33, 15, n.a.
Kenya	Tana	Garissa	76, 80, 83–4	53, 40, 27, 40
Madagascar	Maeverana		68–75	17
Madagascar	Mandrare	Amboassary	68–75	12 (68–75), 34 (72–5)
Mali	Niger	Koulikoro	70–7	20
Niger	Niger	Niamey	70–7	20
Senegal	Senegal	Bakel	70–8	37
Senegal	Gambie	Gou Loumbo	80, 82–4	23 (79); 24; 61; 43
Senegal	Senegal	n.a.	68–73	65
Sudan	White Nile	Roseiris	75, 76, 78, 82–4	0, 3, 0, 21, 8, 31.6
Sudan	White Nile	Khartoum	79	22
Zambia	Zambezi	Livingstone	71–2, 81–7	20, 32

Note: Drought years shown in the table do not necessarily coincide with drought years listed in Table 38.4 because hydrological drought typically lags behind meteorological drought. In addition, drought definitions may differ depending on the data source
[a]See Appendix 1 in Keck and Dinar 1996 for a complete list of sources
[b]Unless otherwise specified, values are averages of all years in related drought periods
n.a. = station unknown

are Burkina Faso, Chad, Ethiopia, Ghana, Kenya, Mali, Niger, Senegal, and Sudan. Findings in the table suggest that countries within clusters 1 and 2 (which have more variable rainfall and generally drier conditions) generally experience greater declines in river flow during drought. For example, river flow was more than 50 per cent below long-term averages in Burkina Faso, Chad, Senegal, and Kenya. Furthermore, the table values do not always reveal the lowest single-year deficiency in annual discharge. The Niger River in Mali averaged 20 per cent below-normal flows from 1970 to 1977. However, in 1973 and 1977, flows on the same river were 39 per cent and 42 per cent below average, respectively. Although wetter countries also experience river flow deficits in times of drought, the more severe deficits often occur in dry areas of these countries (e.g., the Benue River in northern Cameroon).

Although data on African lakes is less comprehensive than rainfall and river flow data, the impact of drought on surface water storage is fairly well documented. Lake Volta, created by the construction of the Volta Dam at Akosombo in 1965, has a long-term mean annual inflow of 36,268 km³. The annual inflow went from 150 per cent above the mean in 1968 to less than 60 per cent of the mean in 1972. From 1972 to 1990, Lake Volta's annual inflows were below the long-term average in all but four years (World Bank and UNDP 1992). The sustained low water inflow and storage during the long-running drought culminated in a crisis when the rain failure in 1983–4 necessitated reductions in power generation (World Bank and UNDP 1992).

The persistent drought conditions in the Sahel have also created problems for developments around Lake Chad. Although expansive, Lake Chad is extremely shallow, with average depths of 1.5–5 m. The Sahelian drought in the 1970s witnessed a remarkable reduction in the size of the lake. The largest water development scheme in the region, the South Chad Irrigation Project in Nigeria, has a gross area of 66,000 ha. However, the decreasing size of the lake has meant that only 40,000 ha were actually prepared for cultivation and no more than 7,400 ha have been irrigated in any given year (World Bank and UNDP 1992).

In comparison to precipitation, lakes, and rivers, there is relatively little knowledge of the impact of drought on aquifers of SSA. The country reports prepared as part of the World Bank/UNDP hydrological assessment in SSA often list the number of boreholes and tubewells and their associated flow rates. This information is important, but it is not sufficient to explain how drought affects groundwater quantity and quality in SSA. At a more general level, Beran and Rodier (1985) note that although groundwater is less sensitive than surface water to evaporative loss, it is also extremely slow to recharge. Moreover, overdrawn aquifers are susceptible to land subsidence, saline intrusion, and degradation of the fissure network (Beran and Rodier 1985). This suggests that groundwater dependency during drought should be carefully managed to avoid excessive depletion of the resource. Excessive surface water consumption or diversion can also lead to overdraw of aquifers.

ASSESSING THE IMPACT OF DROUGHT IN SSA

Overview

Drought events can have serious economic, social, and environmental consequences (e.g., relocation, famine, diseases, land degradation, loss of vegetation, loss of wildlife resources, and loss of human lives). Drought-affected countries in the region also experience a serious reduction in agricultural production and herd sizes. For example, in 1983, twenty-two countries in the region experienced a significant decline in food production because of droughts (UN 1986).[2] In 1986, about 185 million people living in the African dryland were at risk, with 30 million immediately threatened. Environmental impacts of drought in the region have also been significant. Over the past half-century, 65 million ha of productive land have become desert on the southern edge of the Sahara region alone (UN 1986). Estimates of the impacts of the 1973 drought in Africa include 100,000 deaths in Ethiopia (UN 1975); a drop of 2–15 m in water table levels of aquifers; and decreased flow rates in all rivers in the Sahel (UN 1975).

Drought impacts on agriculture, livestock, and human life are often reported as national or even regional figures. These figures, although helpful, are rarely sufficient to accurately assess drought impact. However, there are numerous instances in which researchers have made detailed assessments of drought impact on an individual country or even in specific regions or communities within a country. This section attempts to bring the two types of information together to provide a broad review of the magnitude of drought in SSA, as reported in the literature.

Tables 38.6 and 38.7 summarise the findings. The figures on agricultural and livestock loss are staggering. More shocking is the number of deaths during prolonged drought. The resulting response costs are often equally disproportionate to normal development assistance expenditures. A combination of lost production, livestock, and estimated assistance costs may be a viable basis for computing the value of mitigation and planning measures for governments and donors.

Agricultural impacts

Agricultural drought occurs when there is not enough moisture available at the right time for the growth and development of crops (Glantz 1987). This results in lower yields and/or total production. Moisture deficits also reduce the level of biomass and browse that pastoral communities depend on to feed their livestock. Table 38.6 illustrates the degree of agricultural and livestock losses due to droughts in SSA.

With the exception of Central African Republic and Uganda, the examples of drought impact on agriculture and livestock are in more arid countries in SSA. The declines in production of various crops range from 17 per cent in Mauritania to 70 per cent in Kenya. Most agricultural declines from drought range from one-third to one-half of average annual production. The implications of the lost production are more obvious when expressed in monetary terms. For example, Botswana's 1982–3 drought is estimated to have cost $68.9 million in lost agricultural production. The 1982–3 drought is estimated to have cost the whole of southern Africa approximately $575 million in lost agricultural production alone. These estimates include only direct effects of drought on agricultural production (lost yields). Direct effects are easy to estimate; indirect effects that might have a greater effect are more difficult to estimate.

In SSA, similar climate conditions sometimes prevail over enormous distances. As a result, drought may affect several countries simultaneously. Table 38.7 presents recent figures on the impact of the 1991–2 drought on cereal production and people in the ten SADCC countries. Across the region, total cereal production was 6.7 million tons below the annual requirement for the population. This shortfall is believed to have affected an estimated 20 million people across ten countries (SADCC 1992).

Livestock impacts

Pastoralism necessarily entails risk because of the uncertainty over the quantity and quality of fodder available for livestock from year to year. But at what point during a drought must pastoralists change their management strategies or risk loss of valuable livestock? One analysis in Niger found that two consecutive years of severe drought represents a threshold for the carrying capacity of pastoral communities as the residual biomass becomes insufficient to support herds (Sollod 1990, after Greenwood and de Leeuw 1983). At this point, massive animal mortality begins and herders begin to seek camps and food relief (Sollod 1990). In Lesotho, drought in the 1980s simultaneously reduced range forage and destroyed the herbage around livestock watering points. As springs and streams dried up, grass shortages became worse and herd sizes, production, and reproduction rates all declined (Molapo and Sekoli 1989).

Table 38.6 also demonstrates the degree of livestock loss that accompanies severe drought. For example, in an 82,000 km^2 region in Niger, the cattle population fell 88 per cent between 1981 and 1985 while total animal population plummeted from 535,000 units to 100,000 units (Sollod 1990). The 1968–73 Sahelian drought destroyed about 50 per cent of livestock in Mauritania and 40 per cent of livestock in Mali (DuBois 1974, cited in Oladipo 1993).

The susceptibility of herds and pastoralists depends on numerous management and environmental factors. In terms of management, herders are almost certainly going to move their cattle in search of more favourable grazing land if conditions deteriorate.

Table 38.6 Drought impacts on agriculture and livestock

Country	Drought year(s)	Estimated agricultural costs (in tons or $)	Agricultural decline as a portion of normal production	Livestock losses (number or per cent)
Botswana	1981–8		1/3 decline in tonnage (81–6)	30% (82–8)
	1982–3	$68.9 million		
Burkina Faso	1974			100,000 bovine, 135,000 sheep/goats
	1983		30% decline in cereals	
Central African Rep.	1971		50% of coffee	
Chad	1972–4		10–15% of cotton	1.5 million head
Ethiopia	1970–4			20–30% of original stock
	1984	300,000 tons		
The Gambia	1983		30% decline in cereals	
Kenya	1970–1	K£11.2 million[a]		1 million cattle; 300,000 other livestock valued at K£10.3 million[a]
	1982–4		50% less maize; 70% less wheat and potato	25%–75% losses in the north; 51% cattle and 50% small stock (84)
Lesotho	1982–3	$45 million		
Mali	1968–73	356,000 tons of millet and sorghum	42% less millet and sorghum	40% lost by 1974
Mauritania	1968–73	loss equivalent to 1.5 times GNP in 'normal' years		
	1974			50% lost
	1983–4		1/6 of normal cereal production	
Mozambique	1980–5	$75.1 million (83–4)		
Niger	1968–74			100% loss near Agades
	1980–4			In 82,000 km[2] area, 12% of 1981 cattle still alive in 1985
Nigeria	1968–73	706,000 tons in northeast (72–4)	12%–40% of the average (72–3)	300,000 head (northeast in 72–3); 4.5 million cattle in Sokoto State (72–4)
	1987	5 million tons		
Senegal	1968–73	435,000 tons of groundnut	44% of groundnuts	
Sudan	1982–4			90% of cattle and 25% sheep in semiarid belt
Swaziland	1982–3	$26.4 million		
Tanzania	1972–3		12–40%	300,000
	1982–7		56–75%	
Uganda	1986–7	5 m tons/US$4 million		
Zambia	1968–73			500,000 bovine (20%)
Zimbabwe	1982–3	$360 million		250,000 cattle died in communal areas
REGIONAL				
Sahel	1968–73		70% of predrought level	30–40% of cattle lost
	1984			30% of all livestock
Southern Africa[b]	1982–3	$575 million		
	1984	1.4 million tons	41% less cereal than 'normal' years	
	1992			75% of maize; most millet/ sorghum

Source: Keck and Dinar 1996

Notes:

[a]Expressed in Kenyan pounds. Figures are likely nominal 1971 values

[b]Southern Africa includes Angola, Botswana, Lesotho, Malawi, Mozambique, Swaziland, Tanzania, Zambia, and Zimbabwe

Table 38.7 The impact of the 1991–2 drought on cereal supplies in the SADCC region

Country	Annual requirement (million tons)	1991–2 production (million tons)	Deficit (million tons)	Number of persons affected
Angola	0.985	0.451	0.485	1,000,000*
Botswana	0.311	0.020	0.225	350,000*
Lesotho	0.406	0.079	0.295	120,000
Malawi	1.999	0.679	0.941	6,000,000
Mozambique	1.621	0.273	1.310	3,000,000
Namibia	0.191	0.033	0.124	250,000
Swaziland	0.195	0.042	0.120	325,000
Tanzania	3.846	3.253	0.327	150,000*
Zambia	1.729	0.872	1.040	2,800,000
Zimbabwe	2.814	0.721	1.860	6,000,000
SADCC	14.097	6.387	6.727	20,000,000*

Source: SADCC (1992)
Notes: *Estimate

Evidence from Zimbabwe indicates that herders are inclined not to sell their livestock if they believe the dry conditions will only persist a single season. When drought does persist, pastoralists are often forced to sell or slaughter some of their herd. Decisions depend in part on the composition of the herd and of the local economy. Susceptibility to drought is likely to be greater in areas where the entire community's livelihood is confined to livestock (Sollod 1990). In such circumstances, as the condition of livestock gradually deteriorates during drought, the livestock market price declines. The decreasing income from livestock increases the relative costs of grains and cereals, which may also rise in price during drought (Sollod 1990). Because cattle populations also typically recover slowly, the impact is felt well after the drought. Smaller livestock can reduce the duration of the impact since females can reproduce twice in a year (Fratkin and Roth 1990).

There are also apparent links between death rates of cattle and different ecological conditions. The clay soils in Zimbabwe have high potential productivity and grass production and so are preferred areas for grazing livestock. But when drought occurred in 1982–4 and again in 1987, death rates were highest in the clay soil areas because they require good rains to maintain high grass production. The survival rates of cattle improved in sandy soil zones whose grass productivity is not as sensitive to decreased rainfall. Scoones (1992) found that the survival rate from the 1982–4 drought was 17.8 per cent in the clay soil zone compared to 35.7 per cent in the sand soil zone. Given the differences between the quality of fodder under different soil conditions, it is not surprising that as the grass productivity collapsed in clay soil areas, pastoralists shifted herds to more reliable grassy areas in edge and sandy soils. Statistical analysis of movement strategies (Scoones 1992) found that the probability of cattle survival was greatly improved ($\chi^2 = 82.13$; Sig = 0.000 . . .), being 40 per cent if moved early, 22.9 per cent if moved at the height of drought, and only 3 per cent if not moved at all. In other words, the earlier herders responded to drought by moving their herds, the higher the survival rate of their livestock.

Human impacts

The lost agricultural and pastoral production during extended droughts frequently have repercussions for large numbers of people. Some more immediate impacts include food shortages, health-related low water flow problems (such as increased spread of waterborne disease), social unrest, forced migration, increased poverty, and loss of life (Wilhite 1993). Some statistics on drought-affected people and drought-related deaths in Africa are summarised in Table 38.8.

Table 38.8 provides perhaps the clearest indicators of the most severely drought-prone countries since OFDA only reports those countries that required US

Table 38.8 Social consequences of drought in sub-Saharan Africa

Country	Year(s)	Total affected population	Deaths	Country	Year(s)	Total affected population	Deaths
Angola	1985	500,000	na	Madagascar	1981	1,000,000	na
Benin	1972	115,000	na		1988	116,500	na
Botswana	1965	60,000	na	Mali	1969–73	1,900,000	na
	1968	60,000	na		1980–4	1,500,000	na
	1969–70	87,600	na	Mauritania	1965	46,000	na
	1982–7	2–3,000,000	na		1969–73	1,300,000	na
Burkina Faso	1969–73	300,000	na		1976–7	1,420,000	na
	1977	442,000	na		1978–9	27,000	na
	1983–4	2,500,000	na		1983–4	1,600,000	na
	1988	200,000	na	Mozambique	1980–5	2.5–6,000,000	100,000 in 1981
Cameroon	1971	400,000	na	Niger	1968–74	1,600,000	na
Cape Verde	1900,20,40,46	na	85,000		1983–5	3,500,000	na
Chad	1969–73	900,000	na		1988	1,000,000	na
	1976–7	1,900,000	na	Rwanda	1976–7	1,700,000	na
	1980–4	2,100,000	3,000	Sao Tome and Principe	1984	93,000	na
Djibouti	1980	145,000	na	Senegal	1969–73	1,400,000	na
	1983	80,000	na		1977–8	3,715,000	na
	1988	30,000	na		1979–80	950,000	na
Ethiopia	1965	1,500,000	2,000		1983	1,200,000	na
	1973	3,000,000	100,000	Somalia	1964	700,000	50
	1977–8	1,400,000	na		1969–77	230,000	19,000
	1983–4	7,750,000	300,000		1987–8	553,500	na
	1987	330,000	367	Sudan	1983–4	8,500,000	na
	1989	5,000,000	na	Tanzania	1967	53,483	na
The Gambia	1968	180,000	na		1977	20,000	na
	1971	150,000	na		1984	1,900,000	na
Ghana	1971	12,000	na	Togo	1971	150,000	na
Kenya	1965	260,000	na		1989	400,000	na
	1971	150,000	na	Uganda	1967	25,000	na
	1980	40,000	na		1987	331,000	na
	1984	600,000	na		1988–9	600,000	na
Lesotho	1968	204,000	na	Zaire	1978–9	500,000	na
	1984	500,000	na		1984	300,000	na

Source: Office of Foreign Disaster Assistance 1990

government relief assistance for drought. A quick review of countries in the table reveals that eleven out of twenty-seven are among the more humid countries included in the typology clusters 3 and 4. Of the thirteen countries that received US drought relief assistance at least three times (through 1989), all but two (Uganda and Tanzania) are within clusters 1 and 2, and five of them are among the driest countries in cluster 1.

Although it is clear that drought can lead to famine,

death, and relocation, there are numerous compli-cating political and economic factors that can exacerbate the impacts of drought and extend them over a much longer time horizon than might other-wise occur.

Economic impacts

The list of potential economic impacts of drought is extensive. The more immediate losses in agricultural production (crops, livestock, forestry and fisheries) may consequently decrease national income; increase food prices and unemployment; increase the costs of water supply, energy provision, and industrial processes; and decrease government revenues (Wilhite 1993). The links between drought and the economy can be difficult to distinguish and require in-depth investigation.

Despite the complications of tracing drought's impacts on gross national product (GNP) or gross domestic product (GDP), the direct costs of drought response are often easy to determine. Drought can lead to massive public expenditures as well as increases in loans. Government costs can include emergency subsidy programmes, direct food aid, loans, and emergency medical services, among others. For example, the 1991–2 drought in Zimbabwe led the government to propose a multifaceted drought recovery and mitigation project at a cost of US$1.044 billion (World Bank 1993). Following the 1992 drought in Kenya, the government pursued a drought recovery programme estimated to cost nearly US$30 million (World Bank 1993).

The total drought-related costs incurred by the government of Botswana and donors from 1979 to 1989 is presented in Table 38.9. In Botswana's case, the six-year drought programme (1982–3 to 1987–8), accounted for 14 per cent of the government's development expenditures during the period (Valentine 1993). Over the same period, the real, nonrecurrent expenditures of the government and donors on drought relief were equal to nearly half of the contribution of the agricultural sector to GDP (Valentine 1993).

Besides trying to quantify direct and indirect response costs, some researchers have sought to quantify the impact of drought on economic activity. Numerous techniques have been applied. Simplified approaches include a regression of GDP or agricultural production against rainfall (see Webb, von Braun, and Yohannes 1992 or Wisner 1976). More complex techniques include detailed analysis of livestock and macroeconomic modelling.

A recent analysis by the Overseas Development Institute of the impact of drought on macroeconomic performance in six SSA countries (Burkina Faso, Ethiopia, Kenya, Senegal, Zambia, and Zimbabwe) illustrates the difficulty of isolating drought impact. It shows that drought impact seems to vary with the structure of a country's economy. Burkina Faso and Ethiopia are listed as *simple* economies because agriculture represents a substantial part of GDP and there is a large rural population. Kenya, although similar, has a larger nonagricultural sector and therefore has some characteristics of an *intermediate* economy. Senegal also is closer to an intermediate economy. The relatively developed manufacturing sector in Zimbabwe moves it distinctly into the category of intermediate economy. Finally, Zambia's important minerals sector categorises it as a more *dualistic* economy.

Of the six countries, it appears that the lowest income, simple economy countries (Burkina Faso and Ethiopia) are possibly less vulnerable economically than more complex economies (Benson and Clay 1994). More specifically, the study finds that drought had the least impact on nonagricultural GDP in these two countries. Zambia's dualistic economy is also believed to have acted as a buffer against serious drought impact. However, this does not imply that drought has less of an impact on individuals and households in the simple economy countries; rather, 'due to the weak inter-sectoral linkages, a high degree of self-provisioning and relatively small non-agricultural sectors, the multiplier effect throughout the rest of the economy is fairly limited . . . and the effects of drought are likely to be concentrated in the rural economy' (Benson and Clay 1994). Thus the effect of drought on the simple economy countries, Burkina Faso and Mali, is different in nature from that experienced in the more complex economies in Senegal and Zimbabwe.

Beyond agriculture, drought also creates problems for urban water supply and industrial/energy production. Benson and Clay (1994) note that the 1991–2 drought in Zimbabwe reduced the country's manufacturing output by 9.3 per cent in 1992. The decline arose because of water shortages through rationing, a shortage of electricity, changes in supply of inputs, reductions in demand, and poor macroeconomic conditions.

Table 38.9 Combined drought relief and accelerated rain-fed arable programme (ARAP) expenditures, in drought and recovery periods in Botswana (millions of Pula)[a]

	1979–80	1980–1	1981–2	1982–3	1983–4	1984–5	1985–6	1986–7	1987–8	1988–9
Rainfall of previous year: arable areas (%)	−26	+7	+28	**−16**	**−18**	**−21**	**−38**	**−34**	**−19**	+41
Govt. development expenditure on drought programmes	3.05	2.67	0.98	**5.41**	**11.95**	**30.29**	**44.31**	**56.83**	**88.40**	92.73
Donor funding on drought programmes[b]	0.81	0.39	0.23	**0.74**	**0.71**	**2.2**	**3.35**	**6.65**	**12.85**	
Total govt. development expenditures	3.86	3.06	1.21	**6.15**	**12.66**	**32.49**	**47.66**	**63.48**	**101.25**	
Government drought expenditure as percentage of total development expenditure (%)	3.10	0.20	0.81	**3.37**	**8.50**	**14.44**	**17.90**	**14.02**	**15.84**	11.63
Donor funding as percentage of total expenditure on drought (%)	26.6	14.6	23.5	**13.7**	**5.9**	**7.3**	**7.6**	**11.7**	**14.5**	

Source: Republic of Botswana (various years) and Rural Development Unit, Ministry of Finance and Development Planning, Botswana. Reported in Valentine (1993)
Notes:
[a]Figures in bold are drought years (1982–3 to 1987–8). Negative values imply a reduction in rainfall compared to previous year
[b]Excludes donor support in-kind (i.e., food aid)

Environmental impact

In general, the relationships between drought and environmental problems are somewhat contentious. Drought events typically serve to intensify or extend existing environmental problems such as soil erosion, desertification, and salinisation. These problems, in turn, are often the result of human overuse or mismanagement of available resources. For example, arid, semiarid, and even subhumid zones are susceptible to desertification during times of dry climate conditions. But this susceptibility is often linked to human activities in those areas. Waterholes can be overused by grazing livestock, boreholes can be overexploited where groundwater is too shallow, and, in general, clearing land of vegetation can lower the water table and make it impossible to live off the land.

Pastoral strategies of maximising herd size for unexpected events such as drought are often criticised by ecologists (Pratt and Gwynn 1977) for contributing to range land degradation from overstocking. Where overstocking occurs, drought events can be unusually harsh on land quality. In South Africa, where the natural veld is overstocked by approximately 50–60 per cent, widespread land degradation has occurred. There are recommended normal stocking rates (e.g., 6 ha/livestock unit) that are intended to maintain a balance between pro-duction potential of land for fodder and livestock (Bruwer 1993).

Wetlands and natural habitat are also likely to be affected by drought. Unfortunately, to date we are unable to obtain relevant information documenting the impact of drought on wetlands and natural habitat.

DROUGHT MONITORING, WARNING, AND RESPONSE

Conceptual issues

The impact of drought in Africa has obviously been severe over the past twenty-five to thirty years. Many SSA countries have responded with drought miti-gation programmes and famine early warning systems. With continued population growth, the increasing demand for water (particularly in urban areas) will make comprehensive water policies and planning a key element in drought mitigation. This section takes a look at drought monitoring, warning, and response systems in SSA, with a special interest in how water resources management is incorporated into those systems. Examples from India, Israel, and the United States are included in Appendix 3 of Keck and Dinar (1996) to illustrate how countries in other regions describe how they manage water resources during drought.

There are two basic perspectives that countries might take in the process of planning for drought. One perspective is to consider drought as a random natural disaster. Based on this approach, planning tends to be ad hoc, with a focus on implementation of assistance measures such as subsidies and food aid only when drought has created a noticeable problem for all or part of the population. Similarly, weather-dependent producers fail to take precaution-ary measures (e.g., grain stocking, increasing water efficiency, or diversifying sources of income) that can buffer their losses when drought recurs. As long as weather conditions are favourable, governments are often apathetic and reluctant to develop long-term drought mitigation plans (Wilhite 1993).

An alternative perspective is to treat drought as a recurring phenomenon with likely effects on the population and the economy. This suggests a more proactive approach to drought management based on assessment of the potential for drought and esti-mation of its duration and severity. Such a system entails defining strategies and policies to implement both before and during a drought. The recurring long-term droughts of the 1970s and 1980s and the recent drought across southern Africa have increased the awareness of governments and donors of the advantages such an approach can offer.

In general, a crisis management approach to drought long dominated policy making in developed and developing countries alike (Wilhite 1993). Perhaps because of the devastating impacts of drought in the 1970s and 1980s, an increasing number of countries are pursuing a more proactive approach that empha-sises the principles of risk management and sustain-able development (Wilhite 1993).

From scrutiny of the available data in Keck and Dinar (1996), some patterns of best drought prepared-ness practices in the region have been observed. These best practices are organised according to the three drought-prone typologies (Table 38.10).

WATER MANAGEMENT FOR DROUGHT

Discussions of drought impact and how to mitigate and respond to drought typically focus on agricultural and pastoral aspects. The country cases from SSA illustrate this tendency. This approach to the problem is not unique to African countries. However, better water management is critical, for reasons clearly explained in Benson and Clay (1994). From a per-spective of water use, hydrological drought can affect available water for an ever-expanding irrigated area in Africa. Similarly, hydroelectric services (particularly important in Zambia, Zimbabwe, Ghana, and Mozambique) can be affected. Adequate and safe water for domestic use can become increasingly problematic as Africa's urban populations continue to grow rapidly. It already has been a problem in places like Windhoek, Namibia. Finally, tourism and related services might be affected by water shortfalls. All these sectoral demands point to the growing importance of monitoring and managing water storage and supply systems. The India case study (Appendix 3, Keck and Dinar 1996) illustrates the

Table 38.10 Best drought preparedness practices in SSA countries, by typologies

Typology 1	Typology 2	Typology 3
Long-term drought prediction (rain)	Ad-hoc responses Early warning	Early warning for food (yields)
Satellite, early warning	Data collection, interpretation	
Household and industry restriction and penalty tariffs	Restrictions on GW pumping, irrigation and connections	
Public campaign		
Pumpdown storage	New water sources Dam construction	
Livestock subsidies	Agricultural production support Rehabilitation: – agricultural inputs – livestock restocking – water reservoir development	
Food for work	Food for work	
Free food	Food distribution	
Emergency water supply units (pipes, pumps, tankers)	Rural emergency programmes (drilling wells)	drilling boreholes

Source: After Keck and Dinar 1996

potential interventions that African countries should consider for a water resources master plan.

Typically, rural communities in drought-prone areas have managed their vulnerability by storing harvests and diversifying their livelihoods (e.g., crops, cattle, and off-farm employment). Population growth and the sometimes resulting degradation of natural resources is one set of circumstances that can undermine the ability of communities to cope with drought. This is particularly true in dryland areas. It is often recommended that economies diversify to include agro-industry or various tertiary products, which could move some of the population out of direct farm employment and create new forms of income.

DISCUSSION

In SSA, many countries already face scarce and/or highly variable water supplies. The high population growth in the region has increased competition for the available water among agriculture, urban, hydropower and industrial, and environmental interests. Drought in Africa aggravates these particular prob-

lems through its negative impacts on agricultural production and livestock and the subsequent food scarcity that tends to destabilise communities. There are also urban and industrial water supply problems associated with drought. Combined, these impacts can harm overall economies through a reduced GDP, higher unemployment, skewed prices, and lower government revenues. The environmental impacts of drought include higher soil erosion, desertification, salinisation, and wetlands loss.

The repeatedly devastating effect of drought in SSA accentuates the importance of improving water resources management strategies in the region. This chapter focuses on the high variability of rainfall and water availability in Africa and understanding how they are related to drought. In doing this, we have developed a typology of countries based on their total annual rainfall and interannual rainfall variability. The working hypothesis was that the countries in clusters 1 and 2 face both high water variability and an acute susceptibility to drought. Countries in clusters 3 and 4 were expected to be much less prone to drought and therefore have less pressing need for comprehensive water management strategies.

Although the typology clusters are based on relatively limited information on water resources and drought impact in Africa, there is strong evidence to support the claim that countries with higher water variability experience more frequent and longer droughts. Drought affects the countries found throughout the Sahel and southern and eastern Africa. Most of the countries in those regions are the same ones identified as having highly variable water supply (clusters 1 and 2). However, many countries with higher rainfall and more stable water supplies (clusters 3 and 4) at an aggregate level are also prone to severe and repeated drought. In these countries (i.e., Tanzania, Zambia, Ghana, and Nigeria), the droughts typically occur only in those regions where rainfall appears to be well below the long-term national average.

The typology 1 and 2 countries were more likely to have drought serious enough to warrant international assistance. These countries were also more likely to have droughts lasting three or more consecutive years (see Table 38.11).

Interestingly, the countries with more frequent and geographically extensive drought are also more likely to develop comprehensive drought preparedness measures and emergency drought response systems. Strategies that might be adopted include:

- assessment programmes
- relevant water protection legislation
- water supply augmentation
  - public awareness campaigns,
  - technical assistance for water conservation,
  - demand reduction programmes,
  - emergency response programmes, and
  - drought contingency plans, including worst-case scenarios.

The countries in clusters 1 and 2 were often more likely to support the hydrological monitoring systems needed as an information base in designing drought preparedness strategies. In contrast, some less drought-prone countries have more ad hoc approaches, strongly relying on emergency response systems. Regardless of the country category, water manage-

Table 38.11 Drought effects by typology*

	Typology 1	Typology 2	Typology 3	Typology 4
Countries that requested US drought relief (through 1990)	Cape Verde Djibouti Mauritania Niger Somalia Sudan	Angola Botswana Burkina Faso Chad Ethiopia Kenya Lesotho Mali Senegal	Benin The Gambia Ghana Madagascar Rwanda Tanzania Togo Uganda Zaire	Cameroon
Countries experiencing drought three or more consecutive years	Cape Verde Mauritania Namibia Niger Somalia Sudan	Botswana Burkina Faso Chad Kenya Lesotho Mali Senegal South Africa Swaziland Zimbabwe	The Gambia Ghana Mozambique Nigeria	Guinea-Bissau

Source: Keck and Dinar 1996
Notes: *Political factors likely influenced US aid decisions. Most typology 3 countries in this table form part of the 'low' subcategory of average annual rainfall less than 1,242 mm (see Table 38.2)

BOX 38.1 BOTSWANA AND SOUTHERN AFRICA'S 1994–5 DROUGHT

Southern Africa has not yet fully recovered from the 1991–2 drought when parts of it have been hit by another drought in 1994–5. Assessment of the impacts of the 1994–5 drought and preparedness efforts in countries in the region (USAID 1995) concluded that, although efforts to improve drought preparedness are being made in some countries, the drought is still being handled on an emergency basis in most southern African countries. Ad hoc responses are straining the administration and financial capacity of national governments. The fact that southern Africa has a significant, recurrent risk of regional droughts with measurable, detrimental impacts on development makes it imperative that strategies be developed to mitigate drought before it becomes an emergency causing human suffering and requiring outside assistance.

The 1994–5 drought has forced on the one hand the governments of Zimbabwe and Zambia to divert funds from development programmes, to jeopardise food and water management policies, to borrow at high interest rates, and to appeal for foreign aid. Botswana on the other hand handles drought differently. Botswana's approach can be used to improve drought management in the rest of the region.

Botswana treats drought as a recurrent phenomenon. Therefore, a permanent inter-ministerial subcommittee for drought management is enplane, allowing for long-term planning rather than unanticipated and ad hoc response. Botswana's drought management plan emphasised early warning based on post-rainy-season assessments. Additional elements in the drought management strategy include: flexibility in expanding and modifying regular developmental programmes as needed, and drought mitigation and relief programmes.

---

ment appears to play a relatively small part in the strategies employed in sub-Saharan Africa to respond to drought. Finally, the literature does not reveal the extent to which the drought response programmes of the various countries were devised before drought occurred. It is thus very difficult to determine whether countries had preconceived strategies for minimising drought impact, or if they created water management strategies at the crisis stage. A recent work (USAID 1995) provides some insight into such issues in southern Africa (Box 38.1).

NOTES

1 This is an admittedly subjective approach to classifying the two countries. The authors believe the value of 2 is appropriate, however, because it recognises the presence in both countries of semiarid and subhumid agroecological zones where drought can frequently occur.

2 Of the twenty-two countries, seven, ten, and five were among cluster 1, 2, and 3, respectively.

REFERENCES

Benson, C. and Clay, E. (1994) *The Impact of Drought on Sub-Saharan African Economies: A Preliminary Examination*, paper prepared for ODI workshop Regent's College, London 14 June 1994.

Beran, M.S. and Rodier, J.A. (1985) *Hydrological Aspects of Drought*, Paris: UNESCO and WMO.

Bruwer, J.J. (1993) 'Drought policy in the Republic of South Africa', in D. Wilhite (ed.), *Drought Assessment, Management, and Planning: Theory and Case Studies*, Boston, MA: Kluwer Academic Publishers, pp. 199–212.

DuBois, V. D. (1974) 'The drought in West Africa. Part I. Evolution, causes, and physical consequences', *West African Series* 15: 1–6.

Dyer, J.A. (1989) 'A Canadian approach to monitoring for famine relief in Africa', *Water International* 14, 4: 198–205.

Engelman, R. and LeRoy, P. (1993) *Sustaining Water. Population and the Future of Renewable Water Supplies*, Washington, DC: Population Action International.

FAO (Food and Agriculture Organization) (1984) *Agroclimatological Data for Africa*, Rome: FAO.

—— (1987) *Irrigation and Water Resources Potential for Africa*, Rome: FAO.

Fratkin, E. and Roth, E.A. (1990) 'Drought and economic differentiation among Ariaal pastoralists of Kenya', *Human Ecology* 18, 4: 385–402.

Glantz, M. (ed) (1987) *Drought and Hunger in Africa*, Cambridge: Cambridge University Press.

Greenwood, G. and de Leeuw, P. (1983) 'Annex 10: Natural resources management', *The Niger Integrated Livestock Production Project Paper*, North Grafton, MA: Tufts University.

Johnson, G.E., Rao Achutuni, V., Thiruvengadachari, S., and Kogan F. (1993) 'The role of NOAA satellite data in drought early warning and monitoring: Selected case studies', in D. Wilhite (ed.), *Drought Assessment, Management, and Planning: Theory and Case Studies*, Boston, MA: Kluwer Academic Publishers.

Keck, A. and Dinar A. (1996) *Water Supply Variability and Drought in Sub-Saharan Africa: Physical and Economic*

Perspectives for a Comprehensive Water Strategy, African Water Resources: Challenges and Opportunities for Sustainable Development, Working Paper No. 7, Washington, DC: World Bank.

Molapo, L.L. and Sekoli, B.T. (1989) 'Lesotho's experience with drought', paper prepared for the Drought Preparedness Seminar in Gaborone, Botswana.

Nicholson, S.E. (1982) 'The Sahel: A climatic perspective', Dissemination Paper of the CILSS and OECD.

Office of Foreign Disaster Assistance (OFDA) (1990) *Disaster History: Significant Data on Major Disasters Worldwide, 1990–Present*, OFDA/USAID, Washington, DC.

Oladipo, O.E. (1993) 'Some aspects of the spatial characteristics of drought in northern Nigeria', *Natural Hazards* 8: 171–88.

Oyebande, L. (1990) 'Drought policy and drought planning in Africa', *Water Resources Development* 6, 4: 260–9.

Palmer, W.C. (1965) 'Meteorological Drought', *Research Paper* No. 45, Washington, DC: US Weather Bureau.

Pratt, D. and Gwynne, M. (1977) *Rangeland Management and Ecology in East Africa*, London: Hodder and Stoughton.

SADCC (1992) *Food Security Bulletin*, Gaborone, Botswana: SADC.

Scoones, I. (1992) 'Coping with drought: Responses of herders and livestock in contrasting Savanna environments in southern Zimbabwe', *Human Ecology* 20, 3: 293–314.

Sollod, A.E. (1990) 'Rainfall, biomass and the pastoral economy of Niger: Assessing the impact of drought', *Journal of Arid Environments* 18: 97–107.

Trewartha, G.T. (1968) *An Introduction to Climate*, New York: McGraw-Hill Co.

UN (United Nations) (1975) *Drought in Africa*, report by the United Nations Development Program, New York: United Nations.

—— (1986) *Countries stricken by desertification and drought*, General Assembly, Economic and Social Council, 9 June, New York.

UNCRD (United Nations Centre for Regional Development) (1990) *Challenges of the IDNDR: International Decade for Natural Disaster Reduction*, Nagoya, Japan.

USAID (United States Agency for International Development) (1995) 'Southern Africa drought assessment', Washington, DC: USAID.

Valentine, T.R. (1993) 'Drought, transfer entitlements, and income distribution: The Botswana experience', World Development 21, 1: 109–26.

Webb, P., von Braun, J., and Yohannes, Y. (1992) 'Drought impact and household response in East and West Africa', *Quarterly Journal of International Agriculture* 31: 230–46.

Wilhite, D.A. (1993) 'The enigma of drought', in D. Wilhite (ed.), *Drought Assessment, Management, and Planning: Theory and Case Studies*, Boston, MA: Kluwer Academic Publishers.

Wisner, B. (1976) 'An overview of drought in Kenya', *Natural Hazard Research Working Paper* 30, Boulder, CO: University of Colorado.

World Bank (1993) *Projects in Progress: The World Bank at Work*, No. 8, Washington, DC: World Bank.

World Bank and UNDP (1989–93) 'Hydrological assessment for sub-Saharan Africa', unpublished country reports.

WDA (World Disc Associates, Inc.) (1988) *The World Weather Disc*, data compiled from the National Climate Data Center and the National Center for Atmospheric Research, Seattle: WDA.

39

STATE ACTIONS TO MITIGATE DROUGHT

Lessons learned[1]

Donald A. Wilhite

INTRODUCTION

Drought is a normal, recurrent feature of the climate of virtually all portions of the United States. Because of the country's size and the wide range of climatic regimes, it is rare for drought not to exist somewhere in the country each year. The most recent series of drought years that has plagued the country since 1986 has extended almost uninterrupted to the present. During this time, drought has affected all or a portion of nearly all states; in some instances, states were affected for six or seven consecutive years. The per cent area of the contiguous United States, according to the Palmer Drought Severity Index (Palmer 1965), that has been in severe and extreme drought (i.e., ≤ -3.0) from 1986 to 1995 is shown in Figure 39.1. During 1988, the most severe drought year, nearly 40 per cent of the nation was in severe to extreme drought. In 1996, the drought in the Southwest and southern Great Plains states affected approximately 20 per cent of the nation.

The occurrence of severe drought, especially when extended over several seasons or a series of consecutive years, often results in serious economic, environmental, and social consequences. During 1995–6, for example, drought plagued large portions of the Southwest and southern Great Plains states during the winter, spring, and summer months. For some parts of this drought-stricken region, 1996 was actually the second or third consecutive water-short year. Impacts on agriculture, energy, water supply, and other sectors were significant throughout the region. In Texas, costs and losses were the most dramatic; impacts through mid-summer were esti-

mated to be approximately $6.5 billion (Boyd 1996).

In response to recent droughts, states have implemented numerous measures to mitigate some of the most serious drought impacts. Collectively, these responses help provide a catalogue of options now available to states to lessen the burden of drought. These options, in many cases, may be transferable to other states or countries, with appropriate modifications.

This chapter has two objectives. First, it will update the reader on the status of state-level drought planning efforts in the United States. There has been a rapid increase in state-level planning efforts in recent years in response to numerous factors, including the pattern of severe drought (Wilhite and Rhodes 1994) and the existence of models for states to follow in developing a plan (Western States Water Council 1987, Wilhite 1991a). Second, the chapter will

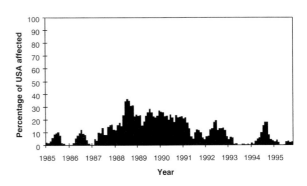

Figure 39.1 Percentage area of the United States experiencing severe to extreme drought, January 1986–October 1995. (Data source: National Climatic Data Center)

highlight the types of mitigative actions taken by drought-stricken states in response to droughts that occurred during the late 1980s and early 1990s. The chapter will conclude with some recommendations for future directions regarding state-level drought planning efforts.

STATE-LEVEL DROUGHT PLANNING: CURRENT STATUS

The number of states with drought plans has grown from three in 1982 to twenty-seven in 1996 (Figure 39.2). In 1991, twenty-three had drought plans (Wilhite 1991b). In addition to the states that now have plans, six states (Alabama, Arizona, Louisiana, Pennsylvania, Texas, and New Mexico) are at various stages of plan development. Texas undertook a comprehensive feasibility study in 1994 to consider an appropriate drought management plan (Water Demand/Drought Management Technical Advisory Committee 1994). This study recognised the need for a statewide plan and recommended the development of a drought planning and response framework as part of the state water plan. Largely as a result of the 1996 drought, Texas is now moving forward with a major drought planning effort. New Mexico and Arizona have received funding to develop statewide drought contingency plans. Pennsylvania is planning to develop a statewide plan. The eastern portion of that state is included in the drought plan for the Delaware River Basin. Alabama and Louisiana began drought planning efforts before the 1996 drought. Two additional states allocate drought planning authority to regional (Florida) or local (California) authorities. Constraints to plan development were discussed by Wilhite and Easterling (1987), Wilhite (1992), and Wilhite (1996). Although the increase in the number of state drought plans is an extremely positive sign, these plans are still largely reactive, treating drought in an emergency response mode.

This pattern of state-level drought planning is quite complex and cannot be explained adequately on the basis of drought climatology alone. A state's decision to develop (or not to develop) a drought plan is based on specific climatological, political, economic, environmental, and demographic factors. Wilhite and Rhodes (1994) constructed a typology of state behaviour in an attempt to explain the current pattern of drought plans that existed in the early 1990s and found that social, political, and institutional influences may be more important than recent drought experiences. They speculated that the increase in state drought planning activities may also have been the result of improved capabilities of state governments in conjunction with the Reagan administration's 'New Federalism' initiative and concurrent federal regulatory mandates to state and local governments, states' concerns about federal intrusion into state-level water resource planning and water rights, and some states' early experiences in working with the newly formed FEMA. Issues such as these may have contributed to an increased awareness of the value of drought planning within some state governments.

The basic goal of state drought plans is to improve the effectiveness of state response efforts by enhancing monitoring and early warning; impact assessment; and preparedness, response, recovery, and mitigation programmes. These plans are also directed at improving coordination within agencies of state government and between local, state, and federal government. The growth in the number of states with drought plans suggests an increased concern about the potential impact of extended water shortages and an attempt to address those concerns through planning. In the United States, states are clearly the policy innovators for drought management (Wilhite 1991b), in contrast to Australia, where the federal government has provided most of the leadership, in concert with the states, for the development of a national drought policy (White et al. 1993).

State drought plans take many forms. Some concentrate largely on impacts in one principal sector (e.g., agriculture, municipal water supply), while others attempt to address a full range of impacts within the state. One of the first states to develop a drought plan was Colorado. This plan was developed in 1981 at the request of the governor and is quite comprehensive. Since development, the plan has undergone revisions to improve the state's capacity to deal with extended periods of water shortage. The Colorado Drought Response Plan is administered by the Office of Emergency Management under the authority of the Colorado Natural Hazards Mitigation Council (Truby and Boulas 1994).

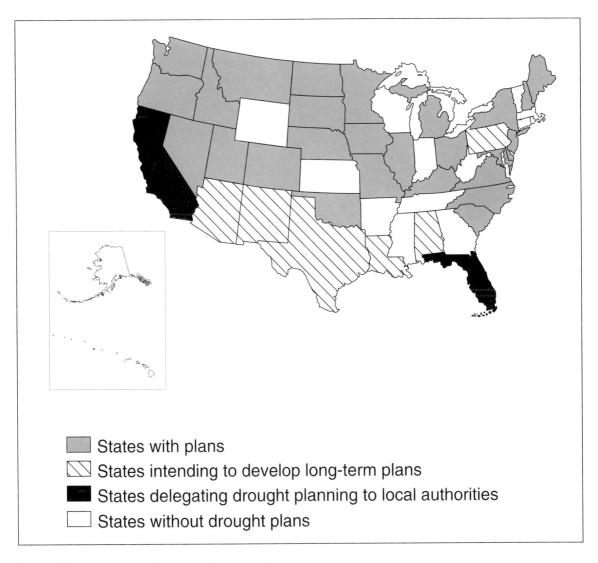

Figure 39.2 Status of state drought plans as of August 1997

LESSONS FROM RECENT DROUGHTS: STATE-LEVEL MITIGATION TOOLS

Wilhite (1993a) recently assessed ongoing and developing federal, interstate, and state drought mitigation technologies, programmes, and policies in the United States. This study was based on the assumption that the roles of federal and state governments in drought mitigation needed to be reexamined, given the severity of drought experienced in the United States between 1986 and 1992; the economic, social, and environmental costs associated with these droughts; and the mitigation actions and policy efforts underway at all levels of government. The impacts of the 1987–9 drought have been reviewed by Riebsame *et al.* (1990). One of the goals of the study was to identify opportunities to improve the effectiveness of drought mitigation efforts by the Soil Conservation Service (now called the Natural Resources

Conservation Service) of the US Department of Agriculture and other federal agencies. A premise of this study was that the nation's ability to cope with and manage water shortages resulting from drought would only be improved if an integrated approach within and between levels of government, involving regional organisations and the private sector where appropriate, were adopted.

This section of the paper reports on emerging drought assessment, response, and mitigation technologies employed by state government to lessen the effects of severe droughts in recent years. Numerous innovative institutional technologies were introduced during this period to manage water more effectively and efficiently in response to drought and increased demand. These data were collected through a survey of states and key federal agencies with responsibility for the management of water and other natural resources. The survey was directed at specific drought mitigation actions taken or programmes adopted during the period from 1986 to 1992.

Mitigation is defined in several ways in the natural hazards literature. Hy and Waugh (1990) referred to mitigation as activities that reduce the degree of long-term risk to human life and property. These actions normally include insurance strategies, the adoption of building codes, land-use management, risk mapping, tax incentives and disincentives, and diversification. Drought is not often directly responsible for loss of life and its impacts are largely nonstructural. Therefore, this definition is not appropriate in this case. For the purpose of assessing mitigative actions specific to drought, this definition was modified as follows: short- and long-term actions, programmes, or policies implemented in advance of drought that reduce the degree of risk to people, property, and productive capacity.

In the study referred to above (Wilhite 1993a), the survey instrument purposely did not define the term mitigation. States were given flexibility to define mitigation by including actions or activities that they felt were appropriate. However, the definition given above was used to help understand and cluster the actions and activities reported by states. Mitigation activities identified by states and/or local municipalities during recent droughts were diverse, reflecting regional differences in impacts, legal and institutional constraints, and institutional arrangements associated with drought plans. The diversity in responses was also related to the wide range of state agencies with principal authority for drought planning and mitigation (e.g., agriculture, natural resources, water resources, emergency or disaster management).

State mitigation actions used to address issues during recent droughts are clustered into nine primary areas in Table 39.1. These actions represent a full range of possible mitigative actions, from monitoring and assessment programmes to the development of drought contingency plans. Some of the actions included were adopted by many states, while others may have been adopted only in a single case.

Assessment programmes adopted by states range from the development of improved criteria or triggers for the initiation of specific actions in response to drought to the establishment of new data collection networks. Automated networks such as those that exist in Nebraska, California, and Oklahoma have significantly improved the states' monitoring capabilities. One of the three critical components of a drought plan is a comprehensive early warning system. Parameters that must be monitored to detect the early onset of drought include temperature and precipitation, stream flow, reservoir and groundwater levels, snowpack, and soil moisture. Each of these parameters represents different components of the hydrologic system and, therefore, impact sectors (e.g., agriculture, energy, transportation, recreation, and tourism). To assess emerging drought conditions, these data must be integrated to provide a comprehensive snapshot of water availability and outlook. Many recommendations for the development of a national drought watch (Riebsame et al. 1990) or integrated climate monitoring system (US Congress OTA 1993, Wilhite and Wood 1994, FEMA 1996) have been offered, but not implemented. Some states have also undertaken vulnerability assessments of public water supplies in conjunction with drought planning efforts. This is an especially critical issue in states with many small water supply systems that may be quite sensitive to extended periods of water shortage. It is important to identify vulnerable systems in advance so that adequate mitigation measures can be adopted.

Legislative actions included the passage of measures

to protect instream flows and guarantee low-interest loans to farmers. Low-interest loans, a common federal response to drought, are not generally state financed. Many states have been reexamining aspects of water rights doctrine in response to growing water use and associated conflicts. Water banks have been used in some states (e.g., California) as a means of temporarily modifying water allocation procedures during water shortages. The California Drought Water Bank programme is an example of an innovative and successful mitigation action (California Department of Water Resources 1992). This programme was created in 1991. It allowed the Department of Water Resources to acquire water in three ways: (1) by purchasing water from farmers who chose not to irrigate; (2) by purchasing surplus water from local water districts; and (3) by paying farmers or water districts to use groundwater instead of surface water. MacDonnell *et al.* (1994) present a review of water banking in the West.

Augmentation of water supplies during recent droughts included rehabilitating reservoirs to operate at design capacity and reviewing reservoir operation plans. Cities also worked with self-supplied industrial users on programmes to reallocate some water for emergency public water supplies.

One of the key responsibilities of state government during periods of drought is to keep the public aware of the severity of the situation through timely reports. These reports must provide a clear rationale for mitigative actions that are being imposed on either a voluntary or mandatory basis. During recent droughts, states organised informational meetings for the media and the public, implemented water conservation awareness programmes, prepared and distributed informational materials, and organised workshops on drought-related topics. Sample ordinances on water conservation were also prepared and distributed to municipalities and rural suppliers.

Most states lack the financial resources necessary to provide drought relief to individual citizens during times of emergency. However, it is often within the mission and capacity of state agencies to provide technical assistance to municipalities and others. During recent droughts, states assisted by providing advice on potential new sources of water and evaluating the quality and quantity of those supplies. Agencies also assisted municipalities in assessing the vulnerability of water supply systems. States encouraged the adoption of voluntary water conservation measures and established stronger economic incentives for water conservation within the private sector. Water metering and leak detection programmes were implemented.

Emergency response programmes would not be considered by some as a mitigative action. However, if these measures are implemented to reduce immediate impacts or the risk of future impacts as part of a long-term mitigation programme, they represent a proactive approach to drought management. State responses included a wide range of measures such as lowering of well intakes on reservoirs for rural water supplies, establishing water hauling programmes for livestock, extending boat ramps in recreational areas, and creating a tuition assistance programme to enable farmers to participate in farm management classes.

Conflicts between water users increase during water-short periods. Timely intervention to resolve these conflicts will become increasingly necessary as demands on limited water supplies continue to expand in number and complexity. The best approach is to anticipate these conflicts well in advance of drought and initiate appropriate actions to avoid conflict. Many of the actions taken focused on the growing conflicts between municipal and agricultural water use.

As mentioned previously, the growing number of states with drought plans is an indication of greater concern about the impacts of drought and the acceptance by states of the role that planning can play in reducing some of its most adverse effects. The optimal time to plan for drought is during non-drought periods; however, considerable progress in establishing a basic response framework is often accomplished during the period of peak severity, as occurred in several drought-stricken states in 1996. The challenge is to transform this framework into a response/mitigation plan during the post-drought period. A brief window of opportunity usually exists to initiate a longer term mitigation programme between the panic stage of the hydro-illogical cycle at the peak of drought severity and the beginning of the apathy stage when rainfall returns to normal. The hydro-illogical cycle is often used to explain the crisis management approach to drought management and is discussed in detail at the National Drought Mitigation Center's home page

Table 39.1 Drought-related mitigative actions of state government in response to recent episodes of drought

Category	Specific action
Assessment programmes	• Developed criteria or triggers for drought-related actions • Developed early warning system, monitoring programme • Conducted inventories of data availability • Established new data collection networks • Monitored vulnerable public water suppliers
Legislation/public policy	• Prepared position papers for legislature on public policy issues • Examined statutes governing water rights for possible modification during water shortages • Passed legislation to protect instream flows • Passed legislation providing guaranteed low-interest loans to farmers • Imposed limits on urban development
Water supply augmentation/development of new supplies	• Issued emergency permits for water use • Provided pumps and pipes for distribution • Proposed and implemented programme to rehabilitate reservoirs to operate at design capacity • Undertook water supply vulnerability assessments • Inventoried self-supplied industrial water users for possible use of their supplies for emergency public water supplies • Inventoried and reviewed reservoir operation plans
Public awareness/Education programmes	• Organised drought information meetings for the public and the media • Implemented water conservation awareness programmes • Published and distributed pamphlets to individuals, businesses, and municipalities on water conservation techniques and agricultural drought management strategies • Organised workshops on special drought-related topics • Prepared sample ordinances on water conservation for municipalities and domestic rural supplies • Established drought information centre as a focal point for activities, information, and assistance
Technical assistance on water conservation and other water-related activities	• Provided advice on potential new sources of water • Evaluated water quantity and quality from new sources • Advised water suppliers on assessing vulnerability of existing supply system • Recommended that suppliers adopt water conservation measures
Demand reduction/water conservation programmes	• Established stronger economic incentives for private investment in water conservation • Encouraged voluntary water conservation • Improved water use and conveyance efficiencies • Implemented water metering and leak detection programmes
Emergency response programmes	• Established alert procedures for water quality problems • Stockpiled supplies of pumps, pipes, water filters, and other equipment • Established water hauling programmes for livestock from reservoirs and other sources • Compiled list of locations for livestock watering • Established hay hotline

	• Provided funds for improving water systems, developing new systems, and digging wells
	• Provided funds for recovery programmes for drought and other natural disasters
	• Lowered well intakes on reservoirs for rural water supplies
	• Extended boat ramps and docks in recreational areas
	• Issued emergency surface water irrigation permits from state waters
	• Created low-interest loan and aid programmes for agricultural sector
	• Created a drought property tax credit programme for farmers
	• Established a tuition assistance programme to enable farmers to enrol in farm management programmes
Water use conflict resolution	• Acted to resolve emerging water use conflicts
	• Negotiated with irrigators to gain voluntary restrictions on irrigation in areas where domestic wells were likely to be affected
	• Established a water banking programme
	• Clarified state law regarding sale of water
	• Clarified state law on changes in water rights
	• Suspended water use permits in watersheds with low water levels
	• Investigated complaints of irrigation wells interfering with domestic wells
Drought contingency plans	• Established statewide contingency plans
	• Recommended to water suppliers the development of drought plans
	• Evaluated worst-case drought scenarios for possible further actions
	• Established natural hazard mitigation council

Source: Wilhite 1993b

(http://enso.unl.edu/ndmc) and by Wilhite (1993b). Several states in the Southwest and southern Great Plains are attempting to capture the interest in this past summer's crisis and direct it toward a longer term planning process.

Many of the mitigative programmes implemented by states during recent droughts can be characterised as emergency or short-term actions taken to alleviate the crisis at hand, although these actions can be successful, especially if they are part of a preparedness or mitigation plan. Other activities, such as legislative actions, drought plan development, and the development of water conservation and other public awareness programmes, are considered actions with a longer-term vision. As states gain more experience assessing and responding to drought, future actions will undoubtedly become more timely and effective

and less reactive. Viewed collectively, the mitigative actions of states in response to recent drought conditions are numerous, but most individual state actions were quite narrow. In the future, state drought plans need to address a broader range of mitigative actions, including provisions for expanding the level of intergovernmental coordination. Table 39.1 is illustrative of the arsenal of mitigation programmes and actions currently available to states. One of the goals of the NDMC is to facilitate this process. Improved coordination will require a greater commitment by federal agencies to work together and with states to promote an integrated approach to drought planning. Coordination at the federal level will likely require the establishment of an interagency task force, as recommended by the US Congressional Office of Technology Assessment (1993).

CONCLUSIONS AND RECOMMENDATIONS

The trend is clear. Societal vulnerability to natural hazards such as drought is increasing, and at an alarming rate. Increasing demand for water and other shared natural resources is real and illustrates the necessity of learning to cope more effectively with both short-term and extended periods of drought in the United States and elsewhere. During the past decade in the United States, widespread and severe drought has resulted in an increased awareness of the nation's continuing vulnerability to this creeping natural hazard. This experience has resulted in numerous initiatives by state government to improve the timeliness and effectiveness of response efforts.

Progress made by states in the past fifteen years in the field of drought planning has been impressive, but these plans continue to stress emergency response. Although these plans generally provide for a more coordinated and effective response to the emergency, they are still largely reactive (i.e., crisis management) rather than proactive (i.e., risk management). Little thought or attention has been given to actions that could be taken or programmes that could be implemented in advance of the next drought to reduce impacts. What is needed is a thorough and systematic assessment of vulnerable sectors by each of the states.

As noted in this paper, states have developed and implemented a wide range of mitigation measures, but the transition from crisis to risk management is a difficult task. Each state must assess its own unique experiences (i.e., lessons learned) and share these lessons with other states. The collective experiences of states in responding to and preparing for drought is a unique archive of information that, if applied systematically, can help mitigate the effects of future drought.

NOTE

1   This chapter is reprinted from *Journal of the American Water Resources Association*, vol. 33, no. 5, October 1977, pp. 961–8.

REFERENCES

Boyd, J. (1996) 'Southwest farmers battle record drought', United Press International, 30 May.

California Department of Water Resources (1992) *Report to the California Water Commission*, Sacramento, California, 1 May.

FEMA (1996) *Drought of 1996: Multi-State Drought Task Force Findings*, Federal Emergency Management Agency, Region VI, Denton, Texas.

Hy, J.H. and Waugh, W.L. Jr. (1990) 'The function of emergency management', in W.L. Waugh, Jr., and R.J. Hy (eds), *Handbook of Emergency Management: Programs and Policies Dealing with Major Hazards and Disasters*, New York: Greenwood Press, Chapter 2.

MacDonnell, L.J., Howe, C.W., Miller, K.A., Rice, T.A., and Bates, S.F. (1994) *Water Banks in the West*, Boulder, CO: Natural Resources Law Center, University of Colorado.

Palmer, W.C. (1965) 'Meteorological drought', *Research Paper* No. 45, US Weather Bureau. Washington, DC.

Riebsame, W.E., Changnon, S.A. Jr., and Karl, T.R. (1990) *Drought and Natural Resources Management in the United States: Impacts and Implications of the 1987–89 Drought*, Boulder, CO: Westview Press.

Truby, J.O. and Boulas, L.A. (1994) 'Formulation of a mitigation system for long-term drought in Colorado', in D.A. Wilhite and D.A. Wood (eds), *Drought Management in a Changing West: New Directions for Water Policy*, IDIC Technical Report 94–1, Lincoln, NE: International Drought Information Center, University of Nebraska, pp. 111–21.

US Congress, Office of Technology Assessment (1993) *Preparing for an Uncertain Climate*, Volume 1, OTA–O–567, Washington, DC: US Government Printing Office.

Water Demand/Drought Management Technical Advisory Committee (1994) *Consideration of an Appropriate Drought Management Plan for the State of Texas*, Austin, TX: Texas Water Development Board.

Western States Water Council (1987) *A Model for Western State Drought Response and Planning*, Midvale, UT: Western States Water Council.

White, D.H., Collins, D., and Howden, M. (1993) 'Drought in Australia: Prediction, monitoring, management, and policy', in D.A. Wilhite (ed.), *Drought Assessment, Management, and Planning: Theory and Case Studies*, Boston, MA: Kluwer Academic Publishers, pp. 213–36.

Wilhite, D.A. (1991a) 'Drought planning and state government: Current status', *Bulletin of the American Meteorological Society* 72: 1,531–6.

—— (1991b) 'Drought planning: A process for state government', *Water Resources Bulletin* 27: 29–38.

—— (1992) *Planning for Drought: A Guidebook for Developing Countries*, Nairobi: Climate Unit, U.N. Environment Program.

—— (1993a) *An Assessment of Drought Mitigation Technologies in the United States*, Final Report to the Soil Conservation Service/USDA, *IDIC Technical Report* 93–1, Lincoln, NE: International Drought Information Center, University of Nebraska.

—— (1993b) 'Planning for drought: A methodology', in

D.A. Wilhite (ed.), *Drought Assessment, Management, and Planning: Theory and Case Studies*, Boston, MA: Kluwer Academic Publishers, Chapter 6, pp. 87–108.

Wilhite, D.A. (1996) 'A methodology for drought preparedness', *Natural Hazards* 13: 229–52.

Wilhite, D.A. and Easterling, W.E. (eds) (1987) *Planning for Drought: Toward a Reduction of Societal Vulnerability*, Boulder, CO: Westview Press.

Wilhite, D.A. and Wood, D.A. (1994) *Drought Management in a Changing West: New Directions for Water Policy*, IDIC Technical Report 94–1, Lincoln, NE: International Drought Information Center, University of Nebraska.

Wilhite, D.A. and Rhodes, S.L. (1994) 'State-level drought planning in the United States: Factors influencing plan development', *Water International* 19: 15–24.

40

RESPONDING TO DROUGHT

Common threads from the past, visions for the future[1]

Donald A. Wilhite

INTRODUCTION

Severe drought affected large portions of the United States during the winter, spring, and summer months of 1995–6. This event triggered a significant response effort by both state and federal government in the drought-stricken states of the Southwest and southern Great Plains. A federal interagency multistate drought task force was formed in late May. This task force, coordinated by the Federal Emergency Management Agency (FEMA), organised a workshop (FEMA 1996a) in late June to evaluate and assess drought-relief programmes available from federal, state, and local agencies for the states of Arizona, California, Colorado, Nevada, New Mexico, Oklahoma, and Texas. Other federal agencies participating in this task force included the Department of Agriculture, Corps of Engineers, Department of Interior, and Small Business Administration. The goal of this task force was to develop 'an overall strategy to mitigate the effects of this devastating situation' (FEMA 1996b). This strategy was intended to include both short- and long-term actions that could be applied in the drought region.

Simultaneously, the Western Governors' Association (WGA) unanimously passed a resolution calling for the creation of a drought emergency response task force composed of the WGA staff council and state emergency managers 'to coordinate a comprehensive, integrated response effort' (WGA 1996). This task force met in September and began preparing a document of recommended short- and long-term actions. These recommendations will lead to the development of an implementation/action plan.

Both of these activities epitomise the 'crisis management' approach to dealing with severe drought, an approach that has characterised federal and state response in the United States since the 1930s. Under the crisis management approach, response measures are reactive; they are hastily prepared and executed during the peak of drought severity and usually do little to lessen impacts. Most of these response measures are in the form of post-impact government interventions (i.e., emergency assistance), which serves to reinforce existing, possibly nonsustainable, resource management practices. Relief is generally considered to be a disincentive to the adoption of management methods that are more resilient to drought and more economically and environmentally sustainable in the long term.

The response of state and federal government to the 1996 drought was fairly typical of previous response attempts. However, this response differed from earlier efforts in several critical ways. First, coordination and communication between state agencies and with appropriate federal agencies was improved in those states with drought plans in place. Unfortunately, Oklahoma, Texas, and New Mexico, all located in the core of the drought-affected area, did not have drought plans in place at the onset of drought. Those states were, in most cases, able to set up temporary response authorities using organisational and communication structures in place in other states as models. Second, the severity of the drought led the states mentioned above to reexamine the need for a more permanent structure or plan; these states have subsequently initiated a process to develop a drought plan. Third, the FEMA drought workshop was timely and proved to be worthwhile for both federal agencies and state governments. The workshop assembled all appropriate state and federal representatives and some representatives from regional organisations to discuss the status of impacts, available assistance programmes, and appropriate responses. This workshop also brought significant media attention to the impacts associated with drought and the importance of addressing this issue at the regional and national scale. Fourth, the decision of the FEMA task force and the WGA to include both short- and long-term measures in their recommendations to the president and the congressional leadership is a significant step forward. This decision reflects the higher profile now being given to mitigation when addressing natural hazards and disasters. The WGA's decision to fully incorporate ideas from all western states in the report formulation and recommendation process reflects one of the lessons learned by the western states in response to the 1977 drought: federal action is more timely and comprehensive when states speak with one rather than many voices (Crawford 1978, Wilhite *et al.* 1986).

The purpose of this chapter is to review the recommendations that have emanated from several key evaluations of state and federal responses to recent episodes of severe drought in the United States. These evaluations were selected for review because each identified a number of key issues and impediments that needed to be addressed to improve the nation's ability to cope with and prepare for future drought episodes. The goal of this analysis is to identify those fundamental issues common to all the evaluations. The premise of this chapter is that the series of drought years that occurred between 1986 and 1992 and recurred between 1994 and 1996 increased awareness of our nation's continuing and apparent growing vulnerability to drought. This increased awareness has led to greater consensus among the principal constituents and stakeholders, and also a greater sense of urgency to implement these actions now to reduce future vulnerability to drought.

RESPONDING TO DROUGHT: COMMON THREADS FROM THE PAST

In the United States, the federal government became the principal player in the provision of drought relief during the 1930s in response to a drought that was nearly nationwide in extent and coexisted with severe economic conditions (Wilhite 1983). Before the 1930s, assistance was provided primarily by the private sector (e.g., churches, Red Cross) but the level of assistance required during the 1930s far exceeded the response capacity of this sector. The federal government has continued to be the principal provider of drought assistance during subsequent drought events, most notably the 1950s in the Southwest, southern Great Plains, and Midwestern states; the 1960s in the Northeast; the mid-1970s in the Midwest and western states; and the recent series of drought years beginning in 1986. More than $7 billion in drought relief was provided by the federal government during the period from 1974 to 1977 (Wilhite *et al.* 1986); nearly $5 billion was provided in 1988 (Riebsame *et al.* 1990). Until recently, state government assumed a relatively passive role in drought management. States have now assumed a greater responsibility for drought planning, but drought relief remains largely a federal responsibility.

Post-drought evaluations or audits are not routinely completed in the United States. However, following the severe droughts of 1976–7 and the demonstrated inability of federal government to adequately cope with the problems that emerged, scientists and policy makers expressed considerable concern about the inefficiencies of this effort and repeatedly issued 'calls for action' for the development of drought plans, including the development of a national drought policy and plan. These calls include recommendations from the Western Governors' Policy Office (1978), General Accounting Office (1979), National Academy of Sciences (1986), Great Lakes Commission (1990), American Meteorological Society (Orville 1990), and Interstate Council on Water Policy (1987, 1991). In light of a possible increase in the frequency and severity of extreme events in association with changes in climate, an Environmental Protection Agency report (Smith and Tirpak 1989) called for the development of a national drought policy to coordinate federal response to drought.

In addition to these 'calls for action,' several studies completed in the late 1970s, 1980s, and 1990s evaluated specific response efforts and offered recommendations for improving future drought management in the United States. These recommendations placed greater emphasis on federal response initiatives to address many of the problems and issues identified, but the role of state government, regional organisations, and the private sector was not ignored. A content analysis of the each of the following studies was completed for this paper: General Accounting Office (GAO) (1979), Wilhite *et al.* (1986), Grigg and Vlachos (1989), Riebsame *et al.* (1990), Wilhite (1993), Office of Technology Assessment (US Congress, OTA 1993), Wilhite and Wood (1994), and the Federal Emergency Management Agency (FEMA 1996a).

GENERAL ACCOUNTING OFFICE

(Federal Response to the 1976–77 Drought: What Should be Done Next?)

GAO (1979) characterised the response programmes implemented in 1976–7 as largely untimely, poorly coordinated, and inequitable. The GAO found that assistance provided by federal agencies to farmers, communities, businesses, and water user organisations was available too late to lessen the effects of drought. GAO recommended that Congress direct the four principal agencies responsible for administering relief programmes in 1976–7 (Departments of Agriculture, Interior, and Commerce, and the Small Business Administration) to consider the problems identified and formulate a national plan to provide future assistance in a more 'timely, consistent, and equitable manner.' Issues to be addressed in the development of the plan included the identification of the respective roles of each agency in order to reduce duplication and overlap, legislation needed to more clearly define those roles, and standby legislation that might be necessary to allow for more timely response to problems associated with drought. GAO suggested that effectively implementing a national plan required establishing uniform criteria for determining 'priorities for the type of projects to be constructed; eligibility of applicants; and interest rates, terms, and repayment requirements for loans.' No action was taken on these recommendations.

WILHITE, ROSENBERG, AND GLANTZ

(Improving Federal Response to Drought)

Wilhite *et al.* (1986) confirmed the GAO findings and also concluded that the decision-making process for determining eligibility for drought assistance was seriously flawed. For example, the designation and revocation process for determining eligibility for the more than $5 billion of disaster relief expended in 1976–7 was confusing and was not based on consistent, established criteria. In total, sixteen federal agencies administered forty separate assistance programmes in 1976–7. Wilhite *et al.* (1986) concluded, based on lessons learned during the 1976–7 response effort, that a more effective federal response effort must address four basic issues. First, information on drought severity must be provided to decision makers and other users in a more timely manner. This requires better coordination of data collection efforts between federal agencies, information sharing between and within levels of government, and improved delivery systems. Second, impact assessment procedures must be more reliable and timely. Better indices are required to capture the severity of drought, particularly in the spring planting period. Improved estimates of drought impact on yield would help trigger assistance to the stricken area, and improved impact estimates are also important in other sectors such as fire protection, transportation, energy, and recreation and tourism. Third, objective and timely designation (and revocation) procedures are necessary to target assistance to drought areas. Decisions on drought disaster designations during 1977 were based largely on the Palmer Drought Severity Index (Palmer 1965), an index that often does not accurately reflect the severity of the drought, particularly in its early stages (Alley 1984, Wilhite *et al.* 1986). Fourth, disaster programmes must be more efficiently administered and programmes must match specific regional needs. In other words, the 'one size fits all' of federal drought assistance was not considered effective in addressing the needs of regions with different resource management issues. It was concluded that a national drought plan would help coordinate the activities of federal government in responding to the effects of future droughts. It was also suggested that state governments and regional organisations should play a more active role in drought management and that their activities be coordinated between levels of government. The growth in the number of states with drought response plans (Wilhite 1991a) has been a positive sign and an indication of greater awareness of drought planning and the resources available to facilitate that process (Western States Water Council 1987, Wilhite 1991b, Wilhite 1996).

GRIGG AND VLACHOS

(Drought Water Management: Preparing and Responding to Drought)

Grigg and Vlachos (1989) analysed local, state, region (i.e., river basin), and federal responses to the droughts of 1986 and 1988 and derived a series of 'next steps' to improve future response efforts. These steps expressed the importance of learning from previous experiences and treating drought management as a process rather than a discrete event. They emphasised the critical role of state government in drought management and recommended that states evaluate existing plans and their effectiveness in responding to recent droughts. It was suggested that federal government improve the analysis and integration of drought-related data and information and how this information is presented to various audiences. Grigg and Vlachos recommended that existing administrative structures be streamlined and communication between organisations improved. This could be accomplished by a vertical restructuring between levels of government and a horizontal restructuring within levels of government to achieve greater integration in water management. Better information on the origins and patterns of drought, the interrelationships of natural and human-induced water shortages, and the implications of climate change for drought frequency and severity were considered necessary to improve understanding and decision making. Grigg and Vlachos stressed the importance of contingency planning and the use of monitoring techniques to improve drought management to sustain the natural resource base. The challenge, in their view, was to make planning and management more effective within the current administrative and governmental system.

RIEBSAME, CHANGNON, AND KARL

(Drought and Natural Resources Management in the United States: Impacts and Implications of the 1987–89 Drought)

Riebsame et al. (1990) reviewed the climatology of the 1987–9 drought and evaluated the impacts and responses to this event. They concluded that the response effort was seriously deficient. Most of these deficiencies had been observed in previous droughts. Several critical issues were identified and recommendations were proposed to address these problem areas: (1) conduct a post-drought evaluation of the 1987–9 experiences; (2) develop an improved drought watch system, linking federal, state, and local agencies; (3) evaluate the reliability of indices in detecting emerging drought; (4) develop an integrated impact assessment programme for all primary sectors; (5) increase drought contingency planning to provide greater guidance to resource managers and others in response to extreme events; (6) develop improved record keeping on heat mortality and morbidity and conduct studies of the impact of drought on mental health; and (7) improve the delivery of information on drought and its impacts to users, especially in the business sector. Riebsame et al. (1990) suggested that since many of these recommendations were embodied in the National Climate Programme Act of 1978, this legislation, if fully implemented, could serve as a vehicle to address many of these issues.

WILHITE

(Drought Mitigation Technologies in the United States: With Future Policy Recommendations)

Wilhite (1993) reviewed drought mitigation technologies recently implemented in the United States in response to the series of severe drought years between 1986 and 1992. The primary goal of this study was to review and evaluate ongoing and developing federal, interstate, and state drought mitigation technologies, programmes, and policies to determine ways to improve the effectiveness of future Natural Resources Conservation Service (NRCS, formerly the Soil Conservation Service) drought mitigation initiatives. Although this study was initially focused on NRCS programming, the scope extended to all federal agencies and other levels of government in an attempt to identify initiatives that would improve the nation's ability to manage droughts through a more integrated approach within and between levels of government, involving regional organisations and the private sector where appropriate. Feedback from federal and state government and regional organisations was obtained from a series of survey instruments.

Six recommendations were forthcoming from this study. First, it was recommended that a national drought policy and plan be developed to improve the effectiveness of future response efforts and the efficiency of resource allocation during times of water shortage. This action is intended to improve coordination by integrating planning activities within and between levels of government and to reduce duplication between federal agencies. Second, development of a national drought watch system was recommended to achieve a more comprehensive assessment of drought and other extreme climatic conditions. This system would support and reinforce the tenets of a national policy and plan. Third, it was recommended that a national drought mitigation centre be created to assist state and other levels of government in the development of appropriate mitigation technologies. The centre would also be responsible for establishing a clearing-house that would serve as a resource for government, regional organisations, and the private sector for a broad range of drought-related information. Fourth, the study recommended that all federal drought relief programmes be reviewed to ensure consistency with national drought policy. The goal of this action is to redefine emergency assistance available during periods of drought to guarantee that it provides adequate incentives for the adoption of proactive management and planning strategies that minimise risks associated with drought. Fifth, post-drought audits of previous response efforts must be conducted to identify the successes and failures of recent efforts and provide a rational basis for recommending the continuation or discontinuation of assistance programmes. Sixth, educational programmes and training workshops that promote water conservation and management should be developed for all age groups and the media.

OFFICE OF TECHNOLOGY ASSESSMENT

(Preparing for an Uncertain Climate)

The Office of Technology Assessment conducted a study (US Congress, OTA 1993) at the request of Congress to address how the United States can cope with projected changes in climate, given the high level of uncertainty about what the future climate is likely to be. This study sought to identify natural and managed natural resource systems at risk from climate change, how to incorporate the uncertainty of climate change into planning decisions, and whether the US Global Change Research Programme will provide information to decision makers in a timely manner. OTA based its assessment on six systems: coastal areas, water resources, agriculture, wetlands, federally protected natural areas, and forests. The water section of this study specifically addresses the issue of drought management and federal initiatives that would improve future response and preparedness.

OTA noted that a first step to improved water management would be improved management of extreme climatic events such as floods and droughts. One institutional recommendation to improve drought management was to create an interagency task force to develop a national drought policy and plan. Other actions recommended to improve water management were to provide the Bureau of Reclamation and the Corps of Engineers with greater administrative flexibility to manage reservoirs on a basin wide level and to promote water marketing as a means of facilitating water transfers. The use of new analytical tools for water modelling and forecasting, as well as demand management, were also recommended. OTA also recommended that the scope of the Western Water Policy Review Commission (P.L. 102–575) be expanded to include a wide range of issues that are relevant to drought management. OTA further recommended that the nature of the Commission's review be expanded to address national water policy issues.

More specific to the issue of drought management, OTA suggested that a national drought policy and plan be created under Executive Order 12656, created to guide emergency water planning and management responsibilities of federal agencies. The national drought policy and plan would be developed under the leadership of the interagency drought task force mentioned previously. OTA recommended that a national drought policy and plan identify 'specific, action-oriented response objectives' and an implementation plan. Given the numerous federal agencies with drought and water management responsibilities, a lead agency or the Office of the President would need to be appointed to direct this process. Federal agencies would be expected to review, as part of this policy and plan formulation process, all drought assistance programmes, the identification of eligibility requirements for these programmes, and the programmes' overlapping responsibilities. The distribution of financial resources to relief recipients and the timing and effectiveness of relief should also be included in this review process.

OTA also recommended that three additional components be part of a national drought policy and plan. These were the adoption of risk management practices to promote self-reliance and protect the natural and agricultural resource base, the conduct of post-drought audits to evaluate the effectiveness of these efforts, and the development of a national drought watch system in support of a more proactive, anticipatory approach to drought management.

WILHITE AND WOOD

(Drought Management in a Changing West: New Directions for Water Policy)

In 1994, a conference was held to examine the future of western water and natural resources management and the region's growing vulnerability to extended periods of water shortages because of the sequence of drought years that occurred between 1987 and 1992 (Wilhite and Wood 1994). Participants of this conference offered a series of recommendations to improve drought management and reduce vulnerability to future drought episodes. First, participants recommended that a national drought policy or

framework be adopted that integrates actions and responsibilities between levels of government and promotes preparedness and mitigation. This policy should include actions that promote development of utility and locally based drought plans. Second, funds currently expended on drought relief should be re-allocated to preparedness and mitigation programmes. Third, region-specific drought policies should be developed and the missions of federal agencies modified as necessary to implement these policies. Fourth, FEMA should be encouraged to include drought planning and preparedness as a part of overall hazard planning at the state and local level. Fifth, human and technological resources should be redistributed within and between state and federal agencies to promote collaborative institutional relationships that improve productivity and eliminate redundancy on drought and water policy and management issues. Sixth, an integrated climate monitoring system should be created to better detect emerging drought and other climate-related extreme events. Seventh, seasonal forecast skill for drought and water supply should be improved through increased support for research.

FEMA

(Drought of 1996: Multi-State Task Force Findings)

In 1996, FEMA was asked to chair the Multi-State Drought Task Force to address the drought situation in the Southwest and southern Great Plains states. The purpose of the task force was to coordinate the federal response to drought-related problems in the stricken region by identifying needs, applicable programmes, and programme barriers. The task force was also directed to suggest ways to improve drought management through both short- and long-term national actions. To accomplish these objectives, a workshop was held in June 1996 that included representatives from many federal agencies, the drought-affected states, regional organisations, universities, and the Navajo Nation. The final report of this workshop (FEMA 1996a) divided short- and long-term recommendations and issues into three categories: policy, legislative, and executive branch. These recommendations are the product of intensive discussions and represent the opinions of all participating parties.

This discussion of the FEMA report will present only long-term issues and recommendations. First, participants recommended the development of a national drought policy based on the philosophy of cooperation with state and local stakeholders. They emphasised that this policy should be developed now even though 'regional interests and states' rights advocates may occasionally throw up roadblocks.' Participants emphasised the need for a contingency plan to help apply lessons from the past to future drought events. This policy should include a national climate/drought monitoring system to provide early warning of the onset and severity of drought to federal, state, and local officials. This policy would also include an institutionalised organisational structure to address the issue of drought on a national scale. Second, it was suggested that a regional forum be created to assess regional needs and resources, identify critical areas and interests, provide reliable and timely information, and coordinate state actions. It was suggested that multistate and impact-specific working groups be established under this forum to identify critical needs. Third, FEMA was asked to include drought as one of the natural hazards addressed in the National Mitigation Strategy (FEMA 1995), given the substantial costs associated with its occurrence and the numerous opportunities available to mitigate its effects. Fourth, states strongly requested that a single federal agency be appointed to co-ordinate preparedness and response to droughts. The states recommended that FEMA be given this respon-sibility; FEMA suggested that USDA should be the agency in charge given its programme responsibilities in agriculture, often the first sector affected.

In summary, these eight studies are in general agreement on the primary challenges and oppor-tunities that lie ahead if we are to achieve a higher level of preparedness and a more effective response to drought in the United States. In other words, there seems to have been a convergence of ideas on how to improve the management of drought. The next section of this paper will synthesise these themes into some specific recommendations for improved drought management and preparedness.

RESPONDING TO DROUGHT: VISIONS FOR THE FUTURE

What common threads or recommendations from the studies discussed above could define a new direction for drought management and preparedness in the United States? Several recurring themes emerged from this analysis:

- **Create a national drought policy and plan**
  An interagency task force should be established to develop an integrated national drought policy and plan that emphasises a preventive, anticipatory (i.e., risk management) approach to drought management and promotes self-reliance. The Australian National Drought Policy could be used as a model for the United States (White *et al.* 1993). The interagency drought task force would coordinate the activities of the federal government in responding to and mitigating the effects of drought. A lead federal agency would need to be appointed to direct this effort.

The interagency task force should identify ways to streamline current administrative structures between levels of government (i.e., vertical) to improve communication and information flow and within levels of government (i.e., horizontal) to achieve a more integrated approach to water management (e.g., reservoir management on a basin wide scale).

The national policy or framework would integrate actions and responsibilities between all levels of government and would be developed through a participatory process. This policy and plan should lead to a more coordinated and timely response while concurrently promoting self-reliance. A national plan would include an institutionalised organisational structure to address drought on a national scale with mitigation and response pro-grammes that are regionally appropriate.

Most funds expended on drought relief should be redirected to programmes that encourage planning and mitigation or to provide more timely and reliable information to decision makers.

This task force should conduct a review of all federal drought assistance programmes to ensure that they are consistent with national policy.

- **Develop a comprehensive, integrated national climate monitoring system**

  Develop a comprehensive, integrated climate monitoring system to provide early warning of emerging drought and other climate-related (e.g., floods) extreme events. This system would be an invaluable resource for planners, managers, and policy makers nationwide in preparing for and responding to a broad range of climatic events that occur simultaneously each year. This system would be an integral part of the national drought plan.

  The goal of this system would be to integrate data from federal and state collection networks. It would include the following parameters: precipitation and temperature; stream flow; reservoir and lake levels; groundwater levels; snowpack; and soil moisture. Satellite remotely sensed data (e.g., Advanced Very High Resolution Radiometer – AVHRR) should be used to monitor vegetation stress to help derive early estimates of impacts.

- **Incorporate drought in the national mitigation strategy**

  The National Mitigation Strategy (FEMA 1995) includes all major natural hazards, except drought. Steps should be taken, in conjunction with formulation of a national drought policy and plan, to incorporate drought in this strategy.

- **Conduct post-drought audits of federal/state response efforts**

  Post-drought audits of federal and state drought response efforts should be conducted to determine successes and failures, and recommendations from these studies should be incorporated into national and state-level policies and plans.

- **Establish regional drought forums**

  Regional forums or councils should be established to consider drought-related issues on an ongoing basis to keep policies and plans current, share lessons learned, and avoid a return to the reactive approach to drought management. This is an especially relevant issue in the drought-prone western states.

- **Encourage development of state drought mitigation plans**

  States should evaluate existing drought response plans and revise them to place greater emphasis on

mitigation. States without drought plans should develop plans. The federal government could provide incentives to states to develop plans.

CONCLUSIONS AND RECOMMENDATIONS

During the past decade in the United States, widespread and severe drought has resulted in an increased awareness of the nation's continuing vulnerability to this creeping natural hazard. This experience has resulted in numerous initiatives by state and federal government to improve the timeliness and effectiveness of response efforts. Although some progress has been made, much remains to be done. For the most part, government continues to deal with drought in a reactive, rather than proactive, mode. The dilemma facing government, particularly federal government, is whether to continue with the approach of the past (i.e., crisis management) or seek a new direction. Given that previous attempts to mitigate drought in the United States have been largely unsuccessful, it seems clear that fundamental and sweeping programme and policy changes must occur in order for the nation to more adequately address existing drought management problems. As a nation we can no longer afford to tinker with a system that is seriously flawed. For this transition to a more proactive, risk management approach to be successful, the deficiencies of previous drought response attempts must be addressed in a systematic way.

A review and synthesis of studies that have evaluated recent drought response efforts shows that there is broad agreement on the need for an integrated national drought policy and plan. The first step in this process would be the establishment of a federal interagency task force with the authority to develop and implement the plan. The task force must develop the objectives of a national policy in concert with extensive public involvement. This policy should promote the concept of risk management, although it cannot ignore the need for government assistance for some sectors during extended periods of severe drought. The policy should promote self-reliance while at the same time protecting the natural and agricultural resource base. The interagency task force should coordinate the drought-related activities of the federal government (i.e., forecasting, monitoring, impact assessment, response and recovery, and planning). The national policy should also include incentives for all drought-prone states to develop plans that promote a more proactive, anticipatory approach to drought management. Lessons learned from previous drought response attempts need to be documented through post-drought audits and shared with all levels of government. Regional drought councils could be used as a forum for keeping policies and plans current and sharing lessons learned.

In support of the national drought policy and plan, it is recommended that a comprehensive, integrated national climate monitoring system be established to provide early warning of emerging drought and other extreme climate events. This system would integrate data from federal and state collection networks, including information on precipitation and temperature, stream flow, reservoir and lake levels, groundwater levels, snowpack, and soil moisture.

Drought inflicts considerable pain and hardship on society. The impacts of contemporary droughts have demonstrated this fact again and again over the past several decades. Drought illustrates in innumerable ways the vulnerability of economic, social, political, and environmental systems to a variable climate. It also illustrates the dependencies that exist between systems, reinforcing the need for improved coordination within and between levels of government.

Extended periods of normal or benign weather conceal the vulnerability of societies to climate variability, while drought exposes these sensitivities. Projected changes in climate because of increased concentrations of CO_2 and other atmospheric trace gases suggest a possible increase in the frequency and intensity of severe drought in the future. Any increase in the incidence of drought will aggravate drought management problems further. Coupled with increasing population and the associated rise in demand for water and other shared natural resources, there is a sense of urgency for reducing the personal hardships and economic and environmental impacts of drought.

NOTE

1 This chapter is reprinted from *Journal of the American Water Resources Association*, vol. 33, no. 5, October 1977, pp. 951–9.

REFERENCES

Allen, W.M. (1984) 'The Palmer Drought Severity Index: Limitations and assumptions', *Journal of Climate and Applied Meteorology* 23: 1,100–9.

Crawford, A.B. (1978) 'State and federal responses to the 1977 drought', in N.J. Rosenberg (ed.), *North American Droughts*, AAAS Selected Symposium, Boulder, CO: Westview Press.

FEMA (1995) *National Mitigation Strategy: Partnerships for Building Safer Communities*. Washington, DC: Federal Emergency Management Agency.

— (1996a) *Drought of 1996: Multi-State Drought Task Force Findings. Report of a Workshop*, Washington, DC: Federal Emergency Management Agency.

— (1996b) 'FEMA Region Six director appointed to chair drought task force', press release, Washington, DC.

General Accounting Office (1979) *Federal Response to the 1976–77 Drought: What Should Be Done Next?*, Report to the Comptroller General, Washington, DC.

Great Lakes Commission (1990) *A Guidebook to Drought Planning, Management and Water Level Changes in the Great Lakes*, Ann Arbor, MI: Great Lakes Commission.

Grigg, N.S. and Vlachos, E.C. (1989) *Drought Water Management: Preparing and Responding to Drought*, Ft. Collins, CO: International School for Water Resources, Colorado State University.

Interstate Council on Water Policy (1987) *Statement of Policy 1986–87*, Washington, DC: Interstate Conference on Water Policy.

Interstate Council on Water Policy (1991) *Statement of Policy 1991–92*, Washington, DC: Interstate Conference on Water Policy.

National Academy of Sciences (1986) *The National Climate Program: Early Achievements and Future Directions*, Washington, DC: National Academy of Sciences.

Orville, H.D. (1990) 'AMS Statement on Meteorological Drought', *Bulletin of the American Meteorological Society* 71: 1,021–3.

Palmer, W.C. (1965) 'Meteorological drought', *Research Paper* No. 45, US Weather Bureau, Washington, DC.

Riebsame, W.E., Changnon, S.A. Jr., and Karl, T.R. (1990) *Drought and Natural Resources Management in the United States: Impacts and Implications of the 1987–89 Drought*, Boulder, CO: Westview Press.

Smith, J.B. and Tirpak, D. (eds) (1989) *The Potential Effects of Global Climate Change on the United States*, EPA–230–05–89–050, Washington, DC: Environmental Protection Agency.

US Congress, Office of Technology Assessment (1993) *Preparing for an Uncertain Climate*, Volume 1, OTA–O–567, Washington, DC: US Government Printing Office.

Western Governors' Association (WGA) (1996) Draft strategy for development of western drought policies and regional response plans, Denver, Colorado.

Western Governors' Policy Office (WESTPO) (1978)

Managing Resource Scarcity: Lessons from the Mid-Seventies Drought, Denver, CO: Institute for Policy Research.

Western States Water Council (1987) *A Model for Western State Drought Response and Planning*, Midvale, UT: Western States Water Council.

White, D.H., Collins, D., and Howden, M. (1993) 'Drought in Australia: Prediction, monitoring, management, and policy', in D.A. Wilhite (ed.), *Drought Assessment, Management, and Planning: Theory and Case Studies*, Boston, MA: Kluwer Academic Publishers.

Wilhite, D.A. (1983) 'Government response to drought in the United States: With particular reference to the Great Plains', *Journal of Climate and Applied Meteorology* 22: 40–50.

——— (1991a) 'Drought planning and state government: Current status', *Bulletin of the American Meteorological Society* 72: 1,531–6.

——— (1991b) 'Drought planning: A process for state government', *Water Resources Bulletin* 27: 29–38.

——— (1993) *An Assessment of Drought Mitigation Technologies in the United States*, Final Report to the Soil Conservation Service/USDA, *IDIC Technical Report* 93–1, Lincoln, NE: International Drought Information Center, University of Nebraska.

——— (1996) 'A methodology for drought preparedness', *Natural Hazards* 13: 229–52.

Wilhite, D.A., Rosenberg, N.J., and Glantz, M.H. (1986) 'Improving federal response to drought', *Journal of Climate and Applied Meteorology* 25: 332–42.

Wilhite, D.A. and Wood, D.A. (1994) *Drought Management in a Changing West: New Directions for Water Policy*, IDIC Technical Report 94–1, Lincoln, NE: International Drought Information Center, University of Nebraska–Lincoln.

41

DROUGHT RISK MANAGEMENT IN SOUTHERN AFRICA

Developing institutions to transform 'belated disaster response' into 'informed preparedness'

Jim Williams

OVERVIEW

Recent developments in long-lead forecasting offer drought-prone developing countries (DCs), like those in southern Africa, the novel prospect of *managing* climatic variability rather than always being the passive, surprised victim of 'unexpected' drought. Although such an opportunity offers major economic and social benefits, these will not be achieved without important changes in the operational practices of many institutions. In particular, DC government departments will need to become more proactive, incorporating risk factors as part of a broader requirement for government institutions to improve information management for more timely decision making.

Drought mitigation through long-lead climate forecasting is one potential benefit among several arising from improved monitoring and understanding of *global* weather and climate. The existing meteorological infrastructure in southern Africa, however, does not yet deliver full benefit from long-lead climate forecasts and other equally promising new opportunities. Many services are caught in transition between traditional working practices and the new global meteorology. Meteorological and climatological observation networks, however, are fundamental components of monitoring the natural and human-affected environment. Considerable advantages could accrue from enabling meteorological services to fulfil a wider role as national real-time environment monitoring units, including a range of hazard warning capabilities. Strong demand for drought risk management could be the catalyst for an important process of institutional development.

INTRODUCTION TO THE ISSUES

Hazards and disasters present responsible authorities with difficult decisions. Where resources are chronically scarce, as in many African countries, institutions find coping with actual disasters disruptive enough, let alone investing in hazard warning. In countries where drought recurs all too frequently, preparedness for early mitigation of the worst effects is politically important, and can be highly cost effective, but institutional resolve tends to weaken when rains are good and drought risk is apparently remote again.

By international convention, to release a forecast of natural disaster for a foreign country is an unfriendly action: evidence should be passed to the relevant national authorities for appropriate response. Modern technology (e.g., satellites), however, now enables many more potential disasters to be forecast remotely and warnings to be disseminated (e.g., global TV networks) before local authorities are even aware of the problem. At an International Decade for National Disaster Reduction meeting (Hunt 1994), discussion touched this difficult topic. It was estimated that given the good offices of the World Meteorological Organization (WMO), it might take only another ten years to evolve agreements to cope effectively with meteorological disaster forecast dissemination. For other hazards like volcanoes, earthquakes, and landslides, for which no global organisation coordinates international relations, similar agreements could take much longer to develop. Technological capability now evolves much faster than institutions can adapt and cope. Similarly, developments in drought forecasting are progressing faster than institutions in many DCs can incorporate this new and powerful information into their decision making. It is important to take stock of such constraints and examine them in conjunction with social, political, and technical issues, because they are crucial to effective disaster reduction everywhere.

Historical context

In the past, societies in Africa were generally self-sufficient in food and had coping strategies sufficient to mitigate all but the worst excesses of drought. It was not until the 1970s that imbalances in food production became large enough to necessitate 'structural food aid', whereby certain countries in Africa required significant annual imports of food aid. At the same time, expensive strategic grain reserves were established in many countries to maintain national food security in the event of drought.

Drought proofing

During the long-term structural adjustment programmes subsequently adopted in several southern African countries, with support from the World Bank and donors, it became clear that the impact of drought on development was disproportionally large. Attempts to 'drought-proof' agricultural systems required new thinking, part of which reached toward earlier drought warning through climate forecasting. Although recent developments in long-lead forecasting in parts of the world, including southern Africa, had shown increasing skill (e.g., see Cane *et al.* 1994, Ropelewski and Halpert 1987, WMO 1986), there appeared to be little impact on operational decision making outside Australia. To see whether such a new technology was ready to contribute to drought proofing economies in southern Africa, a team was commissioned to explore the technical and institutional issues. This chapter is based largely on the findings of the team (see Gibberd *et al.* 1996).

THE IMPORTANCE OF DROUGHT IN SOUTHERN AFRICA

The impact of drought[1]

The predominance of rain-fed subsistence agriculture and an overdependence on water-demanding maize serves to ensure that food security across southern Africa is inextricably linked to the quality of each rainy season. Both agricultural and livestock production are extremely susceptible to seasonal rainfall and, as a result, have shown considerable volatility in recent years.

Drought shock, however, extends well beyond the confines of agriculture and livestock and directly affects the performance of many nonagricultural sectors, ranging from electricity generation to industry, urban development, and health, through their heavy dependence on water. In the future, as demand increases and resources become scarcer, water will increasingly become the limiting factor in economic and social development across the subcontinent. The implementation of Structural Adjustment Programmes in a number of southern African countries during the 1980s and the occurrence of a number of droughts since then has highlighted the economy-wide impact of rainfall variability and has increased awareness amongst planners of the need to include climate variability in the planning process, at all levels within the economy.

Drought management in the national economy

Economic impact or drought shock affects countries differently, depending on their economic structure (Benson and Clay 1994). For example, low-income countries with the highest proportion of population in subsistence agriculture, like Malawi and Zambia, are severely affected by drought, with a danger of famine. Intermediate and complex economies like Zimbabwe and South Africa, respectively, are generally affected less severely, but increased cash cropping results in a decrease in food production and the national economy may be more vulnerable, especially from water shortages. In addition, recovery is not immediate on the return of the rains. Complex or dualistic economies (i.e., with large mining sectors, such as Namibia and Botswana) appear to be affected least severely by drought, with the effects being largely confined to the agricultural sector. The effects of drought, however, are wide-reaching and long-term.

The occurrence and frequency of drought

Other chapters in this book will explore the occurrence and frequency of drought. Suffice it here to say that recent evidence (assessed in Gibberd *et al.* 1996) suggests that droughts are becoming not only more common in the region of southern Africa, but also larger in scale and impact. In addition, there is concern that the twentieth-century 'normal' rainfall pattern is now being disturbed by global warming. Recent research (Mitchell *et al.* 1995) with improved climate models indicates that overall conditions in southern Africa are likely to be drier and warmer in the mid-twenty-first century than during the past few decades. Increased variability is predicted for the 'transition' period.

DROUGHT MANAGEMENT OPPORTUNITIES

Comparing potential benefits from three time scales of long-lead forecasts (i.e., a month, a whole wet season, a multiyear outlook), it is clear that in southern Africa, the ability to predict, with confidence, the quality of the next wet season is, without doubt, the single most sought-after item of climatic information for drought risk management, both at macro and micro levels.

At macro level, improved seasonal forecasts could:

- enable governments to build climate variability into *macro economic management* processes;
- *transform early warning systems* from their current function of supporting drought relief and recovery interventions into proactive agents guiding drought mitigation and preparedness;
- encourage *trade in agricultural commodities*, both in the Southern African Development Community (SADC) and with the rest of the world; and
- enable *national-level food security* without having to maintain expensive grain stocks.

Improved multiyear forecasts would diminish uncertainty in long-term planning and facilitate:

- development and sectoral planning – especially for water, an increasingly scarce regional resource;
- drought preparedness and mitigation strategies – governments need justification and confidence to embark on long-term approaches; and
- capital investment projects – through a more certain environment for investors throughout the economy.

Reliable long-lead forecasts would also enable improvements in a large number of strategic planning decisions in the public and private agricultural support services. For example, the availability of reliable seasonal forecasts should vastly extend the scope of response farming, allowing researchers to develop a limited range of different agronomic packages; in any particular year, the most appropriate extension packages could be promoted in accordance with the actual forecast for the area. In southern Africa, demand for water – urban, rural, industrial, agricultural, and ecological – is increasingly outstripping supply. Options to satisfy future requirements increasingly demand international collaboration. Potential benefits from better *regional* water resource planning and management would themselves justify major investment in improving the reliability and precision of long-lead forecasts.

At micro level, the potential benefits of improved seasonal forecasts are extremely numerous and diverse, but seemingly the seasonal forecast again provides the best fit with people's planning processes and priorities. Multiyear forecasts, while useful, are more remote and a bit ominous. Reliable forecasts of weeks or a month ahead would be useful, but options for response would be less numerous. It is the seasonal forecast, issued a few months in advance of wet season commencement, that offers the most opportunity.

Demand for better drought forecasting

Useful skill in long-lead forecasting is very new. It is only recently that understanding of global climate and weather relationships has become sufficiently good for both meteorologists and potential users to begin to believe that seasonal forecasting (that dream since biblical times) may be developing into a practical proposition. This evolving belief is dampened in many instances by the perceived poverty of service currently provided by national weather organisations.

Farmers, however, have a major preoccupation with the weather, and frequently seek a seasonal outlook. During this work, a great majority of those consulted (from subsistence farmers to futures dealers) were strongly interested in the possibility of long-lead forecasting and most keen that its further development be promoted as an extremely high priority for southern Africa. The extraordinary dependence of the Zimbabwe stock exchange on rainfall is a clear indicator of need. For such a new technology, this is strong demand indeed.

Long-lead forecasting does present problems, however, to people of superstitious or strongly religious persuasions. Forecasting the quality of the next wet season is very much the domain of gods, and suffering the inflicted drought can be seen as an important part of the atonement process. That said, ethno-meteorological reports describe a wide variety of traditional forecast systems based on plant or animal behaviour, testifying to the strong desire for farming people to be able to forecast the quality of the next season. In a somewhat similar vein, since 'unforeseen drought problems' are reported to cover a multitude of incompetencies and economic mismanagement, it is argued that at a certain level *people actually do not want to be advised of future climate*, because that would make them more accountable for their (lack of) actions.

Delivering benefits

There is an interesting paradox here. Seasonal forecasts are not only in great demand and potentially the most beneficial, but are also the easiest to deliver of the three long-lead forecasts explored. Already, seasonal drought forecasting in southern Africa is probably about 80 per cent reliable at macro level. People, however, have little awareness of current forecast skill levels and even less confidence that they are getting the best deal from their weather service, while other government institutions don't really want to know. This suggests a dislocation: in southern Africa, new meteorological products are ahead of current capacity to deliver and use them.

NEW METEOROLOGY: CHANGING TECHNOLOGY, ROLES, AND NEEDS

Meteorology is going through an unprecedented period of development. It has become an increasingly reliable and beneficial science, but relatively few developing countries make best use of the available products. To do this requires changes in working practices.

Changing technology

Weather forecasting has always been technology-constrained, in terms of communications, processing power, and observational capacity. The relatively recent conjunction of satellites, ever-improving telecommunications, and high-powered computers allows modelling of global weather systems, the natural scale of world weather. This has resulted in a veritable revolution in meteorology, and has led to drought forecasts, among other products. Since weather systems move around the world in a matter of days, any reliable forecasting of more than two or three days ahead needs to consider the total global weather situation and how it is evolving. Local meteorology and climatology has now become interpretation of the local situation within the dynamic global context.

Although much of the progress in meteorology is driven by new technology, concern over anthropogenic-induced global warming and consequent climate change has been another major stimulus to understanding global influences on local weather. In a warmer world with human-affected rainfall patterns, it is essential that droughts be better predicted and managed.

Changing roles

About thirty years ago, there were 150 meteorological services around the world, all trying independently to analyse 'their' weather to predict imminent changes. Today, with the abundance of quality products from global models, the role of most national institutions is radically different. WMO is an excellent example of international collaboration with the development of a genuine network of participants that all gain from their mutual collaboration. It is also a good example of subsidiarity in operation, since there are marked benefits from pooling efforts to work cooperatively at global, regional, and local levels. The essential feature of meteorology today is that local synoptic data are collected from all over the world as input for global scale models, the outputs from which are disseminated back to the original data providers. At the global scale, there is need for a few operational modelling centres, and already there are several. At the regional scale, the South African Weather Bureau runs a regional model calibrated from the global models, which provides outputs useful to all within the limited region. At the local level, the national services obtain global and regional products and interpret them for detailed use within their local area.

To date, the developed economies have benefited more than developing countries from the new global meteorological network. Successful participation requires that each national service provide basic observations in timely fashion and then interpret and make best use of the resultant global and regional model outputs *for the greatest benefit of its customers*. Corporate attitudes of meteorological services tend to be rather traditional, and this fundamental change in role (more service and less meteorology) has yet to be accepted by many small services. The transition process can be difficult.

Changing needs

In most countries, meteorology evolved to serve the needs of aviation security, both civil and military. Although an obligation remains to maintain minimum meteorological standards at international airports, this is no longer the primary raison d'être. The core business of a meteorological service is likely to include providing timely information for:

- *Response management* All governments are under growing pressure to manage economies with more sensitive response to changing circumstances and recurrent events like drought and flood.

- *Water resource management* In many countries, water is increasingly becoming a more scarce resource highly prone to disruption by drought. Its increasingly high value in urbanising and

industrialising economies requires better management of its allocation and use.

- *Agriculture* Agriculture is still the most important economic sector in many of the countries of SADC, and it is critically drought prone. Serving the needs of agriculture with information to improve weather-sensitive decisions has become a priority need of meteorology.

- *Environment monitoring* Meteorological services are de facto the real time environment monitoring units in southern Africa. With the advent of meteorological satellites providing free daily data, the ability of meteorological services to monitor environmental change has markedly increased.

- *Social and health issues* Increased understanding of the effects of weather on diseases, and the changing epidemiology of diseases like malaria, offers opportunities for meteorological services to use the information available to them for important quality-of-life decisions.

INSTITUTIONAL ISSUES: NEW PRODUCTS FROM OLD SERVICES

The importance of weather and climate information for managing resources and the national economy is widely recognised, but doubts exist as to whether meteorological institutions in their existing state can ensure that early and maximum benefit is derived from emerging technologies such as drought forecasting. Governments, donors, and commercial customers all expressed reservations (Gibberd *et al.* 1996) about the capacity, attitude, and performance of national meteorological services.

Comparative advantage

In general, meteorological services are unique as government bodies:

- They do not make end-point decisions themselves, but are information providers to a wide range of users. This means they do not belong naturally to any one branch of government.
- They work with weather, which is part of the environment and of major interest to many, if not

all, people in the countries concerned.

- They must function in real time, all day and every day. The value of their information is highly perishable and needs to be communicated, in timely fashion, to a diverse range of customers.
- They operate as part of a coherent, operational global network to which they contribute data and from which they receive information. Without the global network, the ability of individual services to function effectively is very limited. With good access to global weather products, their *potential* for providing timely and reliable information is growing rapidly, and will continue to do so.

It is *this extraordinary potential that needs development* so that best use can be made at national and local levels of drought forecasts and other products of the global weather network. *Until recently, meteorological services needed to be large to be effective*, hence their emphasis *on capacity development*. This is no longer the case. *Future emphasis must be on capacity utilisation.*

Meteorological institutions in southern Africa

Besides the national meteorological services in each of the countries in the SADC, there are several other organisations at the regional level with interests in meteorology. These include the Drought Monitoring Centre (DMC), the Regional Early Warning System, the SADC Environment and Land Monitoring System, and several universities undertaking research, including those in Witswatersrand, Cape Town, Natal, Pretoria, and Harare. If progress is to be made in adapting outputs from global centres such as the recently created International Research Institute for Seasonal Climate Prediction in the United States, then scope exists for using existing research capability in SADC and rationalising diverse regional interests.

Subsidiarity

Just as in Europe there are moves toward a European-wide meteorological service, in SADC, similar steps toward a regional service operating from the South African Weather Bureau are progressing. National services will concentrate more on local users, and may find more reward and better long-term access to resources in a Department of Water Affairs or Ministry of the Environment.

DMC

Within SADC, the Drought Monitoring Centre appears to have more of a future as a drought *management* centre. It could help national services to:

- take advantage of the new meteorology and long-lead forecasts in particular;
- restructure themselves to focus activities more on users and their needs;
- develop business plans; and
- seek support for taking on new initiatives, such as timely warning of hazards/environmental change.

Universities

In a similar way, there is need for development of a more active regional research network in existing universities, to explore and develop drought forecasts and coping mechanisms in collaboration with both potential users and the meteorological services in the region.

The transitionary process

Meteorological services in SADC, as elsewhere, are currently at various stages of transition between traditional and modern working techniques. Satellite and global model output products are still relatively new and not yet fully accessible, so services are at different stages in the process of incorporating the new data sources into operational practices. One service was routinely faxing the five-day forecasts received from the European Centre for Medium-Range Weather Forecasts (ECMWF) directly to customers, emphasising the essential role of the service as information provider. Meteorological services need support – investment for restructuring and retraining – to assist them through this important and productive change.

Institutional development

Drivers for institutional reform are the objectives, orientation, and expectations of outputs from the new service-to-be. This defines requirements and guides options for new structures. Although information management and decision making by governments everywhere is characteristically weak, several governments in SADC have demanded a more timely information service better tuned to their rapidly changing needs. External factors influencing the debate include:

- the extent to which a national natural resource management strategy or system exists;
- the level and development of the national information system or network;
- national data policy and government attitude toward cost-recovery processes in the public sector;
- the extent to which government, NGOs, or the private sector are the main users of information;
- the extent to which commercial companies could develop and provide complementary services; and
- the need to sustain national participation in the global network.

In SADC, the meteorological service of the future is likely to be one of a set of small dynamic public sector agencies, closely networked with (and accountable to) their customers and each other. The greatest potential for meteorology in the future lies in an expanded environment monitoring role, an arrangement that would allow services to develop their potential and use their comparative advantages to best effect while sustaining essential core activities for long-term benefit. Taking on new roles and other (hazard warning) responsibilities would be made easier with a clear lead from WMO.

Policy: data and information management

An important element of operating an effective system of this nature is data policy. Incentives toward cost recovery can restrict both data availability and net benefit for the country concerned. To encourage greatest *utilisation* of basic data in an era of super-abundance, a clear data policy is required. The American meteorological partnership (Friday *et al.*

1996) appears to offer one of the most effective working models. This open arrangement guarantees the basic level of service through government support and at the same time encourages individual enterprise to develop and market new products wherever there is a buyer.

THE WAY FORWARD: INTEGRATED DROUGHT RISK MANAGEMENT

Improvements in climate forecasting and meteorological service productivity are not sufficient to ensure better drought risk management. Rather, a number of concurrent developments need to take place to ensure that such information can be taken up by a wide range of decision makers and put to effective use *across the economy*. Certain widespread obstacles to response exist, which need to be addressed through a comprehensive strategy in parallel with reform of meteorological institutions.

Confidence

A lack of confidence in forecasts rather than a lack of recognition of their potential applications is the underlying reason why climate forecasts are little utilised today. From a user's perspective, the prime requisites for a forecast are *reliability* and *timeliness*, and people are often prepared to trade geographic and quantitative precision for greater reliability and timeliness, particularly in the case of multiyear and seasonal forecasts.

Evolving use

How reliable is 'reliable enough'? The propensity to use long-lead forecasts depends on the individual decision makers' own risk profile. Historically, the level of forecast reliability has been too low to be included in serious decision making. At a certain threshold of reliability and user awareness, however, depending on the vulnerability of the decision both to drought and to the forecast being incorrect, forecasts will begin to be used *in support of other factors and pressures*. Thus a simple but sufficiently reliable forecast of 'significant drought' or 'no significant drought' for the next wet season could be surprisingly useful if it is available when decisions are made (or if it serves to stimulate them). It is not logical to wait until forecast skill (in virtually any domain) is '100 per cent reliable' before beginning to incorporate forecasts into decision making.

Systematic release

The release of forecasts on an infrequent and often ad hoc basis can contribute to the *shock effect* of drought. In the present system, the sudden issuance of a drought pronouncement, after months of apparent inactivity, can create overreaction and does little to stimulate confidence in forecasters' abilities. A system is needed that regularly updates long-lead forecasts in a transparently open and reliable way, even if it states 'at the moment there is no clear indication that the next wet season will be abnormal in any way'.

Thus, forecasting centres should give primary attention to improving the *reliability of seasonal forecasts*, since such products offer the greatest utility. The *immediate goal* of forecasters should be to issue *a reliable and comprehensible national-level seasonal forecast by the beginning of July each year*. Forecasting centres should issue *regular* and *frequent forecasting* bulletins for free and widespread dissemination. As a general principle, forecasting centres should issue rolling forecasts to minimise the shock effect of sudden unexpected forecasts.

Owning the service and the forecasts: 'User Consultative Panels'

Efforts are needed to ensure that improvements in forecasting are *user driven*. One way to facilitate this would be to establish *consultative panels* made up of representatives from various user groups to advise forecasting services on the quality of existing forecast products and on the types of improvements needed. User Consultative Panels could be integrated with benefit to national meteorological services as well as to regional institutions such as the SADC Regional Early Warning System and the Drought Monitoring Centre.

Resources to respond

The ability to use climate forecasts depends on the size and diversity of the decision maker's *resource base*. Resource-poor decision makers have less scope and fewer opportunities to use forecasts, even if they have a high degree of confidence in them. Special measures would need to be directed toward strengthening *the response capabilities of resource-poor user groups*, particularly *subsistence farmers*. Apart from the need to ensure that forecasts are issued in sufficient time to enable resource-poor groups to respond, mechanisms need to be put in place to support less well endowed users. In particular, research and extension services need to become much more forecast-responsive in their approach to small farmers. They need to be able to translate seasonal forecasts into specific options for the subsistence and smallholder sectors, in co-ordination with other agricultural support services, such as input suppliers and credit institutions. Evidence of relatively sophisticated coping strategies obtained from farmers groups, NGOs, and the University of Witswatersrand Geography Department suggests that scope for beneficial response to long-lead forecasts by subsistence farmers may be larger than is sometimes supposed.

Free market

Opportunities for responding to long-lead forecasts are also influenced by the *market environment*. In the past, central government control restricted opportunities by the private sector to respond: market liberalisation is an important prerequisite for enterprising uptake and use of forecasts.

Economic management

Finally, as experience in the region with early warning systems has shown, improvements in the quality of information does not guarantee better drought management. *Good government*, *fiscal responsibility*, and *effective organisation* are important prerequisites for effective response. These requirements, in particular, should not be underestimated.

User awareness for improved decision support and information management

Even after ensuring that all the above preconditions for the effective use of improved forecasts are satisfied, the integrated national benefit from application of forecasts in drought risk management will depend on whether enough users have a sufficient understanding of how to use the new information and, ultimately, an incentive and willingness to apply the forecasts. An important part of any initiative to encourage the use of climate forecasts must therefore include organised *user awareness education*. Decision makers throughout government and the private sector need to be encouraged to examine their own risk profiles and the sensitivity of their decision making to the vagaries of weather and climate, and develop strategic options, precautions, or contingency arrangements appropriate to a limited range of forecast scenarios in advance of the next ENSO drought forecast. In this way, individual decision makers or managers can affirm that existing decision making is appropriate to an uncertain and possibly changing climate, and also accept ownership of drought risks and recognise their responsibility to use available forecasts to minimise losses.

Good governance

In 1994, at least one government in SADC tried to suppress the release of seasonal forecasts in advance of the ENSO-related drought. Drought mitigation strategies must be designed to take into account a country's economic circumstances and structure, and likely future weather. In intermediate and complex societies where drought shocks are widely diffused, balance of payments and budgetary support are most effective. In simple economies where drought impact is concentrated in rural areas, more targeted interventions are required. Both responses can be aided by reliable advance knowledge of conditions. Since fiscal responsibility and improved economic management across the board can also reduce the effects of drought, *the development and widespread uptake of reliable long-lead forecasts* and their *incorporation for improved decision making throughout the economy* is rapidly becoming *of the utmost priority* for the countries of southern Africa.

CONCLUSIONS AND CHALLENGES

The general conclusion is that the magnitude of the economic and social benefit to be gained from improved drought risk management in southern Africa through long-lead climate forecasting justifies further investment in measures to improve forecasting reliability together with accessibility, uptake, and utilisation. As one senior decision maker put it, *information* of such fundamental *economic value* must be easily available in the *public domain* as early as possible, so as to *maximise benefits* from the *broadest possible range of investment decisions*.

Particular conclusions

1 Seasonal forecasting capability is already skilful enough to start being incorporated in decision making, and is on the threshold of becoming vital for better drought risk management in southern Africa. Improving this capability is a very high priority indeed.
2 For countries of southern Africa to benefit from more of the considerable potential offered by modern meteorological services when networked into the global system, meteorological institutions in SADC need appropriate investment together with institutional development. Such action, however, needs to be part of a more comprehensive approach to strengthen natural resource information management and decision making in developing countries.
3 By addressing the use of long-lead forecasting for drought risk management in a systematic way, developing countries will refine methods of immediate benefit that will also help them to adapt more easily to systematic climate change.

Challenges

1 The challenge for the scientific community is to improve reliability and timeliness of long-lead forecasting toward meeting priority user needs in southern Africa, as soon as possible.
2 The challenge to government administrators and decision makers is to respond intelligently to the new technology, which carries its own obligations

toward better economic management, fiscal responsibility, and good governance.

3 The challenge to the meteorological community in SADC is to put their house in order with imagination and make the most of the many powerful new opportunities presented.

4 The challenge to the general public and private sector is to demand a better service from government bodies in the supply and use of information.

5 The challenges to donors are to recognise the major potential benefit to be derived from these and other products of the information revolution, adapt their own machinery to be able to address sweeping multisectoral issues of this nature, and ensure that benefits are incorporated in pertinent ongoing programmes.

6 The challenge to the global community is to accept the likely consequences of anthropogenic global warming and seek to mitigate the effects on those least able to adapt.

ACKNOWLEDGEMENTS

The initial work that provided the backbone for this analysis was supported by the UK Overseas Development Administration (now Department for International Development) and the World Bank. Their advice and support is keenly acknowledged, along with the many people in southern Africa who helped with the assessment.

NOTE

1 Drought can be defined in many ways according to purpose. In this chapter, a drought is 'an occurrence of significantly below normal rainfall which impacts on productive activities'.

REFERENCES

Benson, C. and Clay, E. (1994) *The Impact of Drought on Sub-Saharan African Economies: A Preliminary Examination*, London: Overseas Development Institute.

Cane, M.A., Eshel, G., and Buckland, R.W. (1994) 'Forecasting Zimbabwean maize yield using eastern equatorial Pacific sea surface temperatures', *Nature* 370: 204.

Friday, E.W., Gross, E.M., and Yerg, M. (1996) 'The public-private partnership in the USA for the delivery of weather services and its relationship to the international exchange of meteorological and related data and products', *WMO Bulletin* 45, 1: 39–45.

Gibberd, V., Rook, J., Sear, C.B., and Williams, J.B. (1996) *The Potential of Long Lead Climate Forecasts for Improved Drought Management*, NRI, University of Greenwich, ME4 4TB, UK.

Hunt, J.C.R. (1994) 'Forecasts and warnings of natural disasters and roles of national and international agencies', in G. Wadge (ed.), *Natural Hazards and Remote Sensing*, Proceedings of an IDNDR conference [8–9 March 1994] at the Royal Society, London, pp. 26–33.

Mitchell, J.F.B., Johns, T.C., Gregory, J.M., and Tett, S.F.B. (1995) 'Climate response to increasing levels of greenhouse gases and sulphate aerosols', *Nature* 376: 501.

Ropelewski, C.F. and Halpert, M.S. (1987) 'Global and regional scale precipitation patterns associated with the El Niño/Southern Oscillation', *Monthly Weather Review* 115: 1,606.

WMO (1986) *The Global Climate System, A Contribution to the Global Environmental Monitoring System*, CSM R84/86, Geneva: World Meteorological Organization.

42

DROUGHT HAZARDS IN ISRAEL AND JORDAN

Policy recommendations for disaster mitigation

Hendrik J. Bruins

INTRODUCTION

Planning and development intrinsically require an approximation of the future, which is often based on *the standard of the average and the normal.* However, such an approach is not realistic, as it neglects the abnormal and the extreme, both in the physical and human environment. Historical analyses provide a required perspective about the frequency and impact of extreme natural events as well as human-made calamities. It is, therefore, essential that planning for the abnormal and extreme be included in the scope of both regional and national development strategies, particularly with regard to water (Bruins 1996).

The hazard of severe drought ought to be taken seriously in Israel and Jordan. Both countries are situated at the northern fringe of the largest desert belt on earth, which stretches from the Atlantic coast of northern Africa eastward through the Sahara, Arabian, and Iranian deserts to the Thar desert of India. Large parts of Israel and Jordan form part of this formidable planetary desert belt (Figure 42.1). Aridity in both countries is related to descending air masses (sub-tropical high) of the Hadley cell circulation during the long hot summer (Alpert *et al.* 1990), the distance from the oceans, and the frequency and trajectory of precipitation-bearing depression systems in autumn, winter, and spring. The summer months are usually completely dry from May to October.

Interannual rainfall variations in the region are quite large, which is not surprising in such a transitional geoclimatic situation. Natural drought is a prevailing hazard that may strike with various degrees of severity. The available resources of fresh water in

Israel and Jordan are rather small in relation to the respective population sizes. A comparison with the other countries in the Near East (Table 42.1) shows the precariousness of the water situation in Jordan and Israel, as well as in the West Bank and Gaza Strip.

The prevailing water shortage in Jordan is even more severe than that in Israel. It is, therefore, understandable that water-related matters form an important part of the Peace Treaty between the two countries, signed on 26 October 1994. Rather detailed agreements were drawn up concerning the sharing of water resources. Israel is obliged to halt the diversion into the Jordan River of 20 million cubic metre (mcm) of saline water per year, derived from springs. This water is to be desalinated and half of it (10 mcm/year) supplied to Jordan. Pending completion of such a desalinisation plant near these saline springs in the

Table 42.1 Relation between population and average sustainable yield of fresh water in the Near East for 1992

Country	Population (million)	Fresh water (mcm/yr)	Fresh water per capita (cm/p/yr)
Israel	5	1,600	320
West Bank, Gaza	2	250	125
Jordan	4	750	188
Syria	13	10,500	800
Lebanon	3	3,700	1,230
Turkey	59	105,000	1,800
Egypt	55	60,000	1,100

Source: Fishelson 1995: 45–8

Kinneret basin, Israel will supply Jordan in winter with 10 mcm/year of good-quality Jordan River water. Both countries will cooperate in finding an additional amount of 50 mcm of drinkable water for Jordan.

An analysis is made in this chapter of drought hazards in Israel and Jordan in relation to climate and water resources management. The definition and classification of dry climates and drought are treated in considerable detail. Suggestions are made for a scientifically accurate, convenient, and globally comparable system to classify bioclimatic aridity, which is useful on a local and global scale. Policy recommendations are given to reduce and mitigate potential

drought disasters in Israel and Jordan, also through regional development cooperation.

DROUGHT CONCEPTS AND DEFINITIONS

The phenomenon of drought has been described as the most complex and least understood of all natural disasters (Wilhite 1993). Drought is a recurring, natural part of climatic variability, but scientific prediction of both its beginning and termination is virtually impossible. The frequency and severity of drought can, however, be linked to the various types of climate on earth. Drought can occur in each

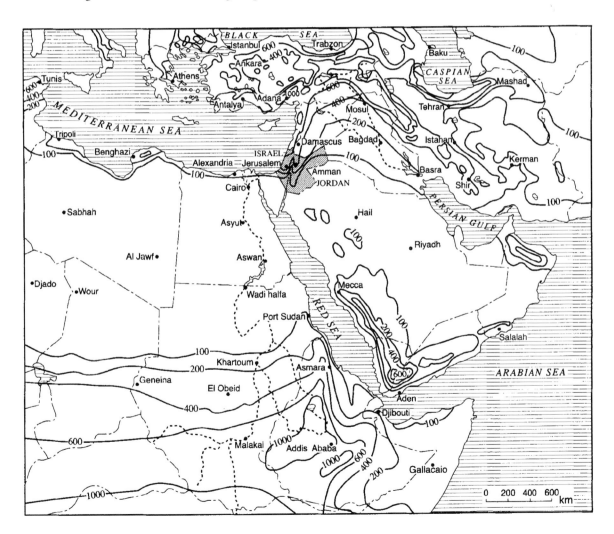

Figure 42.1 Israel and Jordan are situated at the northern fringe of the largest desert belt on earth

climatic zone, including in very wet regions. The frequency of its occurrence is usually related to an important empirically observed rule: the drier the climate, the larger the interannual variability of precipitation. Drought, therefore, tends to occur more often in subhumid and dry climates.

How dry is dry? It is important to classify bioclimatic aridity in a globally comparable way as a basis for land-use planning, proactive drought planning, and interactive management (Bruins and Lithwick 1998). A numerical representation is able to express dryness in much greater detail than language. Average annual precipitation (P) divided by average annual potential evapotranspiration (ETP) is the preferred mathematical way to classify bioclimatic aridity (or humidity), according to the classification system developed by UNESCO (1979). The sophisticated Penman (1948) approach was adopted by UNESCO (1979) as an accurate estimate for potential evapotranspiration. However, certain geophysical data required to calculate Penman's formula are often not available at every site. UNEP (1992) opted, therefore, in its *World Atlas of Desertification*, for the simplified Thornthwaite (1948) approach, which is a step backward. UNESCO (1979) and UNEP (1992) definitions are compared in Table 42.2.

Bruins and Berliner (1998) prefer to retain the numerical boundaries between the above arid zones as established by UNESCO (1979), basing P/ETP ratios on Penman-related methods only. Discussing the above problems, they suggested a more convenient way to establish ETP data in line with Penman's approach. Berliner (manuscript in preparation) collected measurements that clearly show that Penman's ETP is very well represented by data from Class A evaporation pans, which are widely available throughout the world. 'We, therefore, suggest to base globally comparable P/ETP ratio calculations in the future on Class-A evaporation pan data as a standardised system to define bioclimatic aridity throughout the world' (Bruins and Berliner 1998: 102).

Both Israel and Jordan have large areas with a hyperarid (P/ETP < 0.03) and arid climate (P/ETP 0.03–0.20). These areas, unsuited for rain-fed agriculture, have been used since time immemorial for extensive livestock raising by (nomadic) pastoralists, such as the Bedouin. Central Israel and northwestern Jordan have a semiarid climate (P/ETP 0.20–0.50), in which rain-fed farming is feasible but quite sensitive to drought. The transition from hyperarid to semiarid occurs in both Israel and Jordan over a rather short distance of 30–150 km. The subhumid zone (P/ETP 0.50–0.75) in the Levant includes part of northern Israel, but does not reach Jordan, because it does not extend as far north (Figures 42.1 and 42.3). Drought frequency in the subhumid zone is somewhat less than in the semiarid zone, rendering the former zone more secure for rain-fed agriculture.

Wilhite and Glantz (1985) distinguish four main categories of drought according to disciplinary or causative perspectives: meteorological, agricultural, hydrological, and socioeconomic drought. Two additional categories are added here: 'pastural drought' and 'human-made calamity drought'. Meteorological drought can be regarded as the most basic form of drought, resulting from dynamic and complex geo-

Table 42.2 Comparison between UNESCO (1979) and UNEP (1992) definitions for bioclimatic aridity and the boundaries between the various arid and subhumid zones

Climatic zone	P/ETP ratio (Penman method) UNESCO (1979)	P/ETP ratio (Thornthwaite method) UNEP (1992)	Interannual rainfall variability
Hyperarid	< 0.03	< 0.05	~ 100%
Arid	0.03–0.20	0.05–0.20	50–100%
Semiarid	0.20–0.50	0.20–0.50	25–50%
Subhumid	0.50–0.75	0.50–0.65	< 25%

Source: Bruins and Berliner 1998

physical processes in the earth atmosphere. Drought develops passively as the rains fail to come or if the amount of precipitation is significantly less during a certain time period than the average amount in a specific area. More precise drought definitions are necessarily site specific. Precipitation records enable time-series analysis of drought occurrence and severity (Lee *et al.* 1986, Sharma 1994). The Palmer Drought Severity Index (PDSI) is widely used in the United States (Palmer 1965, Wilhite and Glantz 1985, Wilhite and Hayes 1998).

A certain year cannot be classified as a meteorological drought year if total annual precipitation reaches the average amount or above. Yet drought damage may have occurred to crops as a result of bad rainfall distribution within that year. The term *agricultural drought* (Wilhite and Glantz 1985) becomes useful to characterise such dry periods in areas where farming is practised. Livestock raising is a rational land use in many parts of the world, often taking place in areas that are too dry for rain-fed agriculture. Such pastoral or livestock regions are found in the Near and Middle East, including Jordan and Israel; the African continent; Central Asia; Australia; and North and South America, including the southwestern United States. It would be inappropriate to speak of agricultural drought in such regions, where natural pasture, rather than agricultural crops, is affected by dry spells. *Pastural drought* would seem the logical term in such cases (Bruins 1996).

Hydrologic drought relates to shortages in the flow of water at the surface or in the subsurface, which causes problems for societies depending on such water (Wilhite and Glantz 1985). Egypt is a classic example of a civilisation receiving virtually all its water supply from a so-called allochthonous or exotic river, the Nile. Egyptian agriculture, therefore, is not affected by local meteorological drought in the eastern Mediterranean or north African region. However, an extended meteorological drought in the catchment of the Nile in central and east Africa can cause a hydrologic drought in Egypt.

Socioeconomic drought, as defined by Wilhite and Glantz (1985), is in fact a human-made drought, although not unrelated to the basic structure of meteorological water supply and geohydrological water reserves. It occurs when the government and/

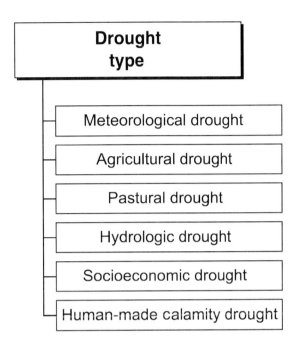

Figure 42.2 Overview of different categories of drought
Sources: Wilhite and Glantz 1985, Bruins 1996

or the private sector, in the economic development of a region, create a demand for more water than is normally available (Hoyt 1942, Wilhite and Glantz 1985). The relationship between supply and demand of water is not static, but may vary with time in response to changes in government policy, such as legislation to prevent overpumping of aquifers, development of hitherto untapped water resources (including desalinisation of brackish water and seawater), and water price and other socioeconomic criteria.

If constructive, albeit unwise, human activities in the socioeconomic realm can lead to drought in developed water management and delivery systems, it is but one step to move (in conceptual classification and definition) to destructive human activities as the cause for drought. Modern chemical industrial production and the problem of waste disposal may lead to pollution of groundwater, which can render such water unfit for human consumption or agricultural use. This may lead to a shortage of potable water in a certain area. Moreover, modern warfare and weapons of mass destruction pose a veritable threat not only in terms of direct lethal capability and destructiveness, but also in terms of environmental pollution. The concept of *human-made calamity drought* is introduced (Bruins 1996) to identify shortages of potable water resulting from destructive human activities. Human-made calamity drought is hereby defined as pollution of water resources and/or destruction of water-supply networks in a certain area, either accidentally or purposefully, resulting in a shortage of potable water for domestic and agricultural use.

GEOGRAPHY, CLIMATE, AND LAND USE IN ISRAEL AND JORDAN

Israel and Jordan are situated at the northern fringe of the planetary desert belt that lies between the tropical precipitation zone in the south and the Mediterranean precipitation zone in the north (Figure 42.1). Both Israel and Jordan are characterised by a variety of landscapes and climatic zones within a rather small geographical area. The Hashemite Kingdom of Jordan comprises an area of 89,213 km², which is about four times larger than Israel. Jordan has a maximal north-south length of about 395 km (245 miles) and a maximal width from east to west of about 355 km (221 miles). The maximal length of Israel from north to south is about 425 km (264 miles); its maximum width from east to west reaches only 115 km (71 miles).

The main geographic regions in Israel are the coastal plain, foothills (Shefela), and central mountain ridge, which is the backbone of the country. The central hills are bound in the north by the Jizreel Valley and in the south by the Beer-Sheva basin. The hills and mountains of Galilee continue farther to the north, to the border with Lebanon, while the hilly and rocky Negev desert makes up southern Israel.

The leeward eastern side of the Galilee, central mountain ridge, and Negev hills become increasingly drier toward the great Syro-African Rift Valley, which forms the border between Israel and Jordan. The area around the Dead Sea is the lowest spot on the continental surface of the earth, more than 400 m below ocean level. The climate in the Rift Valley is hot and dry, being hyperarid in the south and around the Dead Sea and becoming arid more to the north.

The Jordanian mountain ridge rises sharply on the eastern side of the Rift Valley, running from north to

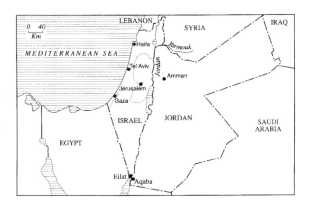

Figure 42.3 Location of Israel and Jordan in the Near East

south over the entire length of the country. These mountains are higher than on the western side of the Rift Valley, resulting in considerable precipitation despite the greater distance from the Mediterranean Sea. However, precipitation drops sharply at the eastern leeside of the Jordanian mountain ridge. A hyperarid and arid desert climate prevails over much of Jordan, which is reflected in the very low amount of cropland, only 2–4 per cent (Table 42.3). The northeastern plateau, which borders Syria and Iraq, is partly composed of basaltic rocks and hills. The southeastern plateau, having a higher ridge (Ard as-Suwwan) in its centre, is even drier. It gradually descends to Wadi al-Sirhan, a large valley shared by Jordan and Saudi Arabia, being important in the annual cycle of extensive livestock raising by Bedouin pastoralists.

There is very little agricultural land in the Near

Table 42.3 Land use in the region

Country	Cropland (%)	Pasture (%)	Forest (%)	Desert (%)
Israel and PA*	21	7	6	66
Jordan	4	9	1	86
Jordan **	2	97	1	–
Near East	4	20	2	74

Sources: World Resources Institute as cited in Bureau for the Near East US Agency for International Development, *Water Resources Action Plan for the Near East: Background, Issues and Options*, January 1993
Notes:
* PA = Palestinian Authority
** Data according to Nesheiwat 1995

East because of widespread aridity. Israel has more cropland than Jordan, because it has a somewhat wetter climate and more water resources. The alternative classification for Jordan by Nesheiwat (1995) clearly underlines the use of the desert for extensive livestock raising by Bedouin pastoralists, as the entire desert area of Jordan is included as pasture land. The range lands in Jordan support a population of 184,000 people. The number of sheep increased during the period 1983–91 from 1,100,000 to 2,671,000 and the number of Baladi goats from 360,000 to 888,000. This increase in herding animals by more than 140 per cent was accompanied by a decrease in forage production of 50 per cent, according to Nesheiwat (1995). He states that a few years ago the range lands provided 85 per cent of total feed requirements, but now provide less than 40 per cent. Changes in traditional herd management, drought coping mechanisms, and the intensified exploitation of the grazing lands by the Bedouin of Jordan are discussed by Lancaster and Lancaster (1993).

Precipitation in the region is usually related to depression systems coming from the west. Rainfall in Israel and Jordan decreases from north to south and from west to east. The average annual precipitation in Israel ranges from only 30 mm in the south to 800 mm in the elevated parts of Galilee in the north. Precipitation in Jordan ranges from a minimal average annual amount of 30 mm in the south at the Gulf of Aqaba to a maximum of 600 mm in the north. Areas receiving more than 500 mm are largely restricted to the Ajloun and Balqa mountains.

The Mediterranean coastal plain of Israel receives considerable rainfall, ranging from 587 mm in Haifa (elevation 10 m), to 556 mm in Tel-Aviv (elevation 20 m), to 371 mm in Gaza (elevation 45 m) in the south (average annual amounts for the period 1921–51, Katsnelson 1964). The Old City of Jerusalem (elevation 760 m) in the central hills has an average annual rainfall of 561 mm (for the period 1846–1953, Amiran 1994), whereas Jericho, just 25 km to the east, has only 143 mm (1921–51, Katsnelson 1964), because it lies in the Rift Valley at an elevation of –260 m below ocean level. Going farther east into Jordan, the topography rises sharply above the Rift Valley. Annual precipitation in Amman at the central part of the mountain ridge is 474 mm

(at the University of Jordan). However, just 10 km to the southeast, at Amman Airport, precipitation decreases to 290 mm, mainly because of adiabatic heating on the leeward side of the hills (Salameh 1997). The topography gradually descends into the eastern desert of Jordan, as average annual precipitation drops below 100 mm in large parts of this area. Aridity in Jordan stretches over a proportionally larger region than in Israel, owing to its distance from the Mediterranean Sea. Most (93 per cent) of Jordan receives on average less than 200 mm annual precipitation (Salameh 1997).

WATER RESOURCES IN ISRAEL AND JORDAN

The main water resources of Israel comprise one surface water basin, Lake Kinneret, and two groundwater basins, the Coastal Aquifer and the western Mountain Aquifer. About 80 per cent of all the water used in the country is derived from these three sources. Other important aquifers are found in Western Galilee, the Carmel region, Eastern Galilee, the Golan, the Yizreel Valley, Beit Shean Valley, and, in the south, the aquifers of the Negev and the Arava Valley (Gilead and Bachmat 1973, Grinwald and Bibas 1989).

The Yarmouk and Jordan rivers are the main surface water resources for the Hashemite Kingdom of Jordan and are shared with Jordan's neighbours. The average annual flow of the Yarmouk is about 470 mcm. Average utilisation of these waters by Syria, Jordan, and Israel amounts to 80 per cent of the total potential. During the rainy winter months an estimated average amount of 90 mcm of Yarmouk water flows unused into the Dead Sea. The use of Yarmouk water by Jordan, conveyed through the King Abdallah Canal to the eastern part of the Rift Valley, is mainly in the summer months.

The Jordan River, flowing in the Rift Valley, forms the border between Israel and Jordan from the confluence with the Yarmouk River to the Dead Sea. The water quality in this part of the Jordan River is poor, because 20 mcm of saline water from springs in the Kinneret basin and additional waste water are diverted by Israel into the lower Jordan River. The overall cocktail, diluted by flood waters in winter, usually has a very low quality, unsuited for agriculture. The 1994 Peace Treaty between Israel and Jordan contains articles to improve water quality in the lower Jordan River. The 20 mcm of saline water are to be desalinated by Israel for joint use by both countries, thus removing a major source of pollution (Ministries of Foreign Affairs and Finance 1996).

The groundwater aquifers of Jordan are divided into three main groups, the Deep Sandstone Aquifer Complex, the Upper Cretaceous Aquifer, and the Shallow Aquifer Complex (Salameh and Khdier 1985). A regional groundwater division differentiates the following groundwater basins, separated by aquifer limits or geomorphologic and geologic features: Yarmouk basin, Northern escarpment to the Jordan Valley, Jordan Valley floor, Zerqa River basin, Central escarpment to the Dead Sea, Escarpment to Wadi Araba, Red Sea basin, Jafr basin, Azraq basin, Sirhan basin, and Wadi Hammad basin (Salameh and Khdier 1985).

The current demand for water in Jordan is well above the so-called safe yield of presently used water resources, which are overexploited. The deficit in 1995 amounted to 543 mcm, which is expected to rise further, despite intentions to increase the available water resources from 700 mcm in 1995 to 1,070 mcm in 2010 (Table 42.4). These figures underline the more severe aridity in Jordan as compared to Israel. The territory of Jordan is about four times larger than Israel, but the average safe yield of available water (about 700 mcm) is less than half the amount of Israel's fresh water resources (about 1,600 mcm).

Irrigation is important in enabling Jordan to grow some of its own agricultural crops, as the area suited for rain-fed agriculture is very small (Table 42.3): 93 per cent of the country receives less than 200 mm of average annual precipitation (Salameh 1997). The first major irrigation project in Jordan was the construction of the King Abdallah Canal in the eastern part of the Rift Valley from the Yarmouk River to near the Dead Sea. The project began in 1958 and was completed in 1964. Large dams were also constructed, such as the King Talal Dam on the Az Zarqa River (Nyrop 1980). The total area irrigated in Jordan in 1990 was about 70,000 ha, nearly half of it situated in the Jordan Valley. The large relative agricultural demand of the national water budget is expected to decline in relative terms from 72 per cent to 63 per cent, while municipal water use is bound to increase. The urban sector already suffers from acute shortages, particularly in Amman, where regional artesian reservoirs have been overpumped (Water Authority Jordan, cited from Ministries of Foreign Affairs and Finance 1996).

In Israel it became clear in the 1950s that the various regional water projects would not be adequate to meet the water needs of the country in the years ahead, because most of the water resources are concentrated in the wetter northern part of the country. Thus the National Water Carrier (Figure 42.4) was planned and completed in 1964 to distribute and regulate the water supply in spatial and seasonal terms. Water is pumped from Lake Kinneret and transported southward, as the lake supplies about 50 per cent of potable water in the country. The National Water Carrier system integrates most of the regional water resources in Israel, and it also has an important seasonal and interannual regulation function. In the rainy winter season, it is used to transport surplus water to underground reservoirs for storage in the aquifers as buffer stocks for the dry summer season and to store excess water from wet years for use during drought years (Ministry of Agriculture 1973). However, in reality, overexploitation of the groundwater aquifers did occur in the 1970s and 1980s (State Comptroller 1990, Bruins 1993).

Plate 42.1 The beautiful desert landscape of Wadi Ram in southern Jordan. The nearby region contains fossil water, which is becoming increasingly important for drought mitigation

Table 42.4 Water demand, available water resources (safe yield) and water deficit in Jordan

	1995	*2000*	*2005*	*2010*
Municipal	300 mcm/24%	390 mcm/25%	455 mcm/28%	530 mcm/30%
Industrial	43 mcm/3%	80 mcm/5%	100 mcm/6%	120 mcm/7%
Agricultural	900 mcm/72%	1,088 mcm/70%	1,088 mcm/66%	1,088 mcm/63%
Total demand	1,243 mcm	1,558 mcm	1,643 mcm	1,738 mcm
Safe yield	700 mcm/56%	843 mcm/54%	970 mcm/59%	1,070 mcm/62%
Deficit	543 mcm/44%	715 mcm/46%	643 mcm/39%	668 mcm/38%

Sources: Water Authority Jordan, Ministry of Water and Irrigation; and Ministries of Foreign Affairs and Finance 1996

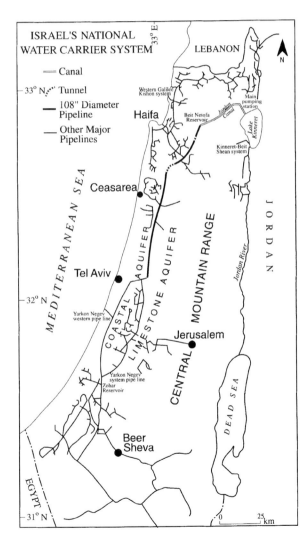

Lake Kinneret is situated in the Rift Valley (Plate 42.2). Its water level at maximum capacity stands at –208.9 m (below ocean level), above which flooding would occur in the town of Tiberias and other villages around the lake. The minimum acceptable level, the so-called red line, has been set at –213 m, below which water quality in the lake, particularly salinity, is expected to deteriorate to unacceptable levels. Lake Kinneret covers an area of 165 km² and holds at maximum capacity almost 4,000 mcm of water. Each metre represents about 170 mcm of water. An average amount of 450 mcm is pumped from the lake annually. The overflow into the Jordan River at the southern end of the lake is controlled by a sluice gate to keep the lake at desired levels (Grinwald and Bibas 1989).

Plate 42.2 Lake Kinneret is the major source of fresh surface water in Israel and the major water supplier to the National Water Carrier System, which begins here. The Golan Heights are visible in the background

Figure 42.4 The National Water Carrier and its distribution system (after Doron 1993 and Shanan 1998)

The Coastal Aquifer began to be used in the beginning of this century. The amount of water pumped from the aquifer was about 250 mcm in 1948, reaching a record 493 mcm in 1958. With the opening of the National Water Carrier in 1964, less water was initially withdrawn from the Coastal Aquifer. However, pumping later increased again, reaching 470 mcm in 1984–5 (Grinwald and Bibas 1989). The continuous overpumping of the Coastal Aquifer caused a drop in the water table, increased penetration of seawater, and caused a general reduction in water quality. The hydrological deficit at the end of the 1980s was estimated at 1,100 mcm (Schwarz 1990). However, the very wet year 1991–2 replenished some of this deficit. The average safe yield is about 283 mcm per year (Melloul and Bibas 1990, State Comptroller 1990), but to restore the aquifer, even less water should be withdrawn – about 210 mcm/year, according to Schwarz (1990).

The western Mountain Aquifer of the central hills is composed of hard calcareous rocks of Cenomanian-Turonian age. Its main reserve is situated in the Yarkon-Tanninim basin east of the coastal plain, extending south to Beer-Sheva. The aquifer is of a karstic nature with high conductivity and swift flows (Grinwald and Bibas 1989). Use of the Yarkon-Tanninim aquifer increased rapidly since the 1950s, reaching annual withdrawal levels of more than 400 mcm. Water levels in the aquifer dropped by more than 8 m in the period 1970–90, passing the so-called red line in 1986 and 1990, while the water quality deteriorated because of pollution. Every metre in the level of the aquifer represents an estimated 100 mcm of water. Lowering of the water level in the aquifer beyond the red line may introduce salinity problems in this largest groundwater reservoir of the country. The 'miracle' rainy season 1991–2, the wettest year since recordings began in Jerusalem in 1846, resulted in considerable recharge of the aquifer. The long-term safe yield is estimated at 310 mcm per year (Schwarz 1990).

Artificial recharge of both the Coastal Aquifer and the Mountain Aquifer can be done in winter with water pumped from Lake Kinneret, about 35 mcm/month (Schwarz 1990), and transported through the National Water Carrier. Additional regional aquifers in Israel produce 510 mcm/year, an amount that is expected to increase to 560 mcm/year. Schwarz (1990: 59) notes: 'Most of these aquifers suffer from overexploitation and part of them, especially in the inner valleys, suffer from salinity increase. Pumping will be reduced in these aquifers. However, in other aquifers that are not yet fully utilised due to excessive costs, pumping will increase in the future'. Table 42.5

Table 42.5 Short-term water potential in Israel in million cubic metres (mcm) per year, as compared to actual supply in 1984–5 and planned supply for the year 2000

Water source	Fresh water	Saline water	Total	1984–5	2000
Boreholes	768	132	900		
Springs	82	100	182		
Total groundwater	850	232	1,082	1,340	1,115
Hula Valley use	122		122		
Lake Kinneret	490		490		
Saline water		20	20		
Outflow Kinneret	−20		20		
Total Kinneret basin	592	20	612	620	660
Floodwater	160		160	40	80
Recycled waste water	241		241	110	275
Losses				−60	−40
Total water supply	1,843	252	2,095	2,050	2,090

Sources: State Comptroller 1990, Schwarz 1990

shows Israel's potential water availability compared with past usage (1984–5) and projected requirement (2000).

The demand for fresh water by the domestic sector is expected to rise to 640 mcm by the year 2000, compared to 420 mcm in 1984–5. The supply of fresh water to agriculture is supposed to decline to 740 mcm in 2000, as compared to 1,200 mcm in 1984–5. This loss is to be only partly compensated by an increased amount of reclaimed waste water of 320 mcm for agriculture in the year 2000. The potential of treated sewage and runoff water is expected to reach about 500 mcm in 2010 (Schwarz 1990).

WATER SHARING BETWEEN ISRAEL AND JORDAN ACCORDING TO THE PEACE TREATY

Annex II of the Israel-Jordan Peace Treaty of 26 October 1994 deals with water-related matters. Concerning the Yarmouk river, Israel is allowed to pump 12 mcm in the summer period (15 May–15 October) and Jordan gets the rest of the flow. During the winter period (16 October–14 May) Israel can pump 13 mcm and Jordan gets the rest of the flow. However, Israel may pump an additional 20 mcm from the Yarmouk in winter, if it supplies Jordan during the summer with the same amount of water (20 mcm) from the Jordan river upstream from the Deganya gates. Israel is to desalinate, within four years from the entry into force of the Peace Treaty, the 20 mcm of saline spring water currently diverted into the Jordan River. Half the amount of this desalinated

water (10 mcm) is to be suppled to Jordan. Until the desalinisation facilities are operational, Israel will supply Jordan during the winter period with 10 mcm of Jordan River water, derived upstream from the Deganya gates.

Moreover, Israel and Jordan are to cooperate in finding an additional 50 mcm of water of drinkable standards for Jordan. Other articles in the Peace Treaty deal with water storage, quality, and protection, as well as groundwater in the Arava Valley, situated between the Dead Sea and the Gulf of Aqaba. Proposed water projects to further the stipulations in the Peace Treaty are presented in more detail in a report (Version IV) by the Government of Israel (Ministries of Foreign Affairs and Finance 1996).

THE HAZARDS OF NATURAL AND SOCIOECONOMIC DROUGHT

It is possible to distinguish three main types of meteorological drought in Israel. The three types can also be considered applicable to Jordan, as both countries form part of the southern Levant: (1) annually recurring seasonal summer drought; (2) regularly occurring annual to multiannual drought of light to medium severity; and (3) occasional multiannual drought of great severity (Bruins 1993). Time spectrum analysis of Jerusalem rainfall data by Zangvil (1979) revealed a prominent peak at 3.0 to 3.3 years, similar to the frequency of drought years in the Negev based on rainfall-runoff data (Bruins *et al.* 1986). A study about rainfall variability in Israel by Amiran

Table 42.6 Drought periods of three or more consecutive years, having at least one year with a drop in precipitation of 33 per cent or more, based on Jerusalem rainfall records for the period 1846–1993

Drought period of three years or more	Number of consecutive years	Average rainfall decline (%)	Driest year in this period	Largest rainfall decline (%)
1869/70–1872/3	4	−21	1869–70	−43
1898/9–1901/2	4	−16	1900–1	−39
1922/3–1935/6	14	−27	1932–3	−53
1945/6–1954/5	10	−14	1950–1	−55
1957/8–1962/3	6	−37	1959–60	−63
1983/4–1985/6	3	−22	1985–6	−33

Source: Amiran 1994

(1994) showed the average rainfall amount in drought years to be 30–40 per cent less than the long-term average.

The overall average rainfall in Jerusalem for the period 1846–1993 amounts to 556 mm (Amiran 1994). The three wettest years during this period occurred in 1873–4 (1,004 mm), 1877–8 (1,091 mm), and 1991–2 (1,134 mm). The three driest years occurred in 1950–1 (247 mm), 1959–60 (206 mm), and 1962–3 (227 mm). The Jerusalem rainfall record was studied by Zangvil (1979) for the period 1846–1954. Applying a ten-year running mean, he distinguished a relatively wet period with above-average rainfall during 1868–1911 (690 mm) and a relatively dry period during 1912–37 (412 mm).

Analysing the precipitation years of Jerusalem for the period 1846–1993 at face value, without running means or filters, Amiran (1994) distinguished (Table 42.6) six dry periods of three consecutive years or more in which at least one year shows a precipitation decline of more than 33 per cent.

Ben-Zvi (1987) studied hydrologic drought in Israel over the period 1937–84, analysing fourteen rivers in the central and northern part of the country. Severity in terms of decline in the flow of water, duration of the hydrologic drought, and geographic extent are the principle variables. Severe and extensive hydrologic drought in Israel, affecting the majority of the fourteen studied streams, occurred in 1950–1, 1958–9, 1972–3, and 1978–9. Multiannual continuous shortages occurred approximately in the periods 1955–61 and 1971–9, with variations at the beginning and end of those periods with respect to the various streams studied. A third period, around 1967–72, can be recognised for a few streams in central Israel.

An interesting interaction can be observed in Israel between meteorological drought and socioeconomic drought in relation to available water reserves in the main aquifers. Figure 42.5 shows the water consumption in Israel for the period 1958–94 (i.e., the amount of water sold by the state to the domestic, agricultural, and industrial sectors). Assessing the effect of past drought periods of three years or more (Table 42.6) on water deliveries by the state (Figure 42.5), it seems apparent that the drought of 1957/8–1962/3 caused only minor change in water supply to

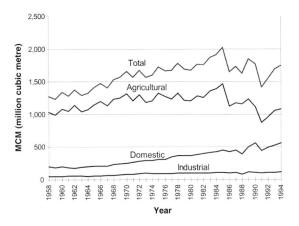

Figure 42.5 Water consumption in Israel, 1958–94, in million cubic metre (mcm), based on data provided by Michael Bibas (Water Commission, Water Allocation Department, personal communication, 1996)

the agricultural and domestic sectors. Following the severe drought year of 1959–60, characterised by a 63 per cent drop in precipitation (Amiran 1994), only a slight drop can be observed the next year in water supply to the agricultural sector, as well as during 1962–3, the last year of the extended drought period. At that time there were still considerable water reserves in the aquifers, particularly in the western Mountain Aquifer. However, socioeconomic drought gradually developed in Israel during the 1970s and 1980s, as the state sold more water from the groundwater reserves than the so-called safe yield (i.e., the amount replenished annually by rainfall). A sustained decline resulted in the levels of groundwater in the aquifers. When the meteorological drought of 1983/4–1985/6 came to pass, groundwater levels in the two main aquifers had already approached the red line. As the meteorological drought exacerbated the creeping socioeconomic drought, there was no alternative for the state in 1985–6 but to make a deep cut in the supply of water to the agricultural sector. However, water supply to the domestic sector dropped only slightly (see Figure 42.5).

The creeping human-made drought in Israel was exposed by the State Comptroller in a report published in 1990. The publication coincided with a meteorological drought of moderate severity of three years duration (1988/9–1990/1). Water reserves in the aquifers had dropped beyond the red line, while Lake Kinneret reached its lowest level in living memory. The increased public awareness and media attention finally caused a shift in government policy, which was long overdue. Water allocations were cut while the price of water was increased. These measures caused the most severe cut in water consumption by the agricultural sector, declining to pre-1958 levels, and the first significant drop in water consumption by the domestic sector. Total water consumption in 1991 was down to 1,420 million cubic metre (mcm), compared to 2,024 mcm in 1985. However, just when the water crisis had reached its most serious condition, 'heavenly' mitigation arrived in 1991–2 with the highest recorded precipitation amounts of the last 150 years (since recordings began in Jerusalem in 1846). These rains replenished the aquifers to a certain extent. Data since 1992 (Figure 42.5) again show an increase in water consumption, but the amount of fresh water made available to agriculture is not allowed to rise to the same levels as before, because the increasing population requires more and more water.

POLICY RECOMMENDATIONS TO MITIGATE DROUGHT DISASTERS

Drought planning and water crisis management need to be proactive, because the overall policy, legislation, and specific mitigation strategies should be in place before a drought or water crisis affects the regular use of the country's water resources. Ad hoc crisis management is inferior and more costly than the implementation of preplanned crisis policy. Hastily prepared assessment and response procedures may lead to ineffective, poorly coordinated, and untimely response (Wilhite and Easterling 1987, Bruins 1993). The basic elements involved in the development of proactive drought contingency planning and their respective relationships are displayed in Figure 42.6.

The analysis of drought risk can be investigated on the basis of meteorological, paleoclimatic, and historical data, in relation to climate variations (Bruins 1994, Issar *et al.* 1995). The time scale of recurrence of severe drought may exceed the average human lifespan. Perception of both risk and impact may

therefore disappear out of public memory, which has its bearing on planning and policy by the authorities. Drought definitions need to be precise, regional, and even specifically targeted at selected economic activities to be useful for proactive planning and government policy.

Assessments have to be made of the impact of drought on the various water resources, economic sectors, towns, villages, and the environment. The different types of drought, shown in Figure 42.2, should all be considered in impact assessment studies. Respective vulnerability of different sections of the environment, economic activities, and social groups needs to be studied at different hierarchic levels – local, provincial, national, regional (Bruins and Lithwick 1998). Drought scenarios have to be drawn up on the basis of available information, including frequency and severity index, if applicable. Finally, proactive drought contingency planning needs to be developed. Wilhite (1993) outlined in considerable detail a generic process with methodological steps that may be adopted by governments (Wilhite 1986, Wilhite and Hayes 1998) to develop comprehensive drought planning and management. Proactive planning needs to be executed through interactive management (Bruins and Lithwick 1998), because planning for future drought situations can never be sufficiently accurate. Actual realisation of the proactive plans in times of drought needs to be adjusted and updated through interactive management.

The National Water Carrier system in Israel forms, in terms of proactive drought planning, an important water management buffer that enables regular water supply during the annually recurring seasonal summer drought, as well as during light to medium types of recurring annual drought. However, the buffering capacity of the present system with the overpumped aquifers is not sufficient to protect the country against the impact of severe multiannual meteorological drought (Bruins 1993).

Management of the water resources in Israel has reached a turning point, according to Schwarz (1990), and both revision and new development plans are needed. The large-scale desalinisation of seawater and brackish groundwater for use by the domestic sector is absolutely essential in view of the growing population and continuous risk of drought in both

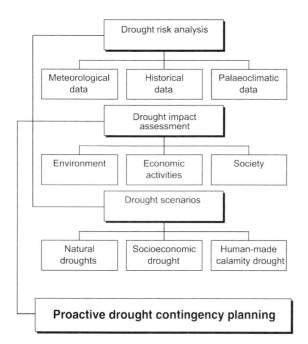

Figure 42.6 Basic elements involved in proactive drought contingency planning (after Bruins 1996)

Israel and Jordan (Bruins 1993, Amiran 1994, Glueckstern 1996, Hoffman and Zfati 1996, Kedem 1996). It is obvious that the virtually unlimited supply of seawater is not affected by meteorological drought. Hence large-scale seawater desalinisation for the domestic sector, which can afford a higher water price, is a very important mitigation factor during drought years, as seawater remains available. The price of desalinated seawater is now estimated at about one US dollar per cubic metre, which is about a thousand times cheaper than a litre of Coca Cola. Moreover, such desalinated seawater for the domestic sector will, in its third cycle (after being seawater and desalinated fresh water), become available for agriculture as treated waste water, even during severe meteorological drought years.

Sewage from the domestic sector must be treated to prevent groundwater pollution. Schwarz (1990) estimates the potential of treated sewage, reclaimed floodwater, and runoff in 2010 at about 500 mcm/ yr. This is already becoming a major water source for the agricultural sector, as the diminishing quantities of high-quality fresh water are increasingly consumed by the domestic sector. Large-scale desalinisation of seawater for the domestic sector and large-scale use of the resulting sewage water, after proper treatment, for agriculture, will allow a significant reduction in pumping from the groundwater aquifers. Thus it is possible to recharge the aquifers to capacity as an important water bank reserve for extended meteorological drought periods. Such a strategy is important for Israel as well as for Jordan, although the latter country only has access to the sea in the south near Aqaba. Development in Jordan of both the southern aquifer and seawater desalinisation near Aqaba could provide much-needed water along a Jordanian national water carrier to the centre and north of the country.

Centralised water distribution systems, however good and useful in normal circumstances, may be vulnerable in times of crisis or very severe drought. The National Water Carrier system in Israel provides piped water to most of the country and reaches the Negev as far south as the town of Mizpeh Ramon. The difference in elevation between Lake Kinneret (–209 m) and Mizpeh Ramon (+890 m), as well as the approximate pipeline distance of some 300 km, gives an indication of both the pumping costs and potential vulnerability in times of crisis. Although the level of Lake Kinneret might be lowered in case of severe drought to one metre below the red line, to –214 m, according to Schwarz (1990), this would not be helpful if the water was to be polluted by chemicals.

It is therefore vital to develop additional water supply systems based on regional groundwater and floodwater resources. Issar (1985) has consistently advocated the use of groundwater in the Negev. Regional and local water planning should provide self-reliance, independent of the centralised system (Gradus 1984), to decrease vulnerability. Local, decentralised water supply systems need to be developed in parallel with the centralised system. Such dual systems can make meaningful contributions in regular years, and their existence becomes absolutely crucial in times of severe meteorological and human-made calamity drought (Bruins 1996).

Local water supply systems exist in the driest parts of southern Israel, situated beyond the reach of the National Water Carrier. There are some forty-four reverse osmosis units in the Arava Valley to desalinate brackish water, while the southernmost town of Israel, Eilat, is now receiving most of its water through seawater desalinisation. Regional cooperation with Jordan in these areas could be extended for the benefit of both countries.

Proactive planning to mitigate human-made calamity drought must be based primarily on water resources that are safely protected against pollution. Deep groundwater reservoirs in sandy geological layers well protected from the penetration of polluted surface water seem best suited in this respect. Such aquifers exist in the Negev as well as in southern Jordan. The mountain aquifers in both central Israel and north-western Jordan are of a karstic nature with high conductivity and swift flows, which makes them much more vulnerable to pollution. As cooperation between Jordan and Israel in the field of water sharing has begun since the Peace Treaty of 1994, cooperation ought to be extended in the associated fields of pro-active drought planning and water crisis management.

Nesheiwat (1995) made some proposals to reverse the process of range land degradation and deserti-fication in Jordan by allowing appropriate resting periods for the vegetation, keeping stocking rates to the sustainable carrying capacity, and discontinuing or changing the present system of subsidies to animal feed. The possible effect of drought on desertification is probably significant in the current state of over-grazing. About 95 per cent of Jordan is pasture land; its proper management, therefore, is important for virtually the entire country. Intensification of local water resource management, particularly the use of runoff water (Bruins *et al.* 1986) and local ground-water, are very important elements in restoring the vegetation and increasing natural forage production, even in drought years. Storage of runoff water in the soil profile through a series of low check-dams in the wadis and through other rainwater-harvesting systems (Bruins *et al.* 1986 and 1987) are excellent measures in terms of proactive drought planning and com-batting desertification.

Finally, the hazard of famine is rather directly related to the hazard of drought in closed and self-contained agrarian economies, although the level of vulnerability varies with complex socioeconomic factors and coping mechanisms. Self-sufficiency in food production proved difficult with increasing popu-

lation size in many arid countries of the Near and Middle East. The limitations of the agricultural sector are obvious in countries with large desert areas. The basic problem of arid-zone water resource manage-ment is the supply of sufficient water to both the domestic and agricultural sector. This water problem in the Levant has so far been partly solved through the imports of food staples, which can be regarded as the import of 'virtual water' (Allan and Karshenas 1996). Food purchased from outside the country saves the equivalent amount of water that would have been necessary to grow that food inside the country. 'Governments of the Middle East have in practice been able to access "virtual water" very readily via world trade in food staples and have not therefore been exposed to the economic catastrophe predicated by those who saw, and in some cases still see, no escape from the imperatives of food self-sufficiency' (Allan and Karshenas 1996: 121).

Water development in Israel and Jordan first intended for agricultural production is increasingly being diverted to the domestic sector because of the rise in population. For example, the King Talal Dam on the Az Zarqa River in Jordan, completed in 1977, was originally intended for agriculture only. The dam, having a reservoir capacity of 58 mcm as well as electric hydrogenerators, made water available in the area throughout the year, including the rainless summer season, and to a certain extent over a period of years. But in 1979 some 17 mcm/yr were already pumped to urban water systems (Nyrop 1980). The diminishing amount of fresh water for agriculture in both Israel and Jordan, due to increasing population size, has indeed been met with growing food imports on the one hand, and increased water use efficiency in agriculture on the other (Shanan and Berkowicz 1995).

Although virtual water may be accessed readily through world trade in food staples (Allan and Karshenas 1996) during good times, there may be problems in bad times. The FAO has been warning already for decades about the low level of world food reserves (Schneider 1976). There is always the risk that world food reserves will decline sharply because of natural or human-made disasters. If food can neither be imported nor produced locally in sufficient quantity, then 'old-fashioned' famine may result.

Such complex hazards can be mitigated by 'old-fashioned' proactive disaster planning: storage of 'virtual water' before the onset of 'bad global times' through the formation of grain reserves locally. This is reminiscent of perhaps the oldest documented case of proactive drought planning in the Near East, termed the Genesis strategy by Schneider (1976), recorded in the book of Genesis (chapter 41). If both local water and virtual water become scarce, it is probably the only viable strategy – very common, by the way, in parts of Ethiopia, where grain reserves for several years are not unusual as a proactive drought mitigation and disaster reduction strategy.

REFERENCES

Allan, J.A. and Karshenas, M. (1996) 'Managing environmental capital: The case of water in Israel, Jordan, the west Bank and Gaza, 1947 to 1995', in J.A. Allen (ed.), *Water, Peace and the Middle East*, London: Tauris Academic Publishers.

Alpert, P., Abramsky, R., and Neeman, B.U. (1990) 'The prevailing summer synoptic system in Israel – Subtropical High, not Persian Trough', *Israel Journal of Earth Sciences* 39: 93–102.

Amiran, D. (1994) 'Rainfall and water policy in Israel', The Jerusalem Institute for Israel Studies, No. 55 (in Hebrew).

Ben-Zvi, A. (1987) 'Indices of hydrological drought in Israel', *Journal of Hydrology* 92: 179–91.

Bruins, H.J. (1993) 'Drought risk and water management in Israel: Planning for the future', in D.A. Wilhite (ed.), *Drought Assessment, Management and Planning: Theory and Case Studies*, Boston, MA: Kluwer Academic Publishers, Chapter 8, pp. 133–55.

——— (1994) 'Comparative chronology of climatic and human history in the southern Levant from the late Chalcolithic to the Early Arab Period', in O. Bar-Yosef and R. Kra (eds), *Late Quaternary Chronology and Paleoclimates of the Eastern Mediterranean*, Tucson, AZ: Radiocarbon, Dept. of Geosciences, University of Arizona, and Cambridge, MA: Peabody Museum, Harvard University, pp. 301–14.

——— (1996) 'A rationale for drought contingency planning in Israel', in Y. Gradus and G. Lipshitz (eds), *The Mosaic of Israeli Geography*, Beersheva: Ben-Gurion University of the Negev Press, The Negev Centre for Regional Development, pp. 345–53.

Bruins, H.J., Evenari, M., and Nessler, U. (1986) 'Rainwater-harvesting agriculture for food production in arid zones: The challenge of the African famine', *Applied Geography* 6: 13–32.

Bruins, H.J., Evenari, M., and Rogel, A. (1987) 'Run-off

farming management and climate', in L. Berkofsky and M.G. Wurtele (eds), *Progress in Desert Research*, Totowa, NJ: Rowman & Littlefield, Chapter 1, pp. 3–14.

Bruins, H.J. and Lithwick, H. (1998) 'Proactive planning and interactive management in arid frontier development', in H.J. Bruins and H. Lithwick (eds), *The Arid Frontier: Interactive Management of Environment and Development*, Dordrecht: Kluwer Academic Publishers, Chapter 1, pp. 3–29.

Bruins, H.J. and Berliner, P.R. (1998) 'Bioclimatic aridity, climatic variability, drought and desertification', in H.J. Bruins and H. Lithwick (eds), *The Arid Frontier: Interactive Management of Environment and Development*, Dordrecht: Kluwer Academic Publishers, Chapter 5, pp. 97–118.

Doron, P. (1993) *Development: The Eventful Life and Travels of an Engineer*, Jerusalem: Gefen.

Fishelson, G. (1995) 'International Conference on the Peace Process and the Environment', Tel-Aviv University, *Book of Abstracts*, pp. 45–8.

Gilead, D. and Bachmat, Y. (1973) 'Israel's groundwater basins', in J. Bonné, S. Grossman-Pines, and Z. Grinwald (eds), *Water in Israel – Part A, Selected Articles*, Tel-Aviv: Ministry of Agriculture, Water Commission, Water Allocation Department, pp. 37–51.

Glueckstern, P. (1996) 'Short and long term desalination options for enhancement and quality improvement of water supply', in International Conference of Water Resource Management Strategies in the Middle East, *Book of Abstracts*, Association of Engineers and Architects in Israel, Society of Water Engineers, Herzlia.

Gradus, Y. (1984) 'The emergence of regionalism in a centralized system: The case of Israel', *Environment and Planning D: Society and Space*, Vol. 1, pp. 87–100.

Grinwald, Z. and Bibas, M. (1989) *Water in Israel*, Tel Aviv: Ministry of Agriculture, Water Commission, Water Allocation Department.

Hoffman, D. and Zfati, A. (1996) 'Considerations governing the selection and design of optimal seawater desalination plants for integration within conventional regional water supply systems', in International Conference of Water Resource Management Strategies in the Middle East, *Book of Abstracts*, Association of Engineers and Architects in Israel, Society of Water Engineers, Herzlia.

Hoyt, W.G. (1942) 'Droughts', in O.E. Meinzer (ed.), *Hydrology*, New York: Dover Publications, p. 579.

Issar, A.S. (1985) 'Fossil water under the Sinai-Negev Peninsula', *Scientific American* 253, 1: 82–8.

Issar, A.S. (with Zhang Peiyuan, H.J. Bruins, M. Wolf, and Z. Ofer) (1995) 'Impacts of climate variations on water management and related socio-economic systems', Paris: UNESCO, International Hydrological Programme IHP-IV Project H-2.1.

Katsnelson, J. (1964) 'The variability of annual precipitation in Palestine', *Archiv für Meteorologie, Geo-*

physik und Bioklimatologie, Serie B 13, 2: 163–72.

Kedem, O. (1996) 'Desalinating in arid regions', in International Conference of Water Resource Management Strategies in the Middle East, *Book of Abstracts*, Association of Engineers and Architects in Israel, Society of Water Engineers, Herzlia.

Lancaster, W. and Lancaster, F. (1993) 'Sécheresse et stratégies de reconversion économique chez les bédouins de Jordanie', in R. Bocco, R. Jaubert, and F. Métral (eds), *Steppes d' Arabies – Etats, Pasteurs, Agriculteurs et Commerçants: Le Devenir des Zones Sèches*, Paris: Presses Universitaires de France, pp. 223–46.

Lee, K.S., Sadeghipour, J., and Dracup, J.A. (1986) 'An approach to frequency analysis of multiyear drought durations', *Water Resources Research* 22, 5: 655–62.

Melloul, A. and Bibas, M. (1990) 'General and regional hydrological situation in the Coastal Plain Aquifer of Israel and water distribution according to quality standards (chlorides and nitrates) in 1987/88 and expected to 1992', *Rep Hydro 1990/3* (in Hebrew, abstract in English), Jerusalem: Ministry of Agriculture, Water Commission, Hydrological Service.

Ministry of Agriculture (1973) *Israel's Water Economy* (reprints of published papers), Tel Aviv: Ministry of Agriculture, Water Commission.

Ministries of Foreign Affairs and Finance (1996) *Development Options for Cooperation: The Middle East/East Mediterranean Region*, Jerusalem: Government of Israel.

Nesheiwat, K. (1995) *Fact and Figures on the Rangelands in Jordan*, Amman: Agricultural and Policy Department, Ministry of Agriculture, Hashemite Kingdom of Jordan.

Nyrop, R.F. (ed.) (1980) *Jordan, a Country Study*, Washington, DC: The American University.

Palmer, W.C. (1965) 'Meteorological drought', *Research Paper* No. 45, US Weather Bureau, Washington, DC.

Penman, H.L. (1948) 'Natural evaporation from open water, bare soil and grass', *Proceedings of the Royal Society, Section A* 193: 120–45.

Salameh, E. (1997) 'The climate of Jordan', short summary extracted from the *Progress Research Report*, AVI 080 Project 'ACROSS' Analyzed Climatology of Rainfall Obtained from Satellite and Surface data for the Mediterranean Basin.

Salameh, E. and Khdier, K. (1985) 'Groundwater qualities in Jordan', *Newsletter Water Research and Study Centre*, University of Jordan, Amman, Issue 4.

Schneider, S.H. (1976) *The Genesis Strategy – Climate and Global Survival*, New York: Plenum Press.

Schwarz, J. (1990) 'Management of the water resources of Israel', *Israel Journal of Earth Sciences* 39: 57–65.

Shanan, L. (1998) 'Irrigation development: Proactive planning and interactive management', in H.J. Bruins and H. Lithwick (eds), *The Arid Frontier: Interactive Management of Environment and Development*, Dordrecht: Kluwer Academic Publishers, Chapter 1, pp. 251–76.

Shanan, L. and Berkowicz, S. (1995) 'The context of locally managed irrigation in Israel: Policies, planning and performance', *Short Report Series on Locally Managed Irrigation*, Report No. 10, Colombo: International Irrigation Management Institute.

Sharma, T.C. (1994) 'Stochastic features of drought in Kenya, East Africa', in K.W. Hipel (ed.), *Stochastic and Statistical Methods in Hydrology and Environmental Engineering*, Dordrecht: Kluwer Academic Publishers, Vol. 1, pp. 125–37.

State Comptroller (1990) Report on the Management of Water Resources in Israel, State Comptroller, Jerusalem.

Thornthwaite, C.W. (1948) 'An approach towards a rational classification of climate', *Geographical Review* 38: 55–94.

UNEP (1992) *World Atlas of Desertification*, London: Edward Arnold.

UNESCO (1979) 'Map of the world distribution of arid regions. Explanatory note', *Man and the Biosphere (MAB) Technical Notes* 7, Paris: UNESCO.

Wilhite, D.A. (1986) 'Drought policy in the US and Australia: A comparative analysis', *Water Resources Bulletin* 22: 425–38.

—— (1993) 'The enigma of drought', in D.A. Wilhite (ed.), *Drought Assessment, Management and Planning: Theory and Case Studies*, Boston, MA: Kluwer Academic Publishers, Chapter 1, pp. 3–15.

Wilhite, D.A. and Easterling, W.E. (1987) 'Drought policy: Toward a plan of action', in D.A. Wilhite and W.E. Easterling (eds), *Planning for Drought: Toward a Reduction of Societal Vulnerability*, Boulder, CO: Westview Press, pp. 573–89.

Wilhite, D.A. and Glantz, M.H. (1985) 'Understanding the drought phenomenon: The role of definitions', *Water International* 10: 111–20.

Wilhite, D.A. and Hayes, M.J. (1998) 'Drought planning in the United States: Status and future directions,' in H.J. Bruins and H. Lithwick (eds), *The Arid Frontier: Interactive Management of Environment and Development*, Dordrecht: Kluwer Academic Publishers, Chapter 2, pp. 33–54.

Zangvil, A. (1979) 'Temporal fluctuations of seasonal precipitation in Jerusalem', *Tellus* 31: 413–20.

43

DROUGHT PREPAREDNESS AND MITIGATION FOR PUBLIC WATER SUPPLIES

Benedykt Dziegielewski

COPING APPROACHES

During the 1980s and 1990s, hundreds of municipalities across the United States had their water supplies threatened by drought. Many more communities may experience water shortages during future droughts because of increasing demands for water and reduced opportunities for the development of new water supplies. These shortages may be more frequent and more severe if the anticipated changes in the global climate materialise.

In the past, rapid urban growth made it possible to design and build water facilities with substantial extra capacity to accommodate future population growth and industrial development. This extra capacity protected public supplies from droughts by providing sufficient storage of water in times of high rainfall for use during periods of drought. Although the provision of extra storage capacity remains one of the most popular means of protection against drought, several new economic, social, and environmental considerations have placed this alternative beyond the reach of many water agencies. Probably the most important obstacle is the increasing general concern for environmental quality, which has resulted in a more active public role in resource management decisions. The need for new supply development receives unprecedented scrutiny from environmental groups, and even projects that are partially completed may be halted because of their potential environmental impacts.

Because of the current constraints to the development of new and expanded water supplies, many water agencies must look for new ways to prepare for and mitigate the effects of droughts on their water supplies. A new strategy is to consider demand management alternatives aimed at both controlling the growth in water demand over time and achieving significant temporary reductions in water use during periods of drought. Demand-side alternatives, in combination with some unconventional supply augmentation options, have the potential for ensuring adequate future water supply for urban areas during periods of drought.

In managing droughts, public water supply managers rely on both drought mitigation and preparedness for response to a drought that has already begun. Drought mitigation entails a set of long-term measures that are often, but not exclusively, structural. The provision of sufficient storage of water is the simplest and most efficient drought mitigation measure. However, in most cases, drought mitigation measures cannot be implemented quickly enough to deal with the effects of an ongoing drought, and water managers are often limited to drought preparedness measures. During periods of drought, water agencies must carry the burden of responsibility for uninterrupted supply and can take a number of emergency actions to minimise the risk of running out of water. Such drought response actions (or drought management measures) may be (1) planned before the onset of drought or developed ad hoc after a drought becomes apparent, and (2) oriented toward reducing water demand or toward provision of supplemental (emergency) sources of supply. These actions, whether aimed at increasing supply or reducing demand, may result in a temporary increase in the cost of water supply or may cause urban economies and consumers to suffer significant economic losses.

DROUGHT MITIGATION TECHNIQUES

In a broad sense, drought mitigation represents a set of structural and nonstructural adjustments to an established system of water management, which are aimed at protecting the system from adverse effects of future droughts. All public water supply systems are designed with some level of protection against droughts. Regardless of the specific mitigation techniques employed, the level of protection can be characterised in terms of 'vulnerability' to water shortages during drought.

Vulnerability to droughts

The overall vulnerability of water supply systems to the adverse impacts of drought can be assessed based on (1) the types of water supply sources and entitlements to water from these sources and (2) the degree of long-term drought protection as indicated by the severity of drought that would cause significant water shortages. Generally, groundwater supplies are less susceptible than river intakes or surface water impoundments are to drought. Public systems that use groundwater as their major or even supplemental source of supply are afforded some protection against droughts of short duration.

Public water supplies can assess their vulnerability to shortages during drought by comparing average demand to 'safe yield' of their water supply sources. Theoretically, safe yield defines the capability of a water source to sustain a required level of supply over time as the hydrologic input (i.e., reservoir inflows or groundwater recharge) varies both seasonally and annually (Dziegielewski and Crews 1986). Assuming that the hydrologic variability can be described by a reasonably well known probability distribution, and that the desired outcome (i.e., availability of required amounts of water) will take place with a probability of P, the term 'risk' is usually used to denote the probability $(1 - P)$ of other outcomes. In applying the terms of risk and reliability to drought, a concept of safe yield is used to define the output of a water supply system that can be maintained during a severe drought. The estimated probability of such a drought beginning in any given time period is referred to as risk $(1 - P)$, and the value of P defines the reliability of safe yield. For example, if the safe yield of 50 million gallons per day can be maintained during a drought with a return period of 100 years, the reliability of this safe yield would be 99 per cent. This implies that the risk of experiencing a shortage of water supply in any given time period is 1 per cent.

From the perspective of drought mitigation, any water supply system with average demands below the safe yield should not experience water shortages during droughts that are less severe than a 'design drought' used to derive the value of safe yield. In other words, systems with a ratio of safe yield to water use less than one can be considered to have an adequate level of drought mitigation. Table 43.1 is a compilation of water use data and safe yield statistics for selected cities in the United States, developed by Dziegielewski *et al.* (1991).

Table 43.1 Water use vs safe yield statistics for selected cities

City	Current use, mgd	Safe yield, mgd	Water use/safe yield
Binghampton, NY	12.5	43.0	0.29
Springfield, IL	19.3	28.8	0.67
Denver, CO	197.9	266.0	0.74
Indianapolis, IN	102.0	112.0	0.91
Phoenix, AZ	272.0	257.0	1.06
Southern California	3,419.0	3,053.0	1.12
New York City, NY	1,533.0	1,290.0	1.19
Merrifield, VA	78.9	54.0	1.46

Source: After Dziegielewski *et al.* 1991

The ratios of water use to safe yield in Table 43.1 indicate that among the eight cities shown, there is great variability in the level of drought mitigation. Binghampton and Springfield should have low vulnerability to droughts, but New York City and Merrifield draw water from their sources at rates that exceed the safe yield. This indicates that New York and Merrifield would be affected by droughts less severe than the design drought.

Assessment of the level of drought mitigation in a majority of public water supply systems is not possible because the safe yield or the probability of safe yield is not known. For example, Garbharran (1989) conducted a telephone survey of 100 public water supply agencies in Illinois during the summer of 1988, when the Midwest was being ravaged by a severe drought. Forty-two per cent of the responding systems reported that their systems were significantly affected by the drought. Only 70 per cent of respondents knew the safe yield of their system, and many confused safe yield with pumping or treatment capacity.

Dziegielewski et al. (1992a) conducted a survey of 547 local water supply systems serving some 31 million residents of urban areas in the states of Alabama, California, Florida, Oklahoma, Tennessee, and Wyoming. In terms of long-term drought mitigation, approximately one-third of respondents in the three eastern states and one-fourth in the western states believed that a drought that would result in significant supply shortages in their system would have to be at least as severe as the drought of record. Droughts of record are usually of unknown probability of occurrence; however, they can be placed between the recurrence intervals of fifty and one hundred years. Surprisingly, the respondents who used specific recurrence intervals to indicate the critical drought severity for their system were most likely to select the recurrence interval of five years. More than 50 per cent of respondents indicated the critical severity to be equal to or less than one in twenty years, with more than 40 per cent selecting a five-year or ten-year drought as critical. This indicates that approximately half the respondents view their systems as vulnerable and likely to respond to mild or moderate droughts. These respondents seem to place little confidence in the protection built into the concepts of design drought and safe yield.

Drought mitigation measures

Drought mitigation measures can be defined as specific long-term planning actions and investments aimed at reducing the probability of water shortages during droughts. They may involve changes to existing water storage or source infrastructures, conjunctive use of surface water and groundwater, water transfer agreements, and long-term improvements in water-use efficiency. The purpose of mitigation measures is to reduce or eliminate the need for short-term drought response measures and minimise the chances of reaching crisis situations during which emergency measures must be invoked. Table 43.2 shows a roster of long-term options for drought mitigation. The specific mitigation measures in the table are grouped under three broad categories: storing water, regional cooperation in water management, and reduction in demands through long-term conservation.

Water can be captured and stored for use during droughts in many ways. Both surface impoundments and groundwater basins can be used for that purpose. An important aspect of storing water is deciding how much water should be kept in reservoirs at the end of each water year as a measure of protection against the possibility of a drought during the next water year. During the California drought of 1987–92, water supply agencies maintained approximately 60 per cent of average storage in 155 major state reservoirs as carryover storage (Dziegielewski et al. 1993). Although this decision was controversial, it was made to ensure against even greater losses if the drought continued for a longer period.

Water transfers among regions are an effective method of protection against droughts that are limited in geographic extent. With long-distance water transportation systems, water can be 'wheeled' from regions with surplus supplies to drought-stricken areas. Another form of water management for drought protection is conjunctive use of surface and groundwater. In a conjunctive use scheme, surface water is used whenever it is available. When the availability of surface supplies diminishes, groundwater is pumped more heavily. This reduces the average annual pumping of groundwater, and thus can reduce depletion of aquifers by avoiding total withdrawals that exceed the rate of natural recharge.

Table 43.2 Long-term drought mitigation measures

A	Provision of extra storage capacity
	Maintenance of stored water as carryover water
	New surface water impoundments
	Added storage to existing impoundments
	Dredging of silted impoundments
	Storage or recharged groundwater
	Terminal reservoir storage
	Off-stream reservoir storage
B	Integrated regional water management
	Conjunctive use of surface water and groundwater
	Water banking programmes
	Interregional water transportation systems
C	Improvements in efficiency of water use
	Public campaigns to educate consumers on how to modify water use habits
	Promotion or mandatory requirement of the use of water-saving devices and appliances
	Promotion or mandatory requirements of low water-using urban landscaping
	Adoption of efficient marginal cost pricing strategies to discourage inefficient water use
	Adoption of zoning and growth policies to control the number of water users served

Source: Dziegielewski *et al.* 1991

The Salt River Project in Arizona has been relying on conjunctive use for many years.

Improvements in water use efficiency also play a role in drought mitigation. When a portion of current use is conserved, less water is required to support normal activities at all times, including periods of drought. However, water managers are reluctant to use long-term water conservation as a drought mitigation measure because of the possibility of demand hardening. Demand hardening can be defined as the 'diminished ability or willingness of consumers to reduce demand during a supply shortage' (Flory and Panella 1994). Although demand hardening is usually associated with the implementation of long-term water conservation measures, the ability of customers to reduce demand during a period of water shortage may also be related to the presence or absence of significant discretionary uses of water (e.g., landscape irrigation). In other words, if during normal times a large percentage of total urban water use is dedicated to irrigation of landscapes, this water use can be restricted or eliminated during drought without causing major hardships to consumers, allowing the water supply agency to satisfy the remaining demands, despite limited supplies. If all inefficiencies in water use are eliminated through implementation of long-

term demand management measures, then additional reductions in demand during drought will not be achievable without a significant consumer hardship. This perception of demand hardening is a major concern to water supply planners. They believe that long-term water conservation measures take away their flexibility in dealing with potential water shortages. Although the hardening of water demand is to be expected, its magnitude is generally small relative to the potential for reducing water use by changing consumer behaviour during a crisis. Actually, shortage demand management is likely to benefit from long-term water conservation.

PREPAREDNESS FOR RESPONSE

Many drought researchers strongly recommend *proactive* drought management, in contrast to *reactive* activities, which fall into ad hoc crisis management actions (Wilhite and Wood 1985, Dziegielewski 1986, Riebsame *et al.* 1990). Drought preparedness represents an anticipatory approach to drought through development of a detailed drought contingency plan for prompt and efficient response to drought conditions. Proactive drought management and planning can substantially reduce the adverse impacts of drought on public water supply systems, and the development of drought contingency plans can reduce uncertainty in making drought response decisions (Moreau and Little 1989). The need for proactive drought management can best be illustrated by the number of difficult decisions that have to be made during an ongoing drought.

During drought, water supply agencies have to make decisions under a great deal of uncertainty. The source of uncertainty comes from the lack of definitive answers to the following questions:

1   Are we in a drought?
2   How long and severe will the drought be?
3   What can we do to avoid water shortages?
4   When should we implement emergency actions?
5   When should we call off the emergency measures?

These and other questions must be answered before specific drought response actions are taken. Because the information and data needed to provide definitive answers usually are not available, water managers may choose to wait and monitor the development of drought, thus possibly forgoing the opportunity to conserve the available supply.

Once the drought is recognised and the need to take response actions is no longer questioned, the next problem is deciding what actions should be taken. The range of possible drought management measures is affected by many factors. Many options are precluded because their implementation lead time may be too long, they may be technically infeasible, they may not be acceptable to the community, or they may be too costly. Finally, as with most management decisions, there may be a question of the legality of water agency actions.

Drought preparedness measures

During an ongoing drought, water agencies and individual water users must decide what actions to take and when to take them. The specific actions and the timing of their implementation will depend on the existing level of long-term drought mitigation; the severity of drought as indicated by the deficits in precipitation, soil moisture, and streamflow; predictions for near-term weather conditions; and their preferences in terms of risk aversion. Public water supply agencies can select measures to be used in response to drought from a large array of options. Table 43.3 contains a list of preparedness measures that can be used to reduce demand and thus conserve the remaining supply.

Demand reduction measures can be implemented quickly and arranged in combinations that match the required reductions in overall demand. They can also be grouped from less stringent voluntary measures to more stringent mandatory prohibitions and rationing programmes.

Surveys of public water supply systems conducted during and after major droughts are an excellent source of information about the types of short-term measures that were used to reduce the risk of water shortages. DalMonte (1991) conducted a mail survey of 603 public water supply utilities in ten midwestern states in the summer of 1990. The results showed that 83 per cent of the systems that experienced drought conditions employed one or more demand reduction measures. The most commonly employed measures included requests for voluntary conservation, which was used by 244 respondents, and restrictions on non-essential uses, used by 151 respondents. Dziegielewski et al. (1992a) confirmed these findings in a national survey of 547 water supply systems. In their survey, 60 per cent of systems that experienced drought implemented mandatory restrictions on selected uses, and 23 per cent used mandatory rationing plans.

Water agencies can also choose from a large number of options for temporarily increasing the available water supply. Table 43.4 lists short-term preparedness measures for increasing supplies.

The short-term options for increasing supplies are often preferred by water managers because they do not require cooperation of a large number of utility customers to be effective. However, in contrast to demand reduction measures, the availability of supply options is not universal.

PLANNING FOR FUTURE DROUGHTS

Planning for future droughts should integrate the development of long-term plans for drought protection with formulation of detailed drought contingency plans. Long-term planning would involve the selection and evaluation of drought mitigation

Table 43.3 Examples of preparedness measures for reducing water demand

A   Public information and education campaigns
    Mass media campaigns
    School education programmes
    Community relations: tours, speakers' bureau, exhibits

B   Emergency conservation programmes
    Residential indoor plumbing retrofit programmes
    Home water audits for high-quantity users
    Plumbing retrofits for government buildings
    Commercial/industrial/institutional water audits

C   Water service restrictions
    Restriction or elimination of wholesale deliveries
    Discontinuation of sales to water haulers
    Moratorium on new customer connections

D   Restrictions on nonessential uses of water
    Filling of swimming pools
    Car washing
    Lawn sprinkling
    Water hosing of pavements
    Irrigation of parks and street medians
    Operation of public fountains

E   Prohibition of selected commercial uses
    Nonrecycling car washes
    Laundromats
    Irrigation of golf courses

F   Drought emergency pricing
    Drought surcharge
    Excess use charge
    Steep block rate
    Conservation credits

G   Water rationing programmes
    Odd/even-day watering schedule
    Per capita allocation
    Per household allocation
    Allocation based on prior use
    Rationing through inconvenience

Source: Dziegielewski *et al.* 1992a

measures for providing an adequate level of drought protection.

A proper understanding of the distinctive roles of drought mitigation and preparedness for drought response is critical to effective overall drought management. Public water supply agencies tend to emphasise the importance of drought mitigation measures that would limit the need for drought response measures and minimise the chances of reaching crisis situations, during which such emergency measures as declarations of dis-aster areas and provisions of disaster relief must be used. On the other hand, the environmental community tends to favour short-term drought response measures, based on the belief that a greater reliance on such measures will reduce the need for additional water development and withdrawals at the expense of instream uses of water that benefit the environment. However, by definition, a crisis situation cannot be, or should not be, 'planned for', because the reason we pursue planning for droughts is to avoid 'crisis' situations.

Table 43.4 Examples of preparedness measures for increasing water supply

A Water system improvements
Raw water sources
Reservoir evaporation suppression
Reduction of dam leaks
Transfers of surplus water among reservoirs
Providing pumped reservoir storage
Lining of water transmission canals
Water treatment plants
Recirculation of filter washwater
Blending-in impaired quality water
Water distribution systems
Reduction of water pressures
Leak detection and repair
Discontinuing hydrant and main flushing
Meter repair and replacement programmes

B Emergency sources of supply
Interdistrict transfers
Emergency interconnections
Importation of water by trucks
Importation by railroad cars
Cross-purpose diversions
Reduction of reservoir releases for hydropower production
Reduction of reservoir releases for flood control
Withdrawals from recreational water bodies
Relaxation of minimum streamflow requirements
Auxiliary emergency sources
Utilisation of small creeks, ponds, and quarries
Utilisation of dead reservoir storage
Construction of a temporary pipeline
Temporary in-river-channel storage
Reactivation of abandoned wells
Drilling of new wells
Desalination of brackish water
Desalination of sea water

C Management of available water resources
Nonperpetual water transfers from agriculture
Land fallowing programmes
Individual exchange agreements
Emergency water banks
Overdrafting of groundwater aquifers
Precipitation management

Source: Dziegielewski *et al.* 1992a

Water planners are often unclear about what constitutes 'a crisis in water supply'. Some outcomes of a water supply shortage, such as a depressurised and drained distribution system or contaminated water, would likely be seen as a crisis by both water managers and residents. It is less clear, however, whether the imposition of mandatory 'water rationing' represents a crisis situation. In fact, the dispute between water planners and the environmental community may be resolved by finding the answer to this question. If water rationing represents the crisis, then the mitigation and preparedness measures should be adopted to minimise the chances of having to implement mandatory water rationing during future droughts. On the other hand, if rationing is found to be an acceptable drought response measure, then it can become a component of the plan for coping with future droughts. This dilemma can be solved by examining the beliefs and behaviours of the general population, and especially the population served by public water supply systems.

The social behaviour during recent droughts indicates that the general population views severe water rationing with enforcement as a measure taken in response to a 'real crisis situation'. Numerous studies show that individual citizens are likely to change their water-using behaviours and endure significant hardships if they believe that there is a crisis (Bruvold 1979, White 1966, Dziegielewski 1994). In other words, the general public tends to see water supply conditions as either 'crisis' or 'normal' (i.e., non-crisis). As noted by Dziegielewski *et al.* (1993) in a study of the California drought of 1987–92, the reported success of rationing programmes, measured as deep cutbacks in water use, provides proof that the drought situation was viewed by the residents of urban areas in California as a crisis. If the supply shortages caused by the drought were not seen as a 'crisis', then most rationing programmes would fail to produce the called-for reductions in water use. Accordingly, in planning for droughts we can classify rationing programmes as planned-for drought response measures as long as they are aimed at eliminating water waste and improving the efficiency of water use. All rationing plans that call for 'significant sacrifice', by allocating fixed quantities of water to each user that are insufficient for supporting normal lifestyles and that result in property damage, inconvenience, and significant burden, should be classified as emergency measures to be taken only in response to a crisis situation.

While preparing plans for coping with droughts, we can include occasional 'water deficits' in long-term water supply plans, but not water shortages that would result in crisis conditions and require extraordinary measures to recover from the crisis. Such plans can provide guidelines to decision makers as to the proper times to employ drought response measures, and which measures to employ, depending on the status of demand and supply. However, most appropriate drought contingency plans have to be developed as a part of a comprehensive drought planning effort where the long-term and short-term drought management options are considered. A planning framework for finding an optimal balance of long-term drought mitigation measures and short-term drought preparedness measures is described below.

Finding an optimal combination of preparedness and mitigation

The steps that need to be taken while developing a comprehensive plan for coping with potential water supply deficits during periods of drought include: (1) assessment of the reliability of current and new sources of water supply; (2) evaluation of short-term drought response options; (3) evaluation of selected long-term drought mitigation investments; and (4) selection of the optimal combination of long-term and short-term measures for the plan.

The main goal of the drought planning process is to identify the optimal components of a drought mitigation strategy by selecting from a number of alternative strategies aimed at dealing with the risk of water shortages. The development of drought contingency plans must begin with the determination of the vulnerability of a water supply system to water shortages during drought and an assessment of the economic consequences of potential supply shortages. The magnitude of economic damages during a severe drought should dictate the need for and the level of long-term drought mitigation. Economic theory suggests that the incremental cost of long-term drought protection should be balanced with the benefits of reducing economic damages that may result from recurring shortages of water.

In the long term, the vulnerability of a system to drought could be reduced by augmenting supplies or implementing conservation measures to permanently reduce the demand. A system that has to resort to emergency measures fairly frequently can probably mitigate droughts more efficiently by expanding supply or reducing demand through long-term conservation programmes. However, if the risk of drought damages during a planning period is low or moderate, the optimal strategy may involve the formulation of drought contingency plans to cope with actual emergencies. Temporary reduction of demand and reliance on emergency water supplies are two types of preparedness measures that can be incorporated into drought contingency plans. It is important to note that the 'optimal drought plan' can comprise a combination of both mitigation and preparedness measures.

The first step in finding the optimal mix of mitigation and preparedness measures for long-term drought plans is to determine the tradeoffs between the costs of the two types of measures, where the cost represents a sum of economic, social, and environmental costs of each option. The tradeoff can be calculated using the following formula (Dziegielewski *et al.* 1992b):

$$DPIT_m = \frac{CC_o - CC_m}{IC_m} \qquad (43.1)$$

where

$DPIT_m$	=	drought protection investment tradeoff associated with mitigation measure m
m	=	long-term drought mitigation measure
CC_o	=	coping cost *without* long-term drought mitigation alternative m
CC_m	=	coping cost *with* long-term drought mitigation alternative m
IC_m	=	total investment and social and environmental impact cost of alternative m

The coping cost (or the expected and discounted value of the cumulative cost of coping with statistical droughts during the entire planning period) is:

$$CC = E(TC) = \sum_{t=1}^{T} \sum_{i=1}^{k} p_{it} C_{it} (1+r)^{-t} \qquad (43.2)$$

where

CC	=	coping cost (CC_o or CC_m)
$E(TC)$	=	the present worth of the expected cost of coping with shortages during the planning period
p_{it}	=	the probability of drought (i.e., water shortages) in year t also associated with cost C_{it} to cope with that drought
C_{it}	=	cost of coping with water shortage of probability level i occurring in year t
r	=	discount rate
t	=	any future year of the planning period
T	=	number of years in the planning period

p	=	probability of drought event
k	=	number of distinct levels of drought severity

A sample calculation of the drought protection investment tradeoff is shown in Tables 43.5 and 43.6. The example assumes a five-year planning period and information on the cost of coping with drought of various levels of severity during each year of the planning period.

To find the present worth of the expected coping cost, we have to discount each annual cost C_{it} for a drought of given severity to year 0 (using, for example, a discount rate r = 0.04) and then multiply the discounted value by its respective probability.

The coping cost for each year t of the planning period is calculated as:

$$C_t = \sum_{p=1}^{k} p_{it} C_{it} (1+r)^{-t} \qquad (43.3)$$

In this example, the total expected value for the cost of coping with these statistical droughts during the

Table 43.5 Example of calculation of cost to cope with future droughts

Drought year t	Drought severity level	Probability P_{it}	Coping cost C_{it} 1990$ (1,000$)
1	I	0.10	300
	II	0.04	800
	III	0.02	2,000
	IV	0.01	6,000
2	I	0.10	350
	II	0.04	900
	III	0.02	2,300
	IV	0.01	7,000
3	I	0.10	450
	II	0.04	1,300
	III	0.02	3,000
	IV	0.01	8,500
4	I	0.10	600
	II	0.04	1,700
	III	0.02	4,000
	IV	0.01	10,000
5	I	0.10	800
	II	0.04	2,100
	III	0.02	5,000
	IV	0.01	12,500

Table 43.6 Sample calculations of coping cost

Year t	Probability p_{it}	Discount factor $(1+r)^{-t}$	Discounted cost $p_{it}C_{it}(1+r)^{-t}$	Yearly coping cost
1	0.10	0.962	28.860	
	0.04	0.962	30.784	
	0.02	0.962	38.480	
	0.01	0.962	57.720	155.844
2	0.10	0.925	32.375	
	0.04	0.925	33.300	
	0.02	0.925	42.550	
	0.01	0.925	64.750	172.975
3	0.10	0.889	40.005	
	0.04	0.889	46.228	
	0.02	0.889	53.340	
	0.01	0.889	75.565	215.138
4	0.10	0.855	51.300	
	0.04	0.855	58.140	
	0.02	0.855	68.400	
	0.01	0.855	85.500	263.340
5	0.10	0.822	65.760	
	0.04	0.822	69.048	
	0.02	0.822	82.200	
	0.01	0.822	102.750	319.758

five-year planning period is US$1,127,055. The value of US$1,127,055 represents CC_o – that is, total coping cost when using only short-term measures (i.e., without investing in the long-term protection alternative m). If we invest US$500,000 in a long-term alternative and reassess the magnitude of the expected deficits with this mitigation measure, the total coping cost may be reduced to $CC_m = \$420,000$. Therefore, the drought investment protection tradeoff in Equation 43.1 would be:

$$
\begin{aligned}
DPIT_m &= \frac{CC_o - CC_m}{IC_m} \\
&= \frac{1{,}127{,}055 - 420{,}000}{500{,}000} \\
&= \frac{707{,}055}{500{,}000} \\
&= 1.41
\end{aligned}
\tag{43.4}
$$

This ratio represents the tradeoff between the cost of drought mitigation when using alternative m and the cost of relying solely on short-term drought preparedness measures. The magnitude of this tradeoff indicates that for each dollar spent on drought mitigation, we would gain US$1.41 in savings in the cost of dealing with future droughts during the planning period. An application of the tradeoff analysis to the city of Phoenix, Arizona, can be found in Dziegielewski et al. (1992a).

Drought contingency plans

Surveys of water utilities indicate that there is a limited reliance on long-term drought protection and a limited readiness to respond to drought events less severe than the design drought. Dziegielewski et al. (1992a) found that approximately 42 per cent of the surveyed public systems in Alabama, California, Florida, Oklahoma, Tennessee, and Wyoming indicated that their agency had a specific drought contingency plan in place, and an additional 9 per cent indicated that such a plan was under development. Also, more than one-third of responding agencies reported that water conservation ordinances had been adopted in all, or nearly all, communities they serve. An additional 16 per cent reported the adoption of such ordinances in some communities. Four out of five conservation ordinances were reported to have provisions for coping with water shortages. Finally, almost 60 per cent of the systems reported having agreements to rent or purchase water temporarily. California, Florida, and Tennessee have the highest percentage of systems with drought contingency plans, water rental agreements, and water shortage ordinances.

DalMonte (1991) found that 47 per cent of 601 systems in the Midwest had a drought contingency plan in the form of an ordinance or written policy for operating their water supply systems during droughts. A similar proportion of available drought contingency plans was reported by Moreau and Little (1989). These results indicate that approximately half of the systems surveyed engage in planning for water shortages and have formalised their drought management activities. The other half of the systems are likely to resort to ad hoc drought response measures, which may lead to a higher-than-necessary cost of coping with future droughts.

SUMMARY

Urban areas have a number of options for dealing with water shortages caused by droughts. However, these options have to be examined and selected before a drought event to ensure that many unnecessary impacts of a drought event are avoided. Prompt implementation of measures that have been tailored to the conditions of weather and sources of supply can prevent the development of crisis conditions, which would lead to severe hardships and economic losses.

Public water supply systems in the United States are making some progress toward proactive drought management. An increasing number of systems are developing drought contingency plans with specific drought preparedness measures. Drought experiences during the last two decades have demonstrated the ability of urban areas to respond to droughts with short-term measures in ways that minimise the economic, social, and environmental impacts of water shortages. The success of drought response measures prompted a debate about the respective roles of drought mitigation and drought preparedness and response measures in dealing with future droughts. The high investment costs and adverse environmental impacts of the traditional mitigation measures such as water storage force water planners to increase their reliance on drought preparedness. However, a sole reliance on either short-term or long-term options is not likely to be the least costly approach for dealing with droughts. Drought planners must be able to find the optimal balance between the appropriate levels of mitigation and preparedness. This chapter described a method of finding the economic tradeoffs between long-term and short-term measures for dealing with future droughts. However, a practical method for selecting optimal combinations of measures requires a great deal of information about the effects of water shortages on communities and individual citizens. More research should be devoted to measuring the impacts of water shortages and predicting the probability, magnitude, and duration of future droughts. The latter is especially important in light of the recent prediction of global climatic changes that would increase the frequency of extreme weather events such as droughts.

REFERENCES

Bruvold, W.H. (1979) 'Residential response to urban drought in Central California', *Water Resources Research* 15, 6: 1,297–304.

DalMonte, J.A. (1991) 'Midwestern water utility managers' response to drought', unpublished M.S. thesis, Southern Illinois University at Carbondale.

Dziegielewski, B. (1986) 'Drought management options', in Water Science and Technology Board of the National Research Council, *Drought Management and Its Impacts on Public Water Systems*, Washington, DC: National Academy Press.

—— (1994) 'The drought is real: Designing a successful water conservation campaign', in H. Garduno and F. Arreguin-Cortes (eds), *Efficient water use*, Montevideo, Uruguay: UNESCO–ROSTLAC.

Dziegielewski, B., and Crews, J.E. (1986) 'Minimizing the cost of coping with droughts: Springfield, IL', *Journal of Water Resources Planning and Management, ASCE* 112, 4: 419–38.

Dziegielewski, B., Ferrell-Dillard, R., and Beck, R.E. (1992a) 'Coping with urban water shortages during drought: The effects of legal and administrative factors', Research Report sponsored by the United States Geological Survey, Award No. 14-08-001-G1897, Carbondale: Southern Illinois University.

Dziegielewski, B., Garbharran, H., and Langowski, J.F. (1993) *The Great California Drought of 1987–1992: Lessons for Water Management*, Institute for Water Resources Report IWR, Report 93-NDS-5, Fort Belvoir, VA: US Army Corps of Engineers.

Dziegielewski, B., Lynne, G.D., Wilhite, D.A., and Sheer, D.P. (1991) 'National study of water management during drought: A research assessment', Institute of Water Resources Report, IWR Report 91–NDS–3, Fort Belvoir, VA, US Army Corps of Engineers.

Dziegielewski, B., Mee Jr., W.R., and Larson, K.R. (1992b) 'Developing a long-term drought plan for Phoenix', *Journal of the American Water Works Association* 84, 10: 46–51.

Flory, J.E. and Panella, T. (1994) 'Long-term water conservation and shortage management practices: Planning that includes demand hardening', Tabor Caramanis and Associates, Sacramento, CA: California Urban Water Agencies.

Garbharran, H.P. (1989) 'Evaluation of drought preparedness and response measures for public water supply', unpublished Ph.D. dissertation, Southern Illinois University at Carbondale.

Moreau, D.H. and Little, K.W. (1989) 'Managing public water supplies during drought: Experience in the United States in 1986 and 1988', Raleigh, NC: University of North Carolina, Water Resources Research Institute.

Riebsame, W.E., Changnon, S.A., and Karl, T.R. (1990)

Drought and Natural Resources Management in the United States: Impacts and Implications of the 1987–1989 Drought, Boulder, CO: Westview Press.

White, G.F. (1966) 'Formation and roles of public attitudes', in H. Jarrett (ed.), *Environmental Quality in a Growing Environment*, Baltimore, MD: Johns Hopkins University Press.

Wilhite, D.A. and Wood, D.A. (1985) 'Planning for drought: The role of state government', *Water Resources Bulletin* 21, 1: 31–8.

44

AN OVERVIEW OF THE ACTIVITIES OF UNSO IN DROUGHT PREPAREDNESS AND MITIGATION

Tijan Jallow

INTRODUCTION

Drought is a recurrent feature in many African countries, often with devastating consequences for the local populations living in the dry marginal areas. The threat has widened in scope with many more countries and populations affected than previously, partly as result of public policies that have weakened indigenous coping strategies of local populations. Increased poverty has also meant that the vulnerability of rural households has increased, and the ability to recover from the effects of drought has been much reduced (Davies 1993). In addition, the urban poor are increasingly subjected to its effects as well, through drought-induced shocks to the food system. It is clear that more concerted efforts are needed to support the efforts of African countries to confront this problem.

This chapter describes, in broad terms, the activities of the United Nations Development Programme (UNDP) Office to Combat Desertification and Drought (United Nations Sudano–Sahelian Office [UNSO]) with respect to drought preparedness and mitigation in Africa. An overview of the establishment and evolution of UNSO; the recently adopted United Nations Convention to Combat Desertification (CCD), including some of its provisions dealing with drought; and UNSO's past and current activities on drought are presented in this chapter.

ESTABLISHMENT AND EVOLUTION OF UNSO

The United Nations Sudano–Sahelian Office, now known as the UNDP Office to Combat Desertification and Drought (UNSO), was established in 1973 following the west African Sahel drought of 1968–73 to coordinate medium- and long-term assistance of the organisations of the UN system in the subregion. The affected countries in the region also set up, in March 1973, the Permanent Interstate Committee for the Control of Drought in the Sahel (*Comity Inter-Etats de Lutte contre la Sécheresse dans le Sahel – CILSS*), originally consisting of Burkina Faso (then Upper Volta), Chad, Mali, Mauritania, Niger, and Senegal (The Gambia joined CILSS in December 1973, Cape Verde in 1975, and Guinea Bissau in 1985). UNSO has worked closely with CILSS since then.

Following the 1977 United Nations Conference on Desertification (UNCOD) held in Nairobi, Kenya, UNSO's mandate was expanded to include assistance in the implementation of the Plan of Action to Combat Desertification (PACD) in the twenty-two countries of the Sudano–Sahelian zone.[1] This second mandate of UNSO was undertaken through a joint venture mechanism established between UNDP and the United Nations Environment Programme (UNEP) in 1979, and has been one of the successful examples of international collaborative efforts to combat desertification.

Events similar to those that marked the establishment of CILSS in west Africa were also prevalent in much of east Africa in the early 1980s, with the result that in January 1986, the Intergovernmental Authority on Drought and Development (IGADD) was established at a summit meeting of heads of state and governments of Djibouti, Ethiopia, Kenya, Somalia, Sudan, and Uganda. UNSO's responsibility was extended to cover assistance to the IGADD region as well.

The most recent evolution of UNSO's mandate and functions occurred in 1995, following the adoption, in June 1994, of the International Convention to Combat Desertification (CCD). UNSO was transformed into the UNDP Office to Combat Desertification and Drought and made the central entity within the organisation responsible for spearheading and supporting UNDP's efforts in all affected programme countries, within the context of the implementation of the CCD.

THE UNITED NATIONS CONVENTION TO COMBAT DESERTIFICATION

Brief overview of the CCD

The UN Convention to Combat Desertification (CCD) emanated from the Earth Summit held in Rio de Janeiro, Brazil, in June 1992. The Convention was adopted in June 1994 in Paris and entered into force on 26 December 1996.

The objective of the CCD is to promote sustainable development of the world's drylands by strengthening international cooperation and partnerships to combat desertification and mitigate the effects of drought at all levels. The CCD is not only a legally binding international instrument, it also embodies many of the innovative approaches and lessons learnt from many years of experience dealing with desertification and local-level natural resources management issues.

The Convention provides for the formulation and implementation of national action programmes (NAPs), which will constitute the foundation for translating the objectives, principles, and spirit of the convention into concrete actions and measures in affected developing countries. The NAP, as conceived under the CCD, is process-oriented, based on a bottom-up approach, iterative and decentralised. Through the NAP process, a set of integrated actions

encompassing institutional, legal, economic, and technical measures that address the root causes of desertification would be identified and integrated programmes designed and implemented to rehabilitate degraded lands and/or protect vulnerable ones. A strong feature of the CCD is the recognition it gives to national partnership building involving all key stakeholders (in particular, civil society and dryland populations) in identifying, implementing, and monitoring priority actions.

The CCD also provides for preparation and implementation of subregional action programmes to harmonise and increase complementarity between national action programmes as well as facilitate joint programmes for the sustainable management of transboundary natural resources, scientific and technical cooperation, and strengthening of relevant institutions.

To better reflect regional situations and priorities, four regional implementation annexes were also negotiated and agreed to (Africa, Asia, Latin America and the Caribbean, and the northern Mediterranean countries, although the latter do not qualify for financial assistance).

The CCD and drought preparedness and mitigation

Building on Chapter 12 of Agenda 21, the CCD makes specific provisions for addressing the problem of drought in the context of both the national and subregional action programmes. Thus, Article 10 of the CCD proposes that the NAP 'may include, inter alia, some or all of the following measures to prepare for and mitigate the effects of drought':

a) establishment and/or strengthening, as appropriate, of early warning systems, including local and national facilities and joint systems at the sub-regional and regional levels, and mechanisms for assisting environmentally displaced persons;

b) strengthening of drought preparedness and management, including drought contingency plans at local, national, sub-regional, and regional levels, which take into consideration seasonal to interannual climate predictions;

c) establishment and/or strengthening as appropriate

of food security systems, including storage and marketing facilities, particularly in rural areas;

d) establishment of alternative livelihood projects that could provide incomes in drought prone areas; and

e) development of sustainable irrigation programmes for both crops and livestock.

At the subregional level, particularly with respect to the annex for Africa, strengthening drought early warning systems and contingency planning are some of the areas identified for subregional and regional collaboration.

UNSO'S DROUGHT PREPAREDNESS AND MITIGATION PROGRAMME

Previous drought activities

In line with the evolution of its mandate (outlined previously), the focus of UNSO's activities relating to drought has changed over the years. From its establishment up to 1977, most of UNSO's work was concentrated in the CILSS region. The major focus of UNSO during this period was the construction of a network of all-weather feeder roads, which by the end of 1987 amounted to more than 2,500 km. The roads made it possible to deliver food and medical supplies to otherwise inaccessible towns and villages and thus helped in channelling emergency assistance. The feeder roads were also a major factor in opening up these areas to recovery, rehabilitation, and development activities. Other activities undertaken by UNSO during this period included assistance in providing seed supplies and storage facilities as well as other measures to revive agricultural development and boost food production.

Since 1977, UNSO has supported a number of activities related to the implementation of the PACD, such as:

- afforestation and reforestation (including fuel-wood plantation, agroforestry, and woodlots);
- development of alternative sources of energy (e.g., wind energy and peanut shell briquettes) and energy-saving measures (e.g., fuel-efficient stoves) to reduce the demand for fuel wood;
- management, conservation, and use of water resources through small earthen dams, ground-water development, and water harvesting;
- range management projects including fodder production and livestock research and husbandry;
- projects for stabilising both coastal and continental dunes, mainly through vegetative means, and also erosion control programmes;
- assisting governments in ecological monitoring, in preparing national strategies for combatting desertification, and by participating in donor and round-table meetings.

In the two decades of implementing its second mandate (i.e., desertification control), UNSO's activities gradually shifted from sectoral projects in forestry, agroforestry, fuel-wood projects, and sand dune stabilisation to the promotion of integrated village-based land management, pastoral development, and assistance at the national level in the preparation of strategic frameworks for development and implementation of activities on combatting desertification.

Although not focusing on drought as such, these programmes and projects have contributed to reducing vulnerability to drought and improving livelihoods by facilitating the restoration/rehabilitation of degraded lands and other measures. During this period, activities related to drought relief and rehabilitation declined, and greater emphasis was progressively given to anti-desertification activities in response to the PACD. For example, a review of UNSO's project portfolio showed that the ratio between drought and desertification control activities changed from 15:0 in 1977 to 38:167 in 1987.

The renewed UNSO programme on drought

Since the Rio Earth Summit, drought has re-emerged as an important concern in the work of UNSO. Taking into account the persistence of drought in many African countries and the impetus provided by the recently adopted CCD, UNSO is giving a renewed emphasis to supporting the efforts of African countries to plan and respond more proactively to the effects of recurrent drought.

Constraints hampering effective interventions/ strategies for dealing with drought in Africa include the following:

- *Policy* – lack of clearly articulated national policies on drought, which has tended to favour the continuation of relief and food aid over proactive contingency planning. In many cases, drought contingency planning, apart from support for early warning, does not figure sufficiently in development planning processes even in some of the most drought-prone countries.
- *Institutional* – overcentralisation of planning and resources at the national level, resulting in weak capacities at the subnational level.
- *Inefficient use of early warning information for timely responses* – many early warning systems (EWS) are also oriented to supply information for the purpose of relief, as opposed to mitigation and contingency planning.
- *Breakdown/weakening of indigenous coping strategies* – resulting from poor policies and leading to increased vulnerabilities of dryland populations to the effects of recurrent drought.

There have also been some successes in dealing with drought. For example, Cape Verde and Botswana have been recognised as having successfully managed several drought episodes. However, it should be noted that the successes referred to have not resulted in fostering sustainable livelihoods, which in the long run are the key to reducing vulnerability to droughts. More thorough analysis of how drought mitigation policies and interventions are working is needed to provide a sound basis for future planning.

Focus of UNSO's renewed programme on drought

Four aspects of drought management are now recognised: (1) drought preparedness, dealing with collection of information, diagnosis, and contingency planning; (2) drought mitigation, referring to actions undertaken before a drought and aimed at reducing its impacts; (3) drought relief, referring to actions taken during a drought (e.g., food aid); and (4) drought rehabilitation, involving actions taken when conditions improve to re-establish the economic base. Successful drought management requires action on all four dimensions.

Based on the constraints identified, and taking into account the diverse number of actions undertaken at local, national, and international levels to mitigate the effects of drought, UNSO is focusing its efforts on preparedness and mitigation activities, as opposed to relief and rehabilitation (Davies 1993, Wilhite 1993). The long-term goal of UNSO's programme is to contribute to reducing vulnerability of dryland populations to recurrent drought through (among other measures):

- strengthening the capacity of local communities and district and/or regional authorities to plan, develop, and manage effective responses to recurrent drought;
- assisting governments in developing the necessary policies and institutional capacities to monitor and respond to drought at the national level; and
- helping foster greater cooperation among countries on common drought response programmes.

In helping countries formulate and implement drought preparedness and mitigation (DPM) programmes, particular attention needs to be paid to strengthening subnational capacities while not neglecting the need for appropriate reinforcement at the national level. The rationale for this approach is based on the fact that many drought management programmes in Africa are characterised by an overcentralisation of planning and resources. The institutional framework for drought management also is frequently located at the national macrolevel. Current trends in decentralisation and regionalisation in many of the countries, and the fact that droughts with devastating consequences occur more frequently on a local rather than national scale, argue strongly in favour of building DPM capacity at subnational levels, including at the local level. Another important factor is the need to build on indigenous safety nets and coping strategies to ensure long-term sustainability of efforts.

Such an approach could contribute to more successful efforts to reduce the impacts of recurrent droughts by making it possible to:

- situate response capacity closer to the action/need;
- integrate actions into and strengthen complementarity with local strategies;
- increase the likelihood of understanding, evaluating,

and monitoring the impacts of activities undertaken;

- build capacity and create the potential for better management of location-specific interventions; and
- provide opportunities for on-the-job training for district and provincial staff in drought management.

Programme implementation

The programme will be implemented within the framework of the national and subregional action programme processes being developed in the context of the CCD. Priority countries for initial support would be selected through mutual dialogue, taking into account the following factors: (1) demographic vulnerability (i.e., percentage of total population living in drought-prone areas); (2) climatic risk (frequency and intensity of drought occurrences); (3) risk/vulnerability to famine (frequency of famines in the last two decades); and (4) weak institutional capacity, particularly at the local level.

The need for close collaboration between external partners, in the context of the NAP process, is essential in supporting the efforts of affected African countries to develop appropriate responses to drought. For this reason, UNSO will seek to forge collaborative linkages with a variety of agencies such as the World Meteorological Organization (WMO), IFAD, and Food and Agriculture Organization (FAO) as well as bilateral organisations and nongovernment organisations (NGOs). The subregional organisations in Africa (CILSS, IGADD, South African Development Council, and UMA) will also be key partners in these efforts.

CONCLUSIONS

The task of reducing the impacts of drought in Africa poses tremendous challenges in a region where large segments of the population are poor and food-insecure and poverty levels are expected to increase into the next century. The development of appropriate policies and strengthening of institutional mechanisms for drought preparedness and mitigation need to be accompanied by concrete programmes to promote sustainable livelihoods, as well as safety nets to protect lives and livelihoods in the event of major drought episodes. Ultimately, development strategies for dryland areas need to help create increased opportunities for the populations and reduce marginalisation in order to contribute significantly to reducing vulnerabilities to drought.

NOTE

1 Benin, Burkina Faso, Cameroon, Cape Verde, Chad, Djibouti, Ethiopia, Gambia, Ghana, Guinea, Guinea Bissau, Kenya, Mali, Mauritania, Niger, Nigeria, Senegal, Somalia, Sudan, Tanzania, Togo, and Uganda (Eritrea was included later, bringing the total to twenty-three countries).

REFERENCES

Davies, S. (1993) 'Preparing for and mitigating drought: Linking micro and macro levels', report prepared for the United Nations Sudano–Sahelian Office, New York.

UNSO (1988) *The United Nations Sudano–Sahelian Office: Report of an In-house Study*, New York: United Nations Sudano–Sahelian Office.

—— (1992) *Assessment of Desertification and Drought in the Sudano–Sahelian region 1985–1991*, New York: United Nations Sudano–Sahelian Office.

Wilhite, D.A. (1993) 'A framework for developing national drought preparedness and mitigation policies and strategies in the Sudano–Sahelian region', report prepared for the United Nations Sudano–Sahelian Office, New York.

PART VII

LINKING DROUGHT TO OTHER GLOBAL ISSUES

45

DROUGHT DISCOURSE AND VULNERABILITY

Thomas E. Downing and Karen Bakker

INTRODUCTION

Many definitions of drought have been expounded and adopted, as summarised in numerous chapters in these volumes. Equally, vulnerability to drought has been viewed from numerous perspectives, paradigms, and frameworks. This paper reviews frameworks of drought vulnerability, drawing on four sets of literature: agriculture/biology/hydrology, natural hazards, vulnerability and livelihood security, and discourse analysis.

We begin with a regional overview of drought vulnerability to set the stage. The next section presents a set of case studies that illustrate diverse drought situations and applied frameworks. Finally, we reflect on what has been learned in the past decade of research on vulnerability, from the many perspectives.

This discursive approach – from the general to the specific, from case studies to general observations on frameworks and theory – is purposeful. Each framework presented below has merit and applications. It is incautious at present to attempt to impose the definitive framework. Rather, the purpose of this review is to stimulate reflection on actual experience and development of robust applications.

Let's begin with some relatively straightforward observations on drought vulnerability – to set the stage. Anticipating some of the argument below, we can assert that the impacts of drought (for water and food systems) are related to underlying conditions of agricultural resources, economic development, food security, and water use. Indicators of these measures for major world regions are shown in Table 45.1.

Agricultural resources vary widely between regions (Table 45.1a). Africa has relatively low population densities but less cropland than many other regions,

and a low percentage of cropland is irrigated. Cereal yields are highest in the OECD countries and lowest in Africa. Food production has improved in the past decade in all regions except eastern Europe.

Indicators of agricultural incomes (Table 45.1b) highlight the enormous disparity in per capita gross national product (GNP) (from more than US$20,000 to less than US$500). Agriculture is a relatively small share of the wealthiest economies, compared to more than a third of gross domestic product (GDP) in west and east Africa and south Asia. All of the regions have expanding economies, but many are barely (or not) keeping pace with population growth. Investment in agricultural research, a crude indicator of adaptability to future climatic and economic shocks, also varies widely.

The third group of indicators illustrates disparities in household status and food security (Table 45.1c). In agrarian and poorer economies, households spend up to 50 per cent of their income on food, compared to 10–25 per cent in the OECD. However, adult female literacy is improving and infant mortality rates are declining (with exceptions in eastern Europe and the former Soviet Union [FSU]).

Water resources vary widely between regions (Table 45.1d). Africa and the Middle East are much drier than the rest of the world. Asia, the Americas, and the FSU have substantial water resources. However, the lowest rates of water use, expressed as the percentage of withdrawal to resources, are in the Pacific Islands, west Africa, South America, and Mexico. The regions most vulnerable to water scarcity appear to be north Africa (relying on exogenous supplies in many cases) and the Middle East.

Table 45.1 Indicators of food system vulnerability to drought
(a) Population and agricultural resources

	Population density			Cropland	Irrigated land 1980–91 % of cropland	Cereal yields 1990–2 kg/ha	Food production (1979–81 = 100)	
	1950	1995	2025	1000ha			1980–2	1990–2
North Africa	64	196	345	6,609	25	1,757	104	149
West Africa	88	307	689	3,489	3	950	103	133
East Africa	136	475	1,087	3,768	5	1,354	103	121
Southern Africa	54	177	378	3,235	8	930	102	111
South Asia	1,242	3,295	5,052	45,407	31	1,863	102	136
Southeast Asia	430	1,147	1,677	8,054	18	2,580	106	143
Centrally planned Asia	513	1,148	1,433	33,320	42	3,910	102	131
Middle East	141	494	969	6,664	38	2,261	104	188
OECD Asia Pacific	136	230	247	13,485	63	4,585	98	110
Central America	320	887	1,471	1,087	12	1,991	99	114
OECD North America	90	159	196	116,853	6	3,706	105	117
Mexico	143	491	720	24,720	21	2,430	104	128
Southern S. America	65	176	238	23,560	12	2,730	105	128
Northern S. America	61	200	307	2,622	24	2,383	103	125
Eastern Europe	747	1,025	1,116	5,493	22	3,759	103	96
OECD Europe	847	1,084	1,129	5,836	13	4,797	102	113
FSU	13	134	19	41,636		2,178		
Pacific Islands	40	110	192	235		1,932	103	127

(b) Income and agricultural investment

	GNP per capita, 1991 $US	Agricultural GDP, 1991 %	GDP growth, 1980–91 %	Public agricultural research 1981–5 $M
North Africa	1,285	17	3.9	23
West Africa	603	34	2	12
East Africa	516	42	3.3	10
Southern Africa	967	24	2.8	6
South Asia	220	42	5.8	176
Southeast Asia	2,587	24	5.2	50
Centrally planned Asia	364	23	9.4	1,713
Middle East	5,559	14	3.2	30
OECD Asia Pacific	15,618	6	4.6	346
Central America	1,417	16	0.5	4
OECD North America	21,548	3	2.9	923
Mexico	2,971	8	1.2	129
Southern S. America	3,032	10	1.6	96
Northern S. America	1,519	12	1.7	17
Eastern Europe	2,093	14	0.8	
OECD Europe	18,087	6	2.4	86
FSU	2,139	26		
Pacific Islands	1,187	29	2	9

(c) Food security

	H/H food expenditure 1980–5 % share	Refugees 1992	Adult female literacy % 1970	1990	Infant mortality rate 1970–5	1990–5
North Africa	47	213,590	13	39	134	73
West Africa	46	55,279	9	27	155	111
East Africa	41	202,593	23	37	124	82
Southern Africa	45	174,815	30	49	127	92
South Asia	56	237,567	12	24	151	106
Southeast Asia	36	52,000	53	73	92	51
Centrally planned Asia	61	12,500	74	62	69	37
Middle East	37	622,825	27	51	104	53
OECD Asia Pacific	19	8,283	90	94	23	10
Central America	38	7,019	63	77	77	39
OECD North America	12	70,700	99		17	8
Mexico	35	47,300	69	85	68	35
Southern S. America	33	150	84	91	64	31
Northern S. America	30	588	69	86	83	51
Eastern Europe	26	221,267	89	88	37	18
OECD Europe	19	62,947	88	90	20	8
FSU		209,940			17	26
Pacific Islands		3,800	24	38	69	35

(d) Water resources

	Water resources km³/yr	Withdrawal km³/yr	Per capita withdrawal	Withdrawal/ resources %
North Africa	34.62	13.45	561.29	89.21
West Africa	92.65	0.55	81.89	1.18
East Africa	36.39	0.68	97.13	4.81
Southern Africa	173.85	2.12	221.71	5.30
South Asia	1,176.75	101.30	248.25	5.19
Southeast Asia	575.76	10.44	322.10	7.82
Centrally planned Asia	964.00	158.24	794.33	13.25
Middle East	88.82	21.00	995.93	74.42
OECD Asia Pacific	255.75	29.93	426.32	9.28
Central America	302.62	5.03	517.17	4.72
OECD North America	1,417.50	260.60	1,531.50	17.01
Mexico	994.00	27.60	1,059.00	2.78
Southern S. America	1,960.50	13.43	565.50	1.26
Northern S. America	439.63	3.45	1,302.88	2.67
Eastern Europe	162.33	10.44	739.17	6.16
OECD Europe	121.82	17.24	704.06	18.26
FSU	4,684.00	353.00	1,330.00	7.54
Pacific Islands	291.67	0.04	26.67	0.04

Sources: WRI 1996 for (a) to (c), Gleick 1993 for (d)

These regional indicators are not meant to convey complete portraits of individual or household food security or vulnerability to drought. Rather, they suggest four aspects of vulnerability. First, drought does not affect all nations, economies, and households to the same extent or by the same impact pathways. The crude indicators reinforce the conception of vulnerability as a relative construct.

Second, national vulnerability diverges along familiar lines of developed, new industrialised, transitional, and developing countries. Much of Africa is highly vulnerable on all counts; OECD countries suffer drought but can manage the impacts.

Third, drought vulnerability is qualitatively different for different nations (and individuals). In the poorest households and economies, drought can still threaten lives. However, in most of the developing world, drought vulnerability constitutes a threat to livelihoods, the ability to maintain productive systems, and healthy economies. Drought is no longer the dominant cause of starvation and famine. In developed economies, and increasingly elsewhere, drought poses significant economic risks and costs for individuals, public enterprises, commercial organisations, and governments.

And fourth, vulnerability is dynamic. Considerable improvements have occurred over the past several decades, but some regression as well has been noted in eastern Europe and the FSU. Drought is a relatively short-term event (spanning several years); vulnerability changes at a variety of time scales, from within a season to decade-long trends in development.

The probability of most natural hazards changes little over time, with the possible exception of climate change and notwithstanding cycles and clustering of some events. In stark contrast, vulnerability is dynamic and can vary between extreme crises and complete safety (in either direction) in a few months or even days. Trends in such a dynamic state are inevitably specific to individuals, communities, and places. In this section we can provide no more than a sense of the kinds of trends that will shape local vulnerability in the future. Three reference points for vulnerability are essential in this discussion – vulnerability to (1) loss of life, (2) loss of assets and property, and (3) loss of livelihood. The trends in vulnerability for each reference point may differ.

Trends in the major determinants of vulnerability include:

- Population growth: increasing densities in hazardous areas increase the population at risk. The effect of population growth on resource use to create marginal populations in hazardous areas is less clear.
- Settlement patterns and migration: no clear trend away from hazardous locations.
- Economic development: increasing wealth increases the amount and value of property at risk, although it also enables greater investment in protection and mitigation.
- Health infrastructure: most countries have decreasing rates of malnourishment, although the situation among the most vulnerable is not clear.
- Mitigation and preparedness: some progress for specific hazards.
- Early warning, emergency assistance, and recovery: increasing local and global warning and response capabilities reduce the loss of life, at least for hazards where warning is effective.

The outcome of such trends can be illustrated by contrasting two situations. California, no stranger to drought, is served by the largest and likely the most complex human-made water distribution system in the world (see Nevarez 1996, Reisner 1989, Worster 1985). In Santa Barbara, after six years of drought, residents voted in 1991 to extend the State Water Project to their county, one more link in the huge chain of hydraulic projects stretching from northern to southern California. 'Sustainable' options were abandoned by a public unwilling to change to 'drier' lifestyles in the face of severe water shortages. According to one adage, everyone comes to California, but no one brings water with them. While population growth places increased demands on water resources in the West, economic wealth and a highly organised water resource planning system reduce vulnerability to drought.

In contrast, one of the causes of desertification is population expansion in semiarid regions, exploiting fragile resources. The result is soil erosion, reduced organic matter and water-holding capacity of soils, and highly variable crop yields due to moisture stress. Without the economic means and labour resources for protecting the soils or maintaining long fallows, resource-poor farmers accelerate the familiar processes of degradation and vulnerability (see Blaikie and Brookfield 1987 and Kasperson et al. 1995, among many others, for examples and discussion of these processes).

In summary, vulnerability to mortality and morbidity is probably decreasing for most places in the world. Conversely, economic vulnerability is likely to increase quite rapidly in many developing countries as per capita incomes rise. The situation for livelihoods is less clear. Many vulnerable groups are likely to remain susceptible to destitution if they survive a disaster.

INSIGHTS FROM STUDIES OF DROUGHT

The following short case studies illustrate a range of drought situations, definitions, and research frameworks. We begin with the conventional notion of drought as a hydrobiological risk, drawing on the literature of drought monitoring. The human ecology of natural hazards and structural definitions of vulnerability integrate drought hazard and societal vulnerability. Finally, examples of drought discourses draw on literature from political ecology.

Drought monitoring

The premise of most drought monitoring follows a causal chain from monitoring rainfall and temperatures to crop yields and production, and food availability at a national or regional level. A typical agroclimatic analysis is reported by Henricksen and Durkin (1985) for the International Livestock Centre for Africa. They show the utility of using the Food and Agriculture Organisation's length of growing period (LGP) to chart seasonal distribution of rainfall patterns in Ethiopia. The LGP depends on precipitation, evapotranspiration (related to temperature, humidity, wind speed, and radiation), and stored soil moisture. The LGP is readily related to crop yields, as shown for wheat, barley, peas, and lentils at Debre Berhan from 1979 to 1983. The variation in LGP is one indicator of drought risk, particularly important in the lowlands, where less than ninety days in a season results in crop failure.

Such agroclimatic analyses have been extended in recent years. Geographic information systems provide a spatial portrait of agricultural drought (Corbett and Carter 1997). Remote sensing is now commonly used to estimate rainfall (Meteosat monitoring of cold cloud cover duration) and vegetation responses (using NDVI) in operational monitoring of crop production and famine early warning systems.

Agroclimatic analyses are essential for many drought assessments, as indicated by Henricksen and Durkin (1985: 8):

> The present study indicates that the serious famine periods recorded at Mekele and Asmara over the past 20 to 30 years were preceded by 2 or more consecutive years in which the main-season LGP was less than 90 days, and in which the short rains failed. Up-to-date analyses of LGP could therefore constitute the basis of an early warning system to indicate the likelihood of serious famine in drought-prone areas of the country.

However, the link between rainfall and agricultural production does not extend, necessarily, to severe drought stress and famine. Mapping hydrobiological risk may be sufficient where institutional concerns primarily reside in monitoring production. Understanding societal vulnerability is essential to chart human impacts and the likelihood of famine.

Vulnerable groups and food systems in Zimbabwe

The beginning point for recent studies of drought has been a description of who is vulnerable and why. Such assessments recognise the interactions between drought hazard and vulnerability that define the risk of serious impacts. The major famine early warning systems have adopted vulnerability assessment that relies on a wide range of indicators (see Downing 1991 and Maxwell and Frankenberger 1992 for early assessments; World Food Programme 1996 for guidelines on vulnerability mapping; and Caldwell 1993, Hutchinson and Hall 1993, and Ramachandran and Eastman 1996 for case studies of Zambia, Haiti, and west Africa).

Downing (1992) compiled available information on Zimbabwe to portray vulnerability in the context of climatic variations. Four vulnerable groups have been identified in Zimbabwe (Table 45.2). The urban poor total some 6 per cent of the population and are relatively insensitive to fluctuations in agricultural production, as long as urban prices are not inflated and food aid is available. In rural areas, vulnerability among smallholders (occupying present or former communal lands) varies between agroecological zones. Fewer people are vulnerable in the wetter areas (zones I through III) than in the semiarid zones (IV

Table 45.2 Vulnerable groups in Zimbabwe

Group	Average year		Poor year	
	No. h/holds	% of pop.	No. h/holds	% of pop.
Urban				
Unemployment	72,000	3.7	72,000	3.7
Informal workers	53,000	2.7	53,000	2.7
Urban total	125,000	6.4	125,000	6.4
Rural				
Communal farmers				
Zones I and II	20,000	1.0	39,000	2.0
Zone III	22,500	1.0	98,000	5.0
Zones IV and V	137,000	7.0	450,500	23.0
Landless and unemployment	210,000	12.5	210,000	12.5
Rural total	389,500	21.5	797,500	42.5
Total	514,500	27.9	922,500	48.9

Source: Christensen and Stack 1992

and V) because of the conjuncture of better agricultural conditions, improved infrastructure, and access to markets. In all zones, vulnerability is higher in years of drought or poor production, but the increase in vulnerability is largest in the semiarid zones. For all of Zimbabwe, some 28 per cent of the population was determined to be vulnerable on average, based on the analysts' criteria for classifying populations as vulnerable. In years of poor rainfall, almost half of the population would be classified as vulnerable.

The extent of the drought hazard can be illustrated by comparing present agroecological conditions with how they might shift if precipitation were

20 per cent less than at present. Figure 45.1 shows results for a simple soil water balance based on the FAO model. At present, almost 10 per cent of Zimbabwe has an average water balance in which precipitation is greater than average maize requirements ('> 0 mm' in the figure). This area shrinks to less than 2 per cent of Zimbabwe if precipitation is 20 per cent less than the present average. Perhaps more important, the arid and semiarid zones are particularly sensitive to drought. Almost 30 per cent of Zimbabwe has a water deficit of 400 mm or more at present, and this expands to more than half the country in the drought scenario.

Overlaying (at least conceptually) the two analyses illustrates the conjuncture of vulnerability and hazard. The most vulnerable populations are in the semiarid zones (IV and V), and those areas are subject to the largest fluctuations in precipitation, with significant impacts on crop yields.

Revelatory crisis in Kalahari, Botswana

Drought occurs, on average, once every seven years in Botswana. As elsewhere in Africa, drought 'has reputedly been a leading cause of declining production and great human suffering' (Solway 1994). The 1979–87 drought was no exception; indeed, years after the drought, the government had not withdrawn relief to many areas, and had in some areas expanded relief efforts. Was this drought more severe

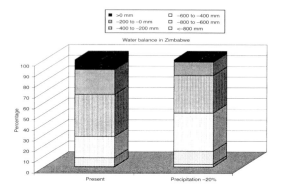

Figure 45.1 Water balance for maize in Zimbabwe, showing the effect of a 20 per cent reduction in precipitation

than preceding dry periods? Solway (1994) argues that nonmeteorological factors are critical to the failure of much of rural Botswana to return to 'normal' after 1987. The differential effects of drought – the distribution of both benefits and disadvantages amongst various classes and races and between men, women, and children – cannot be sought in meteorological factors, but in an examination of the processes by which these benefits and disadvantages are allocated.

Solway identifies important changes legitimated by the drought: both a shift of dependency – from the extended family to the state – and subsequently a deepening of dependency of citizens on the state. Traditional patterns of entitlement[1] that permitted semi-independent production on the part of the poorer majority were significantly eroded during the drought, and have not since been revived. In the case of Kalahari villagers, access to draught animals through a chain of entitlements based on kinship relations was replaced by state-based social security entitlements that were introduced during the drought, and then maintained. This shifting of dependency was, Solway argues, favoured by the rural elite, who saw an opportunity for the consolidation of wealth with the commodification of agriculture and privatisation of production occurring in rural Botswana; this shift was also supported by the government, which viewed traditional patron–client relations as 'backward' and favoured 'an ideal of individualised nuclear family production units which functioned independently of one another but in conjunction with the state' (491), in line with modern systems of taxation, land registration, and government regulation.

With the introduction of 'welfare' and the loss of access to the local means of production, poorer rural residents were no longer able to farm, and overall rural agricultural production dropped, despite the fact that bumper harvests were reported in several villages in Solway's study area during the study period. Falling production statistics provided further 'evidence' of the severity of the drought, and justified the further expansion of government relief programmes.

Solway identifies various critical processes – privatisation, consolidation of economic resources, change in ideology of individualism and kinship – as the basis for this change in social reproduction (Solway 1994: 478–9) in the Kalahari. These processes were supported and sustained by a discourse that embodied a certain vision of proper social and production relations (Solway 1994: 492). Official discourse proclaiming the severity of the drought enabled the processes that were increasing dependency while inhibiting agricultural production to be concealed, allowing change to be attributed to the 'crisis' of drought and not to more fundamental shifts in Botswana society.

In Solway's conceptualisation, the drought was a revelatory crisis, arising from structural contradictions between traditional and modern economies, bringing latent societal tensions to the surface and accelerating changes in the bases of social reproduction (see Allan and Karshenas 1996 for examples of the symbolic functions of drought). These structural contradictions were simultaneously revealed and concealed during the drought; the discourse of crisis allowed them to be hidden from view by claims that 'exceptional' circumstances prevailed. Discourse here served a dual purpose: not only did it obscure deeper processes at work, it also impelled and legitimated innovation with normative codes and regulatory, management, and institutional frameworks.

Drought discourses in Australia

Day (1987) has analysed conceptions and perceptions of 'drought' with reference to water supply policies and the objectives of major water suppliers in the Hunter Valley in New South Wales – an area that has experienced many droughts that have 'severely affected the considerable agricultural base of the region' (Day 1987: 266). Day examines perceptions of water scarcity in the policy-making and public arenas. Her hypothesis – 'that there is a positive causal relationship between the "media agenda" (what is emphasised in the media) and the "public agenda" (what the public sees as important)' (266) – is supported by an analysis of local newspaper reports on the 1979–84 drought, which she attempts to link to public opinion on water resources and management, and to farmers' water use. She finds that the 'substantial pro-agricultural orientation' of the media, with its focus on 'the continued persecution of farmer irrigators' and its neglect of 'the full range of water shortage issues, such as the effects of drought on regional water quality' (272) was of key significance in focusing public demands and government attention on accelerated resource development, rather than 'short- and intermediate-range planning of water supply, demand and consumption' (280). This, in turn, affected the response of government and public sector water development institutions. Evidence suggesting that 'average flow conditions and their attendant water usage patterns and state allocation policies are not relevant to extreme water shortages' (280) was ignored. Emphasis was laid on 'technical and augmentation solutions', with little scrutiny of 'social subsidisation aspects and wider environmental effects' (280). Media construction of the drought as a *farmers'* crisis denied recognition of the problems posed to other communities by the drought, and thus excluded more equitable solutions from public and policy debate.

West and Smith (1996) explore why 'drought' is 'so often invoked as a symbolic threat to the Australian national community' (93). They note that droughts occur, on average, one year in three in Australia, yet droughts are consistently defined as a 'deviant, freakish caprice of nature' rather than a 'normal, expected feature of Australian climate'. Prime Minister Paul Keating encountered great opposition amongst Australia's rural community by arguing in the early 1990s that drought is a normal phenomenon that should be expected by Australia's farmers.

Through an analysis of a sample of media articles, political speeches, government reports, and other texts (books, poems, cartoons, and films), they demonstrate that droughts are 'consistently defined as unexpectedly severe in their intensity or duration' (94); successive droughts, no matter what their absolute intensity, are presented as the 'worst' ever experienced. By appealing to 'interaction effects between the drought and other, contingent circumstances' such as the state of the economy (95), each drought is presented as 'an unprecedented threat to society' (95). In fact, drought discourses are 'relatively autonomous from both meteorological and economic determination' (97), as demonstrated by West and Smith in the loose correlation between rainfall and the amount of drought coverage in the media. People's

perception of a drought bears little relationship to its meteorological and historical significance.

Rather, West and Smith argue, people's perception of drought responds to cultural and symbolic needs, and this is why drought continues to be invoked as a symbolic threat. The continual reinvention of drought as a threat serves as a 'moral drama' in which a litany of indicators of a wider structural collapse – farm bankruptcy, the end of the 'Australian way of life' – are framed (95). Drought is presented as 'an alien force against which society must unite' (95), and serves as a rallying cry for moral unity and discipline, and also as a plea for reconciliation of tensions – rural/urban, conservative/liberal – within Australian society.

FROM CASE STUDIES TO FRAMEWORKS

These four case studies span developed and developing countries. Many other such analyses could be elaborated. Our intention is to illustrate four specific approaches – diverse conceptions of drought and vulnerability to drought are apparent. Each approach is prevalent at present; each has some utility and offers some insight.

Hydrobiological risk

The simplest conception of drought vulnerability is hydrobiological – a linear construction of vulnerability as the consequence of a perturbation in the hydrological cycle and the sensitivity of biological systems. A causal chain of drought leads ultimately to famine, in a progression from human needs to wants, initiating events, exposure, and consequences (Figure 45.2).

One of the oldest traditions in explaining drought follows such a linear set of linked stages, usually beginning with the initiating event – drought in a meteorological or hydrological sense. The emphasis on a linear sequence and end-to-end analysis is straightforward, particularly where drought is seen as a singular anomaly in a more or less static environment, economy, and society. Longer-term perspectives need to search 'upstream' for changes in needs, wants, and technology. More dynamic understanding needs to focus on where and when potential interventions (the bottom row in the figure) are effective.

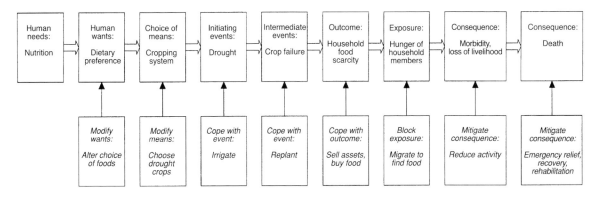

Figure 45.2 Causal chain of hazard development
Source: after Downing 1991

Human ecology of natural hazards

The human ecology of natural hazards conceives of drought risk as the conjuncture of hazard and vulnerability (Figure 45.3). The UN Department of Humanitarian Affairs (UNDHA) (1992) provides accepted definitions (see also Burton *et al.* 1993):

- A *hazard* is 'a threatening event, or the probability of occurrence of a potentially damaging phenomenon within a given time period and area'.
- Vulnerability is the 'degree of loss (from 0 to 100 per cent) resulting from a potentially damaging phenomenon'.
- Risk is the 'expected losses (of lives, persons injured, property damaged, and economic activity disrupted) due to a particular hazard for a given area

and reference period. Based on mathematical calculations, risk is the product of hazard and vulnerability'.

Hazard is the chance of an event, and the chance that the event is potentially damaging. Hazardous weather is distinguished from normal weather by its potential to do damage, and not by its physical or statistical properties. Although the criteria for *hazard* or *extreme* is social and economic damage, hazards are seen as geophysical phenomena.

Vulnerability depends on human infrastructure and socioeconomic conditions. To a large extent, these are shaped by considerations other than natural hazards. Reducing the potential for damage (the hazard) also influences vulnerability.

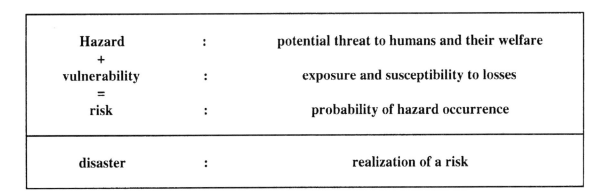

Figure 45.3 Definitions of hazard, vulnerability, risk, and disasters

Coping mechanisms for natural hazards are determined by perceptions of hazard and vulnerability, preferences, and resources. Coping mechanisms are often classified as protection (dealing with physical structures) and mitigation (socioeconomic responses). Examples of protection include water reservoirs, dikes, and irrigation. Examples of mitigation include savings, solidarity, mutual and commercial insurance, crop diversification, alternative sources of income, temporary migration, charity, government support, and foreign aid. *Risk* is the conjuncture of natural hazard and socioeconomic vulnerability. A disaster is a risk that has been realised.

Although the natural hazards paradigm is comprehensive in scope, in practice it tends to focus on individual perception and immediate issues of early warning, rehabilitation, and recovery. This may reflect its western traditions of research on industrial societies, a tendency to focus on individual hazards (particularly sudden events) rather than risk and hazards in general, and an inclination toward applied research.

Structure of vulnerability

What determines the relationship between a hazard and its effects? Who is vulnerable? Why? These questions require a broader analysis of vulnerability than is realised in the natural hazards/perception framework. As research on natural hazards moved from sudden hazards to drought and from western societies to developing countries, approaches to drought and vulnerability emphasised structural explanations. These sought to explain social and spatial difference in vulnerability rather than specific responses to individual events. Variations of explanation focused on entitlements (Sen 1981), political ecology (Watts 1983) and vulnerability (for example, Blaikie *et al.* 1994; Bohle *et al.* 1994; Chambers 1989; Downing *et al.* 1996; Bohle and Watts 1993). As in the natural hazards paradigm, these conceptions sought to integrate natural and social sciences. However, less attention was placed on the hazard itself. The locus of risk was embedded in the social, economic, and political processes that determined vulnerability.

In our view, vulnerability is not simply poverty and marginalisation. Particular vulnerabilities are the conjuncture of social, economic, and political structures.

Bohle *et al.* (1994) suggest a tripartite causal structure of vulnerability (Figure 45.4) based on the human ecology of production, expanded entitlements in market exchanges, and the political economy of accumulation and class processes. Vulnerability *per se* is best viewed as 'an aggregate measure of human welfare that integrates environmental, social, economic and political exposure to a range of harmful perturbations' (Bohle *et al.* 1994: 37–8). This conception of vulnerability supplements and expands the UNDHA's definition quoted above. It shifts the focus of vulnerability away from a single hazard to the characteristics of the social system.

Thinking through the fundamental processes that determine vulnerability is implied in the causal triangle suggested by Bohle *et al.* (1994; see also Bohle and Watts 1993) (Figure 45.4). Vulnerability is the conjuncture of three processes: the human ecology of production, exchange entitlement, and political economy. Vulnerable groups can be located in different sectors of the triangle. For instance, subsistence farmers would be more dependent on their land and labour resources than on market exchanges. The destitute and refugees are closely tied to the political economy of aid. The urban poor are dependent on what they can earn in informal markets.

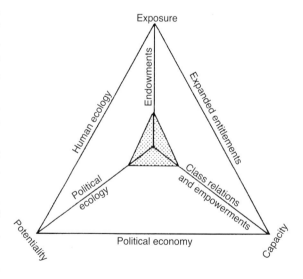

Figure 45.4 Three dimensions of vulnerability
Source: after Bohle *et al.* 1994

In one of the fullest treatments of vulnerability and disasters, Blaikie *et al.* (1994) regard vulnerability as a product of such characteristics as ethnicity, religion, caste membership, gender, and age, all of which influence access to power and resources (Figure 45.5). Dynamic pressures are processes that translate social, political, and economic structures in relation to specific types of hazards into particular forms of insecurity. Regional and global pressures such as rapid population growth, urbanisation, war, foreign debts, epidemic disease, and export promotion have an effect on local conditions. Some of these pressures have a universal character; others are specific to a certain region or society.

Unsafe conditions reflect specific situations and circumstances in a region and time, for a particular group of people, and specific hazards. Examples are groups that are forced to occupy semiarid lands, with marginal economies and a lack of effective preparedness.

By stressing the conjuncture of related factors and the difficulty of developing and proving clear causal connections between root causes, dynamic pressures, and unsafe conditions, the vulnerability approach is less ambitious than more deterministic models. And, by interpreting disaster on the basis of everyday-life situations, which in certain places and times are hazards, social relations and individual choices converge, avoiding the one-sidedness of micro- or macro-analytical approaches.

Vulnerability is not static. Rather, it changes over time, incorporating social responses as well as new rounds of hazardous events. Some researchers have sought to differentiate between background (or structural or slow-changing) and current (or fast-changing) vulnerability (see Downing 1991). However, it is simpler to think of vulnerability as the integral of the recent past and the present, as a dynamic status of the system.

Regarding drought and an ensuing food crisis, Bohle (1993) captures the dynamic nature of vulnerability (Figure 45.6). In this illustration, vulnerability begins to increase at the end of the first year, reaching a crisis at thirty months. Here the outcome of the crisis is uncertain. In a resilient society with appropriate interventions, recovery and mitigation can bring vulnerability back down to baseline (or lower) levels. Unmitigated, or in conjunction with another event such as civil strife following drought, the crisis may become a disaster. Or, some groups and communities may continue in crisis, on the edge of disaster.

Social groups vary in the structure of their vulnerability. For example, the rural landless (without nonagricultural incomes) are typically more sensitive to food shortages, with less on-farm storage and buffering capacity than smallholders. So, the trajectories shown here may be sharper and the outcome different for different groups, even in the same region.

From the causal structure of vulnerability and the access model described above, specific groups of vulnerable peoples can be defined. Although the precise boundaries of vulnerability vary between cultures and environments, the common catalogue, at least for food security in developing countries, often starts with the characteristics of individuals:

- Women, especially those with special nutritional needs during and after pregnancy.
- Children, who are less resilient in terms of nutrition or who may already be malnourished.
- Elderly, who may suffer from a lack of mobility and less mental awareness.
- Disabled and disease-stricken, who have special needs and require routine assistance for survival.

At the household level, vulnerability may be delineated by socioeconomic class and means of securing a livelihood. In rural areas:

- Smallholder agriculturalists may be resource-poor with limited access to land and labour, in marginal lands, with varying degrees of empowerment and access to emergency and development assistance.
- Pastoralists often have little empowerment to recurrent development resources, yet operate in regions with pronounced climatic hazards. However, they often attract international assistance during a disaster.
- Landless labourers relying on casual employment are often at the margin of poverty, with little ability to accumulate savings or invest in more productive activities.
- Destitute peoples have been forced out of productive activities, often because of ill health and

Progression of vulnerability

Root causes	⇒ Dynamic pressures	⇒ Unsafe conditions	⇒ Disasters	⇐ Hazards
Limited access to Resources Structures Power **Ideologies** Political systems Economic systems	**Lack of** Institutions Training Skills Investment Markets Press freedom Civil society **Macro-forces** Population growth Urbanisation Arms expenditure Debt repayment Deforestation Soil degradation	**Fragile physical environment** • Dangerous locations • Unprotected structures **Fragile local economy** Livelihoods at risk Low income **Vulnerable society** Groups at risk • Little capacity to cope **Public actions** Lack of preparedness Endemic disease	RISK = HAZARD + VULNERABILITY	Earthquake Wind storm Flooding Volcano Landslide Drought Virus and pest Heat wave

Figure 45.5 Structure of vulnerability and disasters

Source: Blaikie et al. 1994

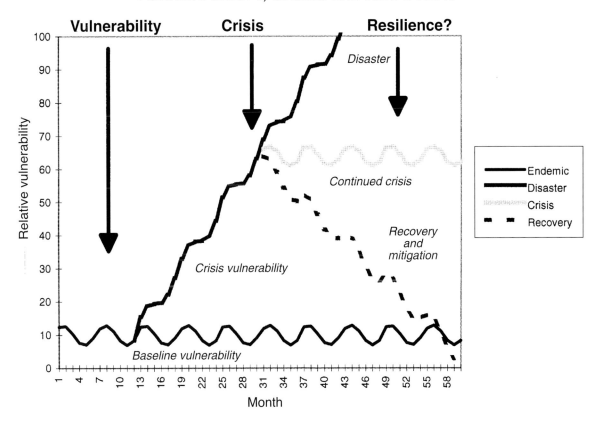

Figure 45.6 Dynamic vulnerability during a food crisis
Source: after Bohle 1993

old age, in addition to being impoverished through natural disasters and other causes. Where the destitute migrate to urban centres, they may have more opportunities for assistance and work, although this depends on the nature of the receiving society.

In urban areas:

- The unemployed destitute in urban areas may be incorporated into social welfare systems (often informal), but suffer significantly in times of disaster if the numbers become too large and if relief fails to target their pressing needs.
- Underemployed poor people, comparable to landless labourers, are on the margins of survival. A slow deterioration in the economy can affect this group, often leading to a major but largely hidden crisis.

- Refugees are the most visible vulnerable population, usually swelling in numbers after a disaster. They may also be vulnerable to further hazards, for instance while attempting to return to their homes and occupations or in camps with inadequate protection against floods, heat, and frost, among other hazards. Yet this group tends to benefit from its visibility and various formal channels of assistance.

Regardless of the nuance of vulnerability frameworks, key concepts are:

- Vulnerability is a relative measure – critical levels of vulnerability must be defined by the analyst (*analyst* may refer to the vulnerable themselves, an external aid worker, or various societies that include the vulnerable and interventionists).

- Everyone is vulnerable, although their vulnerability differs in causal structure, evolution, and severity of likely consequences.
- Vulnerability relates to the consequences of a perturbation, rather than its agent. Thus people are vulnerable to loss of life, livelihood, assets, and income, rather than to specific agents of disaster, such as floods, windstorms, or technological hazards. This focuses vulnerability on the social systems rather than the nature of the hazard itself.
- The locus of vulnerability is the individual related to social structures of household, community, society, and world system. Places can only be ascribed a vulnerability ranking in the context of the people who occupy them.
- Vulnerability is spatially and temporally variable. Vulnerable groups are dispersed over space and change over time. More critically, patterns of vulnerability depend on geographical linkages (such as competition between markets) and are often contingent on past conditions (such as the harvest in the previous season).

Drought discourses

While meteorologists and climatologists tend to adopt the hydrobiological perspective noted above, social scientists tend to focus on drought as a human-made phenomenon rather than a natural event. Political economists, for example, examine regulatory frameworks, the behaviour of farmers, water companies and governments, spatial distribution of industry and population, and the economics of water supply to explain why the amount of water available in certain places at certain times is deemed insufficient. Walker and Williams (1982) argue that analyses that treat water supply in isolation from political-economic forces 'ask the wrong questions' (95). Water supply must be seen in relation to both economic growth and the exercise of class power: 'the [former] generates water demand and the [latter] the political ability to secure it through government action' (112). In so doing, they invert the nature–society dualism, arguing that regional development creates a demand for water supply; it is in this context that shortages in supply must be understood.

Conventional dichotomies between 'natural' and 'social' break down when applied to 'hybrid' environmental phenomena such as drought. Latour (1993; see also Haraway 1991), for example, notes: 'The challenge of analysis of environmental phenomena such as drought arises from their simultaneously multidimensional character – at once "real, like nature, narrated, like discourse, and collective, like society".' This is apparent in European societies, such as the United Kingdom, where unprecedented periods of dry weather and variable climate, shifts in lifestyle patterns, and changes in institutional and regulatory frameworks have combined in recent years to produce droughts of unusual frequency, duration, and intensity (see Letza and Smallman 1996, Haughton 1996, and Marsh 1995 and 1996 for recent treatments of the United Kingdom case). Policy makers have begun to reformulate definitions of drought and scientists are being forced to re-examine conventional models of demand forecasts and question the resiliency of water resource management strategies (see Drought Policy Review Task Force 1990a and 1990b for examples from Australia).

Interdisciplinary and integrated drought research is in many ways a response to the challenge presented by the analysis of environmental phenomena. Of increasing interest to researchers are approaches based on *deconstruction*, a technique that was pioneered in the study of philosophical and literary texts, and theories of *discourse* (drawing on the work of Foucault, Lacan, Giddens, and Bourdieu, among others; see Dijk 1985 and Hajer 1995).

Discourse theorists approach drought as a 'text'; they view drought as a series of narrated, constructed events that are simultaneously emblematic and constitutive of societal norms and power relationships. 'Discourse', in this sense, is more than merely 'ways of talking about the world'. It embraces social practices, concepts, and ideologies as well as narratives, all of which are used not only to interpret reality, but also as a basis on which to make decisions and formulate actions. Specific definitions of discourse vary but include, for example, 'a specific ensemble of ideas, concepts, and categorisations that is produced, reproduced, and transformed in a particular set of practices and through which meaning is given to physical and social realities' (Hajer 1995: 44); 'the ensemble of social practices through which the world is made meaningful and intelligible to oneself and to others' (Johnston *et al.* 1994); or 'frameworks that embrace particular combinations of narratives, concepts, ideologies and signifying practices, each relevant to a particular realm of social action' (Barnes and Duncan 1992).

By using techniques of deconstruction – by showing contradictions within and between concepts, ideologies, narratives, and practices, and by examining assumptions implicit within texts – researchers attempt to understand the various relationships, institutions, and socioecological configurations from which drought emerges and that drought reinforces and destabilises.

This emerging body of research, although eclectic in methodology, is typically motivated by the belief that 'the neglect of socially constructed knowledge, ideology and institutions other than the market as mediators between humans and nature and among humans themselves, represents a major deficiency in the resource management literature' (Emel *et al.* 1992: 38; see also Roberts and Emel 1992). Research aims to demonstrate how socially constructed knowledge is formed, how it mediates our experience and shapes our understanding of environmental phenomena. Emphasis is placed on the 'embeddedness' of discourse in the material conditions of everyday life, the 'naturalising' function of discourse by which a certain set of norms are legitimised, and the 'situated' or partial, contingent nature of knowledge/discourses (Johnston *et al.* 1994). Despite the assertion of the 'embeddedness' of discourse, a reliance on discourse theory often leaves research 'disembodied and suspended from the complex and contradictory material conditions in which discourses about the environment are deeply imbricated' (Peet and Watts 1993: 248); in practice, if not in theory, the 'material'/ 'natural' is often dissociated from the 'discursive'/ 'social'.

Clearly, this approach can yield powerful insights into the social *and* natural forces shaping and sustaining drought, and the links between the social and natural, as shown in the examples for Botswana and Australia.

A closely related research theme involves the study of the ideology of water management. The term 'ideology' is used to denote 'a significant conjuncture

between discourse and political interests' (Eagleton 1991: 221) or an accepted social order. Using the word 'ideology' rather than 'discourse' implies an analytical emphasis on power relations and the relationship between language and social practice. Ideology may serve a legitimating function by offering 'sets of reasons for material conditions' (Eagleton 1991: 209); discourse is the *vehicle* by which common sets of beliefs are created, reinforced, *and* contested. Ideology, in this context, can be seen as 'the struggle of antagonistic social interests at the level of the sign' (Eagleton 1991: 195). Drought is such a sign, and thus discourse about drought is much more than mere language – it is a matter 'of certain concrete discursive effects, rather than of signification as such' (Eagleton 1991: 223). For example, Emel *et al.* (1992) examine the relationship between ideologies of property and the temporal and spatial variation of groundwater resources and their management in Texas and New Mexico. Discourse analysis has been used to explore the social and cognitive basis of the construction of perceptions of drought, at the level of the individual and of institutions. Discourse analysis is also used to examine the creation of 'storylines' (Hajer 1995), sets of ideas that, although sometimes highly contested, nevertheless unite people in a particular way of talking and thinking about environmental phenomena. Through the study of the interaction between storylines and 'the social processes through which actors are mobilised around certain issues' (Hajer 1995: 15), the collective creation and maintenance of common beliefs that distil acceptable 'problems' and 'solutions' from overwhelmingly complex and often conflicting information can be better understood.

Some researchers have gone on to ask: how can drought stimulate people and institutions to think and act in different ways? They approach drought as 'a site where the established institutions of society are put to the test' (Hajer 1995: 39). Here, discourse analysis is used as a means of uncovering the creative potential inherent in current debates over drought and its management. In Hajer's work, for example, the creative potential of discourse is based on Beck's theory of reflexivity. In Ulrich Beck's analysis of our 'risk society' (1992), the project of modernisation has shifted from the goal of the mastery of external threats to the containment of dangers emerging from the practices of industrial society. The emergence of these threats, of an 'ecological deficit', undermines institutions predicated on industrial modernisation. In Beck's theory of 'reflexive modernisation', the further modernisation proceeds, the more these institutions are undermined, forcing a radical alteration in existing institutional and political systems. Modern, industrial societies' 'unintentional self-endangerment' is the source of great conflict, but also of great potential for change, both of which are expressed in discursive practices.

REFLECTIONS AND CONCLUSIONS

Studies of drought, and natural hazards in general, are replete with conceptual frameworks, causal loop diagrams, and boxes and arrows that seek to portray the essence of the problem and point toward essential solutions. And, in recent years, such frameworks have been challenged and supplemented by analysis of discourse and ideology, seeking to define new ways of collapsing the nature/society duality and presenting a coherent view of hybrid environmental problems such as drought. Amidst this plethora of theory, what can we conclude?

We do not have a grand theory, but we glean from this review a sense of scale, an ordering of issues and approaches. In exploring the social and cognitive bases of the construction of perceptions of drought, and in examining the 'storylines' that define our understanding of drought and water scarcity, discourse analysis demonstrates that the manifestation of drought and people's experience of it 'are mediated at all levels by non-meteorological factors' (Solway 1994: 474). An understanding of the discursive production of drought, in addition to the norms and vagaries of weather and climate, is thus critical to societies' preparedness and management of water scarcity.

Shifts in drought discourse are occurring in many regions. For example, in Europe, increasing population density in some regions, increasing per capita demand for water, and an exceptionally dry period over the last five or six years are forcing a re-examination of water resources, water use, and water management. Managed drought in Africa has to a

large extent replaced the drought = food crisis sequence prevalent until the 1970s. Treating drought as a 'norm' rather than an exception requires a focus on scarcity rather than abundance, and on conservation rather than growth. In examining unquestioned assumptions and definitions, discourse analysis can stimulate creative rethinking and require the identification of new 'problems' before new 'solutions' are designed.

At a more applied level, vulnerability analysis, natural hazard paradigms, and hydrobiological approaches offer specific insights. The most common use of a conceptual framework is to structure an argument or summarise a specific situation. The most challenging task is to force the reader to see and analyse drought hazard, vulnerability, and risk in a new way.

So, discourses and frameworks should bring new insight into the social relationships and natural processes that define drought. In conclusion, four facets of drought and vulnerability must be imparted by a conceptual framework:

- Relationships between resource, social, economic, and political circumstances. Drought is a social construct, with multiple attributes in specific contexts. Vulnerability is embedded in life. Sound theory should not reduce drought to simple explanations and should give priority to the important processes.
- Social status and vulnerability. Vulnerability defines drought risk rather than the frequency and severity of weather anomalies on their own. Equally, vulnerability defines the value of climate forecasts and predictions of drought. A conceptual framework should explain who is vulnerable and why.
- Dynamic nature over time. Vulnerability is constantly changing, in response to new situations and the evolution of resources, economies, societies, and political processes. Vulnerability changes more rapidly than drought hazard frequencies. A conceptual theory should be able to explain the continuity that underlines drought and the discontinuities that contribute to crises.
- Analysis and indicators. A conceptual framework should at least suggest analytical modes that would be useful to pursue, ultimately leading to indicators of vulnerability that can be measured or

reported. At present, vulnerability and societal definitions of drought are poorly monitored, especially in comparison to the effort spent on predicting and monitoring hydrobiological conditions.

NOTE

1 Solway is using the concept of entitlement as developed by Amartya Sen: 'A person's legitimately acknowledged right to a certain thing in a specific society' (Solway 1994: 482).

REFERENCES

Allan, J.A. and Karshenas, M.A. (1996) 'Managing environmental capital: The case of water in Israel, Jordan, the West Bank and Gaza, 1947–1995', in J.A. Allan (ed.), *Water, Peace and the Middle East: Negotiating Resources in the Jordan Basin*, London: Tauris Academic Publishers, pp. 75–119.

Barnes, T. and Duncan, J. (eds) (1992) *Writing Worlds: Discourse, Text and Metaphor in the Representation of Landscape*, London: Routledge.

Beck, U. (1992) *Risk Society: Towards a New Modernity*, London: Sage.

Blaikie, P.M. and Brookfield, H.C. (1987) *Land Degradation and Society*, London: Methuen.

Blaikie, P., Cannon, T., Davis, I., and Wisner, B. (1994) *At Risk – Natural Hazards, People's Vulnerability, and Disasters*, London, Routledge.

Bohle, H.G. (1993) 'The geography of vulnerable food systems', in H.G. Bohle, T.E. Downing, J.O. Field, and F.N. Ibrahim (eds), *Coping with Vulnerability and Criticality*, Saarbrucken, Germany: Verlag Breitenback Publishers, pp. 15–29.

Bohle, H.G. and Watts, M.J. (1993) 'The space of vulnerability: The causal structure of hunger and famine', *Progress in Human Geography* 13, 1: 43–67.

Bohle, H.G., Downing, T.E., and Watts, M.J. (1994) 'Climate change and social vulnerability: Toward a sociology and geography of food insecurity', *Global Environmental Change* 4, 1: 37–48.

Burton, K., Kates, R.W., and White, G.F. (1993) *The Environment as Hazard* (2nd edn), New York: The Guilford Press.

Caldwell, R.M. (1993) *A District-Level Food Security and Nutrition-Based Vulnerability Assessment for Zambia*, Rome: World Food Programme and International Fund for Agricultural Development.

Chambers, R. (1989) 'Vulnerability, coping and policy', *IDS Bulletin* 20, 2: 1–7.

Christensen, G. and Stack, J. (1992) 'The dimensions of household food insecurity in Zimbabwe 1980–1991', Oxford, Food Studies Group.

Corbett, J.D. and Carter, S.E. (1997) 'Using GIS to enhance agricultural planning: The example of inter-seasonal rainfall variability in Zimbabwe', *Transactions in GIS* 1, 3: 207–18.

Day, D. (1987) 'An Australian perspective on drought and water management objectives for regional development', *Water Resources Development* 3, 4: 267–83.

Dijk, T.A. (1985) *Handbook of Discourse Analysis*, London: Academic Press.

Downing, T.E. (1991) 'Assessing socioeconomic vulnerability to famine: Frameworks, concepts, and applications', Brown University, Providence, Rhode Island.

—— (1992) *Climate Change and Vulnerable Places: Global Food Security and Country Studies in Zimbabwe, Kenya, Senegal and Chile*, Oxford: Environmental Change Unit.

Downing, T.E., Watts, M.J., and Bohle, H.G. (1996) 'Climate change and food insecurity: Toward a sociology and geography of vulnerability', in T.E. Downing (ed.), *Climate Change and World Food Security*, Heidleberg: Springer, pp. 183–206.

Drought Policy Review Task Force (1990a) *National Drought Policy*, Canberra: Australian Government Publishing Service.

—— (1990b) *Managing for Drought*, Canberra: Australian Government Publishing Service.

Eagleton, T. (1991) *Ideology*, London: Verso.

Emel, J., Roberts, R., and Sauri, D. (1992) 'Ideology, property, and groundwater resources', *Political Geography* 11, 1: 37–54.

Gleick, P.H. (ed.) (1993) *Water in Crisis: A Guide to the World's Fresh Water Resources*, New York: Oxford University Press.

Hajer, M.A. (1995) *The Politics of Environmental Discourse: Ecological Modernization and the Policy Process*, Oxford: Clarendon.

Haraway, D. (1991) *Simians, Cyborgs, and Women: The Reinvention of Nature*, London: Free Association Books.

Haughton, G. (1996) 'Private profits – public drought: The creation of a crisis in water management for West Yorkshire', *Sustainable Urban Development Working Paper Series* 5, Leeds: CUDEM.

Henricksen, B.L. and Durkin, J.W. (1985) 'Moisture availability, cropping period and the prospects for early warning of famine in Ethiopia', *ILCA Bulletin* 21: 2–9.

Hutchinson, C.F. and Hall, R.E. (1993) *Baseline Vulnerability Assessment for Haiti*, Washington, DC: US Agency for International Development, Office of Foreign Disaster Assistance.

Johnston, R.J., Gregory, D., and Smith, D.M. (1994) *The Dictionary of Human Geography*, 3rd edn, Oxford: Basil Blackwell.

Kasperson, J.X., Kasperson, R.E., and Turner, B.L. (eds) (1995) *Regions at Risk: Comparison of Threatened*

Environments, Tokyo: United Nations University Press.

Latour, B. (1993) *We Have Never Been Modern*, London: Harvester Wheatsheaf.

Letza, S. and Smallman, C. (1996) 'Is water thicker than blood? Overcoming the conspiracy of profit over social responsibility in privatised utilities', in L. Montanheir, E. Rebelo, G. Owen, and E. Rebelo (eds), *Public and Private Sector: Partnerships Working for Change*, Sheffield: Pavic Publications, pp. 289–303.

Marsh, T. (1995) 'Drought returns to the United Kingdom', *Drought Network News* 7, 3: 5–6.

—— (1996) 'The 1995 UK Drought – A Signal of Climatic Instability?', unpublished paper, Institute of Hydrology, Wallingford.

Maxwell, S. and Frankenberger, T. (1992) *Household Food Security: Concepts, Indicators, Measurements: A Technical Review*, New York: UNICEF.

Nevarez, L. (1996) 'Just wait until there's a drought: Mediating environmental crises for urban growth', *Antipode* 28, 3: 246–72.

Peet, R. and Watts, M. (1993) 'Introduction: Development theory and environment in an age of market triumphalism', *Economic Geography* 69: 227–53.

Ramachandran, M. and Eastman, J.R. (1996) Applications of GIS to Vulnerability Mapping: A West African Food Security Case Study, Internet document at: www.idrisi.clarku.edu/risk/chapter3/chap3.htm, Worcester, MA: The Clark Labs for Cartographic Technology and Geographic Analysis.

Reisner, M. (1989) *Cadillac Desert*, London: Secker and Warburg.

Roberts, R.S. and Emel, J. (1992) 'Uneven development and the tragedy of the Commons: Competing images for nature–society analysis', *Economic Geography* 68, 3: 249–71.

Sen, A.K. (1981) *Poverty and Famines: An Essay on Entitlement and Deprivation*, Oxford: Clarendon Press.

Solway, J.S. (1994) 'Drought as a "revelatory crisis": An exploration of shifting entitlements and hierarchies in the Kalahari, Botswana', *Development and Change* 25, 471–95.

UN Department of Humanitarian Affairs (UNDHA) (1992) *Glossary: Internationally Agreed Glossary of Basic Terms Related to Disaster Management*, Geneva: UNDHA.

Walker, R. and Williams, M. (1982) 'Water from power: Water supply and regional growth in the Santa Clara Valley', *Economic Geography* 58, 2: 95–119.

Watts, M.J. (1983) *Silent Violence: Food, Famine and Peasantry in Northern Nigeria*, Berkeley: University of California Press.

West, B. and Smith, P. (1996) 'Drought, discourse and Durkheim – A research note', *Australian and New Zealand Journal of Sociology* 32, 1: 93–102.

World Food Programme (1996) WFP Vulnerability Mapping Guidelines, Internet document from www.wfp.org/dm_vam_wfpmapguid.html, Rome: WFP.

World Resources Institute (1996) *World Resources Report*, Washington, DC: WRI.

Worster, D. (1985) *Rivers of Empire: Water, Aridity, and the Growth of the American West*, New York: Pantheon Books.

46

DROUGHT AND DESERTIFICATION

Exploring the linkages

H.E. Dregne

INTRODUCTION

A protracted drought in the Sahel region of West Africa was the immediate reason for a United Nations response that ultimately led to convening the United Nations Conference on Desertification (UNCOD). The 1968–73 drought had brought devastation to the affected region as vegetation dried and disappeared under the pressures of famished livestock and fuel-short humans. Seasonal wells went dry and water tables dropped in permanent wells. There was a mass exodus from the stricken areas as nomadic pastoralists and villagers fled southward to cities and more humid regions. Crude estimates indicate that more than 3 million cattle alone died as a result of the drought. Perhaps as many as 100,000 people succumbed to famine and to diseases brought on by weakened resistance and by unsanitary conditions in refugee camps (Grainger 1990). Humanitarian aid began to flow into the region toward the temporary end of the drought in 1973, and world attention was graphically called to the threat that drought presented. It was feared that the entire Sahel was being turned into a desert as the Sahara expanded.

Droughts are a natural feature of the climate in arid regions, not an aberration. Droughts similar in magnitude to the Sahelian occurrence in 1968–73 had struck the Sahel in the early 1910s and 1940s. The North American drought of the 1930s in the Great Plains produced a major human catastrophe that will live in history for the frightening black blizzards of dust and sand that swept across the region now known as the Dust Bowl. An even worse drought struck the region in the 1950s.

DROUGHT

Although drought was the immediate cause for convening the international conference on desertification, it soon became apparent to conference planners that the land degradation that had occurred in the Sahel and other drylands was not due solely to drought. Rather, destruction of natural resources in the form of vegetation degradation, increased water and wind erosion, and waterlogging and salinisation of irrigated land was at least equally the result of human activities. Drought exacerbated the adverse effects of overgrazing, tree cutting, and fuelwood collection on ecosystems, but it was human intervention that initiated the long-term degradation process. In the absence of human pressures, the relatively frequent six-month or one-year droughts would have little effect on indigenous dryland plants, which are adapted to cope with dry conditions. A two-year drought will slow recovery, and five or more consecutive dry years can seriously delay recovery. Continuation of human land pressures (e.g., overgrazing) during a drought is what greatly impedes restoration and sometimes brings about permanent changes in ecosystems.

DESERTIFICATION DEFINITIONS

Desertification is a term that means different things to different people. It was apparently coined by a French ecologist named Lavauden while he was studying the vegetation of grazing lands in southern Tunisia in the 1920s. Lavauden did not explicitly define desertification but described it as range land degradation that was purely artificial and only caused by man (Lavauden 1927). A very different use of the term was made by Aubréville, a French botanist, who investigated the causes of degradation of tropical forests in Ivory Coast and other French colonies in West Africa in the 1940s. Aubréville also did not define the term explicitly. He referred to desertification as the process of changing productive forested land into a wasteland (desert) as the result of ruination by man-induced soil erosion (Aubréville 1949).

At UNCOD, another meaning was given to desertification. This time, the term was defined as the 'diminution or destruction of the biological potential of the land, and can lead ultimately to desert-like conditions' (United Nations 1978). Although the definition did not expressly mention that desertification was a phenomenon of the world's drylands, the conference report was clearly concerned with land degradation in the arid regions of the world. In 1990, the United Nations Environment Programme (UNEP), the United Nations agency responsible for taking leadership in combatting desertification, attempted to clarify the questions people had by asking a group of experienced scientists to redefine it (Dregne et al. 1991). The new definition explicitly mentions that desertification is land degradation in drylands. Odingo (1990), in an excellent discussion of the disagreements and confusion about what desertification is and its significance, proposed a definition that was a forerunner of the revised UNEP definition. The new UNEP definition says that desertification is 'land degradation in arid, semiarid, and dry subhumid areas resulting mainly from adverse human impact.' Although not mentioned in the definition, drought is understood to be the other significant contributor to land degradation in drylands. Human activities, however, are the main cause.

The importance of attributing desertification to human activities or drought is largely philosophical. If human activities are responsible for the land degradation that plagues the drylands, then humans can stop further degradation. Conversely, if drought is the sole cause, then humans are exonerated of responsibility and nature must take the blame. Since droughts cannot be stopped, land degradation is inevitable (Inshallah: As God wills). All that humans

can do is minimise the impacts of drought on human welfare.

Natural scientists, including agricultural scientists, who are involved in ecological or agricultural research probably are nearly unanimous in believing that vegetation degradation by livestock is due to human manipulation of the livestock. Drought, like locust invasions, is just one (important) natural hazard with which land managers must cope. Range scientists function on the principle that long-term grazing land degradation is a matter of improper management and that an understanding of ecosystem dynamics will allow appropriate management practices to be devised to sustain productivity indefinitely. Soil and water conservation agencies are dedicated to controlling human-induced wind and water erosion within tolerable limits. The same is true for salinisation of irrigated land and rain-fed croplands.

The 1992 United Nations Conference on Environment and Development (UNCED) modified the 1990 UNEP desertification definition by citing 'climatic variations' (not drought alone) as a cause (Anonymous 1993). The change apparently was made to give more prominence to the impact of drought and global warming. The 1990 UNEP definition is the one guiding comment in this chapter, with humans being the principal culprits. Five main implications are derived from the 1990 definition: (1) desertification is land degradation of any kind; (2) the degradation is restricted to that occurring in arid, semiarid, and dry subhumid regions; (3) humans are the main causes of such land degradation; (4) all severity classes of land degradation represent desertification, from slight to very severe; and (5) if humans cause the problem, humans can resolve it.

Despite what seem to be straightforward definitions of desertification by UNEP, there have been numerous different interpretations of what desertification is. Many persons believe that desertification is vegetation degradation of range lands. Others associate it solely with accelerated wind erosion and formation of sand dunes on range lands and farm land. A few even contend that desertification only occurs when once-productive range lands and rain-fed crop lands are reduced to barren wastelands (deserts). If one employs the last definition, desertification is a very minor global problem because little agricultural land has been changed into a desert. Even the poorest rain-fed croplands, when abandoned because of degradation, rarely have no grazing value. Each interpretation does have one thing in common: they all refer to land degradation.

The plethora of interpretation differences means that anyone writing or speaking about desertification needs to make it clear how the term is being used. That clarification is especially needed when statements are made about the extent, severity, and cost of land degradation in the drylands. A few attempts have been made to discredit the concept of desertification as a real-life problem (Thomas and Middleton 1994). It turns out that there is no denial that land degradation in drylands is widespread and serious. Instead, there is a quarrel with calling it desertification. Surely that is a colossal waste of time, given UNEP's widely accepted definitions. Stiles (1995) has written a thoughtful response to the pernicious characterisation of desertification as a myth.

STATUS OF GLOBAL DESERTIFICATION

The first detailed estimate of land degradation in the arid regions of the world was made by Dregne (1983) after the 1977 United Nations Conference on Desertification. That country-by-country estimate was a crude one because good data on the areal extent of land degradation on range lands, rain-fed croplands,

and irrigated lands are grossly inadequate to allow accurate conclusions to be drawn. That situation is still true today, although more information has become available for small areas. In the Dregne study, reliance was placed principally on the informed opinion of knowledgeable scientists. That opinion was supplemented by experimental plot data, maps, and accounts of observers such as explorers and geographers. A second analysis was made for UNEP in 1990 (Dregne and Chou 1992). This one covered a somewhat different climatic region, in accordance with the revised 1990 UNEP definition. The second study also relied heavily on informed (expert) opinion, but the information base was better. Land degradation estimates were made for each country containing drylands (arid, semiarid, dry subhumid zones) by major land use, as in the earlier study. Table 46.1 gives a summary of the global estimates for nearly 100 countries. As Arkes et al. (1997) note, expert opinion analyses can be a valuable tool for quantifying uncertainty, if properly done.

Obviously, the estimates in Table 46.1 are rough approximations for which it is impossible to calculate the error because there are no accurate figures available for comparison. Although the estimates for irrigated land and range land are believed to be reasonable, the estimate for rain-fed cropland almost certainly is too high because it overemphasises the damage wind erosion does to soil productivity. The

Table 46.1 Desertification in global drylands, by continent and land use

Continent	Land use			Percentage degraded of total drylands
	Irrigated[1] % degraded	Rain-fed cropland[2] % degraded	Range land[3] % degraded	
Africa	18	61	74	73
Asia	35	56	76	71
Australia and New Zealand	13	34	55	54
Europe	16	54	72	65
North America	28	16	85	74
South America	*17*	*31*	*76*	*73*
Weighted average	30	47	73	70

Source: Modified from Dregne and Chou 1992
Notes:
1 43,100,000 ha degraded
2 215,600,000 ha degraded
3 3,333,500,000 ha degraded

accuracy of global estimates is not going to improve until other analysts undertake similar country-by-country estimates. Without that background, global numbers are no better than guesses.

Soil and vegetation degradation in the drylands together constitute desertification. The best maps of global soil degradation that have ever been produced are those that came out of a project financed by the United Nations Environment Programme (UNEP) and executed by the International Soil Reference and Information Centre in Wageningen, The Netherlands. The project was called the Global Assessment of Soil Degradation (GLASOD), covering both humid and arid regions of the world (Oldeman *et al.* 1990). The type of soil degradation that was assessed was human-induced degradation, as determined by the scientists involved. Selection of that criterion conforms with the 1990 UNEP definition of desertification, which said that desertification was mainly due to human activities. The definition of soil degradation used in the GLASOD study was 'soil degradation is a process that describes human-induced phenomena which lower the current and/or future capacity of the soil to support human life' (Oldeman and van Lynden 1997).

The result of the GLASOD exercise is three maps compiled from the estimates of about 300 scientists around the world. Informed opinion is the basis for construction of the maps. Calculations of the land area, by continent, in the various classes of soil degradation are presented in the misnamed *World Atlas of Desertification*. The *Atlas* purports to show desertification (land degradation in drylands) but shows only global (drylands and humid lands) soil degradation. There is no evaluation of vegetation degradation of the range lands that constitute nearly 80 per cent of the drylands. The GLASOD survey was never intended to be a desertification study or a land (soil and vegetation) degradation study. It does very well what it was charged to do: estimate human-induced global soil degradation.

DROUGHT AND DESERTIFICATION

There is no question that drought exacerbates desertification and makes desertification control more difficult. Drought has another effect that is seldom mentioned: it confounds the determination of range condition and thus the status of vegetation degradation. Deciding whether a poor range condition is due to improper management or to a previous water deficiency can require considerable local experience.

Range lands

Buffington and Herbel (1965) conducted a study of vegetational changes for the period from 1858 to 1963 on the Jornada Experimental Range in New Mexico, where several short and long droughts had occurred. Mean annual rainfall for the Jornada is about 200 mm. They cited a 1934 report, in the middle of a drought, concluding that black grama, *Bouteloua eriopoda*, the dominant grass, recovered as rapidly from drought when it was conservatively grazed as when it was not grazed. By contrast, heavy grazing year after year weakened the grama, slowed its recovery from drought, and eventually killed it. Even in the absence of grazing, droughts lasting two or more years can cause a marked increase in bare spots (Paulsen and Ares 1962).

Water and wind erosion on upland range land sites of the Jornada increased during droughts and when grazing was heavy. Water erosion became worse because grass cover was reduced. Wind erosion was accelerated both because of the thinner grass cover and the greater dryness of the soil. Temperatures also were higher.

Several very interesting observations on the effect of a protracted drought on range land vegetation were made in a study on the Jornada Experimental Range during the 1950s (Herbel *et al.* 1972). The 1950s drought extended over the southwestern United States and is said to have been the most severe in at least the previous 350 years, worse than the famous 1930s drought. Among the more significant points was the fact that black grama, the climax grass, did better on shallow sands than deep sands. In this case, the shallow sandy soils were underlain by an impermeable caliche (calcium carbonate) layer on which water perched and was readily available to grama roots. In the deep sands, water percolated below the surface 30 cm, where grama roots usually are concentrated.

Other drought effects included a major reduction

Plate 46.1 Denuded grazing land near village well in Niger. Animals are goats, sheep, cattle, and camels. Photo by Dregne

in plant cover, leaving bare areas into which mesquite, a noxious shrub, rapidly invaded; elimination of less drought-tolerant minor grasses in the ecosystem; a reduction of 60 per cent in the yield of grass per unit of precipitation due to less ground cover; and a marked increase in wind erosion, again due to more bare areas but also to the smaller size of the plants. Many of the grass plants were killed by the deposition of sand on top of them, to say nothing about the effect dust storms have on human welfare.

All in all, drought impacts on range lands can be severe, mostly in on-site degradation but off-site, too, due to wind erosion. The longer the drought, the greater the damage. Obviously, reducing drought susceptibility by managing the grazing lands judiciously is incomparably better than trying to mitigate damage on desertified land after a drought is in full swing.

Croplands

Irrigated land seldom is degraded by drought when water supplies are plentiful. In fact, irrigation farmers who have no worries about having enough water would be happy if it never rained on their fields. For that special case, rain is a nuisance that confounds irrigation scheduling, pest control, harvesting, and other operations. Farmers who are not so fortunate pay for droughts by having to irrigate more heavily. When water supplies are limited, as when wells have low discharge rates, it may be impossible to provide as much water as the crop needs to reach its yield potential. Farm income suffers but the drought-accelerated degradation problem will be largely confined to soil salinisation if water supplies are limited.

Rain-fed cropland is different. Droughts not only

Plate 46.2 Wind erosion on cropland in southern Great Plains. Furrows filled with eroded soil. Photo by Dregne

Plate 46.3 Eroded sand encroaching on farm home near Jodhpur, India. Photo by Dregne

Plate 46.4 Sand blowing across highway near Jodhpur, India. Photo by Dregne

Plate 46.5 Severe water erosion in loessial soils of semiarid croplands of Ordos Plateau in Inner Mongolia, China. Photo by Dregne

Plate 46.6 Arroya caused by water erosion in tracks of old wagon road in southern New Mexico. Photo by Dregne

will reduce farm income, they almost certainly will increase wind and water erosion, especially wind erosion. Erosion susceptibility rises because crop cover decreases. Although stories about dust storm frequency lead one to suspect that wind speed rises during droughts, this does not seem to be the case (Lee *et al.* 1993). There are more dust storms, true, but the reason is that soil and vegetation conditions permit wind erosion to occur at lower-than-usual wind velocities. The vegetative cover that is the best protection against erosion becomes smaller and smaller as droughts continue, just the opposite of what is needed to limit soil degradation.

Joel (1937) conducted one of the most detailed analyses of the impact of drought in the US Dust Bowl that has ever been made. He believed that the tremendous damage done to humans, livestock, soil,

Plate 46.7 White lines of salt accumulation in irrigated onion field in southern New Mexico. Photo by Dregne

and vegetation was man-induced in most cases. Depletion or destruction of the native vegetation by cultivation, overgrazing, burning, and other actions made the soil free to blow away. Joel's survey found that 84 per cent of the land was affected by accelerated wind erosion and a further 14 per cent by water erosion. The terrifying black blizzards were the result of land damage and the cause of damage to human and livestock health, roads, cars, buildings, and the economy. All the necessary conditions for massive wind erosion came together in the Dust Bowl: soils ready to blow, frequent strong winds with which to blow it, and little vegetation to slow the wind and protect the soil.

The 1930s US drought demonstrated clearly that agriculture in the marginal area of the drylands was a risky business. When the drought began, few soil and water conservation practices were employed by farmers. By the end of the drought and shortly afterward, many government programmes were initiated in research, extension, education, crop insurance, disaster assistance, and other areas to minimise any recurrence of the Dust Bowl tragedy. Those programmes bore fruit in the 1950s drought, which, although meteorologically worse, had much less adverse effects. It demonstrated that the management tools developed in the years between droughts were effective in controlling or at least reducing soil loss when a drought struck. No-tillage and minimum tillage systems, the adoption of sweep tillage devices that left crop residues on the surface, and invention of a simple but effective tillage implement called a sand-

Plate 46.8 Salt crust due to high water table in ancient irrigated land in oasis of Mary, Turkmenistan. Photo by Dregne

Plate 46.9 Abandoned irrigated land along canal near Hyderabad, Pakistan. Standing water caused by seepage from unlined canal. Photo by Dregne

fighter have done wonders in controlling dryland cropland degradation during droughts and in non-drought years.

CONCLUSIONS

Drought and desertification are closely linked in the world's drylands. Protracted severe droughts that continue for five years or more cause major damage to vegetation and soil on range lands. It probably is impossible to prevent some damage, both on-site and off-site, economically. The likelihood of being able to control or reduce damage is directly proportional to the investment pastoralists have made in good land management before the drought. At best, it is diffi-cult to avoid losses during protracted droughts. It is much easier to do so when the droughts are short-lasting.

On irrigated croplands, the major drought-related problem is the need to apply more water to obtain high yields. Land degradation seldom is a hazard if water supplies are adequate to produce a good crop cover.

Long-lasting droughts on rain-fed cropland commonly cause the most on-site and off-site damage, compared to range lands and irrigated lands. Maintaining a good vegetative cover is essential to reduce wind erosion, the most visible kind of desertification. Yet, in a protracted drought, crop production and vegetative cover become smaller as the drought goes on, thus increasing the potential for damage.

Well-managed lands are minimally affected by the usual short-duration droughts. It is the multiyear droughts that are the major hazards. Droughts, both short and long, are a natural feature of the dryland environment. Prudent land managers remember that the next drought, of uncertain duration, could begin next year. That must be a never-ending component of the planning process. Although droughts are not caused by humans, their effects on the desertification process depend heavily on human actions.

REFERENCES

Anonymous (1993) 'Good news in the fight against desertification', *Desertification Control Bulletin* 22: 3.

Arkes, H.R., Mumpower, J.L., and Stewart, T.R. (1997) 'Combining expert opinions (Letters)', *Science* 275: 463.

Aubréville, A. (1949) *Climats, Forêts, et Desertification de l'Afrique Tropicale*, Paris: Société de Editions Geographiques, Maritime et Coloniales.

Buffington, L.C. and Herbel, C.H. (1965) 'Vegetational changes on a semidesert grassland range from 1858 to 1963', *Ecological Monographs* 35: 139–64.

Dregne, H.E. (1983) *Desertification of Arid Lands*, New York: Harwood.

Dregne, H.E. and Chou, N.T. (1992) 'Global desertification dimensions and costs', in H.E. Dregne (ed.), *Degradation and Restoration of Arid Lands*, Lubbock: Texas Tech Press.

Dregne, H.E., Kassas, M., and Rozanov, B. (1991) 'A new assessment of the world status of desertification', *Desertification Control Bulletin* 20: 6–18.

Grainger, A. (1990) *The Threatening Desert*, London: Earthscan.

Herbel, C.H., Ares, F.N., and Wright, R.A. (1972) 'Drought effects on a semidesert grassland range', *Ecology* 53: 1,084–93.

Joel, A.H. (1937) 'Soil conservation reconnaissance survey of the southern Great Plains wind-erosion area', US Department of Agriculture *Technical Bulletin* 556, Washington, DC: USDA.

Lavauden, L. (1927) 'Les forêts du Sahara', *Revue des Eaux et Forêts* 6: 265–77, 329–41.

Lee, J.A., Wigner, K.A., and Gregory, J.M. (1993) 'Drought, wind, and blowing dust on the Southern High Plains of the United States', *Physical Geography* 14: 56–67.

Odingo, R.S. (1990) 'The definition of desertification: Its programmatic consequences for UNEP and the international community', *Desertification Control Bulletin* 18: 31–50.

Oldeman, L.R., Hakkeling, R.T.A., and Sombroek, W.G. (1990) *World Map of the Status of Human-Induced Soil Degradation*, Wageningen: International Soil Reference and Information Centre.

Oldeman, L.R., and van Lynden, G.W.J. (1997) 'Revisiting the GLASOD methodology', in R. Lal, W.H. Blum, C. Valentin, and B.A. Stewart (eds), *Methods for Assessment of Soil Degradation*, New York: CRC Press.

Paulsen, H.A. Jr. and Ares, F.N. (1962) 'Grazing values and management of black grama and tobosa grasslands and associated shrub ranges of the Southwest', US Department of Agriculture *Technical Bulletin* 1270, Washington, DC: USDA.

Stiles, D. (1995) 'Desertification is no myth', *Desertification Control Bulletin* 26: 29–36.

Thomas, D.S.G., and Middleton, N. (1994) *Desertification: Exploding the Myth*, Chichester: Wiley.

United Nations (1978) *United Nations Conference on Desertification. Round-up, Plan of Action and Resolutions*, New York: United Nations.

47

DROUGHT AND WATER RESOURCES

John C. Rodda

DROUGHT IN A HYDROLOGICAL CONTEXT

Few human activities are unaffected by the weather and climate and their variations. In fact, the extremes have an immediate impact, because they operate directly through the meteorological variables: the devastating winds in tropical storms are one of a number of examples. Other variations operate indirectly, many through changes to the hydrological variables and through the effects of these changes on water resources. At the hydrological extremes, the results are too much or too little water – floods, avalanches, landslides, mudslides, and droughts, which bring death and destruction, followed by famine and epidemic, loss of livelihood, degradation of the environment, and other damaging effects. Drought, however, is unlike other hydrological hazards and, for that matter, it is different from most natural disasters. These are usually short-lived events of limited areal extent, with immediate and obvious effects. Drought, by way of contrast, is prolonged, sometimes even decades in length. It can be small-scale or extensive, a million square kilometres and more, and of variable severity over the area in question. Droughts seem sinister and insidious, with very extensive ramifications, and they can threaten any part of the globe. And where the other hazards are due to an excess of some sort – excessive water, excessive stress, or excessive temperature, for example – drought is uniquely due to an absence or a deficit. Amongst the different natural disasters, drought affects more people than other types (DHA 1994), and it causes large amounts of damage (Figure 47.1).

Drought features frequently in both the written and unwritten records of the past, such as in tree rings and ice cores, but in recent years, probably because of tragic television pictures from Africa, the effects of drought seem to have become steadily more serious. In hydrological terms, most droughts are due to unexpected, unusual, and lengthy periods of little or no precipitation, which can be coupled to high levels of potential evapotranspiration resulting from high temperature, low humidity, and high wind speed. Drought and aridity should not be confused: the first is ephemeral while the second is a permanent feature and relatively easy to define. There are, however, some droughts that are the result of excessive use of water that causes water resources to decline, even when rainfall is near normal. Indeed, Sirculon (1991) has estimated that while the water resources of the west African Sahel may vary between ± 30–40 per cent over the next few decades, the demand for water for the same period is likely to rise by 250–500 per cent. Undoubtedly, the accelerating demand for water for drinking, cultivating crops, producing power, and other purposes, engendered by the needs of the rapidly growing population, has already been a major factor in intensifying the effects of drought in many developing countries. But increased consumption in the developed countries, sparked by the rising standard of living, has also made these countries more vulnerable. In addition, ongoing and worldwide changes to the land surface and their impacts on the hydrological regime must be taken into account. Deforestation, urbanisation, drainage of wetlands, overgrazing (leading to desertification), and other alterations to land use all cause changes to the water

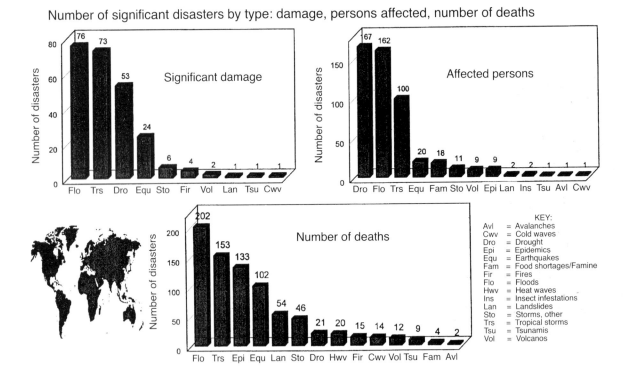

Figure 47.1 Major disasters around the world, 1963–92 (taken from DHA 1994)

balance, which may contribute to drought and exacerbate its effects, particularly on wildlife and the aquatic habitat. Of course, the rising demand for water and the adverse changes in land use have the greatest consequences for drought in the less-developed countries. Warning systems there may be less effective, while the reactions to such warnings are likely to be poor because emergency services are skeletal and badly funded and infrastructures are less sound. Perhaps one hundred years ago, society in these regions was well adapted to drought, but now the increased population means that drought can be accommodated no longer. In such circumstances the development of a drought will cause greater human losses and more severe effects on society. A serious drought could even set back the development of a region or a small nation by five to ten years, and it may make the goal of sustainable development even more elusive. International and bilateral aid is rushed to areas suffering from drought to alleviate its worst effects, often in the face of the fact that the installation and operation of an efficient warning system and investment in the infrastructure of the country concerned would be more effective. But even in developed countries, drought can bring problems. Water supplies are often restricted, crop production may be very low, wildfires can sweep through forested and residential areas, fisheries and wildlife will suffer, and shrinkage of clay soils may cause subsidence of buildings. These events can bring claims on insurance companies and motivate governments to provide funds to relieve the effects of the drought. In addition, drought is likely be a regional harbinger of the world water crisis that is being predicted for the middle of the twenty-first century (Postel 1992, Rodda 1995a), a time when the global demand for water may well be reaching the finite limit of the world's water resources.

The growth of population and the upsurge in economic activities is also adding new dimensions to the problems of drought. The growing volume of untreated sewage, residues from agricultural fertilisers and pesticides, industrial waste, and like materials are causing increasing pollution of surface and ground-waters. This becomes even more serious during drought. Such pollution degrades the biological life of rivers and lakes, especially through the reduction in dilution when flows are diminished by drought and by the increased abstraction that often accompanies it. There is also the threat of climate change and its likely impact on hydrological regimes consequent on changes to global patterns of precipitation and evap-oration. Will climate change cause more frequent drought of greater severity and extent? Will the cli-mate revert to an arid phase, such as during the Holocene? At this stage, to hydrologists the message from climate modellers seems far from clear. And the same applies to the conclusions from the chapters on hydrology and water resources contained in the reports of the Intergovernmental Panel on Climate Change (IPCC 1996). But there is a need to recon-cile the growing weight of opinion with observational evidence, in order to frame future water management strategies in the face of the threat of climate change.

If it were possible to control the weather, then hydrological extremes could become a thing of the past. But for the present, no such control exists apart from the questionable technique of cloud seeding (Kundzewicz *et al.* 1993). As a consequence, the mitigation of drought currently has to rely on the water management techniques that have evolved over the centuries, reinforced by those more recently developed. Such measures as the construction and operation of reservoirs, abstractions from rivers, and pumping from boreholes (with their associated distri-bution systems that carry the water to the point of consumption) are in widespread use. These are supple-mented by dry farming methods, water harvesting, desalination plants in coastal areas, leakage control techniques, re-use of water, and so on. These so-called structural measures have been helped in recent years by nonstructural measures, such as those based on computer-controlled systems for water resources management incorporating models of various types, geographical information systems, decision support and expert systems, and similar tools, in order to sustain water resources under drought conditions.

Some of these measures incorporate hydrological models that may benefit from inputs from improved meteorological forecasts and, in a few cases, from the outputs of long-range climatological models, including the effects of El Niño.

DEFINING DROUGHT FOR HYDROLOGY AND WATER RESOURCES PURPOSES

Drought is one of those words in the English lan-guage that can have several shades of meaning in everyday speech, as well as in poetry, science, and other areas. To the hydrologist, 'the prolonged absence of something' favoured by the *Pocket Oxford Dictionary* (OUP 1978) seems far less appropriate than the definition that appears in the *International Glossary of Hydrology* (UNESCO/WMO 1992): 'a period of abnormally dry weather sufficiently pro-longed to give rise to a shortage of water as evidenced by below normal streamflow and lake levels and/or depletion of soil moisture and lowering of ground water levels'. This definition contrasts with those used by meteorologists, which often express drought simply as a prolonged period when rainfall is below normal or absent. For example, in the United Kingdom, an absolute drought was first defined as a period of at least fifteen days without a daily total of 0.25 mm or more of rain (British Rainfall 1887). In practice, definitions of this kind invariably change from one country to another. In the arid and semiarid regions of the world, where rainfall variability is high, the significance of a lengthy period without rain is usually far less than that of a much shorter period in a humid region.

Drought is also defined differently according to the use made of the water – whether it is for agriculture, industry, hydropower, navigation, eco-logical purposes, and so on. In each case, the main impact of drought is transmitted through changes to the particular hydrological variable or variables (Figure 47.2): reductions in soil moisture for agriculture, low reservoir and river levels in the case of power gen-eration, declining river water and groundwater levels for domestic water supply. But an agricultural drought can be different from a drought affecting power production, while a drought causing problems for navigation may differ from one curtailing water supply. This is not only because of the contrasting interests of the various users and the time (day, season, and year) when their activity occurs, but also because these different droughts can be out of step due to the delays built into the different phases of the hydrological cycle (Beran and Rodier 1985). Precipitation and melt water from snow and ice normally take some time to reappear as river flows, or recharge to aquifers. There is also the matter of the 'critical period of the drought': four months for a farmer wanting seed to germinate and crops to grow, four years for a water manager with a reservoir system containing sufficient storage. Dependent on these factors, the onset of an agricultural drought can be different from those defined in meteorological or hydrological terms, and different from a drought affecting one of the other sectors. Such contrasts point to the value of a more general definition of the type provided by Beran and Rodier (1985): 'the chief characteristic of a drought is a decrease in water availability in a particular period and over a particular area'. Overviews of drought definitions (Palmer 1965, Wilhite and Glantz 1985) offer further insights into the search for a short sequence of words with that elusive sense of a strict and universal definition. Perhaps drought is becoming so multifaceted in terms of causes, impacts, effects, and possible counter-measures that any one definition can be misleading. Perhaps drought defies definition!

Within the scope of the hydrological definition of drought given in the *Glossary* (UNESCO/WMO 1992) and in other similar definitions, a number of characteristics of drought are essential to consider. The areal extent of a drought is an important attribute, but because droughts usually have no clear boundaries, such areas are often imprecise. Duration is also a salient feature, but the start of a drought may only be obvious several weeks or months after the actual point of departure, while in many cases the end is also uncertain. The timing of a drought can also be an important consideration; a drought during the growing season will have a different impact on water resources to one in the rainy season, when recharge of aquifers and reservoirs would normally take place. There are also the variations in drought intensity that can occur within the limits of space and time, variations that can make it difficult to establish a single measure of severity for a particular drought. These characteristics cause problems in estimating the frequency, or return period, of a particular drought. Indeed, Matalas (1991) stresses the multivariate nature of droughts and that there is little or no empirical information regarding the multivariate distribution of measures of drought. In addition to these characteristics of a particular drought, there are a number of other factors to consider that add to the complexity of analysing and understanding droughts as hydrological phenomena. These include auto-correlation within the time series of the variables used to depict drought; the year-to-year independence of

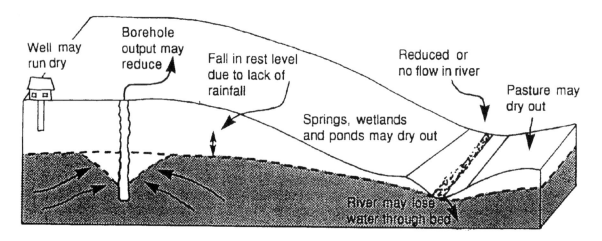

Figure 47.2 Environmental characteristics of drought (taken from Mawdesley *et al.* 1994)

measures of drought; drought periodicity; the effects of persistence; and the teleconnections between extra-terrestrial, atmospheric, oceanographic, and terrestrial conditions that may be shaping these phenomena. Then there are the features of the water resources systems to consider, including the application of risk management to their sustainability (Simonovic 1997). The literature contains references to a large number of studies in these different areas.

Because the record of the flow of a river at a single location integrates the effects registered upstream, hydrologists have been tempted to employ discharge time series to portray and examine drought to a greater extent than records of the other hydrological variables. Low flows, in particular, have been analysed in the context of drought, and Beran and Rodier (1985) have identified three of their numerical characteristics: (1) the minimum flow value averaged over n consecutive days; (2) the dates of their occurrence; and (3) the frequency attributed to the phenomena. They also give the methods of defining frequency in common use: a simple ranking (i.e., the ith lowest in N years of record), an empirical probability of nonexceedence based on sample values, a statistical analysis of all the annual minima using a chosen statistical distribution and plotting position, and expressing the probability in percentage terms or as a return period.

Unfortunately, many droughts do not coincide with the limits of drainage basins or even with the limits for a group of basins, but where they do, such analyses of low flows can be particularly useful. Beran and Rodier (1985) also suggested a six-fold division of hydrological droughts based on variations in duration, season, and severity.

1   A three-week to three-month deficit during the period of germination and plant growth. This can be catastrophic for farming based on irrigation drawn directly from a river without the support of reservoirs.
2   A minimum discharge significantly lower or more prolonged than the normal minimum but not necessarily advanced much in relation to the growing season. Because germination is not affected by this type of drought, it is less important for agriculture.

3   A significant deficit in the total annual runoff. This affects hydropower and irrigation from large reservoirs.
4   A below-normal annual high-water level in the rivers. This may introduce the need for pumping from the rivers concerned. It is a drought related to the type of drought in 3 above.
5   A drought extending over several consecutive years (such as those of the Secas of northeast Brazil). Discharge remains below a threshold and rivers dry up for a long time.
6   A significant depletion of aquifers. Often the true levels are difficult to distinguish because of the excessive withdrawal of water from wells and bore-holes during drought.

MEASURING DROUGHT

Management capacities

A robust and reliable institutional framework is a prerequisite for the proper assessment and mitigation of drought. Because drought is a hydrological extreme, its measurement and monitoring is normally one of the central responsibilities of a national hydrological service, a responsibility that can be carried out in concert with a number of other national bodies at the national, regional, and local levels. Such services are often combined organisationally with bodies that have similar responsibilities for meteorology within a national hydrometeorological service. In countries without a single hydrological or hydrometeorological service, drought monitoring is frequently shared between a number of different agencies of central government, together with provincial and local bodies. Whatever the shape and form of the institution or institutions concerned, they perform a number of tasks (Figure 47.3) that are replicated from one country to another and which together contribute to the continuing assessment of a nation's water resources (Figure 47.4). Because of the importance of drought and other extreme events to society, hydrological services ideally are closely connected to television and radio networks for the broadcast of warnings, and to Civil Protection, the police, and the military for emergency actions.

Timely, easily understood, and reliable hydro-

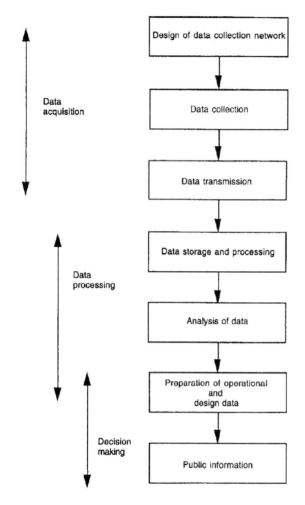

Figure 47.3 Activities of a hydrological service (taken from WMO 1994)

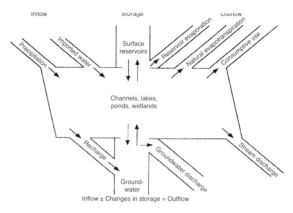

Figure 47.4 Major elements of a hydrological system needed for a water budget of a typical river basin in a subhumid region (taken from WMO 1994)

logical information about drought conditions is paramount so that rapid decisions can be made with confidence. Such information is more readily available in developed than developing countries, the latter being those where the need is greatest. The main hydrological variables important to the measuring and monitoring of drought are shown in Table 47.1, together with the level of accuracy (or uncertainty) recommended by the World Meteorological Organization (WMO 1994). Temperature, humidity, solar radiation, net radiation, and wind velocity measurements are also necessary, should one of the indirect methods of estimating potential evapotranspiration be

employed. Expressions of the quality of surface and groundwaters are also needed, together with data on water resources and water use. The latter would include reservoir inflows, reservoir and aquifer storage volumes, abstraction quantities, water demand, and water use. These data are normally captured by networks of instruments, gauges, meters, and like devices deployed countywide to record the variations in the different variables in space and time. Recommended minimum densities for the instruments and stations in the hydrological network are shown in Table 47.2. Some instruments are observer-read, others record on charts, some record on cassette, and others record on solid-state devices in computer-compatible form. Telephone and radio, both ground based and satellite based, are employed to collect the data from the networks in real time; alternatively, records are removed from recording devices when stations are visited for maintenance. Remote sensing has played an increasing part in recent years, with a growing stream of data coming from ground-based radar and from space vehicles. The different items of data are collected at regional and national centres, where they are quality controlled, processed, and archived, followed by further processing to provide updates of water situation reports and forecasts of the future state of water resources, for use by decision makers in combatting drought and other extreme events.

Unfortunately, the hydrological and allied services

Table 47.1 The hydrological variables and their recommended accuracies

Variable	Recommended accuracy
Precipitation	3–7%
Snow depth	10 mm below 200 mm, 10% above 200 mm
Water content of snow	2.5–10%
Evaporation	2.5–5%
Water level	10–20 mm
Discharge	5%
Soil moisture	1 kg/m³

Source: WMO *Guide to Hydrological Practices*, 5th edn, 1994

in many countries in need, particularly those in Africa and in the former republics of the Soviet Union, have been severely degraded in recent years. The government funding they rely on has been cut, staff numbers and competence have declined, and there has been little or no investment in hardware, particularly computers. The densities of the networks they operate have fallen well below the levels recommended by WMO (WMO 1994). Many of the stations still functioning are in a poor state, and data are not being collected from a number of them. The expertise to assemble, analyse, and interpret data as a basis for decision making has been diminished. Sadly, this situation is limiting the ability of nations to assess their water resources and, in particular, to measure droughts and react to them.

Precipitation

Because precipitation is the primary source of water, it is the forcing function for the remainder of the hydrological variables, and thus it is important to the measures of drought that can be derived from those variables (Mawdesley *et al.* 1994). Notable droughts may last for a week or more in humid regions to decades in the arid zone. Invariably, the precipitation networks that provide the data comprise can-type gauges – there are about 200,000 throughout the world (WMO 1995), supplemented by radar in a few regions, while satellite imagery is available for much of the globe. During drought and hot dry periods, these gauges suffer from evaporation of the catch, which causes them to underregister. In many parts of the world, precipitation networks are dense and records are usually lengthy. Consequently, precipitation data normally provide a good basis for examining and expressing drought. Satellite imagery is also excellent for giving an impression of the spatial extent of drought (Petty and Krajewski 1996). The GOES Precipitation Index (GPI) (Arkin *et al.* 1994) offers one simple way of using infrared satellite imagery for estimating rainfall, or lack of it, in low latitudes, but vegetation indices may be as effective.

For a restricted number of water resources purposes, a simple expression of drought may be sufficient, and there are various examples of how this has been achieved using records of precipitation. One is a statement such as 'Depth of precipitation in Israel in 1989/1990 to 1990/1991 reached only 60 per cent of normal. This value was one standard deviation

Table 47.2 Minimum density requirements for hydrological networks (area in square kilometres per station)

Physiography	Precipitation nonrecording	Precipitation recording	Evaporation	Discharge	Sediment	Water quality
Coasts	900	9,000	50,000	2,500	25,000	50,000
Mountains	250	2,500	50,000	1,000	10,000	20,000
Interior plains	575	5,750	50,000	1,750	17,500	35,000
Hilly (undulating)	575	5,750	50,000	1,750	17,500	35,000
Small islands	25	250	50,000	300	3,000	6,000
Polar	10,000	100,000	100,000	20,000	200,000	200,000
Arid	10,000	100,000	30,000	20,000	65,000	80,000

Source: As Table 47.1
Note: For the present, there are no density requirements for temperature, stage, and groundwater in the *Guide*

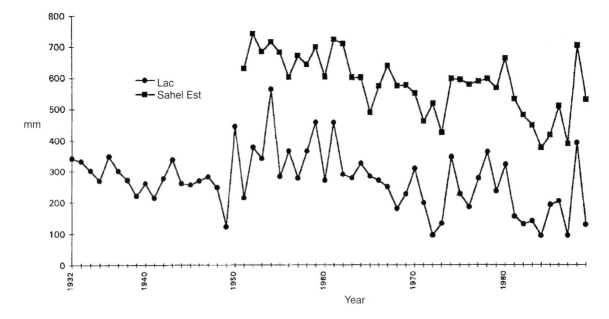

Figure 47.5 Annual rainfall totals over Lake Chad and the eastern Sahel (taken from Olivry *et al.* 1996)

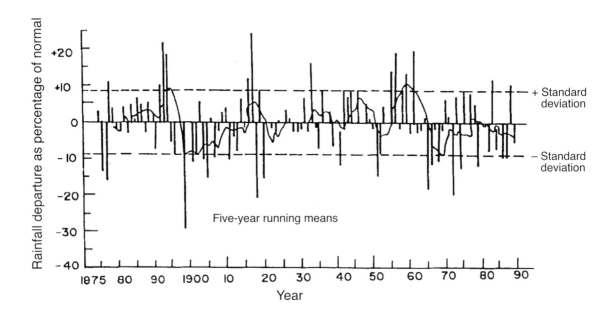

Figure 47.6 Annual rainfall in India, 1875–1989 (taken from Mehotra and Mehotra 1995)

below the mean depth' (Ben-Zvi *et al.* 1997). A graph of annual rainfall totals for the entire record (Figure 47.5) and a plot of their departures from the average (Figure 47.6) can be effective in indicating drought years for a particular station or for an area. The spatial variations in the departures from the mean

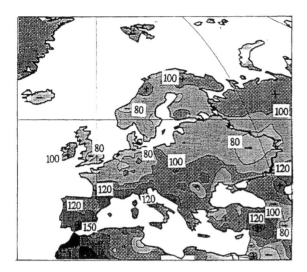

Figure 47.7 Annual precipitation over Europe in 1996 as a percentage of the 1961–1990 mean (taken from ECSN/WMO/ DWD 1997)

can be mapped for a particular drought year (Figure 47.7) to create awareness of drought severity. Droughts ranked by the number of days in the different dry periods and estimates of the return period of a particular drought based on the total precipitation measured during the drought, by comparison with remainder of the record, are means that are often employed, particularly to capture the interest of the public, with the aim of reducing the demand for water.

Potential evapotranspiration

During droughts, potential evapotranspiration rates are high, up to 100 mm a day at the extreme. However, reduced soil moisture limits the water available to the vegetation cover and to the atmosphere, so that actual evapotranspiration rates are usually much lower than potential. Records of open water evaporation produced by pans and tanks – there are about 12,000 globally (WMO 1995) – although the most widespread and lengthy, overestimate the transfer of water from the land surface to the atmosphere, especially during drought. A number of sites around the globe are equipped with lysimeters, and some of these have been employed to assess areal evapo-

transpiration (Green 1970, Venkatasawmy 1985). At present, there seem to be no stations operating where regular observations are made of the flux of water by eddy correlation devices. Data from pans, tanks, and lysimeters and those derived by other methods are not readily available.

Models for estimating potential evapotranspiration, such as the Penman-Monteith model, use the regular observation of the meteorological variables, together with measurements of, or assumptions about, certain physical variables such as aerodynamic resistance (r_a), surface resistance (r_s), and canopy storage capacity (S). The form of the Penman-Monteith model given by Stewart (1989) can be used for determining potential evapotranspiration (E) from:

$$E = [\Delta A + \rho c_p \delta q / r_a] / [\Delta + c_p \{1 + (r_s / r_a)\}\lambda]$$

where

λ is the latent heat of vaporisation of water
Δ is the rate of change of the saturated specific humidity with temperature
ρ is the density of the air
δq is the specific humidity deficit
c_p is the specific heat of the air
A is the available energy

Many of these models have been summarised by Kalma and Calder (1994). Most of them contain assumptions about the way evaporation is moderated as soil moisture content decreases, assumptions that become more important during drought. MORECS (Thompson *et al.* 1981) is one such model that is used operationally to produce weekly estimates of evapotranspiration on a 40×40 km^2 grid covering Britain, employing records from 130 synoptic stations. The model has two reservoirs to simulate the depletion of soil moisture and to estimate actual evapotranspiration. Figure 47.8 shows the potential evapotranspiration over Britain during the 1984 drought and Figure 47.9 shows the difference between the potential and actual evapotranspiration.

In recent years, there has been a proliferation of models and submodels that seek to describe the energy–water interactions at the land surface (Shuttleworth 1997), known as soil vegetation atmosphere transfer schemes (SVATS). These vary in complexity, and many are embedded within general circulation models

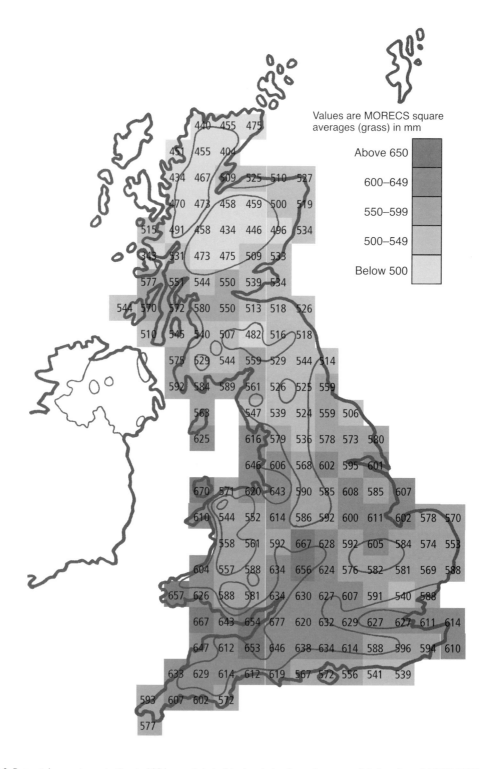

Figure 47.8 Potential evapotranspiration in 1984 over Britain (the isopleths show the average) (taken from IH/BGS 1985)

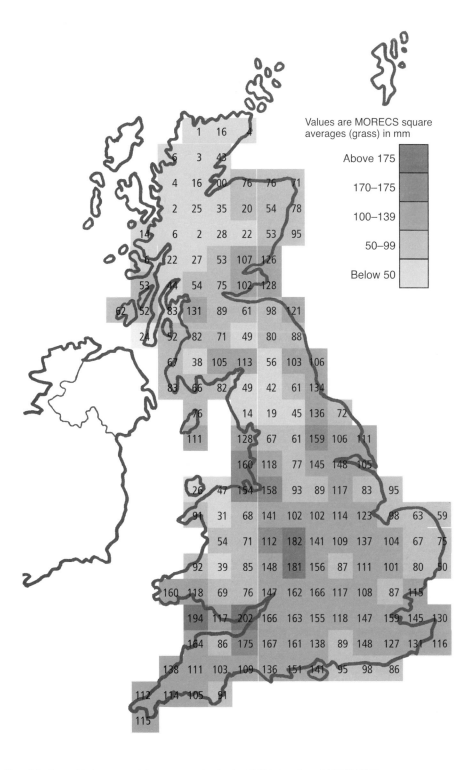

Figure 47.9 Shortfall of actual below-potential evapotranspiration in 1984 (taken from IH/BGS 1985)

(GCMs) to provide linkage between atmospheric and macroscale hydrological models (Vorosmarty *et al.* 1993). SVATS have to simulate a variety of processes, evapotranspiration being an important one, and they may include the effects of extreme conditions, such as drought. Remotely sensed data are employed in many of these models, while some of the processed data are valuable themselves for assessing the extent and severity of drought. One example is the Advanced Very High Resolution Radiometer (AVHRR) data at a 4×4 km resolution, which is processed to provide the Normalized Difference Vegetation Index (NDVI). There are also a number of examples where thermal infrared imagery satellite data has been used for assessing areal evapotranspiration on a daily basis (Kustas and Norman 1996). These employ estimates of the available energy, the net radiation minus the soil heat flux. The operational use of such methods is valuable to the assessment of the impact of drought.

Effective rainfall

This is the term usually given to the difference between the rainfall and the actual evapotranspiration, but because of the difficulties in determining the latter, it is not often used in drought studies (Mawdesley *et al.* 1994). However, in areas where unconfined aquifers occur and in the absence of runoff, the effective rainfall is the control of recharge of groundwater. During drought the effective rainfall is zero and no recharge takes place while it exists.

Soil moisture

During drought, the near-surface soil moisture content declines toward wilting point and beyond, from a previous level that may have been around field capacity. With increasing soil depth, this decline becomes less severe. Measurements of soil moisture are made in the field, particularly to determine irrigation need, by methods such as gravimetric sampling, resistance and capacitance devices, ground-penetrating radar, and neutron probes. However, these in situ approaches suffer from the small-scale variability of soil moisture. Although records of soil moisture may be collected locally for agricultural purposes, there are very few countries where soil moisture records are collected

regionally and nationally to provide a readily accessible archive and where data from these archives are published. Such problems enhance the attractiveness of remote sensing methods.

Passive and active microwave instruments are capable of measuring soil moisture within the surface layers to a depth of 10–15 cm, the volume of water in the soil controlling its dielectric properties. However, this depth is much less than the rooting depth of most vegetation (2 m or more), while the presence of dense vegetation interrupts the signal (Schmugge and Jackson 1996). In addition, the application of these techniques, to drought studies for example, is limited by the currently available and planned satellite instruments (Jackson *et al.* 1996). The consequence is that the assessment of soil moisture is more feasible by one of the modelling approaches mentioned above (a soil moisture accounting model, for example).

Groundwater levels

Levels of groundwater in aquifers can be observed regularly in the wells and boreholes that have been sunk into them. Under natural conditions, these levels represent the equilibrium reached between the water entering the aquifer as recharge and the water draining from it. These levels will be lower than normal during periods of drought, even by 100–200 m in some aquifers, while in other cases the wells may run dry. Obviously the reason is absence of recharge and the continuation of natural drainage to springs, streams, and rivers, together with seepage to the sea in coastal areas, while water may continue to be abstracted for supply purposes. Indeed, the majority of wells and boreholes have been constructed to produce water, and it is not always easy to separate the natural variations in level from those due to pumping, especially where it is intermittent.

Water level is measured in an observation well by lowering a float or electrical probe to the water surface. Some wells are equipped with float-operated recorders to give a continuous record of level, but fluctuations in most aquifers tend to be slow. Because of the heterogeneity of geological conditions, the density of networks of observation wells varies widely, but it is suggested that the maximum distance between stations should not exceed 40 km for basic networks

(WMO 1994). Records of water levels in wells and boreholes have been collected for more than a century in certain countries, and these and shorter records readily demonstrate the severity of each drought (Figure 47.10). Of course, if the volume of water stored in a particular aquifer is required and the fluctuations of that volume, then assessments of the storage coefficient and similar hydrogeological parameters are needed to determine these volumes, in addition to water levels.

River flows

The flow of a river in a basin is maintained principally by aquifer drainage and by surface runoff following precipitation and snowmelt and icemelt exceeding the infiltration rate. During drought, flows generally recess toward zero in proportion to the volume of groundwater remaining in storage. This process may be expressed by one of a number of recession equations, such as:

$$Q = Q_0 K^t$$

where

Q is the discharge at any instant
Q_0 is the discharge at some initial time
t is the time between Q_0 and Q
K is the recession constant (usually with values less than 1)

Of course, certain rivers dry up partly or wholly during drought, their channels being empty, except for a few pools, but where the river has a sand bed, a small amount of flow will occur.

Continuous measurements of river flow are usually made at gauging stations equipped with water-level recorders. Some of these stations contain other devices, such as water quality monitors and flood-level alarms. The record of levels is converted to one of discharge using a relationship between the level and the discharge known as the rating curve, which is often unique for that particular station. During droughts, when flows are low, such records suffer from a number of sources of error, particularly due to growth of weeds and the deposition of sediment. Abstractions from and discharges to rivers can also

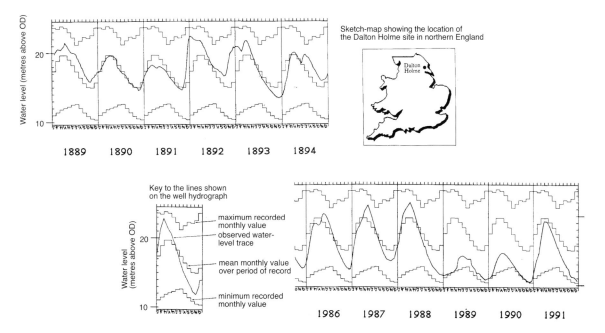

Figure 47.10 Part of the well level record for a site at Dalton Holme, UK, from 1989 to 1991, showing the monthly variations in level against the long-term average and the extremes, with the effects of the drought in 1989 to 1991 (taken from IH/BGS 1994)

cause departures from the natural flow, which may also be altered in time because of changes in the land use of the basin upstream. The continuous record is often summarised as the daily mean flow or the ten-day, monthly, or annual mean. Although records of the Nile exist for more than 1,000 years and records for a number of stations start in the nineteenth century, most flow records were commenced in the twentieth century. There are now approximately 60,000 river gauging stations in operation globally (WMO 1995), and using the records from some of these stations, the total flow into the oceans has been estimated in a number of studies over the last 100 years. From these different estimates, a figure of about 40,000 km³ would seem a reasonable approximation of the average annual runoff to the world's oceans (Rodda 1995a). These records, river flow hydrographs, can be used directly to indicate the severity and length of a drought (Figure 47.11), but there is also a volume of literature on the analysis of these records to assess drought and low flows more precisely.

Low flows have been studied locally and regionally to obtain additional measures of drought, especially for the design of water supply schemes. Several summaries of the resulting analyses have been made – for example, Beran and Rodier (1985), McMahon and Mein (1986), and Gustard (1996). Table 47.3 contains a list of these measures, together with their attributes (including their application). A flow duration curve is one of the measures particularly valuable for characterising drought. It shows, for the duration of the record, the discharge exceeded for specified percentages of time (Figure 47.12), while a flow frequency curve derived from the same data gives the return period when the flow for a given number of days is exceeded (Figure 47.13). When the flows are normalised in some way, such as by expressing them as percentages of the mean flow, then flow duration curves from several rivers can be compared. Rivers that are fed largely by surface runoff are more prone to reduced discharges during drought than rivers relying on groundwater. This point is demonstrated in Figure 47.14, which employs the average discharge during the ten days with the lowest flow in each year of the record in six European rivers. Information about the geology, soils, and other catchment characteristics are the basis for estimation of low flows in basins without records (Gustard et al. 1992). Figure 47.14 also employs an extreme value analysis (Weibull 1939) of the type tailored to the interpretation of minimum values, a topic that first attracted Gumbel (1941) to the analysis of hydrological extremes. He postulated that because the largest daily flow in a year was the upper extreme of the 365 daily flows, this value, with the other annual maxima, forms part of an extreme value series. The largest annual values are termed the annual maximum series and the smallest are the annual minimum series. Figure 47.14 uses the ten-day annual minimum flow series, but an annual series of the longest period when a river was dry would be part of an annual maximum series. There are many examples of applications of extreme value analysis in hydrology, and many of these are reviewed by Cunnane (1989).

Stochastic models, whose parameters have been estimated from the record of flow, have been employed in the study of low flows, including flow forecasting (Krzysztofowicz 1991). Many of these models for simulating monthly, seasonal, and annual flows are first-order Markov models, which assume that the flow in one period t is determined by the flow in the preceding period $t-1$, together with a random impulse $\in$ (WMO 1994). There are also the autoregressive moving average models (ARMA) developed by Box and Jenkins (1970), which have been used to generate synthetic flow sequences by Monte Carlo techniques. The findings that successive flows and other geophysical time series (Hurst et al. 1965) are linked together in some way and that they are nonstationary, as is assumed in Markov models, has led to the development of models that can accommodate this phenomenon of persistence. Because of persistence,

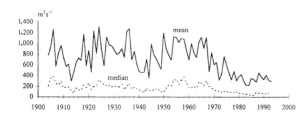

Figure 47.11 Flow of the Senegal Rivers at Bakel, 1904–92 (taken from Albergel *et al.* 1997)

Table 47.3 Summary of measures of low flow

Measure	Property described	Data employed	Application
Flow duration curve	Proportion of time a given flow is exceeded	Daily flows or flows averaged over several days, weeks, or months	Licensing abstractions or discharges, hydropower
Flow frequency curve	Proportion of years in which the mean discharge over a given period is below a threshold for a given duration	Annual minimum flow – daily or averaged over several days	Return period of drought, design of major schemes, storage yield analysis
Low flow spells	Frequency with which the flow remains continuously below a given magnitude	Periods of low flows extracted from the hydrograph, followed by a statistical analysis of durations	Water quality problems
Deficiency volumes	Frequency of requirement of a given volume of make-up water to maintain a threshold flow	As for spells, except the analysis deals with the volume below the threshold	Regulating reservoir design
Storage–yield	Frequency of requirement for a given volume of storage to supply a given yield	Daily flows, flows averaged over several days, or monthly flows	Storage yield design, review old yield from existing reservoirs
Time to accumulate runoff volume	Time to accumulate a given volume of runoff with a given frequency of occurrence	Accumulated runoff volume starting at different times of the year	Probability of reservoir refill under drought conditions
Recession constant	Rate of decay of hydrograph	Daily flows during dry periods	Forecasting flow, hydrogeological studies

Source: Gustard *et al.* 1992

periods of low flow (and high flow) tend to be grouped together in the record, owing to the memory of preceding conditions, to the extent that the observed runs of low flows tend to be greater in length and number than if the data were purely random.

Reservoir storage

This is a most useful indicator of drought (Mawdesley *et al.* 1994), because for most reservoirs, records of level are maintained on a daily or weekly basis. Such records need adjusting for the quantities of water abstracted and, of course, not all the water in a reservoir can be used to meet demands. In many instances the outlet is set above the bottom level, and there are some reservoirs where the water is not directly available, such as river-regulating reservoirs. And levels may have already been drawn down for power generation or flood control before a drought started, while during a drought, the volume stored is reduced by the high rates of evaporation. In addition, for some reservoirs there is a legal requirement to allow a certain specified flow to pass into the river below the dam. Figure 47.15 illustrates the effects of drought on California reservoir storage during the late 1980s and early 1990s. Obviously the control and operation of a reservoir or system of reservoirs and other sources is not solely based on water levels.

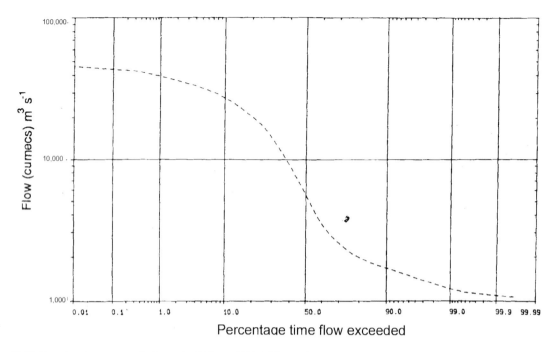

Figure 47.12 Flow duration curve at Paske on the Mekong, 1923–65 (taken from Piper *et al.* 1991)

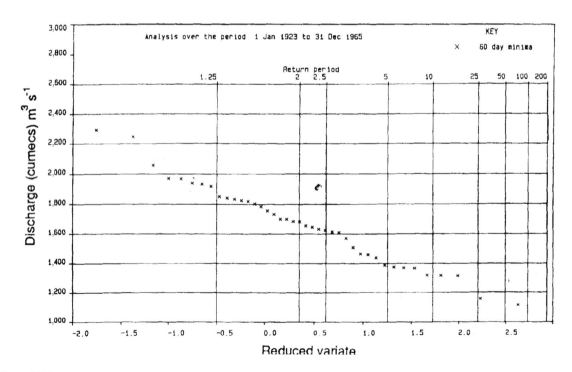

Figure 47.13 Flow frequency curve at Paske on the Mekong, 1923–65 (taken from Piper *et al.* 1991)

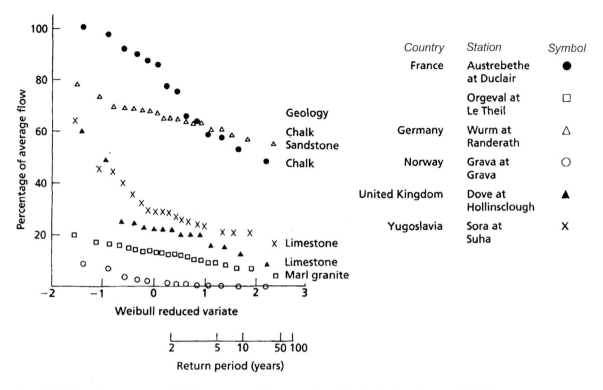

Country	Station	Symbol
France	Austrebethe at Duclair	●
	Orgeval at Le Theil	□
Germany	Wurm at Randerath	△
Norway	Grava at Grava	○
United Kingdom	Dove at Hollinsclough	▲
Yugoslavia	Sora at Suha	X

Figure 47.14 Annual minima series for European rivers with contrasting geology (taken from Beran *et al.* 1990)

Much more information is required – for example, estimates of storage and yield, or whether demand can be managed, or if the water discharged from the reservoir for legal requirements can be cut, or if alternative sources are available.

According to Vorosmarty *et al.* (1997), using data from a series of world dam registers, there are 633 large reservoirs worldwide with a capacity of 0.5 km³ or more, an estimated 60 per cent of the total global capacity, which with the 35,000 smaller reservoirs amounts to world total capacity, approaching 8,000 km³. This represents about 20 per cent of the total annual runoff. With direct river abstractions, groundwater sources, and other local sources such as desalination plants, this storage has to meet the global demand for water. Construction of new large reservoirs has met increasing opposition in many parts of the world, but many new small reservoirs are being constructed, particularly on farms.

Drought indices

Expressions of drought severity, extent, and similar characteristics have been developed into drought indices, using one or more of the hydrological variables and assumptions about other physical factors. Some examples of these indices are:

- Palmer Drought Severity Index (PDSI), USA (Palmer 1965)
- Foley index, Australia (Foley 1957)
- ALERT, USA (Dracup 1991)
- Standard drought index, UK (Bryant *et al.* 1994)

Figure 47.16 displays a drought severity index for eastern and southern Africa (UNDP/WMO 1992), which uses the historical record of rainfall ranked into quartiles, those in the first quarter being considered dry. It shows drought conditions extending over much of the region between Zimbabwe in the south to Ethiopia in the north. Biological indices for fresh waters have been developed for a number of

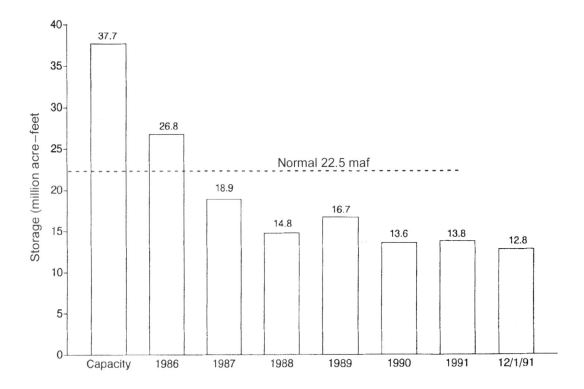

Figure 47.15 Statewide storage in 155 major California reservoirs, 1986–91 (taken from State of California 1991)

purposes, but they can also be useful as drought indices. Figure 47.17 demonstrates the decline of the fish population with the advance of the California drought of the late 1980s (State of California 1991). However, these and similar drought indices can be criticised as one-dimensional attempts to answer a multidimensional question.

DROUGHT – CURRENT AND FUTURE CHALLENGES

Drought is the eternal plague (Sehmi and Kundzewicz 1997) – the scourge of humankind. Each year, droughts cover approximately one-tenth of the surface of the continents outside the Antarctic and the high latitudes of the Northern Hemisphere. During years of extreme drought, such as in 1982, when El Niño peaked, approximately one-sixth of the globe may be affected. As the rising demand for water reinforces and perhaps supplants the climatic controls of

drought, the future must bring an increase in the size of the drought-ridden areas of the world.

Currently, climate change is one focus of attention, partly because of the Framework Convention on Climate Change and the activities of the Intergovernmental Panel on Climate Change. Desertification is another issue where the work surrounding an international convention, in this case the Convention to Combat Desertification, has attracted much attention. It can be argued that in these and similar fora, the importance of water resources has been neglected when water requires far greater emphasis, especially the impact of climate change on water resources and the role of water (or rather the lack of it) in desertification. Perhaps hydrologists (and their funding agencies) are partly to blame – the volume of literature indicates that they prefer to work on floods rather than droughts. But droughts must be studied, to understand and predict them, to evaluate their characteristics, analyse their impacts, and determine

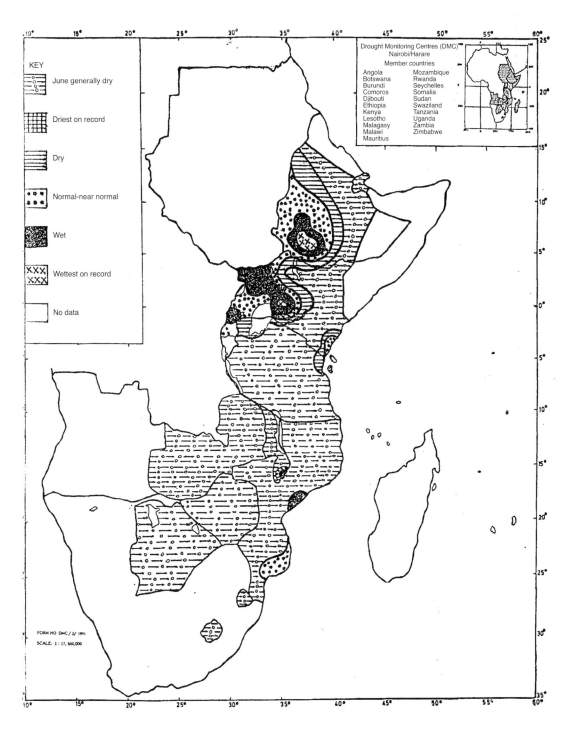

Figure 47.16 Drought severity index over eastern Africa in June 1992 (taken from UNDP/WMO 1992)

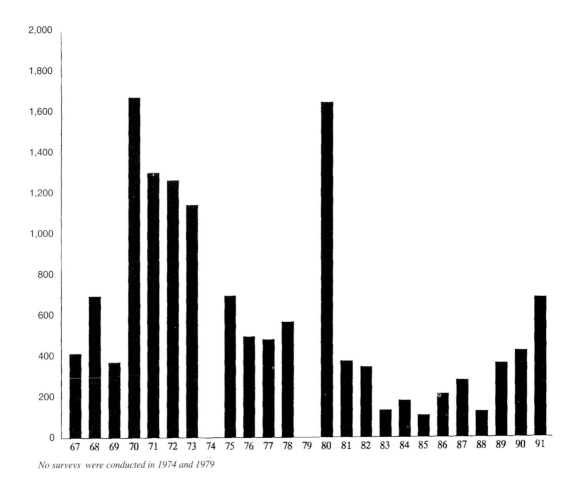

No surveys were conducted in 1974 and 1979

Figure 47.17 Index of abundance of Delta smelt in California, 1967–91 (taken from State of California 1991)

more effective countermeasures. Hydrological data are one of the keys to progress. If it were possible to return to the level of the world's data collection and management systems of twenty or thirty years ago, that would be a significant step forward for many developing regions. The notion that models can do everything and that more data are not needed must be dispelled, because these sentiments have adversely affected data collection systems in other parts of the world (Dozier 1992, Rodda 1995b).

To help overcome these problems, WMO launched the concept of the World Hydrological Cycle Observing System (WHYCOS) (Rodda *et al.* 1993), with the World Bank and UNESCO, to improve networks, upgrade the performance of hydrological ser-

vices, and make hydrological data readily available globally. Such data would allow timely and better assessment of water resources with less risk, and they would permit the perturbations to the hydrological cycle, such as droughts, to be anticipated with greater certainty. Significant progress is being made in implementing WHYCOS in the countries around the Mediterranean and in southern Africa (Pieyns and Kraemer 1997). Other data-supportive initiatives, the Friend Project (Gustard 1997) and the Global Runoff Data Centre (GRDC 1996), for example, will assist in overcoming the difficulties of inadequate data, but such initiatives require more governmental support if they are to succeed.

Shuttleworth (1996) pointed out that year-to-year

variations in local precipitation over the United States, 100 mm or more, are some four times larger than the change in the mean over the last thirty years. He implies that because future changes in precipitation may be of the same order, more effort needs to be directed toward predicting the variations from one year to the next, because of their importance for planning and other purposes. There is also the question that with the error of precipitation measurement being significantly greater than the likely change in the total, will the effect of climate change be detectable in precipitation records (Sevruk 1982)? Nevertheless, these problems should not detract from the research, which aims to connect significant anomalies in the patterns of hydrological variables to the longer-term changes taking place across the surface of the land and ocean. El Niño events and sea surface temperatures, pressure oscillations as described by ENSO, and other measures of the circulation patterns of the atmosphere and the oceans, together with solar activity, have been related to the distribution of precipitation, but also to some of the other hydrological variables. Some recent examples of such studies important to drought in a hydrological context are: for Australia, Cordery 1997; for northeast Brazil, Freitas and Billib 1997; for the western United States, McCabe 1996; and for Europe, Shorthouse and Arnell 1997. These and future research work in similar areas should help to reduce the risk and uncertainty presented by drought and provide a path toward the improved understanding of this phenomena and the goal of sustainable development.

Increasingly, the future is likely to reveal the inadequacies of water management, in developed and developing nations alike, should current attitudes be maintained. At one extreme, there are the geopolitical problems posed by the world's 200 or so shared river basins, where there are few international agreements on the equitable use of the water resources. These resources, stretched to meet the increasing demand and diminished by drought, will fuel confrontation and conflict between the nations concerned. At the other extreme, various local and regional issues emerge during drought, but these may be conveniently forgotten at other times. Demand management (especially during periods of peak water use), the effective control of leakage from water mains and

sewers, a belief that water should be free or very low cost – these are some of the matters that surround the politics of water at the local level. In addition, there is perhaps the more fundamental question of whether governments and their agencies should move now to raise the level of drought security against the prospect of a more uncertain future.

ACKNOWLEDGEMENTS

The author wishes to acknowledge the kind assistance of Mr. Frank Law, Mr. Terry Marsh, and Mr. Martin Lees of the Institute of Hydrology, Wallingford, UK, in the preparation of this chapter. Figure 47.10 (IH/BGS1994) is reproduced by permission of the Director, British Geological Survey. © NERC. All rights reserved.

REFERENCES

Albergel, J., Bader, J.-C., and Lamagat, J.-P. (1997) 'Flood and drought: Application to the Senegal river management', in D. Rosbjerg (ed.), *Sustainability of Water Resources under Increasing Uncertainty*, IAHS Publication No. 240, Wallingford, Oxfordshire, UK: International Association of Hydrological Sciences, pp. 509–17.

Arkin, P.A., Joyce, R., and Janoiwiak, J.E. (1994) 'The estimation of global monthly mean rainfall using infrared satellite data: The GOES Precipitation Index (GPI)', *Remote Sensing Review* 11: 107–24.

Ben-Zvi, A., Dlayahu, E., Gottesmann, M., and Passal, A. (1997) 'Causes and effects of the 1990–1991 water crisis in Israel', in D. Rosbjerg (ed.), *Sustainability of Water Resources under Increasing Uncertainty*, IAHS Publication No. 240, Wallingford, Oxfordshire, UK: International Association of Hydrological Sciences, pp. 89–96.

Beran, M.A., Brilly, M., Becker, A., and Bonacci, O. (eds) (1990) *Regionalization in Hydrology*, IAHS Publication No. 191, Wallingford, Oxfordshire, UK: International Association of Hydrological Sciences.

Beran, M.A. and Rodier, J.A. (1985) 'Hydrological aspects of drought', *Studies and Reports in Hydrology* No. 39, Paris: UNESCO, and Geneva: World Meteorological Organization.

Box, G.E.P. and Jenkins, G.M. (1970) *Time Series Analysis, Forecasting and Control*, San Francisco: Holden-Day.

British Rainfall (1887) 'On the distribution of rain over the British Isles during the year 1887' (compiled by G.J. Symons), London: Edward Stanford.

Bryant, S.J., Arnell, N.W., and Law, F.M. (1994) 'The 1988–92 drought in its historical perspective', *Journal of the Institution of Water and Environmental Management* 8, 1: 39–51.

Cordery, I. (1997) 'Interaction of phenomena to cause drought', in D. Rosbjerg (ed.), *Sustainability of Water Resources under Increasing Uncertainty*, IAHS Publication No. 240, Wallingford, Oxfordshire, UK: International Association of Hydrological Sciences, pp. 83–8.

Cunnane, C. (1989) 'Statistical distributions for flood frequency analysis', *Operational Hydrology Report* No. 33, Geneva: World Meteorological Organization.

DHA (1994) 'Disasters around the world – A global and regional view', *Information Paper* No. 4, UN Department of Humanitarian Affairs, New York.

Dozier, J. (1992) 'Opportunities to improve hydrologic data', *Reviews of Geophysics* 30: 315–31.

Dracup, J.A. (1991) 'Drought monitoring', *Stochastic Hydrology and Hydraulics* 5: 261–6.

ECSN/WMO/DWD (1997) *Annual Bulletin on the Climate of WMO Region VI – Europe and Middle East 1996*, European Climate Support Network/World Meteorological Organization/Deutscher Wetterdienst.

Foley, J.C. (1957) 'Droughts in Australia', *Bulletin* No. 43, Bureau of Meteorology.

Freitas, M.A. and Billib, M.H.A. (1997) 'Drought prediction and characteristic analysis in semiarid Ceara, Northeast Brazil', in D. Rosbjerg (ed.), *Sustainability of Water Resources under Increasing Uncertainty*, IAHS Publication No. 240, Wallingford, Oxfordshire, UK: International Association of Hydrological Sciences, pp. 105–12.

GRDC (1996) *Global Runoff Data Centre – Status Report, 1995*, Koblenz, Germany: Budesanstalt für Gewasserkunde.

Green, F.H.W. (1970) 'Some isopleth maps based on lysimeter observations in the British Isles in 1965, 1966, and 1967', *Journal of Hydrology* 10: 127–40.

Gumbel, E.J. (1941) 'The return period of flood flows', *Annals of Mathematical Statistics* 12: 163–90.

Gustard, A. (1996) 'Analysis of river systems', in G. Petts and P. Callow (eds), *River Flows and Channel Forms*, Oxford and Boston, MA: Blackwell Scientific Publications, pp. 32–50.

—— (1997) 'Preface', *Friend '97 – Regional Hydrology: Concepts and Models for Sustainable Water Resource Management*, IAHS Publication No. 246, Wallingford, Oxfordshire, UK: International Association of Hydrological Sciences, p. v.

Gustard, A., Bullock, A., and Dixon, J.M. (1992) 'Low flow estimation in the United Kingdom', Report No. 108, Wallingford, Oxfordshire, UK: Institute of Hydrology.

Hurst, H.E., Black, R.P., and Simaika, Y.M. (1965) *Long term Storage: An Experimental Study*, London: Constable.

IH/BGS (1985) *The 1984 Drought*, Hydrological Data UK Series, Wallingford, Oxfordshire, UK: Institute of Hydrology/British Geological Survey.

—— (1994) *The 1988–92 Drought*, Hydrological Data UK Series, Wallingford, Oxfordshire, UK: Institute of Hydrology/British Geological Survey.

IPCC (1996) *Climate Change 1995. Impacts, Adaptations and Mitigation of Climate Change: Scientific and Technical Analyses*, Contribution of Working Group II to the Second Assessment Report of the Intergovernmental Panel on Climate Change, Cambridge: Cambridge University Press.

Jackson, T.J., Schmugee, T., and Engman, E.T. (1996) 'Remote sensing applications to hydrology', *Hydrological Sciences Journal* 41: 517–30.

Kalma, J.D. and Calder, I.R. (1994) 'Land surface processes in large scale hydrology', *Operational Hydrology Report* No. 40, Geneva: World Meteorological Organization.

Krzysztofowicz, R. (1991) 'Drought forecasting: Methodological topics from a systems perspective', *Stochastic Hydrology and Hydraulics* 5: 267–79.

Kundzewicz, Z., Rosberg, D., Simonovic, S.P., and Takeuchi, K. (1993) 'Extreme hydrological events in perspective', in Z. Kundzewicz (ed.), *Extreme Hydrological Events*, IAHS Publication No. 213, Wallingford, Oxfordshire, UK: International Association of Hydrological Scientists, pp. 1–7.

Kustas, W.P. and Norman, J.M. (1996) 'Use of remote sensing for evapotranspiration monitoring over land surfaces', *Hydrological Sciences Journal* 41: 495–516.

Matalas, N. (1991) 'Drought description', *Stochastic Hydrology and Hydraulics* 5: 255–60.

Mawdesley, J., Petts, G., and Walker, S. (1994) 'Assessment of drought severity', *British Hydrological Society*, Occasional Paper No. 3.

McCabe, G.J. (1996) 'Effects of winter atmospheric circulation on temporal and spatial variability in annual streamflow in the western United States', *Hydrological Sciences Journal* 41: 873–87.

McMahon, T.A. and Mein, R.G. (1986) *River and Reservoir Yield*, Littleton, CO: Water Resources Publications.

Mehotra, D. and Mehotra, R. (1995) 'Climate change and hydrology with emphasis on the Indian subcontinent', *Hydrological Sciences Journal* 40: 231–42.

Olivry, J.-C., Chouret, A., Lemoalle, J., and Briquet, J.-P. (1996) *Hydrologie du lac Tchad*, Paris: Office de la Recherche Scientifique et Technique Outre-mer (Orstom).

OUP (1978) *Pocket Oxford Dictionary*, Sixth Edition, Oxford: Oxford University Press.

Palmer, W.C. (1965) 'Meteorological drought', Research Paper No. 45, US Weather Bureau.

Petty, G.W. and Krajewski, W.F. (1996) 'Satellite estimation of precipitation', *Hydrological Sciences Journal* 41: 435–51.

Pieyns, S.A., and Kraemer, D. (1997) 'WHYCOS, a programme supporting regional and global hydrology', in *Friend '97 – Regional Hydrology Concepts and Models for Sustainable Water Resources Management*, IAHS Publication No. 247, Wallingford, Oxfordshire, UK: International Association of Hydrological Sciences, pp. 3–11.

Piper, B.S., Gustard, A., Green, C.S., and Sridurongkatum, P. (1991) 'Water resource developments and flow regimes on the Mekong river', in F.H.M. van de Ven (ed.), *Hydrology for the Water Management of Large River Basins*, IAHS Publication No. 201, Wallingford, Oxfordshire, UK: International Association of Hydrological Sciences, pp. 45–56.

Postel, S. (1992) *The Last Oasis*, The Worldwatch Environmental Alert Series, New York: W.W. Norton and Co.

Rodda, J.C. (1995a) 'Guessing or assessing the world's water resources?', *Journal of the Institution of Water and Environmental Management* 9: 360–8.

—— (1995b) 'Capturing the hydrological cycle', in G.W. Kite (ed.), *Time and the River*, Littleton, CO: Water Resources Publications, pp. 25–58.

Rodda, J.C., Pieyns, S.A., Sehmi, N.S., and Matthews, G. (1993) 'Towards a world hydrological cycle observing system', *Hydrological Sciences Journal* 38: 373–8.

Schmugee, T. and Jackson, T.J. (1996) 'Passive microwave sensing of soil moisture', in S. Sorooshian, H.V. Gupta, and J.C. Rodda (eds), *Land Surface Processes in Hydrology*, NATO ASI Series, Berlin and New York: Springer, pp. 239–62.

Sehmi, N.S. and Kundzewicz, Z.W. (1997) 'Water, drought and desertification in Africa', in D. Rosbjerg (ed.), *Sustainability of Water Resources under Increasing Uncertainty*, IAHS Publication No. 240, Wallingford, Oxfordshire, UK: International Association of Hydrological Sciences, pp. 57–65.

Sevruk, B. (1982) 'Methods of correction for systematic error in point precipitation measurement for operational use', *Operational Hydrology Report* No. 21, Geneva: World Meteorological Organization.

Shorthouse, C.A. and Arnell, N.W. (1997) 'Spatial and temporal variability in European river flows and the North Atlantic oscillation', in *Friend '97 – Regional Hydrology: Concepts and Models for Sustainable Water Resource Management*, IAHS Publication No. 246, Wallingford, Oxfordshire, UK: International Association of Hydrological Sciences, pp. 77–85.

Shuttleworth, W.J. (1996) 'Forum: The challenges of developing a changing world', *EOS* 77, 347.

—— (1997) 'Hydrological models, regional evaporation, remote sensing. Let's start simple and maintain perspective', in S. Sorooshian, H.V. Gupta, and J.C. Rodda (eds), *Land Surface Processes in Hydrology*, NATO ASI Series, Berlin and New York: Springer, pp. 331–45.

Simonovic, S.P. (1997) 'Risk in sustainable water resources management', in D. Rosbjerg (ed.), *Sustainability of Water Resources under Increasing Uncertainty*, IAHS Publication No. 240, Wallingford, Oxfordshire, UK:

International Association of Hydrological Sciences, pp. 3–17.

Sircoulon, J. (1991) 'Climate and water development', in J. Jaeger and H.L. Ferguson (eds), *Climate Change: Science Impacts and Policy, Proceedings of the Second World Climate Conference*, Cambridge and New York: Cambridge University Press, pp. 242–52.

State of California (1991) *California's Continuing Drought 1987–1991*, Sacramento, CA: Department of Water Resources.

Stewart, J.B. (1989) 'On the use of the Penman-Monteith equation for determining areal evaporation', in T.A. Black (ed.), *Estimation of Areal Evapotranspiration*, IAHS Publication No. 177, Wallingford, Oxfordshire, UK: International Association of Hydrological Sciences, pp. 3–12.

Thompson, N., Barrie, I.E., and Ayles, M. (1981) 'The Meteorological Office Rainfall and Evaporation System: MORECS', *Met Office Hydrological Memorandum* No. 38, London: Meteorological Office.

UNDP/WMO (1992) *Drought Monitoring Bulletin*, Nairobi and Harare Drought Monitoring Centres, June.

UNESCO/WMO (1992) *International Glossary of Hydrology*, Second Edition, Paris: UNESCO, and Geneva: World Meteorological Organization.

Venkatasawmy, K. (1985) 'Derivation of evapotranspiration maps of a tropical, humid island', in Casebook on Operational Assessment of Areal Evaporation, *Operational Hydrology Report* No. 22, Geneva: World Meteorological Organization, pp. 34–43.

Vorosmarty, C.J., Gutowski, W.J., Person, M., Chen, T.C., and Case, D. (1993) 'Linked atmosphere-hydrology models at the macroscale', in W.B. Wilkinson (ed.), *Macroscale Modelling of the Hydrosphere*, IAHS Publication No. 214, Wallingford, Oxfordshire, UK: International Association of Hydrological Sciences, pp. 3–27.

Vorosmarty, C.J., Meybeck, M., Fekete, B., and Sharma, K. (1997) 'The potential impact of neo-Castorization on sediment transport by the global network of rivers', in D.E. Walling and J.L. Probst (eds), *Human Impact on Erosion and Sedimentation*, IAHS Publication No. 245, pp. 261–73.

Weibull, W. (1939) 'A statistical theory of the strength of materials', *Ing. Vetenskaps Akad. Handl.* 151: 15–29.

Wilhite, D.A. and Glantz, M.H. (1985) 'Understanding the drought phenomenon: The role of definitions', *Water International* 10: 111–20.

WMO (1994) *Guide to Hydrological Practices*, Fifth Edition, Geneva: World Meteorological Organization.

—— (1995) *Infohydro Manual*, Second Edition, *Operational Hydrology Report* No. 28, Geneva: World Meteorological Organization.

48

DROUGHT, VARIABILITY, AND CLIMATE CHANGE IN THE TWENTY-FIRST CENTURY

D. Rind

INTRODUCTION

We live in a time of prospective climate change. Carbon dioxide and various other greenhouse gases are increasing in the atmosphere because of human activities, and the increase is expected to continue through the next century. Greenhouse gases tend to warm the climate, so warming during the twenty-first century is very likely.

How much will it warm? The International Panel on Climate Change estimates that a doubling of atmospheric CO_2 should lead to a global warming of 1.5–4.5°C (IPCC 1990: xxv). One hundred years from now, the climate may well be several degrees warmer, or more (IPCC 1990: xxii). To put this in perspective, the Last Glacial Maximum, when land ice covered much of the northern United States, was estimated to be some 5°C colder on a global average (Rind and Peteet 1985: 1). A return to the present warm conditions took some 10,000 years. During the Little Ice Age several hundred years ago, when the growth of sea ice wiped out the Norse colonies in Greenland and Iceland, the global temperature is estimated to have been 0.5–1.0°C colder (Rind and Overpeck 1994: 371). Thus the prospective warming for the next century is both very large and very fast.

How certain is this warming? The direct radiative forcing of CO_2 can be calculated with confidence; doubled CO_2 would produce about 1.3°C warming (Hansen *et al.* 1984: 135). However, the real question is how will the system respond – that is, what are the 'feedbacks' to this forcing. Estimates of its magnitude derive largely from computerised models of the climate, called general circulation models (GCMs) (e.g., IPCC 1990: 99). These do a reasonable job of simulating the current climate, but they are far from perfect. The IPCC estimated range is derived from different formulations in different models, and hence a different climate sensitivity.

If climate does warm substantially, changes in water availability, in terms of both quantity and quality, are almost certain. Warmer temperatures will allow for more evaporation of moisture from the ocean, because warmer air can hold more moisture. With more evaporation, there will be more precipitation, on a global average. In addition, more moisture will be evaporated from the ground, drying the soil. Snowfall, which provides a reservoir of moisture for spring runoff, will likely decrease in areas of marginal freezing temperatures, and perhaps increase at higher latitudes. All of these effects are bound to change regional water levels, for better or worse.

Climatically induced water changes will be superimposed on a world already experiencing water stress. As reported by the *New York Times* (Lewis 1997: A6), a new United Nations study, 'Comprehensive Assessment of the Freshwater Resources of the World', finds that 40 per cent of the world's population is already suffering from serious water shortages; by 2025, when the world's population is expected to reach 8.3 billion, as much as two-thirds of the population may be affected by moderate to severe water shortages unless water is used much more efficiently. Changes in water availability due to climate have the potential to hinder any increase in efficiency.

Do we know what will happen in any particular area? The answer to this question depends on the quality of the GCMs being used to assess the warming and its hydrologic consequences. The ability of the models in this regard is somewhat dubious. Therefore, in practice, where models tend to agree, such as indicating more rainfall and wetter conditions at the highest latitudes, there is greater confidence in the predictions. Unfortunately, agreements between models are more the exception than the rule. Therefore we are limited in what we can conclude about future changes. We discuss below the nature of the uncertainties.

In addition to changes in time-averaged quantities of moisture or temperature, changes in weather patterns and gradients will likely lead to changes in variability. Variability is defined as deviations from the mean. Since the projected climate change will most likely be a continuing process, changes in both the mean and variability will also be a continuing process. Expectations may have to be readjusted on a decadal time scale.

The IPCC has several different working groups. Working Group 1 assesses the likelihood of climate change, Working Group 2 estimates the potential impacts of climate change, and Working Group 3 evaluates the economic consequences of those impacts. GCMs contribute directly to Working Group 1 results. Output from GCMs is then used by various 'impact models' for Working Group 2, and the impact changes are then fed to Working Group 3.

In this chapter, we review definitions of droughts/ floods adopted by different working groups dealing with the issue of climate change. We discuss the natural and anthropogenically forced variability that can periodically produce hydrologic extremes on different time scales. We then indicate what is expected from the different modelling approaches, and draw conclusions, however tentative, for what the twenty-first century will be like in terms of future water availability.

DROUGHT DEFINITION

A standard definition of drought is lack of available soil moisture. On a practical basis, the quality of the water determines whether it is 'available' for specific purposes, but the primary emphasis historically has been on quantity.

GCMs keep track of a soil moisture diagnostic, so it would be understandable if it were used by IPCC

Working Group 1 to indicate future droughts. However, soil moisture varies greatly over small distances in the real world, and it is difficult to establish what its real value is over any area. Different GCMs have very different values for the current climate (e.g., Kellogg and Zhao 1988: 348), none of which are directly verifiable. Therefore IPCC is sometimes more comfortable in considering elements of the hydrologic cycle in GCMs, like the change in precipitation, or in precipitation minus evaporation, instead.

Impact models have their own hydrologic cycle formulations and therefore their own definitions of effective drought. For example, an agricultural model may define drought as a precipitous decline in agricultural production; an ecosystem model, as a decrease in the health of the forest or grassland; and a river forecast model, as reduced river runoff. The National Meteorological Center (now called National Center for Environmental Programs, or NCEP) issues a 'drought index' that uses a calculation of precipitation minus potential evaporation (the maximum evaporation possible for given atmospheric conditions).

The different definitions of drought, as well as the different hydrological formulations used in the chain of models, opens the possibility for the various IPCC Working Groups to reach different conclusions despite using the same GCM output.

VARIABILITY AND DROUGHT

Variability in the climate system is responsible for much of what we normally think of as drought. Implicit in the definition of drought is a change from expected conditions; we would not, for example, think of the Sahara Desert as undergoing a 'drought', although from a soil moisture point of view it would be an appropriate categorisation. The drought index issued by NCEP indicates deviations from climatological average conditions, not absolute values.

Variability can result from a variety of causes. A particular dry season, or even several consecutive dry seasons, can result from continuing weather patterns, such as the movement of storm systems farther south or north than usual. Such effects can be completely random because of the wide range of possibilities inherent in the movement of a fluid.

If such variations can be related to longer-term cycles or quasi-cycles, it can be said that they are under climatic control. The occasional warming of the sea surface temperatures in the tropical east Pacific Ocean (known as El Niño) has been shown to influence weather patterns; California often receives its heaviest winter rains during El Niño time periods (Sittel 1994). El Niños repeat every four years or so, giving a quasi-periodicity to such weather conditions. It has been hypothesised that the sunspot cycles produce a 22-year cycle in drought conditions in the western United States (Mitchell *et al.* 1979). Although the validity of this claim is still being debated, the actual mechanism by which the solar cycle would produce drought would be by organising the weather systems into a nonrandom pattern, which would then repeat every 22 years. Sediment varves in lakes show cycles of greater/lesser sediment (indicating lake level variations) with periods around 88, 200, and 2,500 years (Stuiver *et al.* 1991); these have been related to longer-term variations in solar radiation, although these too remain uncertain. On even longer time scales, variations in climate and drought conditions of 22,000, 40,000, and 100,000 years (e.g., ice ages) have been associated with the variation in the orbit of the earth around the sun (Hays *et al.* 1976).

Aperiodic events can affect climate, and thus droughts. Volcanoes have been shown to cool the climate, and also force weather patterns into a somewhat different mode. For example, there is some evidence that it is wetter and warmer in western Europe during the winter following a major volcano as systems shift northward (Graf *et al.* 1993).

Therefore, some climate variations in the past have had an effect on the regional hydrologic budgets. This is the perspective from which future climate effects on water availability should be viewed.

CLIMATE CHANGE EFFECTS

As we indicated in the introduction, increasing amounts of greenhouse gases in the atmosphere, primarily CO_2, will likely lead to warming. Uncertainty about the magnitude of the temperature effect makes any hydrologic cycle change equally difficult to estimate. Figure 48.1 shows the global average precipitation increase as a function of temperature increase

that has occurred in different GCM simulations. With greater warming, there is a greater global increase, associated with increased evaporation from the ocean.

Global numbers do not indicate what happens on a regional level, which is the only level that really matters for water availability. Unfortunately, there is less agreement in GCMs concerning regional changes than there is for global changes, and this is true for temperature as well as precipitation. Some models show much more tropical warming than others (Rind 1987). The gradient of temperature between low and high latitudes affects many dynamic processes in the atmosphere, including monsoon distributions, the strength of midlatitude storms, and even the location of desert regions. Models that predict less warming at low latitudes have a tendency to show decreased precipitation in midlatitudes during summer (Rind 1988), although many models show this effect (IPCC 1995: 338). At higher latitudes, the warmer air can hold more moisture, and precipitation generally increases, especially in winter.

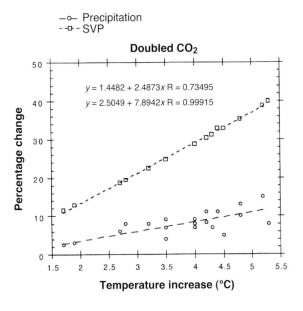

Figure 48.1 Variation of saturation vapour pressure (SVP) (squares, short dashes) and GCM global precipitation change (circles, long dashes) with temperature increase. SVP values are calculated from the Claussius-Clapeyron equation applied to the global mean temperature; GCM precipitation changes for doubled CO_2 climate simulations from different models reported by the IPCC (1990, 1995)

For the doubled CO_2 equilibrium climate, the IPCC (1990: 135), using a confidence scale ranging from one (low certainty) to five (virtual certainty), concluded that a confidence level of three pertained to the prediction that precipitation and soil moisture would increase at high latitudes in winter. A confidence level of two was appropriate for the prediction that northern hemisphere midlatitude soil moisture would decrease in summer. No other result had sufficient commonality among the models to warrant mentioning.

Climate change will likely occur gradually, so modellers are now concentrating on transient climate change effects. An additional uncertainty in this regard arises from questions concerning the response of oceans as climate starts to warm. As shown by the IPCC (1995: 304), some models predict a reduction in poleward ocean heat transports for the next century, leading to relative cooling at high latitudes in the North Atlantic. This result affects the temperature and moisture projections for northwestern Europe. Ocean modellers are not capable of simulating the current ocean structure without artificial corrections, so any such result is highly tentative. Coupled ocean–atmosphere models responding to gradual increases in greenhouse gases tend to show reduced soil moisture in summer over southern Europe, due to enhanced evaporation (IPCC 1995: 309), and the result is amplified when precipitation also decreases. Many models also produce more rainfall over India and/or southeast Asia, associated with the increased moisture in the warmer atmosphere (IPCC 1995: 309). The temperature and precipitation changes that occur at the time of CO_2 doubling (circa 2070 with a 1 per cent/year emissions increase) in different models and select regions are shown in Figure 48.2a (from IPCC 1995: 338).

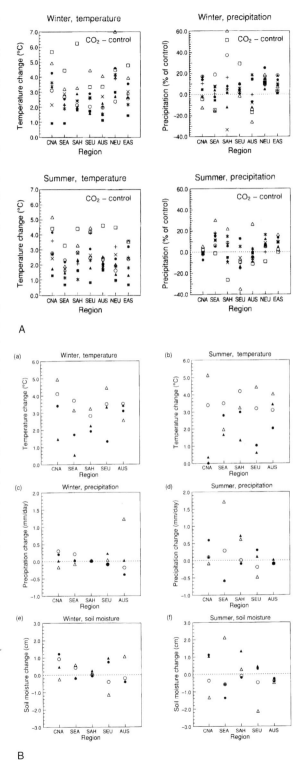

Figure 48.2 (a) Winter and summer temperature and precipitation changes at the time of CO_2 doubling in different GCM simulations, for different regions. CNA = Central North America, SEA = Southeast Asia, SAH = Sahel, SEU = Southern Europe, AUS = Australia, NEU = Northern Europe, EAS = East Asia. From IPCC (1995); for the specific GCMs involved, see IPCC (1995: 338). (b) Simulated regional changes in winter and summer temperature, precipitation, and soil moisture from 1880–9 to 2040–9 in the Max Planck Institute (triangles) and the United Kingdom Meteorological Office (circles) GCMs (from IPCC 1995: 306). Open values include greenhouse gas forcing only, while filled values also include direct sulphate aerosol effects

Another factor to be considered is the likely future increase of tropospheric aerosols, primarily sulfate aerosols associated with fossil fuel burning. When the projected climate forcing for the next century is modified to include this effect, the patterns of soil moisture change in northern winter are weaker and summer soil moisture actually increases over North America and southern Europe in several models (IPCC 1995: 310), and Asian monsoon precipitation now decreases. Aerosol effects are highly regional; they reduce the warming in and downstream of industrial areas, limiting evaporation changes and altering land/ocean temperature contrasts. These results emphasise the value of including all possible climate perturbations when considering likely future impacts. Winter and summer temperature, precipitation, and soil moisture changes for several models with and without aerosol forcing are reproduced from IPCC (1995: 338) in Figure 48.2b.

Without more certainty about the magnitude of the expected warming and its latitudinal distribution, there is little hope that we can accurately project how rainfall will vary in the future. However, there are certain overall guidelines we can establish. As climate warms, the ocean is likely to warm more slowly than the land: water has a larger heat capacity than does land, and it can use any excess energy to evaporate moisture rather than to warm itself. With less warming of the ocean water, there will be less warming of the air above the ocean. Since the ability of air to hold moisture is an exponential function of its temperature, evaporation of moisture into the air above the ocean can only increase as rapidly as the ocean temperatures do. And because evaporation from the ocean provides much of the water for rainfall, the increase in rainfall in a warming climate (e.g., Figure 48.1) is somewhat limited by the slow response of the ocean.

In contrast, the air above land warms more rapidly, and therefore its ability to draw moisture from the air increases more rapidly. Also shown in Figure 48.1 is the increase in saturation vapour pressure (the amount of moisture air can hold) as a function of temperature change. For a 4°C warming, the air above the land can hold some 30 per cent more moisture. Contrast this percentage with the results from GCMs, which show global precipitation increases only 10–15 per cent for the same magnitude temperature change. Therefore, in a warming climate, the precipitation increase is at a disadvantage relative to the increased moisture demand over land, which should lead to drying conditions.

Where will this drying occur? Once again, that depends on the magnitude of the warming and its latitudinal distribution. With significant low-latitude warming over land, drought index calculations show that the increase in moisture demand will outweigh the increase in precipitation, leading to an increase in droughts, first near the equator and then, as the warming increases, spreading poleward (Figure 48.3, adapted from Rind *et al.* 1990: 9,994). At the highest latitudes, the air is sufficiently cool that an increase in temperature does not increase demand (potential evaporation) as much, and the increase in precipitation leads to wetter conditions. At midlatitudes, drying may eventually occur as well; with sufficient warming magnitude, demand may exceed supply, and reduction in snowfall will mean less of a snowmelt reservoir (Wetherald and Manabe 1995: 3,104). This pattern may be analogous to (although we know little about the distribution of warming for ancient climates) the warm climate of the Mesozoic (180–60 million years ago) that was characterised by arid conditions from low to middle latitudes and wet conditions at high latitudes (Hallam 1985).

In agricultural models, the pattern of response discussed above is seen in projections of future food production. Estimates for the change in productivity during the next century indicate much worse conditions for Third World countries, primarily at low and subtropical latitudes, with muted or benign effects at the highest latitudes (Rosenzweig and Parry 1994) even when the ability of some plants to grow better with higher CO_2 is fully included. The effects due to just climate change alone (using simulations from three different GCMs) are shown in Figure 48.4. In this case the 'drought' is manifested as deterioration in the health of the vegetation for all three models, even with the GFDL climate change that produced the least tropical warming.

Interestingly, a similar effect is not seen in GCM soil moisture responses, which indicate little consistent change at low latitudes even when significant warming occurs (IPCC 1990: 135). One reason for

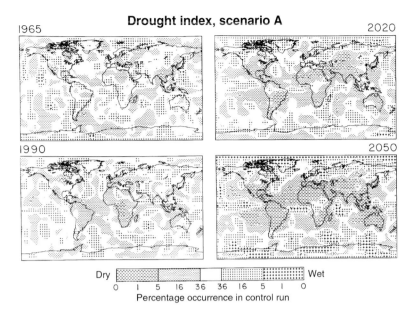

Figure 48.3 Drought index associated with projected climate change due to increasing trace gases in the next century. Dry conditions that occur less than 5 per cent of the time for the current climate control run (dark dashes) can be considered severe drought, and wet conditions less than 5 per cent currently (dark pluses) represent severe floods. Adapted from the results in Rind *et al.* (1990)

this discrepancy with the drought and impact model results is the different formulations used for evaporation among the models, which then tend to have a different sensitivity to climate change (Rind *et al.* 1997). Which sensitivity is more accurate is the subject of continued research, although some problems with the formulations in both GCMs and drought index approaches have been identified (Rind *et al.* 1997). Another facet of the problem is that as the climate starts to dry, GCMs effectively reduce their water loss efficiency, limiting subsequent drying. Since the health of 'vegetation' in the GCM is not interactive, such a reduction has no influence other than conserving soil moisture. In reality, and in agricultural models, reduction in water loss efficiency is achieved by closing of leaf stomata, which also limits uptake of CO_2 for photosynthesis. Reduced photosynthesis and the warming of the plant leaf would both negatively affect the health of the vegetation. This is an effect seen in the agricultural impact models, and it is lost with current GCM formulations.

So far we have been concerned with changes in mean quantities. Changes in variability will also depend on variations in the magnitude and gradient of the warming. In a warmer climate, rainfall will increase, and therefore the range between no rain and the 'normal' rain will increase, in absolute terms. Hence our perception of precipitation variability, as absolute change relative to a norm, will likely increase, although the percentage rainfall change may show less variation (Rind *et al.* 1989: 16). An increase in extreme precipitation intensities in GCMs has been reported in several studies, with the return periods of heavy rainfall events decreasing by factors of two to five, and rainfall intensities increasing by 10–30 per cent in doubled CO_2 conditions (IPCC 1995: 335).

Another effect that should not be ignored is potential changes in hurricanes, which depend on the sea surface for their energy. With warmer sea surface temperatures, hurricanes may increase in intensity/frequency, although other factors may limit such a response (Lighthill *et al.* 1994). An increase in hurricanes will add to hydrologic variability in potential landfall regions, and potential impact areas may move farther poleward along with the higher sea surface temperatures.

Potential change in grain yield

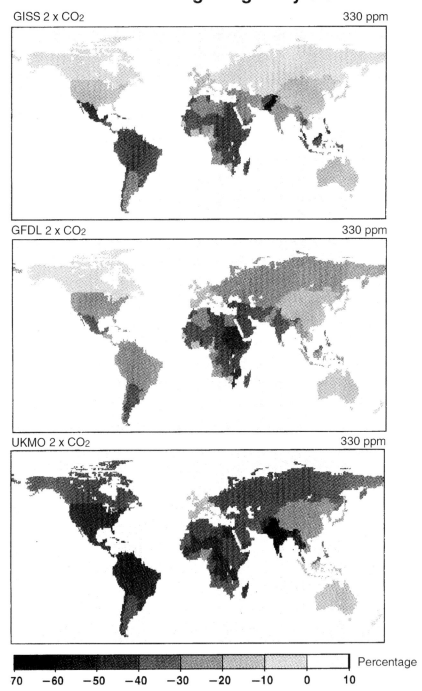

Figure 48.4 Potential change in grain yield calculated from agriculture models using the doubled CO_2 climate change simulations from GISS, the Geophysical Fluid Dynamics Laboratory (GFDL), and the United Kingdom Meteorological Office (UKMO). Notice the strong negative impacts in the tropics in all three cases. Figure courtesy of C. Rosenzweig and R. Goldberg (1997)

If temperatures warm considerably more at high latitudes than at low latitudes, day-to-day temperature variability (and changes in evaporation) should decrease (Rind *et al.* 1989). For example, if the air temperature in Canada during winter is more similar to the air temperature above the Gulf of Mexico, then it will make less difference whether the wind is from the north or the south on any particular day.

In general, then, while changes in the time-averaged mean water availability will depend on the magnitude of the warming, driven by the increase in evaporation demand over land, changes in variability may well be driven by the overall increase in precipitation range possible in a warmer climate.

When will any such influences become observable? For that to happen, the change in mean effects must exceed the variability already present in the system, both the random variations and those driven by other climate forcings. If we knew with greater certainty what the 'footprint' of the global warming effect was, we could compare natural and 'CO$_2$-induced' effects and more quickly ascertain when something significant was happening. This may be possible for the expected high-latitude precipitation increases, for example, and for the global precipitation value (if it were accurately known). It obviously also depends on how fast global warming occurs; without a significant increase in the global temperature, none of the hydrologic effects is likely. Currently there are indications that the warming of the last several decades is the beginning of the expected greenhouse signal (IPCC 1995: 5), although given the variability in the signal, it is likely that this will be more certain in hindsight (that is, if it continues) than it is now. The same is likely true for presently occurring hydrologic variations.

CONCLUSIONS

With significant global warming we can be sure that there will be large changes in the hydrologic cycle, with the potential for increasing droughts and floods. Global precipitation will increase, driven by warmer sea surface temperatures, but evaporation over land will generally increase more, as the warming over land should exceed that over the oceans. In regions where the precipitation itself decreases, such as perhaps

middle latitudes during summer, or where snowfall decreases, the combined effect will be substantial increases in drought. Additional drought increases may be expected if tropical warming over land is substantial. At higher latitudes, and in areas vulnerable to hurricanes, a more active hydrologic cycle will likely lead to an increase in floods. Most effects, however, cannot be more tightly constrained without a better estimation of the future magnitude and latitudinal pattern of the warming.

Therefore the first step is to refine our understanding of the sensitivity of the climate system, in particular the feedbacks to the increased greenhouse gas forcing. A principle uncertainty centres on how clouds will respond, for they could amplify or diminish the projected warming. Another uncertainty concerns the response of sea ice, which when it melts allows more of the sun's radiation to reach the surface rather than being reflected out to space. The likely magnitude of the global warming is the number one requirement for predicting future water availability.

Next most important is understanding the latitudinal gradient of the warming. If we know how much the tropics/subtropics will warm, we will understand what is likely to happen to evaporation from these regions of the ocean, which provide the moisture for the global precipitation. We will also have a better chance of estimating how hurricanes will change. If we know how high latitudes will warm relative to low latitudes, we will be in a position to understand changes in midlatitude storm systems, storm tracks, and daily temperature variability.

We also need to have better formulations of the transpiration of moisture from vegetation. GCMs and impact models have very different approaches, with different sensitivities to temperature changes. This leads to discrepancies between the results of IPCC Working Groups 1 and 2, even though both ostensibly use GCM temperature and precipitation output. GCMs must allow for interactive vegetation. Soil moisture is not the only indicator of drought; the change in health of vegetation must also be assessed.

If warming is significant, increases in droughts and floods, defined as changes from what we now consider normal, are certain, and this will likely be occurring in a world already stressed for water. Further work is needed to characterise the regional distribution of these changes and the timing of their arrival.

ACKNOWLEDGEMENTS

Climate modelling at GISS is supported by the NASA Climate Program Office.

REFERENCES

Graf, H.-F., Kirchner, I., Robock, A., and Schult, I. (1993) 'Pinatubo eruption winter climate effects: Model versus observations', *Climate Dynamics* 9: 81–93.

Hallam, A. (1985) 'A review of Mesozoic climates', *Journal of the Geological Society of London* 142: 433–45.

Hansen, J.E., Lacis, A., Rind, D., Russell, G., Stone, P., Fung, I., Ruedy, R., and Lerner, J. (1984) 'Climate sensitivity: Analysis of feedback mechanisms', in J.E. Hansen and T. Takahashi (eds), *Climate Processes and Climate Sensitivity*, Geophysical Monograph 29, Washington, DC: AGU, pp. 130–63.

Hays, J.D., Imbrie, J., and Shakleton, N.J. (1976) 'Variations in the Earth's orbit: Pacemaker of the ice ages', *Science* 194: 1,121–32.

IPCC (1990) *Climate Change* (J.T. Houghton, G.J. Jenkins, and J.J. Ephraums, eds), Cambridge: Cambridge University Press.

—— (1995) *Climate Change 1995* (J.T. Houghton, L.G. Meira Filho, B.A. Callander, N. Harris, A. Kattenberg, and K. Maskell, eds), Cambridge: Cambridge University Press.

Kellogg, W.W. and Zhao, Z.-C. (1988) 'Sensitivity of soil moisture to doubling of carbon dioxide in climate model experiments, I, North America', *Journal of Climate* 1: 348–66.

Lewis, P. (1997) 'U.N. report warns of problems over dwindling water supplies', *New York Times*, January 20, p. A6.

Lighthill, J.G., Holland, J., Gray, W.M., Landsea, C., Emanuel, K., Craig, G., Evans, J., Kunihara, Y., and Guard, C.P. (1994) 'Global climate change and tropical cyclones', *Bulletin of the American Meteorological Society* 75: 2,147–57.

Mitchell, J.M., Stockton, C.W., and Meko, D.M. (1979) 'Evidence of a 22-year rhythm of drought in the western United States related to the Hale solar cycle since the 17th century', in B.M. McCormac and T.A. Seliga (eds), *Solar Terrestrial Influences on Weather and Climate*, Hingham, MA: D. Reidel, pp. 124–44.

Rind, D. (1987) 'The doubled CO_2 climate: Impact of the sea surface temperature gradient', *Journal of Atmospheric Science* 44: 3,235–68.

—— (1988) 'The doubled CO_2 climate and the sensitivity of the modeled hydrologic cycle', *Journal of Geophysical Research* 93: 5,385–412.

Rind, D., Goldberg, R., and Ruedy, R. (1989) 'Change in climate variability in the 21st century', *Climatic Change* 14: 5–37.

Rind, D., Goldberg, R., Hansen, J.E., Rosenzweig, C., and Ruedy, R. (1990) 'Potential evapotranspiration and the likelihood of future drought', *Journal of Geophysical Research* 95: 9,983–10,004.

Rind, D. and Overpeck, J. (1994) 'Hypothesized causes of decade-to-century-scale climate variability: Climate model results', *Quaternary Science Reviews* 12: 357–74.

Rind, D. and Peteet, D. (1985) 'Terrestrial conditions at the last glacial maximum and CLIMAP sea surface temperature estimates: Are they consistent?', *Quaternary Research* 24: 1–22.

Rind, D., Rosenzweig, C., and Lynch-Steiglitz, M. (1997) 'The role of moisture transport between ground and atmosphere in global change', *Annual Review of Energy and Environment* (forthcoming).

Rosenzweig, C. and Parry, M.L. (1994) 'Potential impact of climate change on world food supply', *Nature* 367: 133–8.

Sittel, M.C. (1994) *Differences in the Means of ENSO Extremes for Maximum Temperature and Precipitation in the United States*, Tech. Rept. 92–4, Florida State University, Tallahassee.

Stuiver, M., Braziunas, T.F., Becker, B., and Kromer, B. (1991) 'Climatic, solar, oceanic, and geomagnetic influences on late-Glacial and Holocene atmospheric $^{14}C/^{12}C$ change', *Quaternary Research* 35: 1–24.

Wetherald, R.T. and Manabe, S. (1995) 'The mechanisms of summer dryness induced by greenhouse warming', *Journal of Climate* 8: 3,096–108.

49

DROUGHT, THE FAMINE PROCESS, AND THE PHASING OF INTERVENTIONS

John Osgood Field

PROLOGUE

Rather like love and marriage, the linkage between drought and famine has been a subject of fascination – and contention – for years. What once seemed to be a fairly simple, direct cause-and-effect relationship, with drought causing crop failure resulting in a decline in food availability and eventual starvation ('famine'), has become a horrendously complex and highly mediated relationship at best. Drought's centrality to famine has diminished from the status of 'cause célèbre' to that of mere 'trigger', and by no means the only or most important trigger.[1] Students of climatic instability continue to regard drought as a significant factor disposing to famine, and there is much evidence to sustain this view. Those who find trigger mechanisms too superficial to explain something as multidimensional as famine find deeper explanations more to their satisfaction – underlying vulnerabilities, eroded entitlements, overwhelmed coping strategies, harmful public policies, political economy relationships victimising specific groups (if not the poor at large), and – a recent concept – the trauma of 'failed states'.[2] There is much to sustain these perspectives as well.

Appreciating the complexity of famine and its multiple determinants has deepened understanding at the expense of clarity. Drought *may* result in famine, but most droughts do not, in fact, produce famine in their wake. Similarly, if famine *can* emerge from drought, there have also been numerous famines in the absence of drought. Moreover, severity of drought turns out to be an astonishingly poor predictor of famine, even in Africa.[3] Size, diversity, and resilience of a country's economy are potent mediating influences, as are government policies, the presence or absence of civil conflict, and the timeliness and effectiveness of international aid. The variability of drought, the famine-inducing potential of other natural triggers, and the significance of 'manmade' socioeconomic conditions and public policies in the emergence of famine all confound simple causal attributions. The 'famine-drought nexus'[4] is so variable and conditional that generalisation becomes difficult, and this, in turn, has led analysts to explore famine causality beyond drought *per se* and to develop indicators other than drought that a famine process is under way.

By the same token, the complex, multiple patterns associated with the emergence of famine enormously complicate efforts to detect the onset of famine and monitor the process as it unfolds, particularly when the objective of early warning is to induce an early, preemptive response. This essay builds on the conceptual ferment and contextual grounding that characterise the rapidly growing literature on famine, while at the same time highlighting instances of successful famine management. There is an extraordinary irony in this analysis, for the best examples of intervention to prevent famine all reflect official efforts to cushion the devastating effects of drought.

INTRODUCTION

Famine is both process and outcome.[5] Whether the famine process results in famine or not depends on the virulence of the triggering shock (e.g., drought, pests, conflict), the coping capacity of affected people

– itself a function of their vulnerabilities and capabilities – and the timeliness and effectiveness of outside intervention. The irony is that, when famine emerges, it is dramatically clear even to the naked eye, with the camera recording the obvious. However, the camera cannot record what does not yet exist, and the process itself is often shrouded in ambiguity. This has typically led to a response that is late.[6]

This chapter is an attempt to tie together two themes of the analytical literature on famine that have tended to run on separate, if parallel, tracks. One focuses on people's entitlements and their erosion, and on government strategies of entitlement protection.[7] The other focuses on phases of the famine process in terms of coping strategies at the community and household levels.[8] The task at hand is to link these two themes by means of a typology of the specific policies and interventions that are appropriate to each phase in light of what people are, and are not, able to do on their own behalf. The operational hypothesis of this exercise is that if we can appreciate the effectiveness of early intervention, we can move programmatically to protect entitlements and help people cope successfully, thereby preventing the widespread destitution and death that are the culmination of the famine process and hallmarks of famine itself.

The set of linkages involved is the essence of Figure 49.1. This diagram traces the famine process, then posits the focus and functions of early warning systems designed to monitor the process and identify critical points reached along the way by different social groups. It concludes by noting the nature and timing of government action to break the process and prevent further deterioration, along with the specific objectives of intervention at different stages. Although this diagram is empirically informed, as a general conceptualisation it is at best a theoretical extrapolation from a limited number of instances in which famine management has successfully arrested the process, broken its dynamic, and prevented the populations at risk from bottoming out and dying in large numbers. The text that follows is an articulation of this diagram.[9]

THE FAMINE PROCESS

As portrayed in Figure 49.1, the famine process is usually triggered by some disturbance that has, or is perceived to have, a negative impact on crop production and/or animal stocks, and hence the availability of food. Shortfalls in aggregate production may be the clearest instances of a food availability decline (FAD), but, in fact, any significant disruption in the production, distribution, and marketing of food can initiate the process, which is to say that an actual decline in availability need not occur for the process to get under way.[10]

The catalysts of the process are the actual or anticipated adverse movement of food prices, employment, and income, as highlighted in the literature on entitlements. As prices rise (especially for staple grains), as employment erodes, and as incomes decline relatively and absolutely, people adopt a wide range of coping behaviours such as altering planting strategies, seeking alternative employment, curtailing current consumption of food, selling jewellery and other possessions not essential to livelihood, disposing of small animals, and gathering wild foods. The fundamental objective of these early coping behaviours is to avoid destitution by protecting future economic capacity.

If the famine process proceeds – that is, if the coping behaviours are insufficient to ride out increasingly hard times – a point is reached when coping becomes failure to cope. This critical transition comes when households find themselves with no alternative but to begin disposing of productive assets on which future livelihood depends (draft animals, one's plough or loom, ultimately the land itself).[11] 'Famine conditions'[12] now exist in which people in increasing numbers and across different social strata experience a process of destitution. As this process intensifies, it is ever more irreversible. As destitution takes hold, social disintegration occurs in communities, manifest in breakdowns of social reciprocities and supports, hoarding, and increased crime. Social disintegration also occurs inside households, with dependents – wives, children, the elderly – sold or abandoned. Current survival is now the prime motivation, even if it is at the expense of future well-being. 'Famine conditions' often culminate in extensive outmigration from afflicted areas, as people become acutely dependent on charity for food, water, and care. Many never make it or cannot be saved. They experience actual

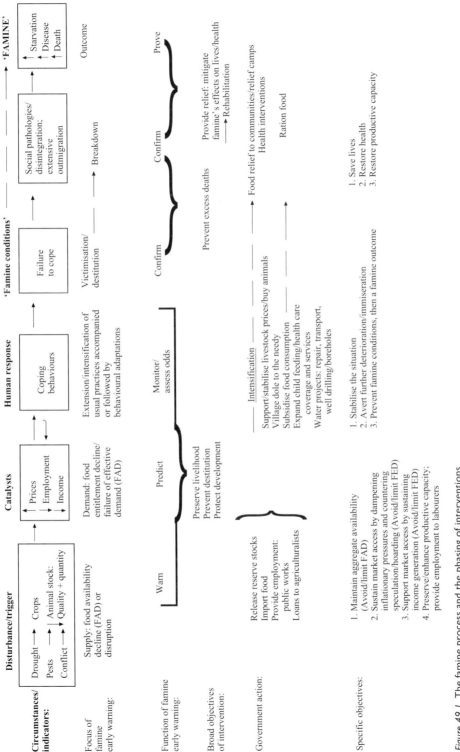

Figure 49.1 The famine process and the phasing of interventions

famine: starvation, disease, and death, with survivors being even more vulnerable to future adversity unless they are successfully rehabilitated. The specifics will vary from case to case, but the overall process is much the same; it is the timing, intensity, scope, numbers involved, and range of outcomes and their long-term effects that differ.

THE FOCUS AND FUNCTION OF FAMINE EARLY WARNING [13]

The logic of the famine process, so conceived, is that the focus of monitoring, or 'early warning', shifts as the process unfolds, as do the functions performed by monitoring.[14] In most instances, the initial focus is on the supply side of famine: crop failure and the factors disposing to it (such as drought). The prevailing concern is with a decline in food availability at local, regional, and national levels – and the anticipated magnitudes of each. At this stage, early warning is just that. Its purpose is to warn of production shortfalls and of the potential that they will result in further entitlement declines on the demand side, reflecting the adverse movement of prices, employment, and income, the actual catalysts of the famine process.

If and when people begin to lose market access to food, and when pastoralists, fishermen, and tradesmen experience increasingly adverse terms of trade in what they sell (animals, fish, goods, and services) relative to the grain they seek to buy to meet nutritional needs, early warning systems are now in a position to assert that, indeed, a famine process is under way and that, left unattended, it could culminate in a famine outcome. Still not known, however, is how well different social and occupational groups will be able to cope with the worsening economic situation in which they find themselves. That, again, will depend on the interplay of their vulnerabilities and capabilities, given the nature and magnitude of the forces at work. Nevertheless, when food entitlement decline on the demand side accelerates, often but not inevitably as a consequence of food availability decline on the supply side,[15] early warning monitoring can, at the very least, predict an intensification of hardship, often group specifically. As people respond to deepening recession and adapt their behaviours in an effort to cope, the focus

of monitoring can be extended to include these behaviours. The task now is to track what people are doing and to weigh its significance.

Cueing off household coping strategies to prevent drought – or any other disruption – from becoming famine is an attractive idea, particularly for the anthropologically inclined.[16] Still, a note of caution is warranted. For this focus of early warning to be applied effectively requires considerable contextual understanding of people in their social and physical environments and of behaviour modification, its meaning, and probable success.[17] This can be a daunting prospect for even the best informed observers; to some it may seem nearly impossible to do with any confidence that one is interpreting (say, the sale of small ruminants by some, but not all) correctly. Moreover, it is not clear that human responses to stress are better indicators than the stresses themselves unless, of course, the human responses precede the stresses by way of anticipation. The best indicators for famine early warning may well be different from the best indicators for verification, with coping strategies typically being among the latter in the early stages.

The monitoring of coping strategies has clear merit when people begin to sell off their productive assets, granted that different people will do so at different times and at different paces. This is the most critical transition in the famine process because it means that the people in question are no longer coping in the positive sense and that 'coping' has become indistinguishable from 'suffering'.[18] When people dispose of factors of production (animals, ploughs, etc.) essential to livelihood, one has a clear signal of failure to cope, of being overwhelmed and forced to mortgage the future to sustain the present. Here one has the onset of 'famine conditions', a process within the larger famine process featuring victimisation and ratchetlike destitution. When monitoring detects this subprocess, in effect it can confirm that the worst is, in fact, happening, and for whom. The same is true as social structures and reciprocities erode and as people abandon hope and leave the land in search of succour elsewhere.[19] At this stage, early warning is no longer warning, predicting, or assessing odds; it is documenting a tragedy.

Needless to say, when actual famine emerges from the famine process – as revealed by expanding starvation, disease, and death among the afflicted – the function of monitoring is no longer to confirm destitution; it is to prove that destitution has itself been transformed into 'famine'. At this point, it makes little sense to speak of early warning, for if early warning reaches the stage when it is proving the reality of famine, no matter how sophisticated and accurate it may be, it has not fulfilled its most basic purpose: to warn early enough to trigger a response early enough to prevent a famine outcome. Early warning solely for relief after the fact is a contradiction in terms. It is also a cruel hoax on the victims of famine.[20]

THE OBJECTIVES OF INTERVENTION

Just as the function of famine early warning shifts across the famine process, so too do the broad objectives of intervention. Here it makes sense to begin at the end of the process and move backward. When intervention is late, as it so often is, especially in terms of an international response, about the best one can do is provide relief to those whose ability to cope has been overwhelmed, whose entitlements have collapsed, and who are in an advanced stage of destitution. It is precisely among such people, particularly the uprooted, that one observes rampant starvation and disease and rising mortality. Because it is so late, the only thing relief can try to do is mitigate famine's effects on lives and health, stabilising a precarious situation that has been allowed to deteriorate to that desperate point.

On a more positive note, relief often – but not always – enables the survivors of famine to experience rehabilitation with outside assistance (provision of seed for the post-famine crop, recapitalisation of the means of production, restoration of animal stock). Rehabilitation rebuilds productive capacity and reestablishes lost entitlements. At its best, it is the second step back to development, the first being relief itself. Rehabilitation has the potential to restore the status quo ante, but in the absence of an actual process of development – the building of new capabilities, improving productive capacity and performance, creating new options for economic enterprise, enhancing income generation, and strengthening entitlements and their protection – rehabilitation does not really address the underlying vulnerability that pushed famine victims over the brink the last time.[21]

So although it is better than no intervention at all, relief is a minimalist intervention that for hundreds of thousands, if not millions, of people is too little, too late. When relief is the only option left, the famine process having run full course or nearly so, early warning has not produced early response and famine victims have been allowed to struggle and fail on their own, experience destitution, and reach the brink of death, with significant numbers falling over.[22]

If intervention is calibrated to 'famine conditions', the subprocess of destitution that ratchets its victims downward at an accelerating pace, it becomes possible to avert the excess deaths associated with famine. Intervention at this stage is the last real opportunity to prevent a famine outcome. In one sense it is preemptive, for decision makers have chosen to act before the existence of famine is apparent and possibly even before social pathologies have passed beyond hoarding and petty thievery. On the other hand, except in rare circumstances,[23] intervention to avert a famine seeks to change the outcome but does little to alter the process leading to it. Intervention to prevent excess deaths is not the same as intervention to prevent destitution. It may forestall the bottoming out associated with destitution, but for the latter to be averted, intervention must come even earlier.

The most ambitious objective of intervention corresponds to the greatest promise of early warning, namely to intervene early enough to prevent destitution. This requires a truly preemptive response capable of breaking the dynamic of the famine process before 'famine conditions' emerge. Intervention to this end must take place soon after the process is underway, and the earlier the better. Even cueing off coping behaviours may be too late, given the need for lead time and the multiple uncertainties of interpretation. Cueing off the catalysts of the famine process – prices, employment, and income – is more timely and promising, especially if terms-of-trade indexes are used and cutoff points established that effectively trigger official action.[24] Clearly the 'best' time for intervention is when crops are threatened (not even waiting to see whether the harvest actually fails), because very early intervention makes possible the protection of entitlements as well as the preservation of livelihood. A major problem is that early intervention at the left side of Figure 49.1 calls for commitment before certainty, indeed commitment at a time of maximum uncertainty. Perhaps only when drought is so recurrent and devastating, as in Botswana, is it politically possible, even necessary, to authorise action so soon.[25]

In sum, in ascending order of ambition, uncertainty, and risk (but also opportunity), the broad objectives of intervention are: (1) to provide relief to famine victims; (2) to prevent famine from occurring; and (3) to preserve livelihood, prevent destitution, and – in so doing – protect a country's investments in rural development. If intervention is early enough, it can protect people's exchange entitlements as well.[26]

If one concurs that this listing is inversely related to the potential of famine management, then clearly we need to move beyond a relief-centred conceptualisation of famine response. Even preventing famine, much to be desired, is too limited a goal. What the governments of famine-prone countries and their international benefactors can aspire to, if they are willing to make the commitment called for, is a type of famine management that seeks to prevent destitution as well as deaths and to preserve people's livelihoods and their entitlements in times of stress. No other approach is more closely attuned to, or part and parcel of, an equity-oriented strategy of rural development. It is the insurance policy to protect vulnerable people should a famine process get under way.

THE NATURE AND SPECIFIC GOALS OF INTERVENTION [27]

Our attention now turns to the actual interventions that have been employed, with success, at different stages of the famine process.[28] In India, Botswana, Cape Verde, Kenya, Zimbabwe, and – most recently – the entire region of southern Africa hit by drought in 1992–3, governments have responded quickly, even preemptively, at the onset of the famine process. Four basic actions have been taken by the governments in question, both on their own and with timely international assistance.

(1) The *release of available reserve stocks of food* and
(2) *importation of food and food aid*, intended to maintain aggregate food availability in the face of actual or anticipated production shortfalls, and to sustain market access by the rural poor through dampening inflationary pressures while also reducing incentives to speculation and hoarding. In each instance, the objective has been to avoid or limit a decline in both food availability and exchange entitlement (FAD and FED, respectively, in Figure 49.1).

(3) *Initiation or expansion of public works* to provide employment and earnings to people who have lost their usual employment or their usual sources and amounts of income, reflecting slackened demand for their goods and services. The explicit objective of employment generation at the earliest stages of the famine process has been to maintain market access and thereby avoid or limit a failure of effective demand (another way of referring to FED).

(4) *Loans to agriculturalists* to help them remain viable when production and earnings are threatened. An added objective has been to preserve and, through timely investment, even to enhance the productive capacity of farm units, and to sustain employment for agricultural labourers.[29]

Two aspects of early intervention are of interest. First, the decision to act early in the manner described indicates a keen understanding of both the supply and demand sides of entitlement failure as well as the need and opportunity to invest in the productive capacity of the land. The presumption that early and late intervention are both likely to be supply oriented (enhancing food availability and providing food relief, respectively), whereas intervention in between is more likely to be demand oriented (providing employment and otherwise maintaining market access),[30] does not hold. Early intervention reveals a reinforcing admixture of both supply and demand considerations and, in the case of the Indian Famine Codes, an in-depth appreciation of the importance of exchange entitlements à la Sen, well before Sen was even born.

Second, it bears repeating that these interventions have been successful, either in snuffing out the famine process at the very onset or in so weakening its dynamic that people have been better able to cope on their own, often with additional supports. If we may generalise, early intervention is possible and feasible, and it works! Moreover, it works by every standard of success. It prevents a famine outcome and all the dislocation and despair that accompany it. It preserves livelihood and prevents destitution among a rural population that is especially vulnerable and so easily overwhelmed. And it protects people's entitlements, thereby dampening, if not always eliminating, the principal catalysts of the entire famine process.

Not only is early intervention cost-effective, it is a wise investment in development. To intervene early is to protect development by preventing economic and social stress leading to collapse in the countryside. Not to intervene early is opportunity foregone.

And yet, for reasons explored elsewhere,[31] early intervention is difficult for many governments and most international agencies. Suffice it to say that decision makers often desire clarity before being willing to commit their resources and institutions to a famine response, but clarity rarely exists early on. So the next threshold of opportunity comes when entitlements have eroded sharply and the people adversely affected have activated their arsenal of coping strategies.

Two things can happen at this still relatively early stage of the famine process. Interventions initiated earlier can be intensified, a pattern typical of Botswana, a country that – almost uniquely – has institutionalised disaster management by incorporating the interventions and administrative systems involved into ongoing development policy.[32] Alternatively, such interventions can be introduced *de novo*. In each case, a plethora of other programmes, such as those noted in Figure 49.1 (stabilising livestock prices, subsidising food consumption, health interventions, water projects), can also be launched and, especially in India, have been, with telling effect both historically and in the current era.[33] Interventions based on terms-of-trade indexes (such as grain-meat, prices-income) and unemployment rates may not prevent entitlement declines (because they cue off them), but they do have the potential to avert entitlement collapse while at the same time protecting – even promoting – health status in the population. Indeed, interventions in response to entitlement declines are commonly the first instances in which the morbidity side of famine receives any concerted attention.[34]

The objectives of intervention at this stage are to stabilise the situation, to avert further deterioration and the onset of severe, often irreversible immiseration, and to prevent a famine outcome, if possible by preventing the emergence of 'famine conditions'. Needless to say, there is no guarantee of success at this stage or any other. But the good news is that there are instances in which intervention toward the middle of the famine process has worked – in shoring up entitlements, supporting people's own coping efforts, minimising destitution, expanding the coverage of health services (including, vitally, provision of water as well as immunisation and nutrition), averting social collapse, and – as a result – preventing famine. The record here is not as good as it is when intervention is earlier, but it is not bad. Moreover, intervention at this point may be necessary anyway, given the virulence of the trigger and the power of the dynamic once under way.

To repeat a sad refrain, all too often the national and international response to famine comes so late that providing relief to its victims is the only remaining option. Again, there are reasons why this is so, not the least of which are lack of preparedness, confusion concerning the nature of famine, and political conflict.[35] The benchmarks of the relief response to famine are thousands of uprooted persons, wretched beyond belief; makeshift camps set up to receive them, provide food, and tend to their worsening health (especially dysentery and respiratory infections superimposed on starvation); and a growing number of draped bodies. Less easily seen and documented by the media are the hundreds of thousands, even millions, more who die silently in their homes without hope and beyond reach.[36]

The objectives of relief are so simple as to defy the difficulty of achieving them: save lives, restore health, and – when possible – rebuild productive capacity. To write these words is to underline how far the situation has deteriorated to reach this end point, how far the famine process has come, and how lacking or inadequate were any earlier attempts to arrest it. Much relief arrives after the fact, often with paeans of self-congratulation, as if nothing effective could have been done earlier. In remote situations beyond normal scrutiny and in situations characterised by unrelenting civil conflict, that may indeed be the case.[37] Conflict, in particular, not only possesses the potential to trigger the famine process. It also enormously complicates the international response both in terms of political decision making and operationally on the ground.[38] But much of the time in today's world, the emergence of famine, and hence the need for a relief response, speaks as much to institutional incapacity and to political inertia or manipulation as to the power of nature and cruelty of contending armies.[39]

CONCLUSION

This essay has traced the famine process and noted the interventions that have successfully been employed at different stages. One insight to emerge is that many of these interventions have strong developmental content and significance until relief becomes the dominant response. In effect, interventions early in the process and during its middle stages are forms of development as well as a protection of development, and should be understood as such. Pre-relief famine management along the lines indicated is actually an investment in development. This insight may come as a pleasant surprise to those steeped in a relief mentality, for whom relief and development are alternative spheres of responsibility. A richer view of famine management that allows for and encourages earlier intervention unites famine management with development.[40]

Second, and more importantly, early intervention has a proven track record. It does work. So too does intervention later in the famine process, after entitlements have shifted negatively but before the sub-process of destitution has proceeded too far. This is extraordinarily good news, and if it can be repeated on a wider scale, we really will have learned something of value and achieved something of consequence.

Finally, it is interesting – and even a bit sobering – to reflect on the fact that the several cases of successful intervention to prevent famine discussed in this chapter all featured a drought trigger. Despite the enormous complexity of the famine process revealed by scholarship in the last two decades, actual performance in managing famine has been best where conceptual simplicity prevailed and could induce an early response. In India since the mid-1960s; in

Botswana from the early 1970s to the present; in Cape Verde, Kenya, and Zimbabwe in the 1980s; and in the entire region of southern Africa in the early 1990s, the 'famine–drought nexus' was sufficiently close, clear, and compelling to warrant public action to deny its fruition. In Botswana and India, in particular, policies to manage drought have become, in consequence, policies to prevent famine, and it is a tribute to both countries that the very interventions initiated to cope with drought have been institutionalised in government and incorporated into ongoing development policy, available to be intensified – not recreated *de novo* – the next time the rains fail. Famine response knows no higher expression than this incorporation of disaster management into the development process.

Also sobering is the fact that famine response predicated on drought is receding in significance in the face of other, more distinctly political factors. In those instances where drought has not been the trigger (North Korea, for example) or where drought's effects have been exacerbated by the dislocations of social engineering (China, Ethiopia) and conflict (Sudan), the record is far less inspiring. Intervention in the new genre of 'complex humanitarian emergencies' exemplified by Somalia, Bosnia, southern Sudan, Rwanda, and eastern Zaire is especially difficult and costly to undertake while being infinitely more problematical in what can be accomplished.

NOTES

1   Others include excessive rainfall and flooding; locusts, other pests, and blights; and social conflict.
2   See, for example, Greenough 1982, Sen 1981, Corbett 1988, Clay 1991, Keen 1994, and Helman and Ratner 1992–3. For a topical review of the literature, see Devereux 1993b.
3   Drèze and Sen 1989, Table 5.2; Berry and Downing 1993.
4   Glantz 1989.
5   Currey 1992, Field 1993. In this chapter, famine as an outcome is characterised by marked increases in starvation, disease, and death afflicting a population. The famine process is the phased series of conditions that dispose to such an outcome. For other conceptualisations, see especially Devereux 1993b and de Waal 1989.
6   These ideas are discussed more fully in Field 1993; see the Introduction and Chapter 11 in particular.

7   The concept *entitlement*, as used here and in the hunger-famine literature, is from Sen (1981; see also Drèze and Sen 1989, 1990a, and 1990b; and Ravallion 1987). It refers to the levels of food consumption that different people can reliably maintain in normal times, along with adjustments induced by changing circumstances. Some entitlements are based on endowment (what people own and produce, as from the land); others are grounded in exchange (purchasing power) and dependency relationships. Much of Sen's work has been to weigh the relative significance in famine of supply and demand failures, with food availability decline (FAD) and food entitlement decline/failure of effective demand (FED) held up as alternative explanations.

8   For example, Corbett 1988, Walker 1989, Bohle *et al.* 1991, Davies 1993, Devereux 1993a.

9   Preceding this diagram is a large funnel of factors – climatological and environmental; demographic, economic, social, and political; macro and micro; historical and contemporary – that feed into it, creating vulnerabilities that are activated and accentuated when the process is triggered. Indeed, people's vulnerabilities and capacities function as a filter through which the force of these background conditions pass, shaping the famine process as it unfolds. Theories explaining famine typically focus on these antecedents, whereas the process itself is a framework for detection, monitoring, and response.

10 This is not a mere repeat of Sen's well-known argument (1981). Disruption includes downturns in aggregate availability, but includes as well timing changes in the sowing and harvesting of crops and their market release, reduced demand for labour in agriculture, a lower return for animal products, and rising transaction costs for merchants (as highlighted by Devereux 1988).

11 The implication of Figure 49.1 is that people first cope and then successively lose their ability to cope, with indicators that are specific to each phase. Although such neat linearity has been challenged so far as the indicators are concerned (see, for example, Devereux 1993a), the transition itself is real, albeit often difficult to pinpoint empirically.

12 Corbett 1988, Field 1993.

13 Like the chapter as a whole, this section is conceptual. It does not examine the institutional framework of famine early warning or the processes by which detection is related to decision making and response. Buchanan-Smith and Davies 1995 provide a thorough assessment of these linkages in practice.

14 Famine early warning systems range from large data gathering and analysis enterprises, such as those managed by FAO's Global Information and Early Warning Unit and USAID's Famine Early Warning System, to various regional, national, and local monitoring efforts. See Walker 1989, Wilhite and Easterling 1987, Torry 1993, Ulrich 1993, and Cekan 1994 for examples.

15 Sen 1981 documents instances in which people have lost market access even when aggregate food availability peaked or at least did not decline. There has been some controversy about this; see, for example, Bowbrick 1986 and 1987, Sen 1986 and 1987.

16 This paragraph is adapted from Field 1993: 268.

17 McCorkle 1987 provides a compelling illustration, as do Devereux 1993a and Davies 1993.

18 von Braun *et al.* 1992: 29.

19 Migration by specific household members – young men especially – in search of alternative employment is often an early form of coping, as is early migration by pastoral nomads and pastoralists who also farm; for the latter, see Franke and Chasin 1980, Timberlake 1985, and de Waal 1989. Reference to outmigration in the text refers to terminal abandonment.

20 The problem is not so much with technical early warning *per se* as with the often tenuous relationship between detection and response. The latter pre-supposes administrative interpretation, political decision, and preparedness. See Field 1993, Chapter 11, and Buchanan-Smith and Davies 1995.

21 This observation is adapted from Field 1993: 22.

22 The most vulnerable to death in a famine are toddlers no longer protected by breast milk, the elderly, and the infirm. Most likely to survive are adults in their reproductive years, females especially because of their greater fat stores unless they are socially victimised. See Bongaarts and Cain 1982 and Young and Jaspars 1995 for the demographic patterns involved and Greenough 1982 and Vaughan 1987 for examples of female abandonment.

23 Such as Botswana; see Holm and Morgan 1985, Hay 1988, Moremi 1988, Morgan 1988, and Drèze in Drèze and Sen 1990b, Chapter 2.

24 Cutler 1986, for example, has proposed that, in drought, a fall in the livestock-to-grain price index by 50 per cent serve as a trigger for administrative response, while predicting massive distress migration on the part of herders should the index fall to 25 per cent of its predrought value. For a dramatic illustration of the shift in market prices for animals *vis-à-vis* grain, see Ulrich 1993.

25 See references in Note 23.

26 McAlpin 1983 documents considerable success in maintaining both the productivity of agricultural land and the size of livestock herds in western India, suggesting that endowments as well as exchange entitlements can be protected through early intervention. Early intervention also has profound effects on health status; see, for example, Berg 1973 regarding Bihar, and Drèze and Sen 1989: 181–2 regarding England and Wales in the context of the

First and Second World Wars.

27 Although Figure 49.1 identifies the types of intervention employed and their approximate timing in the famine process, the text to follow does not describe, much less analyse, the cases themselves. Relevant source materials are referenced for readers desiring more information.

28 This section draws heavily on Drèze's analysis of successful famine management in India, Botswana, and several other countries (in Drèze and Sen, 1990b), supplemented by other case studies (for example, Berg 1973, Moremi 1988, and Downing 1990).

29 McAlpin 1983, Drèze and Sen 1989 and 1990b.

30 As suggested in Field 1993: 257–8.

31 Drèze and Sen 1989, Cutler 1993, Field 1993, Keen 1994, Quinn 1994. This chapter does not address the political incentives and disincentives to famine response. The objective here is to highlight the possible based on actual experience, not the politics associated with earlier or later intervention.

32 Another interesting case is the guaranteed employment scheme piloted in Maharashtra and later extended to other states in India. See Ezekiel 1986 and Echeverri-Gent 1988.

33 In addition to citations already given, see Drèze and Sen 1995 for a detailed assessment of India's overall record in enhancing social well-being through public policy. Of related interest are Rudolph and Rudolph 1987 and Kohli 1987.

34 See Berg 1973 for an example on the positive side, de Waal 1989 for the opposite.

35 Drèze and Sen 1989, Field 1993.

36 This sad phenomenon is graphically described in Conquest 1986. See also Greenough 1982.

37 Examples include China in 1958–61 (Ashton *et al.* 1984, Becker 1996), Cambodia during the Khmer Rouge regime (Shawcross 1984), and Bosnia and Rwanda more recently. See also Watts 1983 regarding northern Nigeria.

38 See, for example, Minear 1991, de Waal 1993, Keen 1994, and Macrae and Zwi 1994.

39 Regarding Ethiopia in the early to mid-1970s and 1980s, see Shepherd 1975 and 1993; Gill 1986; Jansson *et al.* 1987; and Giorgis 1989. Regarding Somalia in the late 1980s and early 1990s, see Jean 1993, Clark 1993, Blumenthal 1993, and Sahnoun 1994. The Sudan qualifies on all points mentioned; see Bonner 1989, Minear 1991, Deng and Minear 1992, and Keen 1994.

40 See Field 1993, especially Chapters 1 and 11, for a discussion of these linkages. The USDA–USAID Famine Mitigation Activity Support Project is a welcome attempt to program officially for famine mitigation; see OFDA 1991a and 1991b.

REFERENCES

Ashton, B., Hill, K., Piazza, A., and Zeitz, R. (1984) 'Famine in China, 1958–61', *Population and Development Review* 10: 613–45.

Becker, J. (1996) *Hungry Ghosts: Mao's Secret Famine*, New York: The Free Press.

Berg, A. (1973) *The Nutrition Factor: Its Role in National Development*, Washington, DC: Brookings Institution, Appendix A: 211–21.

Berry, L. and Downing, T.E. (1993) 'Drought and famine in Africa, 1981–86: A comparison of impacts and responses in six countries', in J. Field (ed.), *The Challenge of Famine: Recent Experience, Lessons Learned*, West Hartford, CT: Kumarian Press, pp. 35–58.

Blumenthal, S. (1993) 'Letter from Washington: Why are we in Somalia?', *New Yorker*, 25 October, pp. 48–60.

Bohle, H.G., Cannon, T., Hugo, G., and Ibrahim, F.N. (1991) 'Famine and food security in Africa and Asia: Indigenous response and external intervention to avoid hunger', *Bayreuther Geowissenschaftliche Arbeiten* 15, Bayreuth, Germany.

Bongaarts, J. and Cain, M. (1982) 'Demographic responses to famine', in K.M. Cahill (ed.), *Famine*, Maryknoll, NY: Orbis Books, pp. 44–59.

Bonner, R. (1989) 'Famine', *New Yorker*, 13 March, pp. 85–101.

Bowbrick, P. (1986) 'The causes of famine: A refutation of Professor Sen's theory', *Food Policy* 11: 105–24.

——— (1987) 'Rejoinder: An untenable hypothesis on the causes of famine', *Food Policy* 12: 5–9.

Buchanan-Smith, M. and Davies, S. (1995) *Famine Early Warning and Response: The Missing Link*, London: Intermediate Technology Publications.

Cekan, J.M. (1994) 'Listening to one's clients: A case study of Mali's Famine Early Warning System – the Système d'Alerte Precose (SAP) – and rural producers', doctoral dissertation, The Fletcher School of Law and Diplomacy, Medford, MA.

Clark, J. (1993) 'Debacle in Somalia', *Foreign Affairs* 72: 109–23.

Clay, J.W. (1991) 'Western assistance and the Ethiopian famine: Implications for humanitarian assistance', in R.E. Downs, D.O. Kerner, and S.P. Reyna (eds), *The Political Economy of African Famine*, Philadelphia: Gordon and Breach, pp. 147–75.

Conquest, R. (1986) *The Harvest of Sorrow: Soviet Collectivization and the Terror-Famine*, New York: Oxford University Press.

Corbett J. (1988) 'Famine and household coping strategies', *World Development* 16, 9: 1,099–112.

Currey, B. (1992) 'Is famine a discrete event?', *Disasters* 16, 2: 138–44.

Cutler, P. (1986) 'The response to drought of Beja famine refugees in Sudan', *Disasters* 10, 3: 181–8.

——— (1993) 'Responses to famine: Why they are allowed

to happen', in J. Field (ed.), *The Challenge of Famine: Recent Experience, Lessons Learned*, West Hartford, CT: Kumarian Press, pp. 72–87.

Davies, S. (1993) 'Are coping strategies a cop out?', *IDS Bulletin* 24: 60–72.

Deng, F.M. and Minear, L. (1992) *The Challenges of Famine Relief: Emergency Operations in the Sudan*, Washington, DC: Brookings Institution.

Devereux, S. (1988) 'Entitlements, availability and famine: A revisionist view of Wollo, 1972–74', *Food Policy* 13: 270–82.

—— (1993a) 'Goats before ploughs: Dilemmas of household response sequencing during food shortages', *IDS Bulletin* 24: 52–9.

—— (1993b) *Theories of Famine: From Malthus to Sen*, Hemel Hempstead, UK: Harvester Wheatsheaf.

de Waal, A. (1989) *Famine That Kills: Darfur, Sudan, 1984–1985*, Oxford: Clarendon Press.

—— (1993) 'War and famine in Africa', *IDS Bulletin* 24, 4: 33–40.

Downing, T.E. (1990) 'Monitoring and responding to famine: Lessons from the 1984–85 food crisis in Kenya', *Disasters* 14, 3: 204–29.

Drèze, J. (1990) 'Famine prevention in India', in J. Drèze and A. Sen, *The Political Economy of Hunger*, Oxford: Clarendon Press, pp. 13–122.

—— (1990) 'Famine prevention in Africa: Some experiences and lessons', in J. Drèze and A. Sen, *The Political Economy of Hunger*, Oxford: Clarendon Press, pp. 123–72.

Drèze, J. and Sen, A. (1989) *Hunger and Public Action*, Oxford: Clarendon Press.

—— (1990a) *The Political Economy of Hunger*, Vol. 1, *Entitlement and Well-Being*, Oxford: Clarendon Press.

—— (1990b) *The Political Economy of Hunger*, Vol. 2, *Famine Prevention*, Oxford: Clarendon Press.

—— (1995) *India: Economic Development and Social Opportunity*, Delhi and New York: Oxford University Press.

Echeverri-Gent, J. (1988) 'Guaranteed employment in an Indian state: The Maharashtra experience', *Asian Survey* 28, 12: 1,294–310.

Ezekiel, H. (1986) *A Rural Employment Guarantee Scheme as an Early Warning System*, Washington, DC: International Food Policy Research Institute.

Field, J.O. (1993) *The Challenge of Famine: Recent Experience, Lessons Learned*, West Hartford, CT: Kumarian Press.

Franke, R.W. and Chasin, B.H. (1980) *Seeds of Famine: Ecological Destruction and the Development Dilemma in the West African Sahel*, Montclair, NJ: Allenheld, Osmun.

Gill, P. (1986) *A Year in the Death of Africa: Politics, Bureaucracy and the Famine*, London: Paladin.

Giorgis, D.W. (1989) *Red Tears: War, Famine and Revolution in Ethiopia*, Trenton, NJ: Red Sea Press.

Glantz, M.H. (1989) 'Drought, famine, and the seasons in sub-Saharan Africa', in R. Huss-Ashmore and S.H. Katz (eds), *African Food Systems in Crisis: Part One: Microperspectives*, New York: Gordon and Breach, pp. 45–71.

Greenough, P.R. (1982) *Prosperity and Misery in Modern Bengal: The Famine of 1943–1944*, Oxford and New York: Oxford University Press.

Hay, R.W. (1988) 'Famine incomes and employment: Has Botswana anything to teach Africa?', *World Development* 16, 9: 1,113–25.

Helman, G.B. and Ratner, S.R. (1992–3) 'Saving failed states', *Foreign Policy* 89: 3–20.

Holm, J.D. and Morgan, R.G. (1985) 'Coping with drought in Botswana: An African success', *Journal of Modern African Studies* 23, 3: 463–82.

Jansson, K., Harris, M., and Penrose, A. (1987) *The Ethiopian Famine*, London: Zed Books.

Jean, F. (1993) 'Somalia: Humanitarian aid outgunned', in F. Jean (ed.), *Life, Death and Aid: The Médecins Sans Frontières Report on World Crisis Intervention*, London and New York: Routledge, pp. 99–107.

Keen, D. (1994) *The Benefits of Famine: A Political Economy of Famine and Relief in Southwestern Sudan, 1983–1989*, Princeton, NJ: Princeton University Press.

Kohli, A. (1987) *The State and Poverty in India: The Politics of Reform*, Cambridge and New York: Cambridge University Press

Macrae, J. and Zwi, A. (1994) War and Hunger: *Rethinking International Responses to Complex Emergencies*, London: Zed Books.

McAlpin, M.B. (1983) *Subject to Famine: Food Crises and Economic Change in Western India, 1860–1920*, Princeton, NJ: Princeton University Press.

McCorkle, C.M. (1987) 'Foodgrain disposals as early warning famine signals: A case from Burkina Faso', *Disasters* 11, 4: 273–81.

Minear, L. (1991) *Humanitarianism under Siege: A Critical Review of Operation Lifeline Sudan*, Trenton, NJ: Red Sea Press.

Moremi, T.C. (1988) 'Transition from emergency to development assistance: Botswana experience', paper presented at the WHO/ACC/SCN Conference on Nutrition in Times of Disasters, World Health Organization, 27–30 September, Geneva.

Morgan, R. (1988) 'Drought-relief programmes in Botswana', in D. Curtis, M. Hubbard, and A. Shepherd (eds), *Preventing Famine: Policies and Prospects for Africa*, London and New York: Routledge, pp. 112–20.

Office of US Foreign Disaster Assistance, Agency for International Development (OFDA) (1991a) 'Concept paper: Famine mitigation activity', 30 September, mimeo, Washington, DC.

—— (1991b) 'On the design of efficient famine-mitigation policies', 20 June, mimeo, Washington, DC.

Quinn, V.J. (1994) *Nutrition and National Development:*

An Evaluation of Nutrition Planning in Malawi from 1936–1990, The Hague: CIP-Data Koninkluke Bibliotheek.

Ravallion, M. (1987) *Markets and Famines*, Oxford: Clarendon Press,.

Rudolph, L.I. and Rudolph, S.H. (1987) *In Pursuit of Lakshmi: The Political Economy of the Indian State*, Chicago and London: The University of Chicago Press.

Sahnoun, M. (1994) *Somalia: The Missed Opportunities*, Washington, DC: United States Institute of Peace Press.

Sen, A. (1981) *Poverty and Famines: An Essay on Entitlement and Deprivation*, Oxford: Clarendon Press.

—— (1986) 'The causes of famine: A reply', *Food Policy* 11: 125–32.

—— (1987) 'Reply: "Famine and Mr. Bowbrick"', *Food Policy* 12: 10–4.

Shawcross, W. (1984) *The Quality of Mercy: Cambodia, Holocaust and Modern Conscience*, New York: Simon and Schuster.

Shepherd, J. (1975) *The Politics of Starvation*, New York and Washington, DC: Carnegie Endowment for International Peace.

—— (1993) '"Some tragic errors:" American policy and the Ethiopian famine. 1981–85', in J. Field (ed.), *The Challenge of Famine: Recent Experience, Lessons Learned*, Kumarian Press, West Hartford, CT: pp. 88–125.

Timberlake, L. (1985) *Africa in Crisis: The Causes, the Cures of Environmental Bankruptcy*, London: Earthscan.

Torry, W.I. (1993) 'Information for food: Community famine surveillance in Sudan', in J. Field (ed.), *The Challenge of Famine: Recent Experience, Lessons Learned*, West Hartford, CT: Kumarian Press, pp. 209–38.

Ulrich, P. (1993) 'Using market prices as a guide to predict, prevent, or mitigate famine in pastoral economies', in J. Field (ed.), *The Challenge of Famine: Recent Experience, Lessons Learned*, West Hartford, CT: Kumarian Press, pp. 239–52.

Vaughan, M. (1987) *The Story of an African Famine: Gender and Famine in Twentieth-Century Malawi*, Cambridge: Cambridge University Press.

von Braun, J., Bouis, H., Kumar, S., and Pandya-Lorch, R. (1992) *Improving Food Security of the Poor: Concept, Policy, and Programs*, Washington, DC: International Food Policy Research Institute.

Walker, P. (1989) *Famine Early Warning Systems: Victims and Destitution*, London: Earthscan.

Watts, M. (1983) *Silent Violence: Food, Famine and Peasantry in Northern Nigeria*, Berkeley, CA: University of California Press.

Wilhite, D.A. and Easterling, W.E. (1987) *Planning for Drought: Toward a Reduction of Societal Vulnerability*, Boulder, CO: Westview Press.

Young, H. and Jaspars, S. (1995) 'Nutrition, disease, and death in times of famine', *Disasters* 19, 2: 94–109.

50

DROUGHT FOLLOWS THE PLOUGH

A cautionary note

Michael H. Glantz

There is a good chance that future generations will look back at the 1970s and 1980s as the beginning of the 'Age of Environmental Enlightenment'. In those decades, worldwide interest in the environment greatly increased, an interest based on a large number of environmental changes increasingly perceived by the public as regional and global threats. An environmental change viewed as a global threat is one that is global in cause, effect, or interest.

During the 1970s, environmental topics such as desertification, water resources, technology transfer, energy needs, food production, population increases, human settlements, and the human environment were of concern to the United Nations General Assembly. In fact, UN-sponsored international conferences on these topics were held during this decade. In the 1980s, the focus of concern shifted to such global issues as ozone depletion, climate change, tropical deforestation, and biodiversity. These issues have since become the focal points of a wide-ranging global change research agenda. In 1987, the ozone depletion issue was seriously addressed by political leaders around the world with the signing of the Montreal Protocol (Benedick 1991). Also in that year, the World Commission on Environment and Development (WCED) issued its report on sustainable development, entitled *Our Common Future* (WCED 1987).

A few years later, rich and poor nations around the globe had to deal with each other on environment and development issues at the United Nations Conference on Environment and Development (UNCED), held in Rio de Janeiro in June 1992. At this Earth Summit, a climate treaty was signed, as were treaties on biodiversity and forest protection.

It seems that governments are beginning to listen to their citizens' pleas to protect the earth. Nations with different and often conflicting interests have been prompted into cooperative action on regional and global scales to address, if not resolve, some of those problems perceived by their citizens to be most important to them.

The collapse of communism in the late 1980s and early 1990s added to pressures on governments everywhere by allowing the world to see how poorly the environment had been treated throughout the former Soviet Union and eastern Europe. Shocking photos of children going to school in gas masks to avoid noxious fumes from polluting industrial plants were matched by horror stories about the aftermath of the Chernobyl nuclear disaster (Glantz and Zonn 1997) or about the adverse health and ecological effects of decades of cotton production in the Aral Basin in Central Asia (Glantz 1998).

Opinion surveys involving people on the street as well as policy makers and scientists in their offices support the contention that environmental degradation is on the minds of many. The media, too, have become increasingly aggressive in their coverage of major global as well as local environmental issues.

It seems as if the interest, if not the will, is there to do something about improving the quality of life by improving the quality of the environment. Some problems considered to be globally threatening are being addressed front and centre, such as ozone depletion. Following the belated 'discovery' of the Antarctic ozone hole, the possibility of stratospheric ozone depletion over the Arctic region, and the linkage of ozone layer depletion with a heightened risk of skin cancer in the midlatitudes of the Northern Hemisphere, governments responded with an international protocol to end the use of chlorofluoro-carbons (CFCs) in the next several years. Societies have also come to realise that many of today's environmental problems will likely be with us throughout the next century. For example, ozone-eating CFCs have a long residence time in the stratosphere (60–100 years), even if their usage were ended today.

The 1980s also witnessed a sharp increase in national and international political concern about the possible implications of a global warming of the atmosphere. Many scientific reports, journal papers, and popular articles on all sides of the issue have appeared on the scene, highlighting global warming as a potential threat to the well-being of the global community. Scenarios generated by general circulation models of the atmosphere suggest that such a global climate change could bring about serious but yet-to-be-identified shifts in climate regimes at the regional level (Houghton *et al.* 1996). However, a considerable number of uncertainties continue to cloud the global warming issue: the rate of temperature change; the ability of human societies and ecosystems to adjust to those rates of change; cloud feedback mechanisms that could reverse the warming trend; the possibility that the anthropogenic enhancement of global warming is countering a natural movement toward an ice age; the level of reliability of scenarios generated by general circulation models of the atmosphere for policy making; and global warming implications for changes in the frequency, intensity, and duration of extreme meteorological events such as droughts, floods, and frosts.

The climate change issue has also drawn attention to the obvious as well as the subtle interactions between poverty of the environment and the environment of poverty. Calls to protect the quality of the earth's atmosphere and, more generally, the earth's environment for future generations to enjoy has raised ethical questions about what we are doing in this regard for those few generations of people alive today (Partridge 1981). In other words, concern about intergenerational equity issues has led to renewed calls for intragenerational equity. How to break this vicious downward spiral of the quality of life and environment at the regional and local level is a key concern.

Nevertheless, although there may be no overwhelming consensus as of today on various aspects of the scientific theories concerning the global warming issue (other than agreement that human activities are adding increasing amounts of greenhouse gases to the atmosphere [especially CO_2] and that such gases can in theory generate a greenhouse effect), there is certainly enough evidence to alarm the global community into realising that precautionary action is warranted. Such action can take many forms. One popular political action is to call for more research to reduce scientific uncertainties (for example, will the warming increase evaporation, which will increase the amount of cloud cover, which will lead in turn to a cooling of the atmosphere?). Another approach is to make decisions to prevent or at least slow down increases in the rate of emissions of greenhouse gases. In fact, there have been numerous suggestions about how to cope with the issue of a greenhouse-gases-induced global warming.

With regard to the call for more research, the scientific community has for some years focused on early detection of global warming. Climate varies seasonally and interannually, and on decadal and longer time scales. Depending on the particular geographic region of concern on the earth's surface, climate variability can range from small to large. Precipitation in arid areas, for example, is skewed to dryness, with a few rainfall episodes that are far above average being balanced out by a larger number of below-average rainfall events; conditions that are statistically average seldom occur. In such regions, rainfall variability is high, making it very difficult to identify a climate change 'signal' in the midst of climate variability 'noise'.

One attempt among several at the early detection of climate change has been to look at a change in the frequency or intensity of extreme meteorological events. Drought and floods, as major extreme natural hazards, have been singled out as possible indicators of changing climate. In the mid-1970s, increases in the number of meteorological stations in India reporting drought were suggested as an early indicator of the regional impacts of a global climate change (at that time scientists focused on the possibility of a global cooling) (Bryson and Murray 1977).

Today many researchers speculate that with global warming of the atmosphere there will likely be an increase in drought-related crop failures in areas already subject to drought. They contend that dry areas will get drier and wet areas wetter. Yet, observations show that people are moving into regions that are relatively less fruitful with respect to agricultural productivity than the lands from which they emigrated. The assumption here is that much of the best rain-fed agricultural land (where agriculture is directly dependent on rainfall) has already been put into production, and that by the movement of farmers into relatively less productive regions, the risk of crop failure would likely increase. This would especially be the case if the same crops that these migrants had grown in the more productive agricultural areas continue to be grown in the marginal areas. In addition, major alterations in the vegetative cover in marginal areas could change regional rainfall patterns as a result of changes, for example, in land-surface properties such as albedo (land surface reflectivity). Thus, we are likely to hear more about crop failures in the future because of human impacts on these fragile environments, whether or not the global climate changes.

The notion that 'drought follows the plough' draws attention to the land-use changes that are taking place – for the worse. Although this notion originally focused on the drier regions of the globe, similar processes can occur in the high rainfall areas as well. Inappropriate land use can reduce agricultural productivity for a variety of reasons and can increase the risk of agricultural and hydrological droughts and associated food shortages. Human activities in different societies around the globe may possibly confound our ability to correctly detect the onset of the projected global warming and its earliest societal and ecological impacts.

The notion that drought might follow the plough also underscores a problem with regard to the early detection of or perceptions about global warming. If the notion proves to be a valid one, it will no longer be a matter, for example, of counting the number of weather stations reporting meteorological droughts or crop monitoring stations reporting agricultural droughts in a given area to determine if the frequency or intensity of extreme events has increased (a pro-

posed sign of climate change). Droughts measured in terms of a decline in crop production or an outright crop failure will have to be carefully scrutinised to correctly identify their cause. Such scientific scrutiny will enable researchers and policy makers to determine which drought impacts might be blamed on physical processes and which might be blamed on socioeconomic factors.

The notion that 'drought follows the plough' was first presented some years ago at an international conference on climate forecasting held in Fortaleza, the capital of the northeastern Brazilian state of Ceará. Following that presentation, a Brazilian economist commented that a similar process of land use was already under way in his country. Researchers from other disciplines and other countries responded similarly to the notion. Each had a similar story to tell about land use in his or her country.

It was almost a century ago that the belief that 'rain follows the plough' was a popular one that accelerated population movements into the region now known as the American Great Plains (Webb 1931). Until the mid-1800s, this region was considered a wasteland, useless for agriculture and human settlement, an inhospitable obstacle to settlers in search of the promised land in the western part of the North American continent.

At the same time that settlements crept westward after the Civil War in the 1860s, rainfall became more prevalent. Suddenly, what had previously been considered a barren waste was seen as a potential garden and a breadbasket for the eastern part of the country. Many attributed the increased rainfall to the effects of human settlement activities, which included ploughing fields, creating ponds, irrigating dry areas, and planting trees on what essentially had been a treeless grassland. The railroad companies and land speculators seized on this explanation to convince easterners to move to the Midwest. The advertising campaigns successfully produced waves of immigrants who came to the sparsely populated plains seeking their fortunes.

During the 1890s, a severe multiyear drought dispelled the 'rain follows the plough' theory. Thousands of settlers abandoned their homesteads to seek livelihoods elsewhere. It seemed that much of the support for the assumption of a causal relationship between rain and population was simply exaggeration by the railroads and other land speculators, intent on selling land at higher prices than it was worth. Before long, people realised that dry and wet periods commonly alternated and that the region's first surge of settlers had accidentally coincided with the onset of a lengthy wet spell. With the return of a prolonged drought, the credibility surrounding the 'rain follows the plough' theory itself evaporated.

The scientific reasoning behind the belief is that a region's atmospheric circulation is positively affected by increased sources of evaporation. These sources derive from breaking the ground with the plough, creating open bodies of water (ponds and tanks), and planting trees whose roots suck the scarce moisture form the ground and whose leaves allow the water to evaporate into the atmosphere, which ultimately returns the moisture as rain.

Today the scientific literature is still filled with articles and studies on how land use has either brought about or eliminated rainfall in a region (Anthes 1984). The belief in the 'rain follows the plough' concept still lives, although the number of its supporters appears to be small. The latest resurgence of interest in this idea resulted from an apparent seventeen-year drought that began in 1968 in the west African Sahel. It was then argued that the reverse process, the removal of vegetation, could create a desertlike environment (Charney 1974). The overgrazing by livestock on vegetation and the collecting of firewood as the only available fuel ensured these conditions in the Sahel. Responding to the plough–rain theory, the United Nations and ALESCO (the Arab League Economic, Scientific and Cultural Organization) suggested that tree belts be built along the northern and southern edges of the Sahara Desert to arrest its encroachment, put moisture back into the air, and bring rainfall to desiccated areas.

It is my contention, however, that as agriculture moves into increasingly marginal areas, drought, not rain, is following the plough. Most of the world's best rain-fed agricultural land is already in production or unavailable to production for political or other reasons. Increasing the amount of land for agricultural use requires the destruction of forests, the use of irrigation in arid areas, or the movement of people into marginal agricultural areas.

Recall that only thirty years ago, Nikita Khrushchev, then head of the Communist Party of the Soviet Union, launched his virgin lands scheme in an attempt to surpass US grain production (Zonn *et al.* 1994: reprinted in Chapter 27 in Volume I of this work). The scheme's success would have demonstrated to the developing world that the USSR was as much an agricultural force as an industrial power.

The plan 'encouraged' people to move into Soviet Central Asia and Kazakstan and put arid and semiarid land under mechanised agricultural production. Soon stories of the failure of this approach reached the press, as people began leaving the virgin areas to return home. Drought conditions plagued the virgin lands areas, and since that time, rain-fed agriculture has been supplanted by irrigation farming. The architects of the virgin lands strategy failed to take seriously the marginality of the climate for sustained production; they paid for it at the time, with political humiliation in the economic development community. In fact, Leonid Brezhnev (1979) was intimately involved in the scheme's implementation and later wrote a book about the problems encountered in the virgin lands areas.

The cases presented in the following pages were selected to present examples of an effective, reliable, and credible argument about the likelihood that a process of 'drought following the plough' could become a more frequent and widespread occurrence in future decades. This would occur because of a variety of irrefutable, measurable, ongoing demographic changes, such as high population growth rates in developing areas (within industrialised as well as industrialising countries) and increases in the demand for land to produce basic food stuffs as well as for intensified cash crop production. Such regional and local assessments will enable those researchers searching for regional signals of a global climate change to appropriately attribute to human factors or to climate change any unusual changes in the frequency, distribution, magnitude, and timing of droughts. A more realistic attribution would allow policy makers to better match drought problems and their causes with appropriate solutions to prevent, mitigate, or adapt to drought's consequences.

THE WEST AFRICAN SAHEL (Glantz 1994)

The 1950s and 1960s were relatively wet across the west African Sahel. During this period the increased rainfall encouraged cultivators to move farther north toward the southern edge of the Sahara. The areas that they came to occupy, often with the encouragement of their governments, had traditionally been used as range lands for livestock herds of pastoralists. Annoyed and harassed by these new settlers, the pastoralists shifted their herding activities farther north. With the increased regional rainfall, more vegetation was now available farther north, so the pastoralists had what appeared to be equally good conditions. During this wet period, herds grew larger and required more range lands and watering points. The new technology of drilling deep wells opened up even more land as seasonal pastures became usable with the availability of permanent sources of water. As the wet period continued, more and more cultivators came to the region and began clearing the land for cultivation.

In 1968, an extended drought began, which some argue lasted more than seventeen years. The first intense drought episode lasted from 1968 to 1973, claiming about 100,000 human lives and 12.5 million livestock. With the failure of the rains to move far north into the Sahelian zone, pastoralists and their herds became stranded at the deep wells. The cattle eventually consumed all edible vegetation near the well. As a result, experts have suggested that most of the livestock that died during the drought perished from hunger, not from thirst.

When the drought wiped out their herds, many pastoralists went into refugee camps. Governments then sought to convert them to farming so that their contribution to the national economy could be encouraged and their production taxed. As pastoralists, they were perceived by their governments as independent, and thus a threat to the central governments. Moreover, they were hard to tax and only reluctantly participated in the modern sector of the economy.

It was in the west African Sahel that the image of the deserts on the march was first formulated. Speculation abounded that the region's climate was indeed changing. Rumours suggested that the desert's rate of advance was up to 50 km a year. Closer investigation showed that the overgrazing of the southern edge of the Sahara during the wet period and the cultivation of areas deemed to be only marginally arable had created patches of desertlike conditions and caused sand dunes to form. With little vegetative cover, the dunes encroached on settlements.

In some of the regions where the government had encouraged cultivation, farmers planted grains and resorted to farming practices that did not anticipate the long-term climatic conditions. When the drought recurred, as the region's rainfall history suggested it should, the farmers believed they were the victims of a natural disaster. Instead, they were victims of poor planning and a lack of understanding of the region's climatic record. After all, the 1968 drought was the third major one this century. Clearly, what had happened was that drought followed the plough in the west African Sahel.

BRAZIL (Magalhães and Magee 1994)

The plight of the inhabitants of the drought-plagued Brazilian Nordeste (northeast) has inspired many classic Brazilian novels, such as deCunha's *Rebellion in the Backlands*. Current patterns of landownership and land use were established hundreds of years ago during Brazil's colonial period. Cattle ranching along the coast was supplanted by sugar cane production, forcing ranchers farther inland into the heart of the semiarid *sertão*.

Landownership in the Nordeste is a key factor in the ability of different segments of society to cope with severe drought. There are basically two types of ownership in the region: large estates and small subsistence landholdings. Estates are extremely large, sometimes encompassing a few hundred thousand square miles. In contrast, the poor are restricted to the marginal areas of this semiarid region for subsistence food production and ranching. The scarcity of productive land is primarily a socioeconomic phenomenon; 60 per cent of the population holds less than 10 ha of land and 3 per cent own about 70 per cent of the land.

Subsistence farming takes place on small landholdings or on land leased to poor farmers on the large estates. Even during years of good rainfall, the small farmer population is in danger because of low agricultural productivity. The growth of the population and livestock herds in the region has forced farmers into increasingly marginal areas and has heightened the region's dependence on food produced on these lands. The soils and existing vegetation in these areas have thus become extremely vulnerable to climatic variability, explaining their persistently low and ever-declining levels of productivity.

The region is known to be plagued by recurrent short-term drought, as well as devastating multiyear dry spells. The poor farmers are the first to be hurt by drought, since they barely grow enough food for their own consumption. They must also find work to supplement their income, which they often do by working on the large estates as labourers. During extreme drought, however, the *latifundistas* (large landowners) lay off their workers as a temporary cost-saving measure, making the workers' plight even worse. Although the federal and state governments implement work programmes to construct roads and dams for minimal wages, many men abandon their homes in search of work in other parts of Brazil.

The basic problem in the Nordeste appears to be one of landownership: an expanding population trying to sustain itself on a dwindling resource base. More and more, we hear about the frequency and intensity of droughts and, correlatively, about the prospects of a changing climate. The question remains open, however: Are we not witnessing the effects of a change in land use rather than in the climate, a situation in which drought once again has followed the plough?

AUSTRALIA (Heathcote 1994)

Australia has a long history of drought. In 1982–3, it witnessed its worst drought in more than one hundred years, with property and other losses estimated in the hundreds of millions of dollars. Brush fires were rampant, consuming homes as well as vegetation. One might wonder why a developed country like Australia is still so vulnerable to the impacts of drought.

Since the onset of European settlement in south-eastern Australia, regional industry has shifted from sheep ranching to growing cereals and dairying. These early changes in land use, often driven by market demands and prices, began a process of climatic vulnerability, which advanced with the settlement movement from the humid southern and eastern coasts toward the semiarid and arid interior. In other words, human settlements were working their way down the rainfall gradients to regions where the climate was only barely supportive. Population pressures mounted to put range lands under the plough. As the wheat farmers moved down the rainfall gradient, they encountered increasing likelihood of drought. The influx of farmers was eventually reversed, as many abandoned their land when the intermittent dry conditions, characteristic of the region, returned.

Although government programmes, which bought out farmers on the edge of bankruptcy, alleviated some of the pressures on the land, new technologies encouraged the farmers to plant wheat. This reliance on wheat production further increased their vulnerability in a region known to be drought-prone.

The severity of drought-induced crises in New South Wales can be attributed to the fact that farmers have moved into such a region and have thus put themselves at risk. The same is true for livestock owners who overstock their ranges and make themselves equally vulnerable.

A variable climate in that area caused prospective farmers to believe the climate had changed in favour of sustained agricultural or livestock production. Once drawn there, however, they were surprised by what they should have expected: a return to drier conditions. Yet, invariably, wet periods in the arid and semiarid interior of New South Wales have lulled people into a false sense of security, and when drought returns, farmers believe themselves to be the victims of a natural disaster.

CONCLUSIONS

The attempt to cultivate borderlands tends to marginalise both land and people. Most often, either a push or a pull into these areas initiates the process. Push factors include population pressure, environmental degradation, and government policies. As populations continue to grow in Third World countries, and especially in sub-Saharan Africa, the natural per capita resource base decreases. If the best land is already in production, new farmers must move into previously farmed areas, which become further impoverished by overuse and misuse. Clearly, future generations will find it more and more difficult to support themselves from the land.

The pull factors are relatively few. As mentioned earlier, climates fluctuate, sometimes with long wet or dry spells alternating. During wet periods in arid and semiarid areas, the normally dry areas appear to be capable of sustaining agricultural production. Thus encouraged to move there, farmers often displace herders who have traditionally used these areas as range lands.

The 'drought follows the plough' idea is based on the belief that increased pressures on currently used agricultural areas cause population movement into less productive, often marginal, areas. Consequently, we can expect to hear more in the future than we have in the past about droughts and their impacts on humankind.

REFERENCES

Anthes, R.A. (1984) 'Enhancement of convective precipitation by mesoscale variations in vegetative covering in semiarid regions', *Journal of Climate and Applied Meteorology* 23: 541–54.

Benedick, R.E. (1991) *Ozone Diplomacy: New Directions for Safeguarding the Planet*, Cambridge, MA: Harvard University Press.

Brezhnev, L. (1979) *The Virgin Lands*, Moscow: Progress Publishers.

Bryson, R. and Murray T.J. (1977) *Climates of Hunger*, Madison, WI: University of Wisconsin Press.

Charney, J.G. (1974) 'Dynamics of desert and drought in the Sahel', Symons Lecture delivered to the Royal Meteorological Society, London, 20 March, mimeo.

Glantz, M.H. (ed.) (1998) *Creeping Environmental Problems and Sustainable Development in the Aral Sea Basin*, Cambridge: Cambridge University Press.

Glantz, M.H. (1994) 'The West African Sahel', in M.H. Glantz (ed.), *Drought Follows the Plow: Cultivating Marginal Areas*, Cambridge: Cambridge University Press, pp. 33–43.

Glantz, M.H. and Zonn, I.S. (1997) 'Lessons from the rising Caspian', *The World and I*, August, pp. 174–9.

Heathcote, R.L. (1994) 'Australia', in M.H. Glantz (ed.), *Drought Follows the Plow: Cultivating Marginal Areas*, Cambridge: Cambridge University Press, pp. 91–102.

Houghton, J.T., Meira Filho, L.G., Callander, B.A., Harris, N., Kattenberg, A., and Maskell, K. (eds) (1996) 'Climate Change 1995: The Science of Climate Change', Contribution of Working Group I to the *Second Assessment Report of the Intergovernmental Panel on Climate Change*, Cambridge: Cambridge University Press.

Magalhães, A., and Magee, P. (1994) 'The Brazilian Nordeste (Northeast)', in M.H. Glantz (ed.), *Drought Follows the Plow: Cultivating Marginal Areas*, Cambridge: Cambridge University Press, pp. 59–76.

Partridge, E. (ed.) (1981) *Responsibilities to Future Generations: Environmental Ethics*, Buffalo, NY: Prometheus Books.

WCED (World Commission on Environment and Development) (1987) *Our Common Future*, New York: Oxford University Press.

Webb, W.P. (1931) *The Great Plains*, New York: Grossett and Dunlap Publishers.

Zonn, I.S., Glantz, M.H., and Rubinstein, A. (1994) 'The Virgin Lands Scheme in the former Soviet Union', in M.H. Glantz (ed.), *Drought Follows the Plow: Cultivating Marginal Areas*, Cambridge: Cambridge University Press, pp. 135–50.

PART VIII

CONCLUSIONS AND FUTURE CHALLENGES

51

REDUCING SOCIETAL VULNERABILITY TO DROUGHT

Future challenges

Donald A. Wilhite

INTRODUCTION

The preceding chapters have provided a comprehensive treatment of drought from many disciplinary perspectives, in the context of many economic, social, political, and geographical settings. Although it would be an insurmountable task to synthesise this information in one chapter, it is important is to distill some of the more salient points from previous chapters. The intent of this chapter is to reiterate some of the principal features of drought and the challenges that lie before us in the twenty-first century if we are to make progress in reducing societal vulnerability to drought.

Drought, like many other fields of scientific inquiry, is extremely complex. A full understanding of all aspects of the issue is beyond the grasp of any one scientist. Likewise, addressing the myriad of problems associated with drought is beyond the scope of a single discipline. It requires collaboration between many physical and social scientists to advance our understanding of this phenomenon. Scientists and policy makers must also interact to build awareness and understanding of the issues associated with improved drought management.

IS DROUGHT A NATURAL HAZARD?

One of the primary frustrations that I have experienced over the years is the lack of inclusion of drought as a natural hazard by scientists and emergency managers working in the field of natural hazard management. At times, drought is not totally excluded but is given only token recognition. This lack of recognition of the importance of drought by the natural hazards community has been an impediment to obtaining adequate research support and, in many instances, an obstacle to building awareness among policy makers at the local, national, regional, and international level. This lack of awareness has resulted in an underappreciation of drought and its far-reaching impacts, and it has perpetuated the process of dealing with drought in a crisis management mode when the knowledge and technology necessary to improve preparedness and mitigate impacts is readily available.

US comedian Rodney Dangerfield is well known for the line 'I don't get no respect'. He then proves his point by recounting situations in which he gets no respect. I often consider drought to be the Rodney Dangerfield of natural hazards. It is often ignored because it differs from other natural hazards. These differences include its slow onset and insidious nature, duration, lack of structural impacts, relatively small loss of human life, and spatial coverage. What is important is the recognition that drought produces impacts equal to or exceeding those associated with floods, earthquakes, and hurricanes. These impacts are often more difficult to quantify, but they should not be disregarded in national or global efforts to develop a plan of action to reduce vulnerabilities. Drought is a natural hazard, too.

WHAT ARE THE CHARACTERISTICS OF DROUGHT?

Regardless of geographic setting, many of the authors in these volumes pointed out that drought is a normal part of the climate. The geographical coverage provided by the case studies in this book reinforces the fact that drought occurs in virtually all regions of the world. It is erroneous to consider drought as a problem of subhumid, semiarid, and arid regions alone. Because of its insidious nature, it is difficult to determine its onset, development, and end. This fact emphasises the importance of developing comprehensive monitoring or early warning systems that track all of the essential elements of the hydrologic system for drought-prone regions. Satellite-derived data is also proving to be of significant value in drought monitoring. Use of appropriate and reliable drought indices is critical in summarising many of these elements for decision makers at many levels. Drought predictions, while still imprecise for many regions, are improving and can be an important tool in anticipating drought occurrence and implementing timely and effective strategies well in advance of dry conditions. These forecasts are particularly useful if they are provided a season or more in advance. Our improved understanding of the ENSO phenomenon is greatly enhancing our ability to provide seasonal forecasts for many regions.

CAN WE DEFINE DROUGHT?

Scientists, natural resource managers, and other decision makers continue the search for a universal definition of drought. It is apparent from the numerous case studies included in this volume that the search for a universal definition of drought is a fruitless endeavour. Characterisations of drought must vary by disciplinary perspective, region, economic sector, and application. Although all types of drought originate with a deficiency of precipitation over an extended period of time (i.e., meteorological drought), other types of drought (e.g., agricultural, hydrologic) are associated with deficiencies in other components of the hydrologic system (e.g., soil moisture, reservoir and lake levels, groundwater levels, streamflow, and snowpack). Even within sectors (e.g., agriculture), definitions of drought will vary according to application. For example, crops respond differently to precipitation shortages depending on the timing of the deficiency and other factors. The causes and characteristics of drought also vary according to

climatic regime. Therefore, definitions of drought must be regionally specific.

Four elements are important to include in the construct of a useful definition of drought. First, definitions must include some measure of intensity or the magnitude of the precipitation deficiency. Second, duration is an important distinguishing feature of drought (in comparison to other natural hazards) and must be linked to intensity to determine the severity of the event. Third, a threshold should be selected as a reference point to determine the onset of drought. Fourth, the threshold chosen should be linked to specific impacts in one or more sectors. Thresholds typically have been chosen arbitrarily and, as a result, have not captured the importance of this linkage to impacts in one or more sectors. This factor has limited the usefulness of definitions in triggering specific response or mitigation programmes.

DROUGHT: NATURAL OR SOCIAL PHENOMENON?

It is clear that some of the misunderstanding about drought and society's capacity to mitigate its effects is the direct result of the fact that many people consider drought to be purely a physical phenomenon. We may ask, if drought is a natural event, what control do we have over its occurrence and the impacts that result? Drought results from a deficiency of precipitation over an extended period of time. This precipitation deficiency is a natural event. The frequency or probability of occurrence of these deficiencies varies spatially and represents a location's exposure to the occurrence of drought. Some regions have greater exposure than others, and we do not have the capacity to alter that exposure.

As with other natural hazards, drought has both a physical and a social component. It is the social factors, in combination with our exposure, that determines societal vulnerability. Some of the social factors that determine our vulnerability are level of development, population growth and its changing distribution, demographic characteristics, demands on water and other natural resources, government policies (sustainable versus nonsustainable), technological changes, social behaviour, and trends in environmental awareness and concerns. It is obvious that well-conceived policies, preparedness plans, and mitigation programmes can greatly reduce vulnerability to drought.

WHAT DO WE KNOW ABOUT THE IMPACTS OF DROUGHT?

The impacts of drought are usually classified by type as economic, social, or environmental. Traditionally, greater emphasis has been placed on identifying and quantifying the economic impacts associated with drought, particularly those associated with agriculture. Agriculture is usually the first sector affected and, as a result, these impacts are better understood and more easily quantified. We are becoming more aware of the impacts of drought on other economic sectors such as energy, transportation, water supply, recreation, and tourism, as well as on the development process. However, greater attention must to be directed to these areas. Likewise, social and environmental impacts are not well understood and are difficult to quantify.

It is clear that the impacts of drought are considerable and differ remarkably between developing and developed countries. Early warning systems, preparedness plans, and mitigation programmes must reflect these differences to be effective.

WILL PREPAREDNESS PLANS AND MITIGATION PROGRAMMES REDUCE FUTURE VULNERABILITY?

The information available on the impacts associated with drought is at times sketchy but still illustrates an escalating trend of losses in both developing and developed countries. Factors contributing to this escalation of impacts were discussed previously and do not differ substantially from the causes for escalating impacts for other natural hazards. In the 1990s, for example, the total losses from natural disasters is estimated at US$400 billion. This is up from losses of US$40 billion in the 1960s. Losses attributable to natural disasters in the United States averaged more than US$54 billion per year between 1992 and 1996, or about US$1 billion per week (Natural Disaster Reduction Research Initiative 1997). Losses of this magnitude are unacceptable, and a global collaborative effort is necessary to reduce these losses to more reasonable levels. Although the International Decade for Natural Disaster Reduction (IDNDR) has had a goal of reducing property loss and loss of life, a very small percentage of this effort has been directed specifically to drought.

It is clear that investments in preparedness and mitigation will pay large dividends in reducing the impacts of drought. A growing number of countries are realising the potential advantages of drought planning. Governments are formulating policies and plans that address many of the deficiencies noted from previous response efforts – efforts that were largely reactive. Most of the progress made in drought preparedness and mitigation has been accomplished in the past decade or so. Although the road ahead will be difficult and the learning curve steep, the potential rewards are numerous. The crisis management approach of responding to drought has existed for many decades and is ingrained in our culture. The victims of drought have become accustomed to government assistance programmes. In many instances, these misguided and misdirected government programmes and policies have promoted the nonsustainable use of natural resources. Many governments have now come to realise that drought response in the form of emergency assistance programmes only reinforces poor or nonsustainable actions.

Policies that encourage self-reliance and the sustainable use of natural resources will be more effective in the long term and will reduce the need for government intervention. A challenge for the future is to identify and quantify the sectors and peoples at risk from drought. Once this step is completed, policies, plans, and mitigation programmes can be formulated to address these vulnerabilities in a systematic manner.

WILL GLOBAL WARMING EXACERBATE DROUGHT AND ITS IMPACTS?

One of the conclusions of the Intergovernmental Panel on Climate Change (Houghton *et al.* 1996) is that the warmer temperatures expected with global warming will lead to a more vigorous hydrologic cycle. This change in the hydrologic cycle may lead to more severe droughts for some places and less severe droughts for others. Our skill at projecting which regions may have more severe droughts is not very precise at the moment. Certainly, increasing temperatures will increase evaporation and transpiration and the number of extremely hot days. These changes in conjunction with potential changes in the amount, seasonal distribution, and form of precipitation may result in substantial changes in regional hydrology. It is likely that the frequency of drought and the magnitude and types of impacts that result will be altered. Those nations that adopt preparedness plans in the near term will be better able to respond to longer-term changes in climate, if they occur. Even if the frequency and intensity of drought does not increase, nations that adopt drought policies and plans now that promote risk management and self-reliance will be able to deal more effectively with continuing climate variability and drought, a normal part of climate for virtually all regions.

SUMMARY

Collectively, the chapters in this book provide an abundance of information on the characteristics and impacts of drought, as well as the lessons learned in previous response efforts. Policies, plans, and mitigation measures that have been effective (and ineffective in some cases) have been discussed in the context of many geographical settings and from many disciplinary perspectives. As I reviewed each of these chapters, I was impressed time and time again by the magnitude and complexity of the economic losses, social costs, and environmental damage that results from drought; the difficult task of developing and implementing preparedness plans and mitigative actions; and the progress that has been made in reducing the number of people and systems at risk from extended periods of water shortage. Continuing that progress is the challenge before us.

REFERENCES

Houghton, J.T., Meira Filho, L.G., Callander, B.A., Harris, N., Kattenberg, A., and Maskell, K. (1996) *Climate Change 1995: The Science of Climate Change*, Contribution of Working Group I to the Second Assessment Report of the Intergovernmental Panel on Climate Change, New York: Cambridge University Press.

Natural Disaster Reduction Research Initiative (1997) Fact Sheet, Office of Science and Technology Policy, Executive Office of the President, Washington, DC.

INDEX

adaptation *see* response strategies

Advanced Very High Resolution Radiometer (AVHRR) data 252

aerosols, troposphere 268

Africa: coping strategies (Zimbabwe) 17–28; effective mitigation 3–16; preparedness and mitigation 206–10; severity index 259; *see also* Sahel (Africa); southern Africa; sub-Saharan Africa

agricultural drought 287; definition 181; New Zealand 105–14

agricultural impact: Mexico 39–40; sub-Saharan Africa 138, 139, 140

agricultural indicators 213, 214

agricultural production: Australia 117; Mexico 38; New Zealand 105; sub-Saharan Africa 138

agriculture, management strategies (India) 46–58

agroclimatic analysis 217

aid *see* food aid

aquifers: Israel 184, 186–7; Jordan 184, 191; Zimbabwe 18–19

arid climate, Israel and Jordan 178–81

aridity, classification 180

Arizona (USA), groundwater storage 70, 84

assessment programmes: USA 152; *see also* monitoring

assistance programmes 95, 99, 297; Australia 119, 121–2; deficiencies 90; New Zealand 108, 109–10, 112; USA 153, 160

Australia 59–69, 115–28; 1982–3

drought 290; agricultural production 117; climate 116–18; discourses 219–20; Drought Exceptional Circumstamces (DEC) 121–2; forecasts and management 66–7; government policy 63–6; history 59–60, 118–20; impact 60–2; national drought policy (NDP) 64, 120–7; private strategies 62–3; risk management 115–16, 124–5

AVHRR *see* Advanced Very High Resolution Radiometer

awareness education, southern Africa 176

bioclimatic aridity, definition 180

biophysical vulnerability, Mexico 39

Botswana: 1979–87 drought 218–19; 1994–5 drought 147; economic impact 142, 143; entitlement 219; interventions 279; rainfall variability 131

Brazil (northeast), land ownership 287, 289–90

Burkina Faso, impact 142

bush fires, Australia 61

California (USA): 1987–92 drought 72–3, 196; 1990s drought 75–6; Department of Water Resources 73–5, 77, 153; El Niño 266; environmental impact 77; fish population 258, 260; groundwater recharge and storage 83–4; reservoir storage 258; State Water Project 216;

water prices 73–4; water transfer banks 70, 72–7, 82, 153

CCD *see* United Nations Convention to Combat Desertification

cereals: India 30–1; sub-Saharan Africa 140

Chad, Lake (Chad), water storage 137

characteristics of drought 295–6

Chernobyl nuclear disaster 285

climate: Australia 116–18; and desertification 232; Israel and Jordan 178–80, 182–3; Mexico 36; New Zealand 105–7

climate change 243, 264–72; effects 266–71; impact on water resources 258–60; precipitation 261

climate variability 265–6, 269–71, 286

collector wells, Zimbabwe 18–23, 25

Colorado (USA), drought plan 150

contingency plans: New Zealand 111; USA 203, 204; *see also* preparedness planning

coping cost, US water supplies 202–3

coping strategies: Australia 62–6; famine 274, 276, 281(n11, 19); India 31–2; indigenous 5–8; institutional response 8–11; methodology 89–104; productive water points (Zimbabwe) 17–28; sustainability 7; USA 194–5;